FOREIGN JUDGES IN THE PACIFIC

We often assume that the judges sitting on domestic courts will be citizens. However, across the island states of the Pacific, over three-quarters of all judges are foreign judges who regularly hear cases of constitutional, legal and social importance. This has implications for constitutional adjudication, judicial independence and the representative qualities of judges and judiciaries.

This book explores the use of foreign judges on courts of constitutional jurisdiction in nine Pacific states: Fiji, Kiribati, Nauru, Papua New Guinea, Samoa, Solomon Islands, Tonga, Tuvalu and Vanuatu. Drawing together detailed empirical research, legal analysis and constitutional theory, it traces how foreign judges bring different dimensions of knowledge to bear on adjudication, face distinctive burdens on their independence, and hold only an attenuated connection to the state and its people. It shows how foreign judges have come to be understood as representatives of a transnational profession, with its own transferrable judicial skills and values.

Foreign Judges in the Pacific sheds light on the widespread but often unarticulated assumptions about the significance of nationality to the functions and qualities of constitutional judges. It shows how the nationality of judges matters, not only for the legitimacy and effectiveness of the Pacific courts that use foreign judges, but also for legal and theoretical scholarship on courts and judging.

Hart Studies on Judging and the Courts: Volume 2

Hart Studies on Judging and the Courts

Series editors: Erin F Delaney, James Lee & Andrew Lynch

Hart Studies on Judging and the Courts aims to publish exceptional scholarship examining judges, the judiciary and the courts, from a range of doctrinal and theoretical perspectives. The primary focus is on appellate courts in the common law world, but we welcome submissions beyond this, including those offering a comparative angle, such as from civilian jurisdictions, or jurisdictions in developing nations. The series supports innovative work by emerging and established scholars in the field.

Volume 1: Values in the Supreme Court: Decisions, Division and Diversity
Rachel J Cahill O'Callaghan

Foreign Judges in the Pacific

Anna Dziedzic

•HART•
OXFORD • LONDON • NEW YORK • NEW DELHI • SYDNEY

HART PUBLISHING

Bloomsbury Publishing Plc

Kemp House, Chawley Park, Cumnor Hill, Oxford, OX2 9PH, UK

1385 Broadway, New York, NY 10018, USA

29 Earlsfort Terrace, Dublin 2, Ireland

First published in Great Britain 2021

A catalogue record for this book is available from the British Library.

Library of Congress Cataloging-in-Publication data

Names: Dziedzic, Anna (Law teacher), author.

Title: Foreign judges in the Pacific / Anna Dziedzic.

Description: Oxford; New York : Hart, 2021. | Series: Hart studies on judging and the courts ; volume 2 | Based on author's thesis (doctoral - Melbourne Law School, 2018) issued under title: The use of foreign judges on courts of constitutional jurisdiction in Pacific island states. | Includes bibliographical references and index.

Identifiers: LCCN 2021030055 (print) | LCCN 2021030056 (ebook) | ISBN 9781509942862 (hardback) | ISBN 9781509942909 (paperback) | ISBN 9781509942886 (pdf) | ISBN 9781509942879 (Epub)

Subjects: LCSH: Judges—Selection and appointment—Oceania. | Law—Oceania—Foreign influences. | Judges—Employment—Foreign countries.

Classification: LCC KVC608 .D95 2021 (print) | LCC KVC608 (ebook) | DDC 347.95/014—dc23

LC record available at https://lccn.loc.gov/2021030055

LC ebook record available at https://lccn.loc.gov/2021030056

ISBN: HB: 978-1-50994-286-2
ePDF: 978-1-50994-288-6
ePub: 978-1-50994-287-9

Typeset by Compuscript Ltd, Shannon

Acknowledgements

In 2011, while volunteering at the Samoa Law Reform Commission in Apia, I applied to work with Cheryl Saunders at Melbourne Law School on a project on the challenges of constitutional comparison. This book is a product of these two formative experiences. It reflects both my desire to better understand the complex legal systems of Pacific island states, and the inclusive contextual approach to comparative constitutional law practised at Melbourne Law School.

This book began as a PhD thesis, supervised by Cheryl Saunders and Adrienne Stone, the best supervisors one could wish for. I thank them not only for their expert feedback and comparative insights, but also for their friendship, support and encouragement. I am also grateful to the examiners of my thesis, Hugh Corder and David Feldman, whose comments and reflections shaped this book.

My work has benefited greatly from discussions with colleagues at Melbourne Law School, the Faculty of Law at Hong Kong University, the University of the South Pacific and iCourts at the University of Copenhagen. I am grateful to all those who shared their knowledge and networks with me. Particular thanks are due to Eselealofa Apinelu, Tom Daly, Ros Dixon, Malaea Aloese Feterika, Harry Hobbs, Bal Kama, Zim Nwokora, Will Phillips, Kristen Rundle, Lee-Anne Sackett, Lulu Weis, Julius Yam and Simon Young.

My research was greatly enhanced by the opportunity to conduct interviews and discuss the how and the why of foreign judging with a wide range of people in the Pacific, Australia, New Zealand, Sri Lanka and beyond. Confidentiality prevents me from acknowledging by name the judges and officials who participated in formal interviews and others who provided me with information, but I am grateful to them all for so generously sharing their time, experiences and insights with me.

My PhD was funded by the University of Melbourne Human Rights Scholarship. Additional financial support that allowed me to participate in conferences and conduct interviews was generously provided by Melbourne Law School, the Pacific Constitutions Network, and the Law Faculties at Auckland University and the University of New South Wales. I was also fortunate to receive funding to visit iCourts, the Danish National Research Foundation's Centre for Excellence for International Courts. This book, and my scholarship, greatly benefited from these opportunities to share my research with leading scholars of Pacific laws and societies, judicial studies and comparative constitutional law.

Last, but never least, I thank my family – Annette, James, Rose and Janet – and the best of best friends, Apsari Dewi and Arturo Villagrán. Your willingness to listen, your ability to counsel and your joy in my achievements mean so much and provide the foundation for all that I do.

Table of Contents

Table of Cases

Belize

Botswana

Canada

Fiji

Kiribati

Nauru

New Zealand

Papua New Guinea

Samoa

Seychelles

Solomon Islands

South Africa

Timor Leste

Tonga

Tuvalu

United Kingdom (including Decisions of the Judicial Committee of the Privy Council)

Vanuatu

Table of Legislation

Australia

Federated States of Micronesia

Fiji

Hong Kong

Liechtenstein

Kiribati

Nauru

New Zealand

Papua New Guinea

Samoa

Seychelles

Solomon Islands

Tonga

Tuvalu

United Kingdom

Vanuatu

Currency of Law

THE LAW IS stated as of 1 December 2020. On 15 December 2020, the Parliament of Samoa passed significant amendments to constitutional and legislative provisions relating to the judiciary. These amendments are noted where relevant, but references to the *Constitution of Samoa 1960* and the *Land and Titles Act 1981* are to the provisions as they stood prior to the amendments.

1

Global Exception, Regional Norm

THE USE OF foreign judges is an exceptional phenomenon. It runs counter to the general assumption, taken for granted in most states as well as in constitutional theory, that the judges sitting on courts of constitutional jurisdiction will be citizens of the state they serve. Yet in Pacific island states, foreign judges regularly sit on the highest national courts and determine constitutional matters. Over the past two decades, about three-quarters of the judges sitting on courts of constitutional jurisdiction across the region have been foreign judges. Every constitution in the Pacific region anticipates, and to varying degrees regulates, the appointment of foreign judges. The use of foreign judges is a long-standing practice and likely to continue for some time.

The use of foreign judges, while not unique to the Pacific, is a significant point of difference between the judiciaries of Pacific island states and those of most other countries. It prompts a range of questions that have not been fully explored in constitutional studies. Does the nationality of the judges who determine constitutional issues matter? Do foreign judges bring a special degree of impartiality and independence to the task of judging? Does foreignness affect a judge's sense of responsibility and accountability to the state and its people? How can the conception of the judge and the judge's role accommodate the movement of judges across national borders?

This book explores these questions through a detailed study of the use of foreign judges in nine independent, common law states in the Pacific region: Fiji, Kiribati, Nauru, Papua New Guinea, Samoa, Solomon Islands, Tonga, Tuvalu and Vanuatu. It describes the work of the 225 African, Australian, British, New Zealander, Sri Lankan and Pacific Islander lawyers and judges who have served as foreign judges on Pacific courts over the past two decades. It explains how they are recruited and the terms and conditions of their judicial service. It examines the laws and practices that facilitate the use of foreign judges in the Pacific states, the provision of foreign judges by donor states and organisations, and the distinctive issues that arise for the regulation, independence and accountability of Pacific judiciaries.

Informed by this empirical study of recent practice, this book then examines the implications of the use of foreign judges for the way in which courts approach constitutional adjudication, judicial independence, and the representative qualities of judges and judiciaries in Pacific constitutional systems. Foreign judges bring different dimensions of knowledge to bear on constitutional adjudication, which can be traced in the jurisprudence of Pacific courts. Foreign judges carry distinctive burdens on their independence, deriving from their status as non-citizens and from laws and practices that distinguish between citizen and non-citizen judges for the purposes of appointment, remuneration and tenure. The use of foreign judges attenuates the connections between judges, the state and its people, such that foreign judges are not readily understood as representatives of the people or the state, but rather as representatives of a profession, with transferable legal skills and expertise. All of these findings have implications for the way in which Pacific communities and foreign judges themselves understand their role in the wider constitutional system.

States across the world appoint foreign judges for a range of reasons. In the Pacific, the most compelling rationale for the use of foreign judges is as a transitional measure until states are in a position to constitute courts wholly comprised of citizen judges. The practice affects the legitimacy and effectiveness of Pacific judiciaries. It poses challenges that deserve careful assessment and redress, not only by institutions in the Pacific states that use foreign judges, but also by the external organisations and the states that supply judges to serve on courts overseas.

By exploring these issues, this book not only provides insights for Pacific courts and judges. It also provides a framework for identifying the rationales for the use of foreign judges, assessing the challenges that the practice poses to the legitimacy of judiciaries, and developing good practice initiatives to inform the laws and policies that regulate the use of foreign judges in the Pacific region and beyond. It also sheds light on widespread but often unarticulated presumptions about the significance of nationality to the functions and qualities of constitutional judges and the nature of judging itself. In this way, this book takes advantage of the capacity of comparative constitutional studies to challenge assumptions about the constitutional arrangements of one's own state in the course of better understanding the constitutional systems of others.

I. FOREIGN JUDGES AND COURTS OF CONSTITUTIONAL JURISDICTION

Foreign judges – that is, judges who are not citizens of the state on whose courts they serve[1] – may be involved in national judiciaries in various capacities. This book focuses on foreign judges who are appointed to domestic courts charged with interpreting the constitution and resolving constitutional disputes.

[1] This definition of 'foreign judge' adopted in this book is explained in ch 2. I use the term 'foreign judge' in preference to 'expatriate' or 'international' judge. Expatriates live outside their home country, and in this sense expatriate judges are foreign judges who reside in the state they serve rather than visit temporarily. I use the term 'foreign judge' throughout and distinguish where relevant between resident and non-resident foreign judges. I use the term 'international judge' only when referring to judges who serve on international, rather than domestic, courts.

Constitutional law is a distinctive branch of law, with features that give special significance to the involvement of foreign judges in the determination of constitutional disputes. Constitutions are closely linked to their states, nations or polities.[2] Every state has a constitution that authorises the use of state power, organises the institutions of government, and regulates the relationships between government and the people. Constitutions often also have a symbolic or expressive function, reflecting the values of the state and its people.[3]

Written constitutions tend to be framed in general, abstract language, and embody overarching principles, national aspirations and human rights protections. Legal provisions are supplemented by principles and values that may not be formally expressed in the written document but rather emerge from the culture, legal interpretations and practices of the particular constitutional system.[4] The written and unwritten aspects of constitutions therefore require interpretation. Courts are called upon to provide such interpretations in the course of resolving constitutional disputes. In many states, including the Pacific island states studied here, courts have powers of strong judicial review, which means they can overrule legislation and executive actions that are inconsistent with the constitution. The power of strong judicial review distinguishes constitutional adjudication from other kinds of legal disputes. It means that judges may override the decisions of democratically elected representatives on politically significant issues or contested social values in ways that can be difficult to reverse. On the highest apex courts, the decisions of judges are final and not subject to further judicial review. In common law jurisdictions, they create precedents that lower courts are bound to follow. In many constitutional systems, judicial interpretations may only be countered by formal constitutional amendment. Despite this, constitutional courts have limited powers of enforcement, and compliance, especially by the state itself, relies on the legitimacy and authority of the court and the constitution.[5]

The combination of the status and subject matter of constitutions means that constitutional adjudication raises distinctive questions about the role, function and legitimacy of courts. Focusing on the use of foreign judges on constitutional courts therefore isolates key issues that press on the limits of the judicial function and the place of judiciaries within national constitutional systems.

The use of foreign judges on courts of constitutional jurisdiction must be distinguished from three other ways in which foreign judges might be involved in a state's judiciary. First, foreign judges might be involved because a state permits

[2] C Saunders, 'Towards a Global Constitutional Gene Pool' (2009) 4(3) *National Taiwan University Law Review* 1, 9.

[3] M Tushnet, 'The Possibilities of Comparative Constitutional Law' (1999) 108 *Yale Law Journal* 1225, 1270.

[4] VC Jackson, 'Paradigms of Public Law: Transnational Constitutional Values and Democratic Challenges' (2010) 8 *International Journal of Constitutional Law* 517, 537.

[5] J Goldsmith and D Levinson, 'Law for States: International Law, Constitutional Law, Public Law' (2009) 122(7) *Harvard Law Review* 1792.

appeals from decisions of domestic courts to a supranational or regional appellate court, such as the Caribbean Court of Justice, the Eastern Caribbean Supreme Court and the Judicial Committee of the Privy Council. These supranational appellate courts determine appeals by applying the domestic law of the state in which the matter arose. In some cases, the supranational appellate court is composed almost entirely of judges from outside the state. For example, while senior judges from Commonwealth countries may be appointed to the Judicial Committee of the Privy Council, in practice the 12 judges of the United Kingdom Supreme Court comprise more than 95 per cent of the judges sitting on appeal cases from the diverse jurisdictions it serves.[6] In contrast, the majority of judges on the Caribbean Court of Justice and Eastern Caribbean Supreme Court are drawn from the Caribbean region, although both also include judges from outside the region. The use of foreign judges to decide domestic legal matters means that supranational appellate courts share some similarities with domestic courts comprising foreign judges. However, there are important differences between the two practices. Supranational appellate courts are more distant from domestic governments and peoples. A supranational court may physically sit in another state or even outside the region. National governments have less influence on the appointment and removal of judges and the funding and administration of the court, which may be placed in the hands of a foreign state or a regional body. This stands in contrast to the appointment of judges to national courts, which is formally in the hands of domestic institutions.

Second, and more unusually, a state might designate a foreign court as part of its own judicial structure. For example, between 1976 and 2018, the High Court of Australia served as the final court of appeal for Nauru.[7] In the years immediately following independence in 1978, Tuvalu continued to use the Fiji Court of Appeal pending the establishment of its own Court of Appeal in 1987.[8] While they share some features, these arrangements must also be distinguished from the appointment of foreign judges to national courts. Of most significance, the judges of the foreign court of appeal do not take a separate commission or make an oath to the designating state, but rather continue to be, first and foremost, judges in their own constitutional system.[9]

Third, the use of foreign judges on courts of constitutional jurisdiction can be distinguished from their use on specialised courts, such as post-conflict tribunals and international commercial courts. 'Hybrid' tribunals composed of

[6] D Neuberger, 'The Judicial Committee of the Privy Council in the 21st Century' (2014) 3(1) *Cambridge Journal of International and Comparative Law* 30, 31.

[7] *Agreement between the Government of Australia and the Government of the Republic of Nauru relating to Appeals to the High Court of Australia from the Supreme Court of Nauru*, 6 September 1976. Nauru withdrew from this treaty and established its own Court of Appeal in 2018.

[8] *Constitution of Tuvalu 1978*, s 104(1); B Atkinson, 'Regional Co-Operation in the Courts: A Tuvalu View' in G Powles and M Pulea (eds), *Pacific Courts and Legal Systems* (Suva and Clayton, University of the South Pacific and Monash University, 1988) 241.

[9] G Dale, 'Appealing to Whom? Australia's "Appellate Jurisdiction" Over Nauru' (2007) 56(3) *International and Comparative Law Quarterly* 641, 665.

local and foreign judges have been established in post-conflict contexts in Bosnia Herzegovina, Kosovo, Timor Leste, Cambodia, Lebanon, Sierra Leone, the Central African Republic, and Chad.[10] In addition to their 'mixed' local and international composition, hybrid tribunals have jurisdiction to try cases arising from the conflict according to both international and domestic criminal law. In a development of a different kind, the globalisation of commerce and investment has led several states to establish commercial courts staffed by local and foreign judges.[11] These courts hear international commercial matters, which often engage the laws of foreign states. The involvement of foreign judges in both kinds of courts and tribunals is distinguished from their presence on domestic courts on two grounds. First, these courts exist outside the ordinary national court system, as specialist tribunals with limited jurisdiction. Second, because they apply international or foreign law, there is a particular justification for the involvement of foreign judges that does not apply to the use of foreign judges on national courts that decide cases according to domestic law.

Foreign judges on national courts have the equivalent powers and functions, and exercise the same constitutional jurisdiction, as the local judges with whom they sometimes sit. They interpret and apply national law. At least formally, their appointment is wholly in the hands of local national appointing bodies. Therefore, while supranational and foreign appellate courts and specialised hybrid tribunals share some features with foreign judging, the use of foreign judges on national courts of constitutional jurisdiction is a distinctive practice deserving of its own study.

II. AN UNDEREXPLORED PHENOMENON

In most countries, by law or by practice, only judges who are citizens serve on courts of constitutional jurisdiction. There are exceptions, however, and over the decade from the beginning of 2010 to the end of 2019, foreign judges sat on courts of constitutional jurisdiction in 30 states in Africa, the Caribbean, Europe, the Middle East and Asia, as well as in the Pacific.

In Africa, foreign judges sat on courts of constitutional jurisdiction in Botswana, Lesotho, Namibia, Eswatini, the Gambia and the Seychelles. In the Caribbean, several states and territories are served by different supranational appellate courts, including the Privy Council, the Caribbean Court of Justice[12]

[10] LA Dickinson, 'The Promise of Hybrid Courts' (2003) 97 *American Journal of International Law* 295, 295; H Hobbs, 'Hybrid Tribunals and the Composition of the Court: In Search of Sociological Legitimacy' (2016) 16(2) *Chicago Journal of International Law* 482.

[11] eg Singapore, Qatar and Dubai: A Godwin, I Ramsay and M Webster, 'International Commercial Courts: The Singapore Experience' (2017) 18 *Melbourne Journal of International Law* 219.

[12] The Caribbean Court of Justice was established in 2005 in part as a court of final appeal for states in the region: *Agreement Establishing the Caribbean Court of Justice*, 14 February 2001. As at 2020, Barbados, Belize, Dominica and Guyana are the only states that have opted into the court's appellate jurisdiction.

and the Eastern Caribbean Supreme Court,[13] but Bahamas and Belize continue to appoint foreign judges to their national courts of constitutional jurisdiction. All are relatively small states, have a history of British colonisation and are current members of the Commonwealth of Nations.

In Europe, foreign judges are appointed to sit on the constitutional courts of the small states of Andorra, Liechtenstein, Monaco and San Marino, mainly because there are insufficient numbers of citizens eligible for judicial appointment. In examples of a different kind, the Constitutions of Bosnia Herzegovina and Kosovo require that three foreign judges sit on each state's constitutional court, as a counterbalance to the deeply entrenched ethnic divisions that are reflected in the courts' composition and other state institutions.[14]

In the Middle East, citizens from other Arab states may sit as members of the Supreme Constitutional Court of Qatar. In Asia, foreign judges served in Timor Leste between 2001 and 2014 as the new state, devastated by conflict, built its judicial institutions anew, initially under international administration and then under local control. In addition, while it is not an independent state, the Hong Kong Special Administrative Region of the People's Republic of China provides a well-known example of foreign judging. There, one judge from another common law jurisdiction usually sits with four Hong Kong judges on the Court of Final Appeal.

Finally, foreign judges regularly sit on the courts of constitutional jurisdiction in 14 Pacific island states. Nine of these states are the focus of this book. The other five are the Federated States of Micronesia, the Marshall Islands and Palau (which are states in free association with the United States) and the Cook Islands and Niue (which are states in free association with New Zealand).

This brief survey demonstrates that although the use of foreign judges on constitutional courts might be considered exceptional, it is globally widespread, with examples arising in most regions of the world, spanning common law and civil law legal systems, and wealthy and developing states. The laws, practices and experiences of other jurisdictions that use foreign judges, particularly other small states in the common law world, provide important insights for the Pacific, and later chapters draw on this comparative experience. In turn, this study of foreign judges in the Pacific will provide insights that will enrich understandings of the practice in other jurisdictions and other courts.

The practice of foreign judging and the reasons for it differ across jurisdictions. It is possible to identify four general rationales, which are not necessarily mutually exclusive and in many contexts are likely to overlap. First, many states

[13] The Eastern Caribbean Supreme Court is the appellate court for six states (Antigua and Barbuda, Dominica, Grenada, Saint Kitts and Nevis, Saint Lucia, and Saint Vincent and the Grenadines) and three British Overseas Territories (Anguilla, British Virgin Islands and Montserrat).

[14] C Grewe and M Riegner, 'Internationalized Constitutionalism in Ethnically Divided Societies: Bosnia-Herzegovina and Kosovo Compared' (2011) 15 *Max Planck Yearbook of United Nations Law* 1.

use foreign judges because there are insufficient numbers of local candidates available for judicial appointment. The availability of qualified citizens may be limited because of the small population size, because the legal profession was depleted during conflict or authoritarian rule (as in Timor Leste[15]), or because of the non-representative composition of the legal profession due to historic discrimination (as in Namibia[16]). Sometimes, the rationale for using foreign judges in these contexts goes beyond 'gap-filling' and extends to rebuilding or strengthening judicial institutions through 'capacity building'. Third, foreign judges might be thought to enhance the reputation of the domestic court and to signify the quality and distinctiveness of the jurisdiction's legal system: Hong Kong is the quintessential example.[17] Finally, foreign judges might be used because they are regarded as distant from and therefore impartial to domestic politics and interests. For example, foreign judges sit on the Constitutional Court of Bosnia Herzegovina, in part because they are not connected to the political interests of any of the different ethnic groups within the state.[18]

A polity's receptiveness to the use of foreign judges is influenced by a variety of factors, including legal tradition, history and a state's self-understandings of its place in the world. While foreign judges feature in both common law and civil law legal systems, the practice arises more often in common law states. The experience of colonisation – and British colonisation in particular – also seems relevant. Foreign judging echoes some of the legal institutions of British Empire, including the Colonial Legal Service which dispatched judges to colonial outposts across the Empire, and the use of regional appellate courts and the Privy Council. Conceptions of sovereignty and vulnerability to geopolitical influences also affect whether a state is receptive to the use of foreign judges.

Despite the number and diversity of states in which foreign judges serve on constitutional courts, the use of foreign judges is an under-explored phenomenon. Studies have focused on the transnational movement of constitutional law via 'constitutional borrowing' and the citation of foreign judgments by courts of constitutional jurisdiction,[19] but the movement of judges themselves across national borders has been largely overlooked. Anne-Marie Slaughter's study of a 'global community of judges', arising from judges' engagement in transnational

[15] H Strohmeyer, 'Policing the Peace: Post-Conflict Judicial System Reconstruction in East Timor' (2001) 24 *University of New South Wales Law Journal* 171, 175.

[16] SH Bukurura, 'A Judiciary in Transition: Reflections on the Selection of Judges in Namibia' in PH Russell and K Malleson (eds), *Appointing Judges in an Age of Judicial Power: Critical Perspectives from around the World* (Toronto, University of Toronto Press, 2006) 313, 316.

[17] J Fok, 'The Use of Non-Local Judges in Overseas Jurisdictions' (2017) 23(1) *Journal of the Commonwealth Magistrates' and Judges' Association* 28.

[18] Grewe and Riegner, (n 14).

[19] VC Jackson, *Constitutional Engagement in a Transnational Era* (Oxford, Oxford University Press, 2010); T Groppi and M-C Ponthoreau (eds), *The Use of Foreign Precedents by Constitutional Judges* (Oxford, Hart Publishing, 2013).

legal disputes and networking at judicial conferences, makes no mention of foreign judges on domestic courts, although it is clearly a manifestation of 'judicial globalisation'.[20]

Although international organisations, such as the United Nations Development Programme and the Commonwealth, recruit and fund foreign judges to serve in countries across the world, studies of the practice are incomplete and evaluations limited.[21] For example, a best practice compendium on the appointment, remuneration and tenure of judges across the Commonwealth excluded the issues raised by the use of foreign judges from the scope of its study.[22] Global standards on judicial independence and accountability rarely address the distinctive position of foreign judges.[23]

The use of foreign judges has recently begun to receive the attention of comparative constitutional scholars.[24] Most literature on the practice is found in studies of the judiciaries of particular states or jurisdictions, and considers the rationales for the use of foreign judges; the advantages and disadvantages of the practice in terms of the capabilities, independence and legitimacy of the judiciary; and the effect that foreign judges might have on judicial decision making.[25] A sub-category of this literature consists of reflections by foreign judges themselves on their experiences.[26]

[20] A-M Slaughter, 'A Global Community of Courts' (2003) 44(1) *Harvard International Law Journal* 191.

[21] United Nations Development Programme, Bangkok SURF, 'Global Experiences Using Expatriate Judges' (Substantive Research Piece East Timor, UNDP, August 2002); A Ferreyra, R Mabsout and United Nations Office of the High Representative for the Least Developed Countries, Landlocked Developing Countries and Small Island Developing States, *Best Practices in the Implementation of the Brussels Programme of Action for the Least Developed Countries for the Decade 2001–2010* (New York, United Nations, 2008) 39; Commonwealth Secretariat, 'Evaluation of the Commonwealth Fund for Technical Cooperation' (London, Commonwealth Secretariat, 2008).

[22] J van Zyl Smit, *The Appointment, Tenure and Removal of Judges under Commonwealth Principles: A Compendium and Analysis of Best Practice* (London, Commonwealth Secretariat, 2015), [2.2.15].

[23] These standards are discussed in ch 6.

[24] R Dixon and V Jackson, 'Hybrid Constitutional Courts: Foreign Judges on National Constitutional Courts' [2019] *Columbia Journal of Transnational Law* 283; Y Ghai, 'Themes and Arguments' in Y Ghai and SNM Young (eds), *Hong Kong's Court of Final Appeal* (Cambridge, Cambridge University Press, 2013) 1, 25–27.

[25] Hong Kong: F Lin, 'The Expatriate Judges and Rule of Law in Hong Kong: Its Past, Present and Future' in S Shetreet and W McCormack (eds), *The Culture of Judicial Independence in a Globalised World* (Leiden, Brill Nijhoff, 2016) 279. Bosnia Herzegovina: D Feldman, 'The Independence of International Judges in National Courts: Lessons from Bosnia Herzegovina' in CF Forsyth and S Shetreet (eds), *The Culture of Judicial Independence: Conceptual Foundations and Practical Challenges* (Boston, MA, Martinus Nijhoff Publishers, 2011) 215; A Schwartz, 'International Judges on Constitutional Courts: Cautionary Evidence from Post-Conflict Bosnia' (2019) 44 *Law and Social Inquiry* 1. Lesotho: R Ellett, *Politics of Judicial Independence in Lesotho* (Johannesburg, Freedom House Southern Africa, 2012) 94–98. Pacific: N Baird, 'Judges as Cultural Outsiders: Exploring the Expatriate Model of Judging in the Pacific' (2013) 19 *Canterbury Law Review* 80.

[26] eg M Casey, 'New Zealand Judges in Overseas Courts' in I Barker and G Wear (eds), *Law Stories: Essays on the New Zealand Legal Profession 1969–2003* (Wellington, LexisNexis NZ, 2003) 89; A Mason, 'Reflections of an Itinerant Judge in the Asia-Pacific Region' (2000) 28 *International Journal of Legal Information* 311.

By analysing the practice of foreign judging in the Pacific, this book contributes comparative knowledge on an understudied phenomenon. It provides an analytical framework for understanding the implications of the use of foreign judges and identifying the points at which pressures on the legitimacy and effectiveness of the practice are likely to arise. This framework, can, with care for relevant differences, be used to understand and assess the practice of foreign judging in other contexts. The book also engages directly with an issue that is more often assumed than it is expressly defended – the significance of nationality to the functions and qualities of a constitutional judge. The study of foreign judges in the Pacific therefore makes a significant contribution to comparative, analytical and theoretical studies of courts, judges and constitutions.

III. AN OVERLOOKED REGION

The Pacific is often overlooked in comparative constitutional law. This is partly because the field has tended to focus on the constitutional systems of Europe and North America, although this is changing as experiences from Africa, Asia and Latin America are increasingly included.[27] It might also reflect a presumption that the constitutional systems of Pacific island states are less relevant to global constitutional studies because of their small size and the less-than-statehood status of some polities.[28] Pacific states are rarely represented in collections examining particular issues of constitutional law across different countries. The marginalisation of the constitutional experiences of the Pacific region, and those of other small states, is perhaps one reason why the use of foreign judges has been an underexamined issue in constitutional law scholarship.

This book proceeds on the basis that the constitutional experiences of the Pacific islands are worthy of close attention in and of themselves, as single country as well as regional comparative studies. They have much to contribute to comparative constitutional scholarship. The constitutional laws and institutions of Pacific island states draw on a unique mix of indigenous law, statute, common law and international law. The exigencies of post-colonialism, smallness and remoteness have fostered constitutional innovations that test established assumptions and that can contribute greatly to the development of global constitutional theories. This section identifies the shared characteristics, as well as points of diversity, of the countries of the Pacific region, and explains why the Pacific is a suitable context for examining the practice of foreign judging and its implications.

The Pacific region encompasses the island states and territories situated in the South Pacific Ocean. It contains independent sovereign states, self-governing

[27] P Dann, M Riegner and M Bönnemann, 'The Southern Turn in Comparative Constitutional Law: An Introduction' in *The Global South and Comparative Constitutional Law* (Oxford, Oxford University Press, 2020) 1.

[28] W Veenendaal, *Politics and Democracy in Microstates* (Abingdon, Routledge, 2015) 2–3.

territories and dependencies. This book focuses on nine independent states: Fiji, Kiribati, Nauru, Papua New Guinea, Samoa, Solomon Islands, Tonga, Tuvalu and Vanuatu. It does not cover islands that are territories of an overseas power[29] or states that have entered into arrangements of 'free association' with a foreign state.[30] While the judiciaries in these Pacific jurisdictions share many of the features of judiciaries in independent states, including the use of foreign judges, they have been excluded from this study on the basis that the use of foreign judges in states that are formally and constitutionally independent raises distinctive issues, particularly in relation to conceptions of national sovereignty.[31]

The states of the Pacific region are diverse and distinctive. They do, however, share some characteristics that affect their constitutional systems and the use of foreign judges. All nine states studied here are classified as small island developing states.[32] They have small populations, in many cases dispersed across islands in large ocean areas. Papua New Guinea is by far the most populous state in the region with over eight and a half million people, while the populations of the other states are far smaller.[33] On an economic analysis, small populations, geographic isolation and limited resources constrain development in small island states.[34] These features also affect the structure and capacities of the institutions of law and government, including judiciaries.[35]

All nine Pacific states are members of the Commonwealth of Nations, an association of independent states that evolved out of the British Empire. The nine Pacific states are all former colonies, protectorates or trust territories of Australia, New Zealand or the United Kingdom.[36] With the exception of Tonga, each state became independent during a period of decolonisation from the 1960s to 1980s. Upon independence, they adopted written constitutions,[37]

[29] American Samoa, Guam and the Commonwealth of the Northern Mariana Islands (territories of the United States); French Polynesia, New Caledonia, and Wallis and Futuna Islands (territories of France); Pitcairn Islands (territory of the United Kingdom); Tokelau (territory of New Zealand).

[30] Cook Islands and Niue (in free association with New Zealand); Federated States of Micronesia, Marshall Islands and Palau (in free association with the United States).

[31] For a critical study of the composition of judiciaries in overseas territories, see M Cohen, 'Judicial Colonialism Today: The French Overseas Courts' (2020) 8(2) *Journal of Law and Courts* 247.

[32] *About the Small Island Developing States* (2015), United Nations Office of the High Representative for the Least Developed Countries, Landlocked Developing Countries and Small Island Developing States, available at www.un.org/ohrlls.

[33] Tuvalu 10,200; Nauru 11,000; Tonga 100,300; Kiribati 120,100; Samoa 196,700; Vanuatu 304,500; Solomon Islands 682,500; Fiji 888,400; Papua New Guinea 8,558,800: Statistics for Development Division, Pacific Community, *2018 Pocket Statistical Summary* (2018).

[34] FX Hezel, 'Pacific Island Nations: How Viable Are Their Economies?', *Pacific Islands Policy No 7* (Honolulu, East-West Center, 2012) 3.

[35] L Briguglio, 'Small Island Developing States and Their Economic Vulnerabilities' (1995) 23(9) *World Development* 1615, 1615–18; Veenendaal (n 28) 22–23.

[36] Vanuatu was an Anglo-French condominium from 1906 until independence in 1980.

[37] *Constitution of Fiji 1970* (sch to *Fiji Independence Order 1970* (Imp)); *Constitution of Kiribati 1979* (schedule to *Kiribati Independence Order 1979* (Imp)); *Constitution of Nauru 1968*; *Constitution of the Independent State of Papua New Guinea 1975*; *Constitution of the Independent State of Samoa 1960*; *Constitution of Solomon Islands 1978* (sch to *Solomon Islands Independence Order 1978* (Imp)); *Constitution of Tuvalu 1978* (sch to *Tuvalu Independence Order 1978* (Imp)); *Constitution of the Republic of Vanuatu 1980*.

which generally continued the common law legal system and Westminster form of government introduced by the colonial administrations. The written constitutions made at independence have continued, with some amendment, in all states except Fiji and Tuvalu.[38] Tonga was never formally colonised, but as a protectorate from 1900 to 1970, the British Government assumed responsibility for defence, foreign affairs and some judicial proceedings. Tonga's Constitution, made in 1875, drew upon the constitutional structures of Hawaii and the United Kingdom to create a constitutional monarchy adapted to the context of Tonga.[39]

The use of foreign judges in Pacific states reflects, in part, the influence of their colonial histories. Colonial administrators established British-style courts, which applied statutory and common laws imported from Australia, Britain or New Zealand to deal with issues deemed to affect the interests of the colonisers. Separate 'native' or 'island' courts were established to resolve disputes between Indigenous peoples.[40] The transplanted systems of law and governance were initially administered by foreign experts, including judges, sourced from Australia, New Zealand, the United Kingdom and Europe. Even in Tonga, where Tongans had served for over 30 years as judges on the courts established by its Constitution of 1875, the practice of appointing British judges became entrenched during the twentieth-century protectorate period.[41] Settlers were generally hostile to the idea of submitting to courts presided over by Indigenous judges.[42] In contrast, courts determining customary matters were sometimes staffed by a mix of European settlers and Indigenous peoples appointed by the colonial administration.[43]

After independence, states chose to continue with the judicial systems established during the colonial period. Many also decided to retain colonial legislation and apply Australian, English or New Zealand statutes, at least as a transitional measure.[44] National authorities continued to appoint judges from other Commonwealth jurisdictions, and former colonial powers continued to provide judges as part of their foreign development assistance programmes.

In the Pacific states, as elsewhere, courts hold the primary responsibility for interpreting and upholding the constitution. Pacific courts have powers of strong judicial review, and may declare legislation and executive actions that

[38] New constitutions were made in Fiji in 1990, 1997 and 2013, and in Tuvalu in 1986.

[39] S Lātūkefu, *The Tongan Constitution: A Brief History to Celebrate Its Centenary* (Nuku'alofa, Tonga Traditions Committee, 1975) 43–55, 70–72.

[40] J Corrin Care and D Paterson, *Introduction to South Pacific Law*, 2nd edn (London, Routledge-Cavendish, 2008) 3–4.

[41] G Powles, 'The Common Law as a Source of Law in the South Pacific: Experiences in Western Polynesia' (1988) 10 *University of Hawaii Law Review* 105, 119–20.

[42] In Fiji: T Banivanua-Mar, 'Frontier Space and the Reification of the Rule of Law: Colonial Negotiations in the Western Pacific, 1870–74' (2009) 30 *Australian Feminist Law Journal* 23, 30–32.

[43] In Samoa: M Meleisea, *The Making of Modern Samoa: Traditional Authority and Colonial Administration in the History of Western Samoa* (Suva, University of the South Pacific, 1995) 188.

[44] J Corrin Care, 'Discarding Relics of the Past: Patriation of Laws in the South Pacific' (2009) 39(4) *Victoria University of Wellington Law Review* 635.

contravene the constitution invalid. In addition, courts in several Pacific states have an advisory jurisdiction in constitutional matters, which permits them to provide opinions on questions referred by the Cabinet, Parliament or head of the executive.[45] Pacific states do not have separate specialised constitutional courts with sole and exclusive competence to adjudicate constitutional matters. Constitutional jurisdiction is instead vested in the superior trial court, with a right to appeal to the highest appellate court. In all Pacific states, courts have been called upon to decide constitutional disputes of great political and social significance. These include challenges to the limits of the authority of state and customary decision-making bodies, human rights violations, constitutional proceedings that directly affect the composition of the Parliament and the appointment of officials, and determination of the legality of extra-constitutional actions taken during states of exception and coups. The engagement by Pacific courts in matters of high political and social importance makes the Pacific a good case study for understanding the significance of the use of foreign judges on courts that have, and exercise, constitutional jurisdiction.

Prior to colonisation, the peoples of the Pacific were governed according to custom.[46] The region contains a great diversity of custom, reflected in different legal systems, laws and languages. Indigenous cultural identities do not necessarily map neatly onto state borders. Some states, of which Papua New Guinea, Solomon Islands and Vanuatu are examples, contain within them many different peoples with their own distinctive customs. The historical and contemporary movement of peoples across 'a sea of islands' created cultural diversity as well as cultural connections across what are now state borders.[47] In all states, custom continues to operate, both as an alternative forum to the formal legal system for the resolution of disputes and as an influence upon the content of formal legal rules and procedures, including the constitution.[48] Many constitutions in the region recognise custom as part of the law or as a source of law.[49] The resulting

[45] *Constitution of Fiji 2013*, s 91(5); *Constitution of Fiji 1997*, s 123; *Constitution of Kiribati 1979*, s 66(5); *Constitution of Nauru 1968*, s 55; *Constitution of Papua New Guinea 1975*, s 19; *Constitution of Samoa 1960*, s 73(3); *Constitution of Vanuatu 1980*, s 39(3).

[46] This book uses the term 'custom' to refer to the codes of behaviour and values that constituted the legal systems of Indigenous peoples of the Pacific islands prior to colonisation, and which continue today. As Zorn explains, writers on Pacific legal systems distinguish between 'custom' and 'customary law', but do so for different reasons: J Zorn, 'Custom Then and Now: The Changing Melanesian Family' in A Jowitt and T Newton Cain (eds), *Passage of Change: Law, Society and Governance in the Pacific* (Canberra, Pandanus Books, 2003) 95, fn 3. The preference for the term 'custom' in this book is intended to reflect the sense that custom includes not only codes of behaviour, but also constitutive values of Indigenous peoples.

[47] E Hau'ofa, 'Our Sea of Islands' in E Hau'ofa, E Waddell and V Naidu (eds), *A New Oceania: Rediscovering our Sea of Islands* (Suva, University of the South Pacific in association with Beake House, 1993) 2.

[48] J Corrin, 'Getting Down to Business: Developing the Underlying Law in Papua New Guinea' (2014) 46(2) *The Journal of Legal Pluralism and Unofficial Law* 155; M Forsyth, *A Bird That Flies with Two Wings: The Kastom and State Justice Systems in Vanuatu* (Canberra, ANU Press, 2009); A Va'ai, 'The Idea of Law: A Pacific Perspective' (1997) 21 *Journal of Pacific Studies* 225.

[49] Corrin Care and Paterson (n 40) ch 3; New Zealand Law Commission, 'Converging Currents: Custom and Human Rights in the Pacific', *Study Paper SP17* (2006) 35–36, app 4.

legal pluralism provides a distinctive legal context for the work of judges and courts, and raises particular challenges for foreign judges.

IV. METHODOLOGY, APPROACH AND OUTLINE OF THE ARGUMENT

The practice of foreign judging would reward study from a range of disciplinary perspectives, including history, geography, domestic and international politics, law and development, and colonial and postcolonial studies. This book examines the practice from a legal perspective, considering the phenomenon from the point of view of the domestic legal system that draws judges from beyond its borders. Characterising the phenomenon to be explored as 'foreign judges' deliberately reflects this domestic, internal perspective. It stands in contrast to alternative characterisations of 'travelling', 'overseas' or 'transnational' judges, and alternative points of view such as those of individual judges, donor states, or the international community.

For the reasons set out earlier in this chapter, this book focuses on the use of foreign judges on courts of constitutional jurisdiction. The research methods of constitutional law involve the analysis of legal texts (including constitutions, legislation and case law) and the principles that inform those texts. They also involve the examination of how the operation of these laws and principles affects the practices of government institutions, the relationships between government and the people, and the rights and values of the political community. The methods of constitutional law therefore extend beyond legal doctrine to encompass an assessment of the operation of law in practice.

Like many of the foreign judges studied in this book, I come to the legal systems of Pacific island states as an outsider. In so far as I am studying (what are to me) foreign legal systems from a perspective inevitably informed by my own Anglo-Australian legal training and experience, this book also draws upon the methods of comparative legal research.[50] In order to identify and explain relevant similarities and differences between legal systems, comparative legal scholars need to understand the institutional and socio-cultural contexts in which law operates. In one's own legal system, this kind of knowledge is tacitly assumed. Comparative legal scholarship, however, seeks 'to make explicit the broader social and cultural context and assumptions of a foreign legal system or legal concepts, as they are understood by the people working from within the system'.[51] Analysing and explaining the approach of a foreign legal system to a particular legal phenomenon – in this book, foreign judges on courts of constitutional jurisdiction – therefore requires more than mere description of relevant

[50] On this understanding of comparative law, see M Adams, 'Doing What Doesn't Come Naturally: On the Distinctiveness of Comparative Law' in M Van Hoecke (ed), *Methodologies of Legal Research* (Oxford, Hart Publishing, 2011) 229, 233–34; G Frankenberg, 'Critical Comparisons: Re-Thinking Comparative Law' (1985) 26 *Harvard International Law Journal* 411.

[51] Adams (n 50) 235.

legal rules. A deeper understanding of the operation of those rules in practice and the assumptions and principles that inform them is necessary,[52] and for this I draw in particular on the work of Pacific Islander legal scholars and practitioners. For the purposes of this book, it involves explaining the ways in which the distinctive social and legal contexts of each of the nine Pacific states affect the practice of foreign judging, and its implications for constitutional adjudication, judicial independence, and the role of judges and judiciaries in the region.

For these reasons, this book draws on a combination of empirical, legal analytical and theoretical research methods. Empirical research methods, including interviews with judges and officials, are used to understand the practice of foreign judging in the Pacific and the operation of the laws that regulate it. Legal analytical research methods inform the detailed, comparative analysis of constitutional and statutory provisions relating to the use of foreign judges in the region. Moving beyond description, the book also includes a critical analysis of the constitutional jurisprudence of Pacific courts in order to understand the influence that foreign judges have on the way in which courts approach constitutional interpretation. Constitutional theory is used to better understand the requirements of the three core aspects of the judicial role that may be affected by the use of foreign judges – the processes of constitutional adjudication, judicial impartiality and independence, and the representative qualities of judges and judiciaries – which all contribute to the legitimacy and effectiveness of the judiciary. These qualities, and the concept of legitimacy itself, are the subject of much theoretical debate. This book does not deal with these qualities in the abstract to make normative claims about the propriety of the use of foreign judges. Rather, it seeks to adapt and apply relevant theoretical insights to the use of foreign judges, in order to understand the implications of the practice in the particular context of the Pacific.

The book begins by presenting a comprehensive empirical picture of the contemporary use of foreign judges in the Pacific and the laws and procedures that regulate the practice. Chapter 2 presents a descriptive overview of the foreign judges serving in the Pacific, detailing the number of foreign judges in the region, the nature of their service, their nationality and professional background, the proportion of foreign to local judges, and trends towards localisation (that is, the replacement of foreign judges with local judges). Chapter 3 examines the laws and procedures relating to the selection, appointment and removal of foreign judges, and the terms and conditions of their service. It analyses the constitutional and statutory requirements governing judicial service in each Pacific state, as well as the contractual relationships between judges, governments, courts and funding organisations. It examines how these legal frameworks are applied in practice, drawing on information collected in interviews with judges and other

[52] KL Scheppele, 'Constitutional Ethnography: An Introduction' (2004) 38 *Law and Society Review* 389.

officials, as well as case law and academic scholarship. Together, the information presented in chapters 2 and 3 provides a detailed picture of who the foreign judges of the Pacific are and how they work.

An assessment of the implications of the practice of foreign judging requires an understanding of whether foreign judges are different from local judges, and if so how. Chapter 4 explains the ways in which a judge's nationality matters. It does so by identifying attributes that are understood to accompany nationality – knowledge, membership and identity – and assessing their significance to the role and function of the judges who sit on courts of constitutional jurisdiction. The resulting analysis shows that the nationality of the judge is indeed significant to three aspects of judging. First, the attribute of knowledge is relevant to constitutional adjudication, in that judges are expected to have technical knowledge of the national law as well as wider contextual knowledge of the community in which the law operates. Second, the attribute of membership – the idea that judges are members of the people and the state they serve – underlies assumptions about judicial responsibility and complicates understandings of judicial independence and impartiality. Third, the attribute of identity is significant to the representative function of the judges of the highest domestic courts, in particular as a symbol of sovereignty. It is therefore expected that the nationality of the judge will, prima facie, bear on three aspects of judging: constitutional adjudication, judicial independence, and the representative role of judges and judiciaries.

The following chapters take up each of these three aspects of judging in turn. Chapter 5 considers how the use of foreign judges influences the way in which Pacific courts approach constitutional adjudication. It does so by focusing on two dimensions of knowledge that foreign judges bring to the task. The first is knowledge *reach*, in that foreign judges will have knowledge that extends beyond local circumstances to encompass direct knowledge and experience of their home jurisdiction. The second is a knowledge *gap*, in that foreign judges generally will not have the same depth of knowledge as local judges about the national legal, social and political context of the Pacific state. From a reading of over 80 constitutional cases determined by Pacific courts, I identify three general features of constitutional adjudication in the region: the influence of common law, the limited integration of custom and constitutional law, and a predominantly textualist approach to constitutional interpretation. I explain how these features are, at least in part, explicable in light of the kinds of knowledge that foreign judges, generally speaking, are assumed to bring to the task of adjudication. I suggest that the predominant approach to constitutional adjudication supports a conception of foreign judges as technical legal experts with knowledge and skills that are transferable across jurisdictions.

Chapter 6 assesses the implications of the use of foreign judges on the impartiality and independence of Pacific judiciaries. A common justification for the use of foreign judges is that they bring, or are seen to bring, a greater degree of impartiality than local judges, who, particularly in small Pacific communities, might feel influenced by family, church, political and community ties. I argue, contrary to this claim, that the impartiality of local judges is not compromised by their membership of the Pacific communities they serve, and foreign judges should not be considered more impartial by virtue only of their presumed distance from the local community. A greater threat to judicial independence arises from the insecurity of foreign judges' tenure, resulting from the widespread appointment of foreign judges for short renewable terms and their vulnerability to arbitrary removal from office. I suggest that claims about the impartiality of foreign judges have been overstated, while the risks to judicial independence posed by the insecure tenure of foreign judges have not been properly addressed, but that this dissonance contributes to the conception of foreign judges as *impartial* technical experts.

Finally, paying attention to the nationality of judges highlights the significance placed on judges' allegiance to the state and responsibility to the people, and the expressive functions of judicial office. Chapter 7 uses the lens of representation to examine the different ways in which the individuals who hold judicial office are connected to that office, the state and the people. The significance of allegiance to the state is examined through the formalities of representation, that is, the procedures by which a person is given authority to act as a judge and held accountable in that position. The idea that judges speak for or represent certain values or constituencies in the course of constitutional adjudication provides a way to examine whether foreign judges, through adjudication, might come to represent particular values or concepts. The expressive function of the judiciary is examined by considering the value placed on a judiciary that represents – in the sense of reflecting or resembling – the society it serves. In each case, the circumstances of foreign judging limit the extent to which foreign judges are understood to be authorised by, accountable to, speaking for, or reflective of the people or the state. Instead, greater emphasis is placed on the sense that foreign judges are members of a profession, with shared transnational values of impartiality and commitment to law.

It is only in light of the empirical findings and the analysis of the implications of the use of foreign judges that I am in a position, in chapter 8, to draw conclusions about the rationale for the use of foreign judges and the legitimacy and effectiveness of the practice. As will be seen, the rationales for, and legitimacy of, the use of foreign judges depend on conceptions of what it is that judges do. Chapter 8 examines the most common rationales for the use of foreign judges in the Pacific and suggests that greater clarity about the rationales for using foreign judges would help to justify some of the more problematic aspects of the practice, such as insecure tenure. The chapter then considers the challenges posed by the use of foreign judges to the legitimacy of Pacific courts of constitutional jurisdiction. I suggest that whether or not foreign judges pose any distinctive challenge to legitimacy depends on what it is that judges do, and are expected to do, when adjudicating constitutional cases. I show that the legitimacy of foreign judges is secure when foreign judges are understood as expert and impartial professionals who apply a pre-existing law to resolve constitutional disputes, but that challenges arise when foreign judges are understood to extend or change the law through interpretation, reflect customary and community values, or represent the people. I suggest that this concern underlies the predominant conception of the foreign judge in the Pacific as an impartial, expert professional with transferable skills in adjudication. Based on the empirical and analytical findings of the book, this chapter suggests some good practice initiatives to support the legitimate and effective use of foreign judges in the Pacific.

The book concludes by outlining the significance of this research for understanding the evolving role of judges and judiciaries in contemporary conditions of globalisation.

2

The Foreign Judges of the Pacific

I. INTRODUCTION

ALTHOUGH THE USE of foreign judges is a long-standing practice across the Pacific, there has been no systematic study of the number, proportion and attributes of the foreign judges serving in the region.[1] This chapter, together with chapter 3, addresses this gap by presenting the results of an original empirical study of the composition of the courts of constitutional jurisdiction in Fiji, Kiribati, Nauru, Papua New Guinea, Samoa, Solomon Islands, Tonga, Tuvalu and Vanuatu from the beginning of 2000 to the end of 2019. Over this 20-year period, 225 foreign judges sat on the relevant courts, making up about three-quarters of the total number of judges serving across the region. While the number of foreign judges is large, many serve only for brief periods or on a part-time basis. The most common profile of a foreign judge in the Pacific during this time was male, a citizen of Australia or New Zealand, with judicial experience in his home state. There is, however, variation between Pacific states and notable changes over time, informed by historical and contextual factors, as well as deliberate policy choices by Pacific states about the composition of their courts.

Section II of this chapter sets out the methodology for this empirical study, while section III outlines the number and proportion of foreign judges serving on the relevant Pacific courts. Section IV describes the different kinds of judicial service performed by foreign judges in the Pacific, and explains how the use of both resident and visiting foreign judges inflates the number of foreign judges serving in the region. Section V provides an overview of the personal attributes of the cohort of foreign judges, drawing on data on their nationality, professional background and gender. It identifies some trends regionally and in particular states, and offers some explanations for why some states tend to recruit foreign judges from particular donor states or with particular professional backgrounds. Finally, section VI compares the extent to which the

[1] Smith lists some of the foreign judges sitting on Pacific courts from 2003–12; however, this study covered only foreign judges from Australia, New Zealand and the United Kingdom and did not include Papua New Guinea: SE Smith, 'The Way We Do Things Back Home: Do Expatriate Judges Preferentially Cite the Jurisprudence of Their Home Countries?' (2013) 13(2) *Oxford University Commonwealth Law Journal* 331.

judiciaries of different Pacific states have localised over time by replacing foreign judges with local or citizen judges. Different patterns of localisation in Pacific states are explained on the basis of population size, the different needs of trial and appellate courts, and deliberate localisation policies in some states.

The analysis presented in this chapter is complemented by chapter 3, which describes the laws and practices for recruiting and appointing foreign judges and the terms and conditions of their service. Together, these two chapters provide the evidence required to assess the implications of the use of foreign judges for constitutional adjudication, judicial independence and the representative qualities of Pacific judiciaries, and to draw conclusions about the rationales for and legitimacy of the continued use of foreign judges in Pacific states.

II. METHODOLOGY

A. Defining a 'Foreign Judge'

An empirical study of the foreign judges of the Pacific first requires a clear definition of a 'foreign judge'. In general terms, a foreign judge is a judge from a country other than one's own. The word 'foreign' is based on the Latin word *foras*, meaning 'outside'. The meaning of foreignness is therefore relative, in that it is defined against whatever is considered to be 'inside' or domestic.[2] Legal texts rarely define foreignness. Instead, the law uses concepts such as citizenship, residence or nationality to categorise who is foreign and who is not.

The typical example of a foreign judge is a person who serves as a judge in a state in which he or she does not hold citizenship or usually reside. However, examples arise that strain the equation of foreignness with non-citizenship and non-residence. For example, there is a large Pacific diaspora in New Zealand, and many New Zealand citizens identify as Pacific islanders and maintain strong links to their home countries. Justice Ida Malosi was born in New Zealand to Samoan parents. In 2002 she was appointed a judge of the New Zealand Family Court, becoming the 'first woman Pacific Island judge' in New Zealand.[3] From 2013 to 2014, Justice Malosi served as a judge on the Samoan Supreme Court. The question arises: was Justice Malosi a foreign judge when she sat as a judge in Samoa?

An alternative way to understand foreignness is as belonging to a different national community, and, in the case of foreign *judges*, belonging to a different *legal* community. In this sense, foreign judges are members of a national legal community outside that in which they now serve as judges. Membership of this

[2] R Saunders, *The Concept of the Foreign: An Interdisciplinary Dialogue* (Lanham, MD, Lexington Books, 2003) 3, 6.

[3] M Hewitson, 'Judge Ready to Be Tough but Caring' *New Zealand Herald* (Auckland) (14 September 2002).

legal community might be defined by the jurisdiction in which a person gained his or her legal qualifications or practised law. One problem with this definition is that it would categorise as foreign judges all those citizens of Pacific states who gain legal education and professional experience overseas. There are only three law schools in the region, and it is fairly common for Pacific islander lawyers to have studied and worked overseas.[4] This definition does, however, capture non-citizen judges, most of whom obtained their legal qualifications and professional experience in their home state and not the Pacific state in which they serve as judges. There are some exceptions. For example, Justice David Cannings is an Australian citizen who lived and worked as a lawyer in Papua New Guinea from 1984. He was appointed a judge of the Papua New Guinea National and Supreme Courts in 2004. Despite his long professional experience in Papua New Guinea, under Papua New Guinean law Justice Cannings is classified as a non-citizen judge.[5]

For the purposes of this study, I define a foreign judge as a judge who is not a citizen of the state on whose courts he or she serves. On this basis, both Justice Malosi and Justice Cannings are categorised as foreign judges. Although defaulting to a definition based on citizenship risks glossing the complexities of national identity and the global movement of peoples, it is justified here on the basis that citizenship is the criterion that the laws of Pacific states use to distinguish between local and foreign judges. It must be emphasised, however, that a definition of a foreign judge based on citizenship, while appropriate for this study of the Pacific, is not universally applicable, and studies of foreign judges in other jurisdictions might plausibly take other approaches.[6]

B. Scope of the Empirical Study

For the reasons explained in chapter 1, this study focuses on courts of constitutional jurisdiction. Eighteen courts across the nine Pacific states exercise constitutional jurisdiction. In Kiribati, Samoa, Solomon Islands, Tonga, Tuvalu and Vanuatu, the superior court (designated the High Court or Supreme Court[7])

[4] The University of Papua New Guinea Law School was established in 1965, the School of Law of the University of the South Pacific, which serves 12 member countries, was established in 1994, and the Fiji National University awarded its first law degrees in 2018. On legal career paths in the Pacific, see NN Bilimoria, 'Choices for the South Pacific Region's Bar Associations and Law Societies?' in P Butler and C Morris (eds), *Small States in a Legal World* (Cham, Springer, 2017) 245, 247.

[5] *Organic Law on the Terms and Conditions of Employment of Judges* (PNG), s 2 distinguishes between citizen and non-citizen judges for the purposes of tenure: see further ch 3, section IV.

[6] For example, the *Hong Kong Court of Final Appeal Ordinance 1995* c 484, s 12(4) defines foreign judges by reference to their non-residence in Hong Kong and judicial service in a foreign jurisdiction, avoiding a definition based on citizenship status: see A Dziedzic, 'Foreign Judges and Hong Kong's New National Security Law' (2020) 25(2) *Commonwealth Judicial Journal* 27.

[7] In Kiribati, Solomon Islands and Tuvalu, this court is designated the High Court; in Samoa, Tonga and Vanuatu it is the Supreme Court.

has original jurisdiction in constitutional matters, while the Court of Appeal has appellate jurisdiction in constitutional and other matters.[8] In Fiji, three courts exercise constitutional jurisdiction. The High Court has original jurisdiction in constitutional matters, which must be commenced in that Court.[9] Appeals on constitutional matters may be taken as of right to the Court of Appeal, and from there by leave to the Supreme Court.[10] In Papua New Guinea, constitutional jurisdiction is shared across the National Court and the Supreme Court. The Supreme Court, as the final court of appeal, has original and exclusive jurisdiction to hear any question relating to the interpretation or application of the Constitution.[11] However, both the National Court and the Supreme Court are charged with enforcing constitutional rights, upon an application by an interested person or upon the Court's own initiative, and both have the power to review the constitutionality of legislation.[12] Judges are appointed to sit concurrently on the National and Supreme Courts, and so they are taken to be one court for the purposes of this study.

The structure of the courts of Nauru underwent significant change in 2018. Prior to 12 March 2018, the High Court of Australia served as Nauru's court of final appeal. Appeals that involved the interpretation or effect of the Constitution were excluded from the High Court's appellate jurisdiction by agreement between Nauru and Australia,[13] leaving the Supreme Court of Nauru as the only court of constitutional jurisdiction in that state.[14] Following Nauru's withdrawal from the treaty formalising this arrangement, it established its own Court of Appeal in May 2018, with jurisdiction over constitutional matters.[15]

Kiribati and Tuvalu retain appeals to the Judicial Committee of the Privy Council. Appeals from Kiribati may only be taken in matters affecting the people of Banaba Island, who hold special rights under the Constitution of Kiribati.[16] Appeals from Tuvalu to the Privy Council may be taken by leave from the Tuvalu Court of Appeal.[17] To date, there have been no appeals to the Privy Council from either country. Because the Judicial Committee of the Privy Council is not a national court, it is not included in this study.[18] Tonga has its own Privy

[8] *Constitution of Kiribati 1979*, s 88; *Constitution of Samoa 1960*, ss 73(2), 80; *Constitution of Solomon Islands 1978*, s 83; *Constitution of Tonga 1875*, s 90; *Constitution of Tuvalu 1986*, ss 130, 131, 135; *Constitution of Vanuatu 1980*, s 53.

[9] *Constitution of Fiji 2013*, s 100(4); *Constitution of Fiji 1997*, s 120(2).

[10] *Constitution of Fiji 2013*, ss 98(1)–(2), 99; *Constitution of Fiji 1997*, ss 121, 122.

[11] *Constitution of Papua New Guinea 1975*, ss 18(1), 162.

[12] *Constitution of Papua New Guinea 1975*, s 57; *Dibusa Mining Pty Ltd v Akipe* [1991] PNGLR 265.

[13] *Agreement between the Government of Australia and the Government of the Republic of Nauru relating to Appeals to the High Court of Australia from the Supreme Court of Nauru*, 6 September 1976, art 2; *Appeals (Amendment) Act 1974* (Nauru), s 45.

[14] *Constitution of Nauru 1968*, s 54(1).

[15] *Constitution (Amendment) Act 2018* (Nauru); *Nauru Court of Appeal Act 2018* (Nauru).

[16] *Constitution of Kiribati 1979*, s 123.

[17] *Constitution of Tuvalu 1986*, s 136; *Superior Courts Act 1987* c 7.68 (Tuvalu), s 13.

[18] For reasons explained in ch 1, section I.

Council, which advises the Monarch in the exercise of his or her executive and judicial functions. For much of Tonga's history, its Privy Council served as the court of final appeal, but its judicial function is now limited to hearing matters relating to hereditary estates and titles,[19] and it too is excluded from this study.

This study covers the composition of the relevant courts from the beginning of 2000 to the end of 2019. This 20-year period was chosen in order to understand the use of foreign judges at a time when the courts and other institutions of Pacific states were well established. The nine Pacific states became independent over the period from 1962 to 1980. Not all states were in a position to establish their judiciaries at the date of independence. Until the mid-1980s, Kiribati, Solomon Islands and Tuvalu extended the arrangements made during colonial times, when courts and judges in Fiji served the Western Pacific region.[20] Domestic courts of final appeal for Fiji and Tonga were established in 1990, when both states discontinued appeals to the Judicial Committee of the Privy Council and the Tongan Privy Council respectively. Therefore, by 1990, the court structures described here were in place, and 2000 to 2019 represents a period when the Pacific courts were, collectively, well settled. The exception is Nauru's Court of Appeal, which was established in 2018 right at the end of the time period of this study. This new court is included in this study, although its short period of existence is taken into account when relevant to understanding the data.

C. Techniques of Data Collection

There is no publicly available, comprehensive list of foreign judges who have served in the Pacific. While some Pacific judiciaries produce Law Reports and Annual Reports that sometimes set out the composition of the court for that year, such reports are not produced consistently in each of the nine states. Lacking reliable and comprehensive data, I created my own dataset with the names, dates of service, nationalities and professional backgrounds of all foreign judges who served on the relevant courts during the case study period.

The dataset was compiled using three sources. In order to identify the names of judges and dates of their service, I conducted an audit of all judgments of the relevant courts published by the Pacific Legal Information Institute (Paclii), an open-access online database of legal materials from 14 Pacific jurisdictions.[21] Not every decision of every court is provided to Paclii for publication, and as a result the database is not exhaustive. It is, however, sufficiently comprehensive to indicate the names of the judges – local and foreign – who produced written judgments in each year over the case study period. A second source of information

[19] *Constitution of Tonga 1875*, ss 50(2), 90.
[20] M Pulea, 'A Regional Court of Appeal for the Pacific' (1980) 9(2) *Pacific Perspective* 1, 4–6.
[21] Pacific Islands Legal Information Institute at www.paclii.org.

was notices of judicial appointment. In four states – Kiribati, Nauru, Solomon Islands and Vanuatu – judicial appointments are published in an official government gazette, but not all judicial appointments are gazetted and not all gazettes are readily available. In Fiji, Papua New Guinea and Tonga, judicial appointments are often announced by government media releases, and so media reports were also consulted. Some judges also provided me with copies of their warrants of appointment. Finally, having identified the names of the judges serving on the relevant courts, I used publicly available biographies and media sources to ascertain the nationality, professional experience and dates of service of each judge to the extent possible.[22] Each of these sources has limitations in terms of comprehensiveness, accessibility and accuracy. However, drawing on all three sources provided a comprehensive list of foreign judges and reasonably complete details about each judge's nationality, position at the time of appointment and the years served on each court.

In order to gather information about the day-to-day practices of foreign judging – such as how judges are selected and appointed and the conditions of their service – I conducted 26 interviews. Twenty-two interviews were with people who, between them, had served as judges in all nine Pacific states and on 15 of the 18 courts of constitutional jurisdiction in the region. The judges interviewed were from three donor countries: Australia, New Zealand and the United Kingdom. No foreign judges from Sri Lanka, all of whom served in Fiji, were interviewed because the then Chief Justice of Fiji refused to permit the researcher to approach judges currently serving on the Fijian courts[23] and Sri Lankan judges who had formerly served in Fiji declined or did not respond to invitations to participate. Four interviews were conducted with representatives of organisations involved in the recruitment and appointment of foreign judges in Pacific states or donor organisations.

The interviews were conducted between July 2016 and May 2017. Interviews were semi-structured and covered the pathways to becoming a judge in the Pacific, the procedures for recruitment and appointment, the judge's tenure and remuneration, and the kinds of tasks that judges performed while serving on the Pacific court. The primary purpose of the interviews was to gather information about procedural matters relating to the appointment and service of foreign judges not available from other sources, although participants sometimes also shared their views about aspects of the practice of foreign judging based on their own experiences. In order to maintain confidentiality, information gathered from interviews is framed in general terms without identifying individuals, with citations only to the file note number of each interview (eg F1, F2). The information provided in the interviews was supplemented by reflections shared by foreign judges in memoirs, articles and speeches.

[22] Where public information on the judge's citizenship was not available, nationality was inferred from the judge's place of residence, legal education and professional legal practice.

[23] Letter from AHCT Gates, Chief Justice of Fiji, to Anna Dziedzic, 6 October 2016.

III. NUMBER AND PROPORTION OF FOREIGN JUDGES

During the period from the beginning of 2000 to the end of 2019, a total of 302 judges served on the courts of constitutional jurisdiction in the nine Pacific states. Of these, 225 were foreign judges and 92 were citizen judges, with 15 Pacific Islander judges accounted for in both groups because they served as local judges in their home state and as foreign judges in another state in the region.

The ratio of foreign to local judges varied between states. In Nauru and Tuvalu all of the judges on the relevant courts were foreign. Between 69 per cent and 95 per cent of the judges serving in Fiji, Kiribati, Samoa, Solomon Islands, Tonga and Vanuatu were foreign judges. Papua New Guinea had the lowest proportion of foreign judges, at just 26 per cent. Combining the figures for each jurisdiction separately, and thereby counting the 34 foreign judges who served in several Pacific states more than once, 276 of the 368 (or 75 per cent) of the judges serving in the region over the case study period were foreign judges.

Table 2.1 Number and Proportion of Foreign Judges in the Nine Pacific States 2000–19

State	Number of judges	Number of local judges	Number of foreign judges	% foreign judges
Tuvalu	11	0	11	100%
Nauru	18	0	18	100%
Kiribati	19	1	18	95%
Tonga	26	2	24	92%
Fiji	135	24	111	82%
Samoa	37	7	30	81%
Vanuatu	33	6	27	81%
Solomon Islands	32	10	22	69%
PNG	57	42	15	26%

While it is clear that the number and proportion of foreign judges serving in the Pacific is high, the numbers do not tell the whole story. The remainder of this chapter situates these figures in context, by reference to the nature of foreign judges' service and the political and historical contexts in which Pacific courts operate.

IV. DIFFERENT KINDS OF JUDICIAL SERVICE

It is important to distinguish between three broad categories of judicial service performed by foreign judges in the Pacific.

The first category consists of foreign judges who reside in the Pacific state and serve on the Pacific court full time for the duration of their appointments. This is the case for most foreign judges serving on the superior trial courts in Fiji, Kiribati, Papua New Guinea, Samoa, Solomon Islands, Tonga and Vanuatu. While there are exceptional cases in which a foreign judge permanently resides in the Pacific state and effectively serves his or her entire judicial career in one Pacific judiciary,[24] most serve only for a period of years or months.

The second category consists of foreign judges who do not reside in the Pacific state but rather visit periodically or temporarily. In Nauru and Tuvalu, the two smallest jurisdictions, the superior trial courts sit part time. As a result, judges do not reside in Nauru or Tuvalu but rather visit as required for sittings of the court, generally two to three times a year.[25] Several Chief Justices of Nauru and Tuvalu have held their positions concurrently with other judicial appointments in the Pacific.[26]

This category also includes foreign judges who sit on courts of appeal, which in the Pacific sit only part time. Courts of appeal are convened for sittings as required in very small jurisdictions such as Nauru and Tuvalu, and periodically one to three times a year in the other jurisdictions. Generally, several foreign judges hold commissions to sit on the court of appeal, and three judges from this pool are invited to constitute the court for a particular sitting. These judges will visit the Pacific state for one to two weeks. Some judges of appeal return to sit in the Pacific jurisdiction annually or more frequently; others may sit only once or twice. In Papua New Guinea, Vanuatu and increasingly Samoa, visiting judges of appeal often sit with judges (both local and foreign) from the court below.[27]

The third category consists of visiting ad hoc judges, who are appointed to hear a specific matter or to sit for a very short term.[28] This most often arises when existing judges are unable to hear a particular case because of a conflict of interest.

[24] Examples include Anthony Gates, who served as a judge and then Chief Justice in Fiji on a full-time basis throughout the case study period, and David Cannings, described in section II.

[25] Nauru Constitutional Review Committee, *Naoero Ituga: Report* (2007) 115; Office of the Attorney-General, 'Country Report of the Office of the Attorney General Tuvalu' (Report to the 34th Pacific Islands Law Officers' Network Meeting, October 2015) 7.

[26] Sir Gaven Donne served concurrently as Chief Justice of Nauru and Tuvalu until 2001; Robin Millhouse served concurrently as Chief Justice of Nauru and Kiribati from 2006–10; Sir Gordon Ward served as Chief Justice of Tuvalu concurrently with service as the Chief Justice of Tonga and President of the Fiji Court of Appeal.

[27] In these states, judges appointed to the superior trial court are ex officio judges of the court of appeal: *Constitution of Papua New Guinea 1975*, s 161(1); *Constitution of Samoa 1960*, s 75(2)(a); *Constitution of Vanuatu 1980*, s 50; *Judicial Services and Courts Act 2000* c 270 (Vanuatu), s 45. This is also the case in Fiji, Kiribati, Solomon Islands and Tuvalu: *Constitution of Fiji 2013*, s 98(2); *Constitution of Fiji 1997*, s 128; *Constitution of Kiribati 1979*, s 91(1)(a); *Constitution of Solomon Islands 1978*, s 85(2); *Superior Courts Act 1987* c 7.68 (Tuvalu), s 7(1).

[28] Ad hoc appointments are expressly permitted by *Constitution of Kiribati 1979*, s 93(1); *Constitution of Samoa 1960*, s 75(5); *Constitution of Tuvalu 1986*, s 123. All constitutions in the region permit the appointment of foreign judges on short terms.

These differences in the nature of the judicial services provided by foreign judges have significance for the assessment of the implications of foreign judging undertaken in later chapters. For example, a foreign judge who resides in the Pacific state is likely to have greater opportunity to gain knowledge and experience of that state, which is relevant to the kinds of knowledge that foreign judges bring to the task of constitutional adjudication. There is also likely to be greater stability in the membership of courts composed of resident foreign judges serving on a full-time basis, than in courts constituted by visiting ad hoc or part-time judges, although stability may also be fostered by foreign judges who regularly return to sit on the one Pacific court.

The nature of judicial service is also important for understanding why such a large number of foreign judges have served in the Pacific. The pool of foreign judges who make themselves available to sit on a Pacific state's court of appeal is likely to be much larger than the three judges who compose the bench, to accommodate visiting judges' limited availability and other commitments. Where foreign judges serve for short periods of time only, either as visiting or resident judges, the one position on a Pacific court tends to be filled by a succession of foreign judges on short terms, rather than by a single permanent judge. These practicalities of foreign judging in the Pacific have the effect of inflating the number of foreign judges in the region.

V. WHO SERVES AS A FOREIGN JUDGE IN THE PACIFIC?

The most common profile of a foreign judge in the Pacific is an Australian or New Zealand male citizen with judicial experience. This 'average' foreign judge, however, does not account for all foreign judges across all courts and all time. Mapping the attributes of the judges in each state reveals diversity between jurisdictions in relation to the nationalities of the foreign judges on their courts as well as changes over time. The recruitment of foreign judges from Commonwealth jurisdictions in Asia and Africa and from within the Pacific itself, represents a shift away from the traditional donor countries of Australia and New Zealand, at least in some Pacific states. Further, while the majority of foreign judges in the region have judicial experience, a significant proportion are recruited from legal practice. In relation to gender, there is limited diversity and little change, as male judges predominate in the cohorts of both foreign and local judges. Comparative analysis between Pacific states provides insight into the range of factors that influence the characteristics of the foreign judges serving in the region, including the availability and expertise of foreign candidates for judicial appointment, procedures for recruitment, and the historical links and political relationships between Pacific states and the states and organisations from which foreign judges are sourced.

The nationality, professional background and gender of the foreign judges of the Pacific are not only relevant to understanding patterns in the recruitment of foreign judges, but, as will be seen in later chapters, also affect the kinds of knowledge that foreign judges bring to their role, claims made about judicial independence, and the expressive or reflective qualities of Pacific judiciaries.

A. Nationality

All foreign judges serving in the Pacific are from jurisdictions with common law legal systems. Of the 225 foreign judges serving across the Pacific, 70 (31 per cent) were from New Zealand, 70 (31 per cent) from Australia, 47 (21 per cent) from Sri Lanka and 14 (6 per cent) from the United Kingdom. The remaining 11 per cent comprise 15 judges from other states within the Pacific region (six from Papua New Guinea, four from Fiji, two each from Samoa and Solomon Islands, and one from Vanuatu), six from African states (two judges from Uganda, and one each from Botswana, The Gambia, Nigeria and South Africa) and the remaining three from Hong Kong, India and Singapore. There is, however, considerable variation between Pacific states in relation to the nationality of their foreign judges. As illustrated in Figure 2.1, some states heavily favour judges from one foreign state while others appoint judges of more diverse nationalities.

Figure 2.1 Nationality of Foreign Judges on Pacific Courts 2000–19

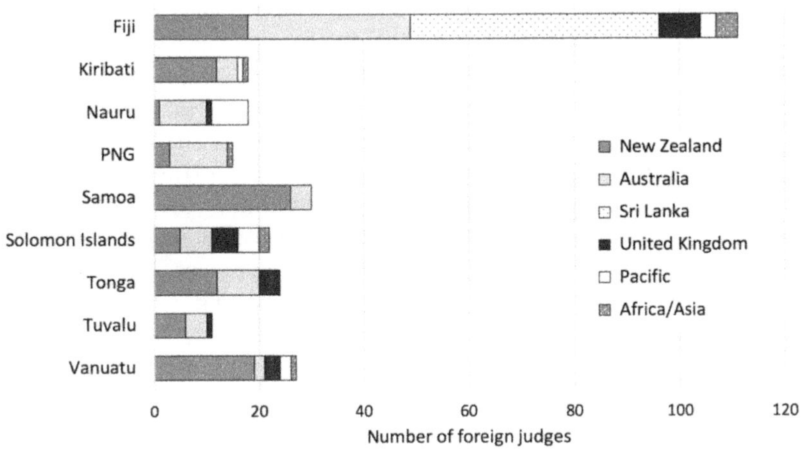

Pacific constitutions provide that in order to be appointed a judge, a person must have held judicial office or practised law in the state itself or another country. Such 'other countries' may be any country,[29] any Commonwealth country,[30]

[29] *Constitution of Kiribati 1979*, ss 81(3), 91(1)(b).

[30] *Constitution of Tonga 1875*, s 85(b)(i); *Constitution of Solomon Islands 1978*, s 78(3)(a); *Constitution of Vanuatu 1980*, s 49(2) with *Legal Practitioners (Qualifications) Regulations 1996* (Vanuatu), s 2.

countries with a similar legal system[31] and/or countries prescribed by law.[32] The legal frameworks therefore permit the appointment of judges from a much wider range of Commonwealth countries than is reflected in practice. The following paragraphs discuss the range of historical, political and pragmatic factors that influence the nationalities of the foreign judges appointed to particular Pacific courts.

i. Historical and Contemporary Links

The use of Australian, New Zealand and British judges reflects continuing historical, political and legal connections between these countries and Pacific states. Prior to independence, these three countries were the colonial administrators: Fiji, Kiribati, Solomon Islands and Tuvalu were British territories, while Tonga was a British protectorate; Nauru and Papua New Guinea were administered by Australia; and Samoa was administered by New Zealand. Prior to its independence, Vanuatu was a condominium jointly administered by Britain and France. These historical links continue to influence the nationality of foreign judges in some states. For example, the fact that 25 of the 29 foreign judges who served in Samoa over the case study period were from New Zealand can be seen as a legacy of New Zealand's position as colonial administrator and the continuing close relationship between the two countries.[33]

Several judges interviewed noted the similarities between their home legal system and Pacific legal systems as a factor that facilitated judicial service in the Pacific.[34] Upon independence, several Pacific constitutions imported and applied the common law of England as it stood at a particular date.[35] Many adopted statutes based on precedents in Australia, New Zealand and the United Kingdom. These historical legal influences also help to explain the high numbers of Australian and New Zealand judges, and the continuing use of British judges.

The legacies of colonisation are echoed in the contemporary movement of foreign judges, which tends to follow the development aid channels that flow from larger 'developed' states to smaller 'developing' states. This in part reflects 'market forces' of supply and demand. Australia, New Zealand and the United Kingdom all have established judicial systems and large numbers of

[31] *Constitution of Samoa 1960*, s 65(5); *Constitution of Tuvalu 1986*, s 124(a); *National Court Act 1975* (PNG), s 2(a)(ii).

[32] *Constitution of Fiji 2013*, s 105; *Constitution of Fiji 1997*, s 130; Judicial Tribunals (Prescribed Countries) Promulgation No 32 of 2007; *Constitution of Solomon Islands*, s 78(3); *Constitution of Nauru 1968*, s 49(3) with *Legal Practitioners Act 1973* (Nauru), s 5.

[33] New Zealand administered Samoa as League of Nations Mandate and later a United Nations Trust Territory from 1914 until its independence in 1962. Upon Samoa's independence, the two countries entered into a Treaty of Friendship.

[34] Interviews F1, F4, F5, F8, F10, F12, F22.

[35] J Corrin Care, 'Cultures in Conflict: The Role of the Common Law in the South Pacific' (2002) 6(2) *Journal of South Pacific Law*, available at www.usp.ac.fj/index.php?id=13220; G Powles, 'The Common Law as a Source of Law in the South Pacific: Experiences in Western Polynesia' (1988) 10 *University of Hawaii Law Review* 105.

qualified judges and lawyers prepared to serve overseas, including judges who have reached the statutory age for retirement but who wish to continue to work. On the demand side, Pacific states are small, developing states, with limited financial and human resources, and several are highly dependent on overseas aid to meet the costs of government. Australia and New Zealand have a strong presence in the Pacific as aid and development donors, particularly in the law and justice sector.[36] Australian and New Zealand judges regularly participate in regional judicial conferences and training, where they meet Pacific judges and some form lasting personal connections.[37] These links, along with geographical proximity, account in part for the higher use of foreign judges from Australia and New Zealand over the case study period.

ii. Procedures for Recruitment

The nationality of foreign judges is also influenced by the procedures used to recruit them. These procedures are described more fully in chapter 3 and range from informal approaches from the Chief Justice, to arrangements between particular courts and processes managed by external funding agencies.

Where judges are recruited through informal approaches, it is to be expected that personal connections will play a part. Foreign judges who are approached for recommendations are likely to suggest candidates from their own jurisdictions, for the simple reason that such candidates are best known to them. This perhaps explains why the Courts of Appeal of Kiribati and Tuvalu predominantly comprise retired judges from superior courts of New Zealand.

Where courts have established formal programmes for the provision of judges, it is likely that a greater proportion of foreign judges will be of that nationality. For example, the Supreme Court of Vanuatu and the District Court of New Zealand have a rolling secondment programme, whereby a District Court judge from New Zealand serves in Vanuatu for two years and is replaced at the end of that term by another District Court judge.[38] This programme accounts, in part, for the higher number of New Zealand judges serving on the courts of Vanuatu.

In contrast, when external aid providers recruit judges on behalf of the Pacific state, there is a greater diversity in the nationality of foreign judges. For example, three of the African judges who served in the Pacific were recruited through the Commonwealth Fund for Technical Cooperation.[39] Under this

[36] eg the Pacific Judicial Development Programme, funded by the Government of New Zealand and managed by the Federal Court of Australia.

[37] JM Van Dyke, 'The Pacific Judicial Conference: Strengthening the Independent Judiciary and the Rule of Law in the Pacific' (2011) 22(1–2) *Western Legal History* 127.

[38] Ministry of Justice, *The District Courts of New Zealand* (2008) 11.

[39] Vincent Zehurikize from Uganda served on the High Court of Kiribati; Nkemdilim Amelia Izuako from Nigeria served on the High Court of Solomon Islands; and Mary Sey from The Gambia served on the Supreme Court of Vanuatu.

programme, the Commonwealth recruited and funded judges and other experts to serve in Commonwealth countries, prioritising south-south exchanges.[40] To take a different example, the Regional Assistance Mission to the Solomon Islands (RAMSI) was established to restore law and order in Solomon Islands after a period of civil conflict from 1998 to 2003.[41] RAMSI sought out a range of foreign legal personnel, including judges, in order to clear the backlog of criminal cases arising from the conflict.[42] RAMSI recruited judges from Australia, Fiji, New Zealand and the United Kingdom. The diversity of nationalities on the Solomon Islands High Court may have been fostered by RAMSI's hiring practices, in which judicial positions were advertised through international development consulting firms.

iii. Intra-regional Appointments

Fifteen of the 225 foreign judges were from other Pacific island states. There is a long history of intra-regional judicial exchanges in the Pacific. Papua New Guinea, as a larger state with a high proportion of local judges, has provided judges to other Pacific states since the early 1990s.[43] After an apparent lapse in the mid-2000s, there are signs that the recruitment of foreign judges from within the Pacific is again increasing.

The intra-regional movement of judges arises in a range of different ways, informed by circumstances in judges' home states and in recruiting states. Two Fijian judges who were unable to serve in Fiji following the 2006 coup sat instead on the Supreme Courts of Nauru and Vanuatu.[44] Sir John Muria, the former Chief Justice of Solomon Islands, was appointed Chief Justice of Kiribati in 2011 after serving as a Commonwealth-funded judge in Belize and Sierra Leone. In 2017 and 2018, the Papua New Guinea Supreme Court entered into formal agreements with Solomon Islands and Nauru respectively to provide Papua New Guinean judges to sit on the courts of appeal in those jurisdictions.[45]

[40] Commonwealth Secretariat, *Report of the Commonwealth Secretary-General 2011–2013* (London, Commonwealth Secretariat, 2013) 21.

[41] A Palmer, 'The Ethnic Conflict in Solomon Islands' in U Dolgopol and JG Gardam (eds), *The Challenge of Conflict: International Law Responds* (Leiden, Martinus Nijhoff Publishers, 2006) 49.

[42] J Fraenkel, J Madraiwiwi and H Okole, 'The RAMSI Decade: A Review of the Regional Assistance Mission to Solomon Islands, 2003–2013' (Solomon Islands Government and Pacific Islands Forum, 2014) 54.

[43] G Hassall and C Saunders, *Asia-Pacific Constitutional Systems* (Cambridge, Cambridge University Press, 2002) 187.

[44] Ratu Joni Madraiwiwi served as Chief Justice of Nauru and Daniel Fatiaki as a judge of the Supreme Court of Vanuatu. Fatiaki was appointed Chief Justice of Nauru in 2021.

[45] 'PNG, SI Sign Agreement on Judiciary Cooperation' *The National* (Port Moresby) (24 August 2017); A Osii, 'Agreement Signed for PNG Judge to Sit in Nauru's Appeals Court' *The National* (Port Moresby) (26 July 2018).

In Fiji, Solomon Islands and Vanuatu, Pacific islander judges serve alongside other foreign judges recruited from outside the region. Nauru's new Court of Appeal, established in 2018, is distinctive for recruiting its judges almost exclusively from other Pacific island states. Five judges were appointed to the Court in 2018: Sir John Muria (a Solomon Islander and at the time Chief Justice of Kiribati); Sir Albert Palmer (Chief Justice of Solomon Islands); Vincent Lunabek (Chief Justice of Vanuatu); Jiten Singh (former judge of the High Court of Fiji); and Michael Scott (a British citizen who has served as a judge in several Pacific jurisdictions for many years).[46] Nicholas Kirriwom, a senior Papua New Guinean judge, was appointed to the Court in 2019 pursuant to an agreement between the Supreme Court of Papua New Guinea and Nauru.[47] The composition of Nauru's new Court of Appeal reflects a deliberate policy choice by authorities in Nauru to create a bench of judges drawn from the region, rather than the traditional donor state Australia. A similar preference can be discerned in the composition of Nauru's Supreme Court, which since 2014 has included visiting judges from Fiji and Samoa in addition to judges from Australia.

Some Pacific authorities have expressed an interest in the greater use of foreign judges from within the region, given commonalities between the legal systems and similarities in the social and cultural contexts in which the law operates.[48] While in the past, the small number of Pacific Islander judges and lawyers has limited the pool for recruitment, the signs are that intra-regional appointments will increase as the number of Pacific islander judges and lawyers also grows.

iv. National and International Politics

Finally, domestic and international politics influence the nationality of the foreign judges serving in a particular jurisdiction. This is seen most clearly in Fiji, where there has been a marked change in the nationality of foreign judges over time. As shown in Figure 2.2, prior to 2009 the foreign judges serving on Fiji's High Court, Court of Appeal and Supreme Court were predominantly recruited from Australia, New Zealand and the United Kingdom. After April 2009, Fiji began to recruit high numbers of judges from Sri Lanka. Forty-seven Sri Lankans were appointed to the Fijian courts between 2009 and 2019, outnumbering both local judges and judges of other nationalities.

[46] Government of Nauru, 'Nauru Announces Court of Appeal' *Media Release* (24 July 2018).

[47] Government of Nauru, 'PNG's Nicholas Kirriwom Sworn in as Judge to Nauru Appeals Court' *Media Release* (12 November 2018).

[48] L Kershaw, 'Presentation to Pacific Constitutions and the Rule of Law Conference' (Auckland, 7 December 2011).

Figure 2.2 Nationality of Foreign Judges Serving in Fiji 2000–19

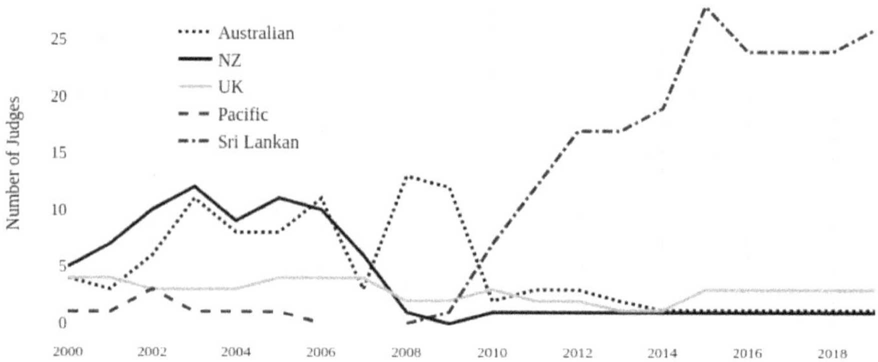

This dramatic change in the composition of the Fijian courts followed a military coup. On 5 December 2006, Commodore Voreqe Bainimarama led a coup, ousting the elected Prime Minister and dissolving the Parliament. Bainimarama then led an interim government that ruled Fiji for nearly seven years. The actions of Bainimarama and other officials involved in establishing the interim government were challenged in court. On 9 April 2009, the Court of Appeal ruled that those actions were contrary to the Constitution and that the interim government had unlawfully assumed executive authority.[49] The following day, the President abrogated the Constitution, revoked all judicial appointments and installed Bainimarama as interim Prime Minister to rule until democratic elections were restored in 2014.[50]

This coup and its aftermath resulted in a great deal of instability for the Fijian courts. It exposed deep polarisations and personal animosities within the Fijian judiciary.[51] Early in 2007, Chief Justice Fatiaki, a Fijian, was suspended and replaced by Anthony Gates, a British/Australian citizen with a long record of judicial service in Fiji.[52] Gates' appointment as Acting Chief Justice and other judicial appointments made under the interim regime were criticised as unconstitutional on the grounds that the Judicial Services Commission was improperly constituted.[53] Over the course of 2007, several foreign judges resigned, citing

[49] *Qarase v Bainimarama* [2009] FJCA 67.

[50] President Ratu Josefa Iloilovatu Uluivuda, Address to the Nation, 10 April 2009; *Revocation of Judicial Appointments Decree* No 4 of 2009 (Fiji).

[51] V Iyer, 'The Judiciary in Fiji: A Broken Reed?' in HP Lee and M Pittard (eds), *Asia-Pacific Judiciaries: Independence, Impartiality and Integrity* (Cambridge, Cambridge University Press, 2017) 109, 124–26.

[52] G Leung, 'The Impact of the Coup on Fiji's Judiciary' in J Fraenkel, S Firth and BV Lal (eds), *The 2006 Military Takeover in Fiji: A Coup to End All Coups?* (Canberra, ANU Press, 2009) 291, 293–94.

[53] *Constitution of Fiji 1997*, s 131 required that the Judicial Services Commission comprise the Chief Justice, the Chair of the Public Service Commission and the President of the Fiji Law Society, but the two former members had been removed from office: International Bar Association, *Dire Straits: A Report on the Rule of Law in Fiji* (2009) 48–49.

concerns about judicial independence and the manner in which Acting Chief Justice Gates administered the courts.[54] Some foreign judges stayed for the duration of their existing commissions but did not seek reappointment under the interim regime.[55] The remaining judges were dismissed on 10 April 2009, by presidential order revoking all judicial appointments.

Fiji needed judges but was unable to recruit them from the traditional donor countries of Australia, New Zealand and the United Kingdom. Following the abrogation of the Constitution in April 2009, Fiji was suspended from the Commonwealth and the Pacific Islands Forum. Australia and New Zealand placed bans on Fijian officials, including judges, travelling into Australia and New Zealand.[56] Professional lawyers' associations in Australia and New Zealand advised their members against accepting judicial appointments in Fiji.[57] In this context, Fiji turned to Sri Lanka to provide a new cohort of foreign judges, and Fijian officials visited Sri Lanka to recruit judges and build connections between the courts.[58] Sri Lanka is a member of the Commonwealth, a mixed common law jurisdiction, and boasts a large number of legally qualified citizens. Fiji is, however, the only Pacific state in which Sri Lankans serve as judges.[59] While Sri Lankans continue to serve in Fiji in high numbers, Fiji has increased the diversity of nationalities represented on its Supreme Court. Since 2018, senior judges from Singapore, India, South Africa and Hong Kong[60] have been appointed to the Supreme Court, creating a multinational profile that is distinctive amongst courts in the Pacific.

Fiji's experience demonstrates how political relationships between Pacific states and the states from which judges are sourced can affect the extent to which certain nationalities are represented on Pacific courts. The issue is not confined to Fiji. It is notable that New Zealand, not Australia, is the primary source of foreign judges to Vanuatu's Supreme Court, in circumstances in which neither country has particularly close colonial ties to Vanuatu. One reason for this is that the ties of nationality between Australian judges and Australian development agencies in particular have been said to 'have a negative impact on the community's and politician's ideas about the independence of the judiciary'.[61]

[54] G Leung, 'The Erosion of Judicial Independence' in Fraenkel, Firth and Lal (eds) (n 52) 301, 303; International Bar Association (n 53) 49–50.

[55] The significance of the acceptance of judicial appointment by foreign judges is discussed in ch 7.

[56] 'Fiji's Chief Justice Condemns Australian, NZ "Interference" and "Hostility"' *Pacific Scoop* (Wellington) (3 November 2009).

[57] C Merritt, 'When Backlogs Lead to Payback' *The Australian* (Canberra) (1 May 2009) 27; 'NZ Lawyers Should Not Work for Fiji Regime, Law Society Says' *NZ Herald* (Auckland) (21 April 2009).

[58] B Sirimanna, 'Fiji Courts Want 6 of Our Judges' *Sunday Times* (Colombo) (16 August 2009).

[59] Although Sri Lankan citizens have been appointed judges in Seychelles.

[60] These judges are Quentin Loh from the Supreme Court of Singapore; Madan Lokur, retired judge of the Supreme Court of India; Fritz Brand, retired judge of the Supreme Court of Appeal of South Africa; and Frank Stock, retired judge of the Hong Kong Court of Appeal and non-permanent judge of the Hong Kong Court of Final Appeal. All serve the Supreme Court of Fiji as visiting foreign judges.

[61] M Forsyth, 'Understanding Judicial Independence in Vanuatu', *Discussion Paper 2015/9, State, Society and Governance in Melanesia* (Australian National University, 2015) 9.

It is reported that this concern, combined with past allegations of spying by Australian police and law officials in Vanuatu and the fact that many cases before Vanuatu courts involve Australian interests, has led Vanuatu to take a cautious approach to sourcing foreign judges from Australia, although Australia provides assistance in other ways to Vanuatu's law and justice sector.[62]

B. Professional Background

Roughly 42 per cent of the 225 foreign judges were sitting as judges at the time of their appointment to a Pacific court. Most of these judges were serving as judges in their home jurisdiction, but nine were serving as judges elsewhere. These judges either serve concurrently in the Pacific state and their home jurisdiction, or take leave from their home court to serve in the Pacific. About 24 per cent were retired judges in their home jurisdiction at the time of their appointment, while 28 per cent were lawyers immediately prior to taking judicial appointment in the Pacific. The remainder were public servants, magistrates or tribunal members, in their home jurisdictions or abroad.

These figures are approximate because the data on which they are based include some generalisations in coding. They record only the judge's position in his or her home country at the date of appointment to the Pacific court and therefore do not account for changes during the period of a judge's service in the Pacific (for example, a judge's subsequent retirement from a judicial position at home), nor do they capture the entirety of the foreign judge's professional career.

It is nonetheless possible to trace some general trends. Appointees to the courts of appeal in the region tend to be either sitting or retired judges in their home states. This preference can be attributed to the prestige, knowledge and authority that experienced judges bring to courts of appeal. It may also reflect some sensitivities about a foreign judge with no prior judicial experience being in a position to overrule judges in the courts below.[63] There is greater variation, however, amongst superior trial courts. In Kiribati, Samoa and Vanuatu, the foreign judges appointed to the superior trial courts generally had previous judicial experience. In Fiji, Nauru, Papua New Guinea, Solomon Islands, Tonga and Tuvalu, the professional backgrounds of foreign judges are more diverse, with judges drawn from both foreign judiciaries and legal practice.

The choice between appointing a retired foreign judge and a judge currently sitting in his or her home jurisdiction depends in particular on the attitude of the head of the relevant court in the judge's home state. Some Chief Justices prefer that judges on their courts do not concurrently serve on courts overseas.[64] Some

[62] ibid.
[63] Interview F7.
[64] Interviews F7, F14, F17.

permit it on the basis that judges serve overseas during periods of leave and as such do not affect the workload of the judge or the court as a whole.[65] Others are in favour of concurrent service as a way of connecting courts and expanding judges' experiences.[66] Some courts have established ongoing relationships with particular Pacific courts, whereby sitting judges are seconded to a foreign court.[67] From the perspective of the recipient Pacific jurisdiction, the decision to appoint a sitting foreign judge or a retired foreign judge will obviously take account of the nature of the judicial position. A judge who continues to sit in his or her home jurisdiction will have limited capacity to serve as a full-time resident judge, but may be able to serve as an ad hoc or part-time judge.

The choice between the appointment of foreigners with judicial experience or directly from legal practice arises principally when recruiting full-time, resident judges to serve on the superior trial court, including, in some cases, the position of the Chief Justice. As with nationality, the nature of the recruitment process might have an effect. Filling a judicial vacancy using a formal advertising and recruitment process might result in a greater diversity of applicants. For example, many of the foreign judges serving on Tonga's Supreme Court were appointed after vacancies were advertised, by either the Tongan Government or donor agencies. In Tonga, four of the 13 Supreme Court judges who served during the case study period were lawyers, five had judicial experience in their home country, while the remainder had judicial experience in the Pacific and elsewhere in the Commonwealth.

Just under half of the foreign judges serving in Papua New Guinea were appointed from legal practice. Unusually, however, most of these judges were recruited from the local Papua New Guinean legal profession.[68] As noted in section II, such judges sit at the edges of the definition of a 'foreign judge'. For present purposes, it is a point of distinction between the Papua New Guinean judiciary and others in the region that several of its foreign judges are drawn from within the local legal community – a familiar path to judicial office in many common law jurisdictions – rather than from foreign courts or legal practice.[69]

Finally, the experience of Fiji's intermediary Court of Appeal illustrates a different context in which foreign lawyers, rather than judges, are preferred. The 2006 coup and its aftermath marked a change in the professional backgrounds,

[65] Interviews F2, F4, F11, F12.

[66] Interviews F2, F3, F5, F12.

[67] For example, from the New Zealand District Court to the Supreme Court of Vanuatu; from the Supreme Court of Queensland to the Court of Appeal of Solomon Islands; and from the National and Supreme Courts of Papua New Guinea to the Nauru Court of Appeal and courts in Solomon Islands. See further ch 3.

[68] Including David Cannings, Graham Ellis, Goodwin Poole, William Neil, Royale Thompson and Teresa Berrigan. See G Ellis, 'Life on the Bench in PNG' [2010] *Bar News: The Journal of the New South Wales Bar Association* 96, 97.

[69] Sitting and retired Australian judges also served in Papua New Guinea during the case study period. These appointments are discussed in section VI.A.

as well as the nationalities, of foreign judges. Until 2007, 17 of the 21 foreign Justices of Appeal were retired or sitting judges from Australia and New Zealand. Two judges were British citizens with long judicial experience in the Pacific, and two more were judges serving in other Pacific jurisdictions. For the reasons previously described, many of these judges resigned or allowed their commissions to lapse over the course of 2007. Because judges were not willing to accept appointments from the interim government, new Justices of Appeal were recruited from a different pool. Three barristers from the Sydney bar were appointed judges in 2008 and 2009,[70] and after April 2009, 11 lawyers, predominantly in government service, were recruited from Sri Lanka along with more lawyers from Australia and the United Kingdom. This shift from a court comprised predominantly of sitting and retired judges to one comprising a majority of judges appointed from foreign legal practice seems to be driven by the exigencies of Fiji's political situation after the coup.

C. Gender

Of the 225 foreign judges who served in the Pacific between 2000 and 2019, only 16 (7 per cent) were women. As such, the proportion of women in the cohort of foreign judges is lower than the proportion of local judges who are women, which across the region over the same period stood at 13 per cent. One reason for the low proportion of women foreign judges is the under-representation of women in the pools from which foreign judges are recruited, namely the judiciaries and legal professions of their home countries. The majority of foreign judges are recruited from Australia, New Zealand and Sri Lanka. In all three states, the number of women law graduates now exceeds the number of men and the number of women lawyers has increased to the point where women outnumber men in some sectors, although not in senior positions.[71] Women are under-represented in the judiciaries in all three states, however, although in no case is the proportion as low as 7 per cent.[72] This in turn affects the diversity of the pool from which foreign judges are recruited. A historical lag is also to be expected: in 2000, the judiciaries and legal professions

[70] Ian Lloyd, Randall Powell and Francis Douglas.

[71] *National Profile of Solicitors*, Report prepared by Urbis for the Conference of Law Societies of Australia (June 2019); G Adlam, 'Snapshot of the Profession' (2018) 915 *LawTalk* 43; D Samararatne, 'Reframing Feminist Imperatives in Adjudication through a Reading of Sri Lankan Jurisprudence' in M Crouch (ed), *Women and the Judiciary in the Asia-Pacific* (Cambridge, Cambridge University Press, 2021) 66.

[72] In Australia in 2017, between 24% and 35% of the judges on the State and federal courts respectively were women (Australian Bureau of Statistics, Gender Indicators: Australia, September 2017). In New Zealand in 2015, 30% of all judges were women: G Adlam, 'New Zealand's Judiciary and Gender' (New Zealand Law Society, 11 November 2015). In Sri Lanka in 2017, 29% of all judges were women: Samararatne (n 71).

of Australia and New Zealand, the primary source jurisdictions for foreign judges at the time, included a much lower proportion of women. The recruitment of retired judges thus extends the effect of historical under-representation of women on the courts of donor countries into the Pacific.

The low number of women in the cohort of foreign judges cannot be wholly explained by the generational lag in gender balance in their home states, however. Additional factors include stereotyped presumptions – in both donor and recipient states – about the suitability of women for judicial appointment in the Pacific, and family and caring responsibilities that make frequent travel or international relocation difficult for some women.[73]

D. The Significance of Identity and Background

The nationalities, professional backgrounds and gender of the foreign judges that serve on Pacific courts are informed by a range of factors, from colonial history to interpersonal relationships, from deliberate decisions of policy by Pacific governments to the exigencies of international politics. All are significant in assessing the implications of the practice of foreign judging for constitutional adjudication, judicial independence, and the role of judges and judiciaries in Pacific states. For example, the discussion in chapter 5 shows how nationality affects the way in which judges approach the task of constitutional adjudication, as foreign judges bring the orthodoxies and assumptions of their own legal systems to bear when determining constitutional matters in an overseas jurisdiction. Similarly, the discussion in chapter 6 identifies ways in which the professional backgrounds of foreign judges inform claims about their independence, and argues that commonly cited assumptions about the independence of foreign judges on account of their holding judicial office in their home state cannot be extended to foreign judges who are legal practitioners at home. Finally, as explored in chapter 7, the nationality of the judges who sit in Pacific states has implications for the expressive or representative qualities of Pacific courts.

VI. LOCALISATION

It was assumed that over time Pacific courts would 'localise', that is, replace foreign judges with local judges, as more citizens became qualified for judicial appointment.[74] The pace of localisation across the Pacific has, with the exception

[73] A Dziedzic, '"To Join the Bench and Be Decision-Makers": Women Judges in Pacific Island Judiciaries' in Crouch (ed) (n 71) 29.

[74] MA Ntumy, *South Pacific Islands Legal Systems* (Honolulu, University of Hawaii Press, 1993) xx.

of Papua New Guinea, been slow.[75] The figures produced in this study, set out earlier in Table 2.1, show that many years after independence and the consolidation of national courts, Pacific states continue to rely on foreign judges. Since independence, no local judges have ever served on the courts of constitutional jurisdiction in Nauru and Tuvalu, while Kiribati and Tonga have appointed just one and two local judges respectively. During the case study period, in Fiji, Samoa, and Vanuatu, local judges comprised 18 to 19 per cent of all judges serving on the relevant courts, while in Solomon Islands 31 per cent of all judges were local. Papua New Guinea has the greatest degree of localisation, with local judges comprising 74 per cent of all judges serving during the case study period. This section examines the various processes of localisation and the forces that facilitate or inhibit it. It does so in order to explain the factors that contribute to the continuing use of foreign judges in the Pacific, which include the small populations of Pacific states, the part-time nature of many Pacific courts, and different political approaches to localisation.

The small size of the population is an important factor in localisation. In small states, the local legal community is also small, with the result that there is both limited supply of and demand for local judges. This is not only a function of population size, but also flows from the isolation and limited resources of small island developing states.[76] In terms of supply, the local legal community from which judges may be drawn is generally small. Many Pacific lawyers obtain their qualifications overseas and some choose to stay overseas, where there is often greater demand for specialist skills and higher remuneration. Judicial salaries are often significantly lower than what lawyers may earn in practice at home or overseas, which presents a further barrier to local candidates taking up judicial appointments.[77] Smallness also limits the demand for permanent, full-time judges. As noted previously, all courts of appeal in the region are part-time, and in the smallest states of Nauru and Tuvalu the superior court also sits part time. Part-time, ad hoc judicial appointments may be cost effective where there is insufficient demand for a full-time court, but they are generally unattractive to local candidates seeking full-time employment.

Table 2.2 shows that localisation generally tracks population size, such that the states with the smallest populations tend to have the lowest number of local judges.

[75] M Scott, 'Fiji's Judicial Department: A Review', ibid 222. One judge predicts that it will be another 60 years before Solomon Islands' judiciary is entirely localised: JA Keniapisia, 'Judges from Other Commonwealth Jurisdictions Serving in the High Court and Court of Appeal of Solomon Islands', Paper presented at the 20th Commonwealth Law Conference, Melbourne (22 March 2017).

[76] L Briguglio, 'Small Island Developing States and Their Economic Vulnerabilities' (1995) 23(9) *World Development* 1615, 1615–18; W Veenendaal, *Politics and Democracy in Microstates* (Abingdon, Routledge, 2015) 22–23.

[77] As acknowledged by the Chief Justices of Solomon Islands and Vanuatu: J Kusapa, 'Expatriate Judges, Not an Answer: Chief Justice' *Island Sun* (Honiara) (21 January 2015); Chief Justice Lunabek, 'Speech on the Official Opening of the Courts of Vanuatu' (Port Vila, 27 January 2012).

Table 2.2 Population Size and Localisation in the Nine Pacific States 2000–19

State	Population[78]	Number local judges	% local judges
Tuvalu	10,200	0	0%
Nauru	11,000	0	0%
Tonga	100,300	1	5%
Kiribati	120,100	2	8%
Samoa	196,700	7	19%
Vanuatu	304,500	6	19%
Solomon Islands	682,500	10	29%
Fiji	888,400	24	18%
PNG	8,558,800	42	74%

Care should be taken when interpreting these figures. A head count of judges does not take account of the different kinds of judicial service provided by (full-time resident) local judges and (visiting part-time) foreign judges. It does not capture the number of cases heard or days worked by each category of judge. Foreign judges serving on courts of appeal sit part time, while foreign judges serving on superior trial courts tend to serve for short terms. In contrast, local judges are generally appointed until retirement, meaning that one local judge may serve alongside a succession of several different foreign judges.

The figures in Table 2.2 also combine the judges sitting on the superior trial courts and courts of appeal in each jurisdiction. In three states in the mid-range population size – Samoa, Solomon Islands and Vanuatu – localisation is much greater in the lower tiers of the court system. For example, over the whole of the case study period, 10 local and eight foreign judges served on the Solomon Islands High Court. However, the number and proportion of foreign judges increased markedly over 2005–10, as foreign judges were hired by RAMSI in order to deal with the large number of prosecutions arising from the civil conflict. Since that time, the proportion of local judges has returned to pre-RAMSI levels, with a steady trend to a court composed entirely of Solomon Islander judges by 2019.

In Samoa and Vanuatu, for the majority of the case study period there was a core group of three to four local judges serving on their respective Supreme Courts. They were supported by successive foreign judges appointed on an ad hoc or short-term basis, with the result that at most points of time, the majority of judges sitting on the Supreme Courts in each state were local. The Samoan Supreme Court has consisted only of Samoan judges since 2017. The reason for

[78] The population figures are as at 2018: Statistics for Development Division, Pacific Community, *2018 Pocket Statistical Summary* (2018).

the greater degree of localisation at this level of the court system again reflects smallness: local judges are likely to prefer appointments to a full-time court in a permanent capacity.

Generally, however, Table 2.2 shows that the larger the population, the higher the number of citizens appointed to judicial office. This is also true of the proportion of local to foreign judges, except in the case of Fiji, which has a larger population but a lower proportion of local judges than Solomon Islands, and, narrowly, Samoa and Vanuatu. Further, while Papua New Guinea's population is significantly higher than all other Pacific island states and it has a greater proportion of local judges, it nevertheless continues to use foreign judges. Exploring the process and degree of localisation in the two most populous Pacific states of Papua New Guinea and Fiji illuminates the significance of reasons other than population size in explaining the continued reliance on foreign judges in the Pacific.

A. Localisation in Papua New Guinea

Of the nine case study countries, Papua New Guinea has the lowest proportion of foreign judges. Of the 57 judges who served on the National and Supreme Courts over the case study period, only 15 were foreign. One compelling reason is its significantly larger population: with over 8.5 million people, Papua New Guinea is by far the largest Pacific state and can support local tertiary-level legal education and a larger local legal profession. Another important reason, however, is the early political emphasis on the localisation of the judiciary.

In 1972, the Constitutional Planning Committee was established to draft Papua New Guinea's independence Constitution. The Committee's Report highlights Papua New Guineans' desire for an autochthonous Constitution tailored to the specific context and needs of an independent Papua New Guinea. The recommendations for the new state's judiciary reflect this and emphasise national sovereignty, localisation and the development of an indigenous jurisprudence. The Committee expressed reservations about the use of foreign judges, stating that it was 'obviously not … consistent with the principle of our national sovereignty'.[79] The Committee considered that 'our own judges' are the best people to judge the cultures and customs of Papua New Guinea, to develop its common law, and to ensure that courts were responsive to the needs and values of Papua New Guinean society.[80]

[79] Constitutional Planning Committee Papua New Guinea, *Final Report of the Constitutional Planning Committee* (1974) ch 8, [34].

[80] ibid ch 8, [37]–[38]. See also B Narokobi, 'The System of Selecting Judges of the National and Supreme Courts: A Proposal', *Occasional Paper No 7* (Law Reform Commission of Papua New Guinea, 1978).

It did, however, recognise that Papua New Guinea would need to rely on foreign judges in the short term, while sufficient numbers of local lawyers obtained legal qualifications and experience.

Following independence, some Australian judges who had served in Papua New Guinea prior to independence continued their appointments and additional judges were recruited from other Commonwealth countries. Localisation of Papua New Guinea's judiciary was accelerated by the 'Rooney affair' in 1979, a conflict between the executive and the judiciary that saw the Minister for Justice sentenced to imprisonment for contempt of court but released by the Prime Minister.[81] By the end of the Rooney affair, five foreign judges, including the Chief Justice, had resigned, leaving Papua New Guinea's courts significantly understaffed. The Prime Minister looked to Australia for new judges, but also approached the local legal profession.[82] The first Papua New Guinean judge, Sir Mari Kapi, was sworn in in late December 1979, followed by the first local Chief Justice, Sir Buri Kidu, in 1980. By 1992, nine of the 14 judges (64 per cent) on the National and Supreme Court were local judges,[83] and by 2019 this had increased to 29 local judges out of 37 (78 per cent).

Despite the early and sustained emphasis on localisation accelerated by the Rooney affair, Papua New Guinea continues to use foreign judges some 40 years later. As noted in section V, Papua New Guinea is distinctive because several of its foreign judges are non-citizen residents recruited from the local legal profession. However, 2011 saw a change in the profile of the foreign judges in Papua New Guinea. That year, two sitting judges from the Federal Court of Australia were appointed to concurrently serve on Papua New Guinea's Supreme Court, pursuant to arrangements agreed by the Chief Justices of Papua New Guinea and the Federal Court of Australia and supported by each country's Attorney-General.[84] Under these arrangements, each Federal Court judge visits Papua New Guinea three times a year, sitting one week at a time on the Supreme Court.[85] In addition, in 2015 Terrence Higgins, a retired Australian judge, was appointed to sit as a visiting judge on Papua New Guinea's Supreme Court.

The appointment of sitting and retired Australian judges as visiting judges of the Papua New Guinean Supreme Court represents a departure from previous practice, which emphasised localisation and preference for recruitment

[81] *Public Prosecutor v Rooney (No 2)* [1979] PNGLR 448. The Rooney affair is discussed in greater detail in ch 7, section V.A.

[82] B Narokobi, 'How Independent Are the Courts in Papua New Guinea? The Somare/Rooney Affair' (1980) 9(2) *Pacific Perspective* 12, 20.

[83] J Nonggorr, 'The Maintenance of Judicial Independence and Integrity in Papua New Guinea: Some Recent Developments' (1992) 18(3) *Commonwealth Law Bulletin* 1181, 1182.

[84] J Logan, 'A Year in the Life of an Australian Member of the PNG Judiciary', *Discussion Paper 2015/16, State, Society and Governance in Melanesia* (Australian National University, 2015) 2.

[85] ibid.

from the Papua New Guinean legal profession. It also stands in contrast to the policies implemented by the Papua New Guinean Government in 2015 to reduce its reliance on non-citizen technical advisers.[86] While the 2015 regulations relate only to the public service and not the judiciary, some of the animating concerns about national sovereignty, costs and effectiveness might nonetheless also apply to the courts. Several reasons have been provided for the renewed use of visiting foreign judges. The growth in the number and complexity of commercial cases before the court requires specific judicial expertise and experience in large commercial litigation, and foreign judges were one way to provide this specialist expertise.[87] Another reason to draw on foreign judges might be the difficulty in attracting local lawyers to judicial office, where the pay and conditions of service are not as attractive as private legal practice. Finally, the arrangements with the Federal Court were instigated by Sir Salamo Injia, who has been described as an outward-looking, modernising Chief Justice keen to expand relationships with other courts in the region.[88] The renewed use of visiting foreign judges on the Supreme Court suggests that the availability of adequate numbers of local judges is not the only rationale for the use of foreign judges. Additional motivations for the appointment of foreign judges include to further develop the knowledge, capacities and international standing of the Papua New Guinean courts.

B. Localisation in Fiji

Fiji has the second highest population of the nine Pacific states. It also has a long judicial history. Fiji was the location of the High Court of the Western Pacific from 1877 to 1962, and into independence Fiji's Court of Appeal was designated the appellate court of several newly independent Pacific states.[89] Fiji has a substantial local legal profession and several Fijians have served as foreign judges in other Pacific states. Despite this, there has not been the same emphasis or progress on localisation as in Papua New Guinea, or indeed as in Samoa or Solomon Islands. As Figure 2.3 shows, while the number of local judges serving on the relevant Fijian courts increased during the case study period, by 2019 it had fallen again, such that there was only one more local judge serving on Fiji's courts in 2019 than in 2000.

[86] M Anderson, J Luma and C Voigt-Graf, 'Recent Developments Regarding Non-Citizen Technical Advisers in Papua New Guinea', *Issues Paper 24* (National Research Institute Papua New Guinea, March 2017).

[87] J Logan, 'Law and Justice in Papua New Guinea', Paper presented at the Australian Institute of International Affairs, Brisbane (23 June 2015) 42.

[88] Interview F24.

[89] Pulea (n 20) 3–4.

Figure 2.3 Number of Foreign and Local Judges in Fiji 2000–19

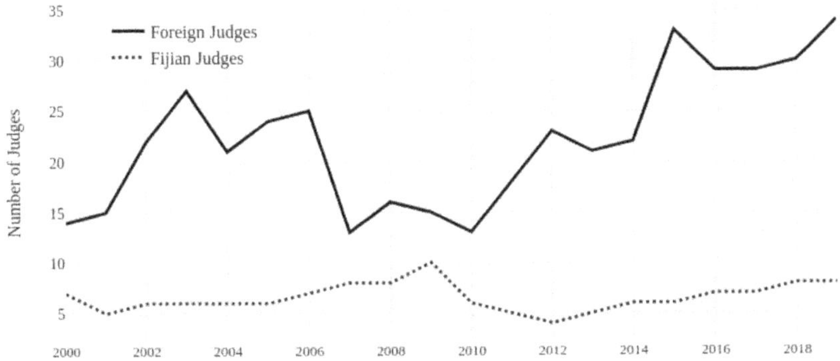

There are several explanations for the limited localisation of the Fijian judiciary. One reason relates to sensitivities arising from the tensions between the Indigenous and Indian Fijian communities. Fiji has a significant population of people of Indian heritage, descended from indentured labourers brought to Fiji during British rule. Prior to independence, more Indian Fijians obtained legal qualifications and served in the Fijian legal profession, and were thus more likely to qualify for judicial appointment.[90] The 1990 Constitution of Fiji, which sought to entrench the political paramountcy of Indigenous Fijians, introduced a requirement that some judicial positions be distributed among ethnic groups, with the majority going to Indigenous Fijians.[91] These requirements were removed in 1997. Iyer notes that while race does 'creep in' to discussions of the administration of justice in Fiji, the use of foreign judges has helped the Fijian judiciary to steer clear of racial politics.[92]

Fiji's political instability has also affected the judiciary and legal profession. Many Indian Fijians emigrated from Fiji in the wake of the 1987 coups,[93] depleting the local legal profession. Several local judges, along with a number of foreign judges, resigned following another coup in 2000.[94] After the 2006 coup – Fiji's fourth – Chief Justice Fatiaki was suspended from office and replaced by a foreign judge, albeit one with significant legal and judicial experience in Fiji. Only some Fijian judges serving prior to the 2006 coup were reappointed after all

[90] BV Lal, *A Time Bomb Lies Buried: Fiji's Road to Independence, 1960–1970* (Canberra, ANU Press, 2008) 17.

[91] *Constitution of Fiji 1990*, s 124(3), (4); P Reeves, TR Vakatora and BV Lal, 'The Fiji Islands: Towards a United Future Report of the Fiji Constitution Review Commission' (Fiji, Parliamentary Paper No 34 of 1996) [13.100].

[92] Iyer (n 51) 128.

[93] RR Premdas, 'The Dynamics of Ethnic Minority Domination in Fiji' in EP Kaufmann (ed), *Rethinking Ethnicity: Majority Groups and Dominant Minorities* (London, Routledge, 2004) 195, 206–07.

[94] T Draunidalo, 'The Rule of Law and Judicial Independence amidst the Coups and Attempted Coups in Fiji since 1987' in Fraenkel, Firth and Lal (eds) (n 52) 311, 312.

judicial appointments were revoked in 2009. Concerns about the erosion of judicial independence under the interim government[95] are likely to have dissuaded local lawyers from accepting judicial appointment since 2006.

The rationale for the use of foreign judges in Fiji, as expressed by government actors and constitution makers, differs markedly from the discourse in Papua New Guinea. In Fiji there is less emphasis on localisation and greater emphasis on the quality and merit of judges. The Reeves Commission's review of the Constitution, undertaken in 1995, stated that localisation was 'an important policy objective' and that the judiciary should reflect the composition of the population as a whole, but left the practice of appointing foreign judges largely unquestioned.[96] In 2016, the Attorney-General was asked in Parliament to justify the large number of foreign judges in Fiji, despite the high number of Fijian lawyers and magistrates. He responded that all judges – foreign and local – must meet the standards of experience, expertise and integrity set out in the Constitution,[97] suggesting that merit, not localisation, was the overriding consideration in the appointment of judges. This rhetoric might, however, be disingenuous: there are claims that the preference for the appointment of foreign judges in Fiji lies in the fact that foreign judges are appointed on short-term contracts and are therefore more susceptible to executive influence.[98]

C. Contributing Factors

No Pacific state has a fully localised judiciary, but the extent of localisation of Pacific judiciaries varies across different courts and different jurisdictions. The reasons for the continued use of foreign judges relate mainly to a shortage of local judges as a result of the various challenges associated with smallness, isolation and limited resources. The examples of Solomon Islands and Fiji demonstrate that other factors, such as increased and unexpected demands on the courts, political instability and discrimination between groups within the population, can also contribute to a shortage of local judges. However, as the study of localisation in the most populous state of Papua New Guinea illustrates, the continued use of foreign judges may also relate to other factors, such as the desire for specialist expertise and to build judicial networks with other courts. The rationales for the continued use of foreign judges in the Pacific are discussed more fully in chapter 8. For present purposes, however, it is clear that localisation is not achieved simply by increasing the number of citizens eligible for judicial appointment, and that foreign judges are used for a range of reasons

[95] Draunidalo (n 94); International Bar Association (n 53); Leung (n 54).

[96] Reeves, Vakatora and Lal (n 91) [13.98].

[97] Fiji, *Parliamentary Debates*, 10 February 2016, 1063–65 (Sayed-Khaiyum).

[98] BV Lal, *Historical Dictionary of Fiji* (Lanham, MD, Rowman & Littlefield, 2016) 24. The appointment of foreign judges for short renewable terms is discussed in ch 6.

including, but not limited to, the need to fill the gaps caused by a shortage of suitably qualified local judges.

VII. CONCLUSION

This empirical study shows that the use of foreign judges is a widespread, prevalent and entrenched practice in Pacific states. Foreign judges serve in large numbers, constituting approximately three-quarters of all judges serving on courts of constitutional jurisdiction in the region. The high number reflects not only the demand for judges, but the part-time ad hoc nature of the practice, in which a succession of foreign judges fill a limited number of judicial positions, with consequences for stability and continuity in the composition of Pacific courts.

The findings present some surprising results that challenge some of the assumptions about foreign judging, in the region and generally. Given historical, legal and development assistance ties between Pacific states and their former colonial administrators, it is not surprising that most foreign judges serving in the Pacific are recruited from Australia, New Zealand and the United Kingdom. The data collected here show, however, a greater diversity of nationalities and an emerging trend towards the appointment of foreign judges from Commonwealth states of the Global South, such as Sri Lanka and common law African states, as well as intra-regional exchanges within the Pacific itself.

In addition, the findings show that Pacific courts are not necessarily 'hybrid' courts, in which local and foreign judges sit together. In two states – Nauru and Tuvalu – there are no local judges on the relevant courts. In Fiji, Kiribati and Tonga, it is common for appellate courts to consist entirely of foreign judges. Progress in localisation in Samoa, Solomon Islands and Vanuatu means that foreign judges increasingly sit with local judges in those states. In contrast, in Papua New Guinea, which has the highest proportion of local judges, only one or two foreign judges might sit on a panel of the Supreme Court, and often not at all. This affects the implications that can be drawn from the use of foreign judges in the Pacific. A commonly cited benefit of the use of foreign judges on hybrid courts in other jurisdictions is the interaction and exchange of knowledge between local and foreign judges,[99] but clearly, this outcome is not generalisable across the Pacific. Similarly, differences in the nature of service (as between resident full-time judges and visiting part-time or ad hoc judges) and the professional backgrounds of foreign judges also caution against making generalisations about the qualities of foreign judges, their motivations and their characteristics.

[99] R Dixon and V Jackson, 'Hybrid Constitutional Courts: Foreign Judges on National Constitutional Courts' [2019] *Columbia Journal of Transnational Law* 283, 311–12.

To properly assess the implications of the use of foreign judges, it is necessary to proceed from an accurate understanding of the practice and the factors that influence the profiles of particular courts. The empirical data and contextual analysis presented in this chapter and chapter 3 permit the examination of the implications of the use of foreign judges based on a comprehensive understanding of the practice, on its own terms and in the particular context of the Pacific.

3

The Regulation of Foreign Judges

I. INTRODUCTION

THE APPOINTMENT AND removal of judges, the conditions of judicial service, and the conduct of court proceedings are critical to the quality and independence of a judiciary. The fact that some or all judges are foreign affects each of these aspects of judicial service. Procedures for selection, appointment, remuneration and removal apply differently to foreign and local judges, sometimes because the law expressly differentiates on the basis of citizenship, at other times because the use of foreign judges raises distinctive issues, resulting in different practices. The operation of Pacific courts has also been shaped by the need for the timing, location and language of court proceedings to accommodate foreign judges.

Understanding the practice of foreign judging requires looking beyond the formal legal requirements that govern judicial service in each of the nine Pacific states. Constitutional and legislative provisions are given effect by the decisions of officials. They are supplemented by contractual relationships negotiated between governments, courts, funding organisations and foreign judges themselves. In addition, a foreign judge's service is affected not only by the laws and practices of the state in which the judge serves, but also by laws and practices in the judge's home country and, in some cases, external funding institutions. The sites and sources of regulation multiply accordingly.

This chapter analyses the layers of law and practice that regulate the use of foreign judges in the Pacific. It is organised around four aspects of judicial service. Section II examines the laws and procedures relating to the selection and appointment of foreign judges. It shows that while the formal procedures of appointment make little distinction between local and foreign judges, processes for recruiting foreign judges differ in practice from those used to recruit local judges. Section III outlines the remuneration and other benefits received by foreign judges and the disparities in pay that can arise as Pacific states compete in a transnational market for judicial services. Section IV considers the tenure of foreign judges and the prevalent practice of appointing foreign judges for short renewable terms under legislative and contractual frameworks. Section V shows how foreign judges are susceptible to removal by extra-constitutional processes as a result of insecure tenure and their status as non-citizens. Finally, section VI shows how the use of foreign judges affects the language, time and place in which Pacific courts conduct hearings. Each section sets out the applicable law and relevant practices in the Pacific states and outside them, and analyses some of the consequences. In order to capture the practices behind the constitutional text and intersecting forms of national, foreign and international regulation, this chapter draws on data collected in interviews with foreign judges and persons from institutions involved in recruiting or appointing foreign judges. The methodology for collecting and presenting this data was explained in chapter 2.

This chapter, together with the empirical analysis of the number and attributes of foreign judges in the Pacific presented in chapter 2, provides the evidence for an informed and contextual analysis of the implications of the use of foreign judges in the chapters that follow.

II. SELECTION AND APPOINTMENT

This section provides an overview of how foreign judges are selected and appointed to judicial office in the Pacific. It is divided into four subsections covering: the formal procedures for the appointment of judges in Pacific states; the strategies used to recruit foreign judges; the criteria guiding the selection of foreign judges; and regulations arising in foreign judges' home states that affect judicial appointment overseas. The analysis shows that while formal appointment procedures make limited distinctions between local and foreign judges, in practice the process for selecting foreign judges differs from that for local judges in at least three respects: first, the appointing authority is less likely to have direct knowledge about a foreign candidate; second, foreign judges might be expected to bring certain qualifications or skills; and, third, the recruitment process may involve the foreign judge's home state or a donor organisation in some way.

A. Formal Appointment Process

In the nine Pacific states, the power to appoint judges is formally vested in the Head of State or a judicial services commission. In Nauru and Tuvalu, all judges are appointed by the Head of State acting on the advice of the government of the day.[1] In Fiji, Kiribati, Samoa and Vanuatu, the Chief Justice is appointed by the Head of State on the advice of the Prime Minister[2] or the Cabinet,[3] while all other judges are appointed by the Head of State acting on the advice

[1] *Constitution of Nauru 1968*, s 49(2); *Constitution of Tuvalu 1986*, s 123. In Tuvalu, the Cabinet consults the Chief Justice before appointing judges.

[2] *Constitution of Fiji 2013*, s 106(1); *Constitution of Samoa 1960*, s 65(2); *Constitution of Vanuatu 1980*, s 49(3).

[3] *Constitution of Kiribati 1979*, s 81(1); *Constitution of Tuvalu 1986*, s 122(2).

of a judicial services commission.[4] In Solomon Islands and Tonga, all judicial appointments are made by the Head of State with advice from the judicial services commission.[5] In Papua New Guinea, all judges other than the Chief Justice are appointed directly by the Judicial and Legal Services Commission.[6]

The membership of judicial services commissions varies across the states. The Chief Justice is a member of all commissions in the region. Many commissions also include the Minister of Justice or Attorney-General. Other members might be representatives of the public service commission, the legal profession, chiefly or tribal leaders, or the general community.[7] Judicial services commissions featured in the independence constitutions of many former British colonies, representing a departure from the system then existing in the United Kingdom, in which the power to appoint judges lay solely in the hands of the executive government of the day.[8] This shift was explained by reference to the expansive power that new Commonwealth constitutions conferred on judges to determine the constitutionality of legislation, which was thought to increase the risk of conflict between the judiciary and the political branches of government.[9] The use of judicial services commissions sought to distance, but not remove, the executive from judicial appointments and limit the risk of undue interference in judicial decision making. It remains a prevalent model across the Commonwealth.[10]

These formal processes for appointment generally apply to foreign and local judges alike. There are two historical examples in which the appointment of a non-citizen to judicial office was subject to a special process. The 1990 Constitution of Fiji required the appointing authority to act in accordance with the Prime Minister's advice when appointing a non-citizen, a requirement that did not apply to the appointment of citizens. The application of this provision to judges was removed in 1997 to address concerns that it was an avenue by which the executive could improperly influence judicial appointments.[11]

[4] *Constitution of Fiji 2013*, s 106(2); *Constitution of Samoa 1960*, ss 72(3), 75(2)(b); *Constitution of Vanuatu 1980*, s 47(2). In Kiribati, judicial appointments are recommended by the Chief Justice sitting with the Public Service Commission, an arrangement akin to a judicial services commission: *Constitution of Kiribati 1979*, ss 81(2), 91(1)(b).

[5] *Constitution of Solomon Islands 1978*, s 78(1), (2), 86(1), (2); *Constitution of Tonga 1875*, ss 85, 86. In Tonga, the King in Privy Council makes judicial appointments after 'receiving advice' from the Judicial Appointments and Discipline Panel.

[6] *Constitution of Papua New Guinea 1975*, ss 169(2), 170(2).

[7] *Constitution of Fiji 2013*, s 104(1); *Constitution of Papua New Guinea 1975*, s 183; *Constitution of Samoa 1960*, s 72; *Constitution of Solomon Islands 1978*, s 117; *Constitution of Tonga 1875*, s 83C; *Constitution of Vanuatu 1980*, s 48.

[8] The *Constitutional Reform Act 2005* (UK) introduced a new process in which an independent Judicial Appointments Commission is responsible for selecting judges. In Australia and New Zealand, the executive has sole responsibility for appointing judges.

[9] SA De Smith, *The New Commonwealth and Its Constitutions* (London, Stevens & Sons, 1964) 137.

[10] J van Zyl Smit, *The Appointment, Tenure and Removal of Judges under Commonwealth Principles: A Compendium and Analysis of Best Practice* (London, Commonwealth Secretariat, 2015) [1.6.1].

[11] P Reeves, TR Vakatora and BV Lal, 'The Fiji Islands: Towards a United Future Report of the Fiji Constitution Review Commission' (Fiji, Parliamentary Paper No 34 of 1996) [13.99].

The second example arose in Papua New Guinea, where the Constitutional Planning Committee recommended that the Constitution include a target date for the localisation of the judiciary, after which non-citizens should not be appointed judges except with the approval of the Cabinet.[12] In the end, however, no such provision was included in the Constitution. While special appointment procedures for foreign judges have been contemplated, Pacific states have, by and large, considered it unnecessary to subject foreign judges to formal processes different from those that apply to the appointment of local judges.

Foreign judges, like local judges, receive a written commission or warrant of appointment signed by the Head of State. They are ceremonially sworn in and take the judicial oath.[13] The significance of the judicial oath in connecting foreign judges to a state to which they otherwise lack the ties of citizenship is considered in chapter 7.

B. Recruitment

In many common law countries, judges are recruited predominantly from the local legal profession.[14] This is also true for local judges in the Pacific states, who tend to be recruited from members of the legal profession working in the public service or private practice. In these cases, members of the appointing authority are likely to have direct knowledge of the candidate, and will certainly have access to judges, the legal profession, employers and members of the wider community who can provide advice on the candidate's qualifications, character and suitability for judicial office. In relation to foreign judges, however, the appointing authority is at a greater distance from potential candidates. As such, Pacific states must use other methods and sources to identify and assess the suitability of foreign candidates for judicial appointment, such as name-tapping via informal connections, advertised positions, registers of judges and arrangements between courts.

i. Informal Methods

Those responsible for recruiting judges in Pacific states will often utilise transnational networks between judges, officials and associations to identify candidates for appointment. Sometimes, the Chief Justice or the Attorney-General in the

[12] Constitutional Planning Committee Papua New Guinea, *Final Report of the Constitutional Planning Committee* (1974) ch 8, [63].

[13] *Constitution of Fiji 2013*, s 109, sch; *Constitution of Fiji 1997*, s 135, sch; *Constitution of Kiribati 1979*, ss 82, 92, sch 1; *Constitution of Nauru 1968*, s 52, sch 4; *Constitution of Papua New Guinea 1975*, s 249, sch 4; *Constitution of Samoa 1960*, s 67, sch 3; *Official Oaths Act 1978* c 24 (Solomon Islands), s 3; *Constitution of Tonga 1875*, s 95; *Oaths and Statutory Declarations Act 1979* c 7.48 (Tuvalu), s 3, sch 1; *Oaths Act 1964* c 37 (Vanuatu), s 6(2).

[14] PH Russell, 'Judicial Recruitment, Training and Careers' in P Cane and HM Kritzer (eds), *The Oxford Handbook of Empirical Legal Research* (Oxford, Oxford University Press, 2010) 528.

Pacific jurisdiction will write to his or her counterparts in foreign countries[15] or to professional lawyers' associations[16] to seek candidates for judicial appointment. At other times the Chief Justice of a Pacific court will approach foreign judges currently sitting on the Pacific court[17] or contacts made at regional judicial conferences[18] to recommend candidates. The Chief Justice or other official might then contact potential candidates directly to seek expressions of interest in judicial appointment. For example, in 2010 the Parliamentary Counsel of Nauru wrote letters to several retired Australian judges to gauge their interest in the position of Chief Justice of Nauru.[19] On occasion, recruitment drives have been targeted to a specific jurisdiction, rather than individuals. For example, Fijian officials visited Sri Lanka in 2009 to recruit judges and build connections between the two jurisdictions.[20] Name-tapping and informal methods of this kind are most often used to identify candidates for appointment as visiting judges on courts of appeal, especially when an additional judge is required at short notice. There are, however, some examples of resident judges serving on superior trial courts who were recruited in this way.[21]

ii. Advertisements

Some Pacific courts have, like many other common law courts around the world, begun to advertise judicial vacancies. Until recently, judicial positions in Pacific states were most commonly advertised where a full-time resident judge was funded by an aid agency or international organisation. Examples include judicial appointments in Tonga funded by New Zealand and Australian aid agencies; appointments in Solomon Islands under the auspices of the Regional Assistance Mission to Solomon Islands; and judicial appointments made as part of the Commonwealth Fund for Technical Cooperation. In the last case, the Commonwealth Secretariat would shortlist candidates for consideration by the head of jurisdiction in the Pacific state, who would settle the final appointment in accordance with local procedures.[22] Although donor agencies have a hand in the recruitment process, officials from the Pacific state concerned are usually responsible for the final selection. There is now an increasing trend towards

[15] Interviews F3, F5.

[16] eg in 2017 the Nauruan Government approached the Australian Bar Association to recommend a retired Australian judge: 'Nauru Bringing in Australian Judge for "Riot" Trial' *Radio New Zealand* (Wellington) (1 August 2017).

[17] Interviews F2, F5, F7, F10, email F27.

[18] Interviews F9, F10, F11.

[19] R Koval, 'Geoffrey Eames, Former Nauru Chief Justice' *The Saturday Paper* (Melbourne) (21 March 2015).

[20] B Sirimanna, 'Fiji Courts Want 6 of Our Judges' *Sunday Times* (Colombo) (16 August 2009).

[21] eg G Winter, 'Judicial Guidelines: The Five Way Test' (2006) 1(2) *International Judicial Monitor*, available at www.judicialmonitor.org/archive_0506/globaljudicialdialogue.html; H Kempton, 'A Busy and Varied Career in Law' *The Mercury* (Hobart) (8 June 2015). Both judges report receiving phone calls from Chief Justices.

[22] Interview F26.

advertising all judicial positions open to local and foreign candidates alike. In Tonga, the Judicial Administration and Discipline Panel established in 2010 advertises vacancies on the Supreme Court, assesses applicants, and makes recommendations to the King and Privy Council.[23] Since 2013, the Government of Nauru has advertised positions for new Supreme Court Judges.[24] The website of the Judicial Department of Fiji has a form entitled 'Expression of Interest in a position as a Judicial Officer on Fiji's Courts or Tribunals', which applicants can submit to the Chief Registrar at any time.[25] In this, Pacific states are part of a wider trend across the Commonwealth towards more open and transparent processes for the selection of judges.[26]

iii. Relationships with Donor Courts and Agencies

Two further methods of recruiting foreign judges focus on building relationships between courts, judges and regional bodies. One approach used in the past was to create a centralised list of foreign judges who were willing to serve overseas.[27] Beginning in 1988, the Pacific Islands Forum Secretariat maintained a Register of Appellate Judges, which it would update and circulate to Pacific governments. It seems, however, that authorities in Pacific states rarely used this list and the Register is no longer maintained.[28] While there is no clear account of the utility of such lists, it illustrates one way in which jurisdictions have attempted to bridge the distance between those wishing to appoint foreign judges and potential candidates.

A second approach is for Pacific courts to establish standing arrangements with overseas courts, under which judges from the donor court are seconded to the Pacific court. For example, there is a programme in which a judge from the District Court of New Zealand is appointed to the Vanuatu Supreme Court every two years. This arrangement has been formalised by an exchange of letters between the Chief Justice of Vanuatu and the Chief Judge of the District Court of New Zealand, and, within New Zealand, by a Memorandum of Understanding between the Court and the Ministries of Justice and Foreign Affairs.[29] Similarly, two judges of the Federal Court of Australia have been appointed to the

[23] Interview F18.

[24] Government of Nauru, 'Expression of Interest Sought for Appointment as Judge to the Supreme Court of Nauru' (October 2013).

[25] 'Expression of Interest in a Position as a Judicial Officer on Fiji's Courts or Tribunals' (20 April 2015) available at www.judiciary.gov.fj.

[26] As reflected, for example, in the *Commonwealth (Latimer House) Principles on the Three Branches of Government* (Nigeria, 2003) guideline II.1, which states that 'judicial vacancies should be advertised'. See also Zyl Smit (n 10) [1.7.5].

[27] A Mason, 'Sharing Expertise with the Developing World' (2001) 26 *Alternative Law Journal* 7, 7. Interviews F4, F5, F19.

[28] Email communication from Lorraine Kershaw, International Legal Advisor, Pacific Island Forum Secretariat (7 November 2018).

[29] Ministry of Justice, *The District Courts of New Zealand* (2008) 11. Interviews F16, F19.

Papua New Guinea judiciary and visit three times a year to sit on the Supreme Court, pursuant to a formal arrangement between the two courts.[30] In 2017 and 2018, Papua New Guinea's Supreme Court signed Memorandums of Understanding for cooperation with courts in Nauru and Solomon Islands respectively, which included, inter alia, provision for a Papua New Guinean judge to serve as a visiting Judge of Appeal in each state.[31] Not all instances of inter-court cooperation are formalised in written agreements. There is a long tradition of sitting or retired judges of the Supreme Court of Queensland serving as judges of the Court of Appeal of Solomon Islands, built on the history of a close association since the establishment of Solomon Islands' Court of Appeal in 1982.[32] To recruit judges to a secondment programme, the Chief Justice of the donor court will call for expressions of interest from judges and propose candidates to the Pacific court. In some cases, the Chief Justice or other representatives of the Pacific state may interview candidates, in others the recipient jurisdiction might simply rely on the recommendations of the donor court.[33]

iv. Analysis and Implications

In relation to all of these methods of recruitment, information gathered in interviews suggests that often it is the Chief Justice who takes on the primary role in building transnational networks, approaching judges from overseas and establishing formal arrangements with donor courts.[34] This role is consistent with the position of the Chief Justice as head of jurisdiction and as a member of the judicial services commission, where one exists. The executive may also exert some influence on judicial recruitment by virtue of membership on the judicial services commission or as the appointing authority. This is especially the case in Nauru, where judicial appointments appear to be handled largely by the executive government, and in Tonga, where the King has considerable discretion and the final say in the appointment of judges. External courts and organisations that provide or fund foreign judges also have a role, ranging from informal influence through shared connections to more formal involvement in recruitment and selection.

Methods of recruitment influence *who* is appointed to be a foreign judge in the Pacific. As explained in chapter 2, the method of recruitment affects the

[30] J Logan, 'A Year in the Life of an Australian Member of the PNG Judiciary', *Discussion Paper 2015/16, State, Society and Governance in Melanesia* (Australian National University, 2015) 2.

[31] 'PNG, SI Sign Agreement on Judiciary Cooperation' *The National* (Port Moresby) (24 August 2017); A Osii, 'Agreement Signed for PNG Judge to Sit in Nauru's Appeals Court' *The National* (Port Moresby) (26 July 2018).

[32] G Williams, 'McPherson JA in the Solomon Islands' in A Rahemtula (ed), *Justice According to Law: A Festschrift for the Honourable Mr Justice BH McPherson CBE* (Brisbane, Supreme Court of Queensland Library, 2006) 632, 632–33.

[33] Interviews F16, F19, F22, F24.

[34] Interviews F3, F4, F7, F9, F10, F11, F14, F17.

diversity of the nationalities of foreign judges serving on Pacific courts. It is not surprising that foreign judges who are approached to recommend other judges for possible appointment to Pacific courts will turn first to judges from their home jurisdictions and their own courts, whom they know best. In contrast, where foreign judges are recruited by donor organisations through open advertisements, the cohort of foreign judges is more diverse, at least as regards nationality.

Several participants commented in interviews that while the calibre of foreign judges appointed to Pacific courts was generally high, there were instances in which persons were appointed who did not have the experience or personal qualities necessary for judicial work in the Pacific.[35] This was said to arise from the challenge of conducting due diligence investigations into candidates whom the recruiting organisations or the appointing authorities did not directly know, and, on occasion, from patronage or self-interest on the part of the executive. Advertisements and open procedures may not always assist Pacific states to identify the best foreign candidate for appointment. Where a candidate is a judge or retired judge in his or her home jurisdiction, recruiters and appointing authorities might assume their qualifications and merit by riding on the rigor and integrity of the process for judicial appointment in the judge's home state. Where a candidate has no judicial experience, appointing bodies must find other ways to assess their suitability, for example by consulting referees or judges' or lawyers' associations in the candidate's home state, a process that may be impeded by lack of access. Recruiting foreign judges through lists presents similar difficulties, especially if the list is compiled using a process in which candidates self-nominate. These difficulties associated with recruitment affect other aspects of foreign judging. A particularly important consequence relates to tenure: one reason given for the appointment of foreign judges on short terms is that it provides an opportunity for appointing authorities to assess the judge's suitability.[36]

C. Qualifications and Selection Criteria

Legal provisions governing eligibility for judicial office facilitate the appointment of foreign judges by recognising legal qualifications and professional experience obtained in foreign jurisdictions. Once the baseline qualifications are met, appointing authorities have discretion to select judges using additional

[35] Interviews F4, F23, F25.

[36] CB Ingram, 'The Length of Terms of Judges in the Pacific and Its Impact on Judicial Independence' in *Land Law and Judicial Governance in the South Pacific: Comparative Studies* (Wellington, New Zealand Association for Comparative Law, 2011) 375, 376; Reeves, Vakatora and Lal (n 11) [13.108]; JM Van Dyke, 'The Pacific Judicial Conference: Strengthening the Independent Judiciary and the Rule of Law in the Pacific' (2011) 22(1–2) *Western Legal History* 127, 160–61.

criteria. These may include the candidate's personal character and integrity, as well as administrative and communication skills relevant to judicial practice.[37] The additional selection criteria that are sometimes applied to the recruitment of judges in the Pacific suggest that foreign judges can be selected on different grounds from local judges and are expected to bring specific expertise or skills to their role.

i. Qualifications for Judicial Office

In the Pacific states, the criteria for the selection of judges – both local and foreign – are principally contained in constitutional provisions. These generally require that a person must have a minimum period of prior judicial or legal professional experience to be eligible for appointment as a judge of a superior court. The appointment of foreign judges is facilitated by recognising judicial or legal professional experience in the state itself or *another country*. In Fiji and Samoa, such other countries may be prescribed by law, although in Samoa the country must have a legal system similar to that existing in Samoa.[38] In Solomon Islands, other countries include any country in the Commonwealth or as prescribed by law.[39] Tonga requires judicial experience in any country, or 10 years' practice as an advocate in any part of the Commonwealth.[40] In Tuvalu, the other country must have a 'similar legal system',[41] while Kiribati accepts legal experience in any country.[42] Nauru and Vanuatu tie eligibility for judicial appointment to the qualifications for admission to legal practice.[43] In effect, this permits the appointment of persons with legal qualifications and experience in specified other countries. In Nauru, this includes those admitted to legal practice in England, Northern Ireland, the Republic of Ireland, Scotland, Australia, New Zealand or any other country as notified by the Minister after consultation with the Chief Justice.[44] In Vanuatu it includes persons admitted to legal practice in a Commonwealth jurisdiction.[45]

In this way, the laws in each state facilitate the appointment of foreign judges as well as citizens who have studied and practised law overseas. The jurisdictions differ as to whether the appointing authority may determine whether another

[37] PH Russell and K Malleson (eds), *Appointing Judges in an Age of Judicial Power: Critical Perspectives from around the World* (Toronto, University of Toronto Press, 2006) 8–9.

[38] *Constitution of Fiji 2013*, s 105, *Constitution of Fiji 1997*, s 130, Judicial Tribunals (Prescribed Countries) Promulgation No 32 of 2007 (Fiji); *Constitution of Samoa 1960*, s 65(5).

[39] *Constitution of Solomon Islands 1978*, ss 78(3), 86(3).

[40] *Constitution of Tonga 1875*, ss 85(1), 86(1).

[41] *Constitution of Tuvalu 1986*, s 124; *Superior Courts Act 1987* c 7.68 (Tuvalu), s 8(1).

[42] *Constitution of Kiribati 1979*, ss 81(3); 91(1)(b).

[43] *Constitution of Nauru 1968*, s 49(3); *Constitution of Vanuatu 1980*, s 49(4).

[44] *Legal Practitioners Act 1973* (Nauru), s 5. Other prescribed countries include India and Papua New Guinea: Nauru, *Government Gazette* No 52, 30 September 1981, 1; Nauru, *Government Gazette* No 60, 29 September 1999, 1.

[45] *Legal Practitioners (Qualifications) Regulations 1996* (Vanuatu), s 2.

country has a 'similar' legal system, or whether this is determined by legislative instrument. Another point of difference is whether the source countries for foreign judges are limited to Commonwealth countries or are more expansive. These differences do not seem to have had much impact on the cohort of foreign judges serving in the Pacific states. As the data presented in chapter 2 show, the vast majority of foreign judges serving in the nine Pacific states between 2000 and 2019 were from Commonwealth countries. The handful of exceptions were judges who had judicial or legal experience in Hong Kong, which, while a common law jurisdiction, is not formally a member of the Commonwealth.

In contrast to the other Pacific states, Papua New Guinea prescribes different qualifications for citizens and non-citizens. Citizens must have recognised university qualifications and at least four years' experience in practice as a lawyer or magistrate. Non-citizens qualify if they have been a judge, or lawyer with at least five years' experience, in a country with a legal system substantially similar to that of Papua New Guinea.[46] The purpose of the distinction, according to the Constitutional Planning Committee, was to provide greater scope to appoint Papua New Guineans, who, at the time of independence, had only recently begun to gain professional legal qualifications.[47] The approach fits with Papua New Guinea's early emphasis on localisation, which was discussed in chapter 2.

ii. Legislative or Policy Guidance on Judicial Appointments

In most Pacific states, the constitutional or statutory qualifications for judicial office, which specify only prior judicial or legal experience, are the only explicit criteria to guide the selection of judges. Kiribati and Vanuatu, however, have prescribed additional considerations that the appointing authority must take into account when recommending judicial appointments. In Kiribati, legislation made in 2017 provided that 'special consideration may be afforded where possible to an I-Kiribati' who meets the generally applicable qualification requirements.[48] This provision, which seeks to promote localisation, is unique in the region. Meanwhile in Vanuatu, legislation requires the Judicial Service Commission to consider candidates' experience and abilities; and their character and standing *in the community in which the candidate usually resides*; and in the case of candidates from outside Vanuatu, their judicial experience.[49] This is a rare example in which the law provides specific guidance on how an appointing authority should assess a *foreign* candidate for appointment to judicial office.

[46] *National Court Act 1975* c 38 (PNG), ss 1, 2.

[47] Constitutional Planning Committee Papua New Guinea (n 12) ch 8, [34]; J Logan, 'Law and Justice in Papua New Guinea', Paper presented at the Australian Institute of International Affairs, Brisbane (23 June 2015) 25.

[48] *High Court Judges (Salaries and Allowances) Act 2017* (Kiribati), s 4.

[49] *Judicial Services and Courts Act 2000* c 270 (Vanuatu), s 33(3).

iii. Specific Selection Criteria for Foreign Judges

In addition to the bare legal requirements governing eligibility for appointment to judicial office, advertisements sometimes specify other qualifications, skills or personal characteristics expected of candidates. Sometimes the selection criteria in advertisements require greater qualifications than the minimum set out in law. For example, an advertisement for a Judge of the High Court of Tuvalu in 2020 required candidates to have 'no less than ten years' experience as a High Court judge in the Pacific', specifying both a longer period of prior judicial service and a narrower range of 'other countries' than required by law.[50] An advertisement seeking a Judge of the Supreme Court of Nauru required candidates to be entitled to practise as a barrister or solicitor in Nauru for at least eight years, 'at least ten years' admission to practice as a legal practitioner in a common law jurisdiction' and experience as a judge in administrative law.[51] This advertisement specified greater qualifications than the minimum five years' practice set out in the Constitution, as well as expertise in a particular area of law.[52] In both Tuvalu and Nauru, the advertisements are clearly targeted at foreign judges. Their approach echoes that of Papua New Guinea, where, as noted, legislation prescribes qualifications of a higher level for non-citizens than for citizens. Unlike Papua New Guinea, however, the goal is not localisation. Rather the selection criteria reflect a desire to recruit a judge with particular skills and experience from the pool of foreign judges.

Advertisements for judicial positions that are placed by donor organisations tend to require a different range of skills and experience of candidates. For example, an advertisement seeking a puisne judge of the High Court of Solomon Islands, a position funded by an Australian government aid programme, sought candidates with at least 15 years' experience as a judge or legal practitioner (10 years more than the minimum experience required by the Constitution). Candidates were also required to have 'proven success in individual and organisational capacity development and sustainability of efforts, ability to share knowledge, and transfer skills'. The position description noted that 'the Judge's efforts should be treated as an opportunity to improve systems and transfer knowledge and skills to National Judiciary and other [Solomon Islands Government] staff, and also to improve the practice of practitioners'. The candidate was further 'expected to demonstrate a good understanding, appreciation and empathy of the local cultures and mores of the society and be able to encourage and assist legal practitioners and other judicial and support staff in improving their work performance, practices and aptitudes'.[53]

[50] 'Judge of the High Court' *Government of Tuvalu* (November 2020). The *Constitution of Tuvalu 1986*, s 124 requires only that a person appointed to the High Court have prior judicial experience of an unspecified period, or have been qualified to practise for at least five years.

[51] 'Justice of the Supreme Court' *Seek* (4 August 2017).

[52] *Constitution of Nauru 1968*, s 49(3).

[53] 'Puisne Judge of the High Court of Solomon Islands (Civil Cases)' *Devex* (6 November 2015).

An advertisement for a judicial position in Kiribati funded by the Commonwealth Fund for Technical Cooperation was less detailed but similarly required the judge to review and implement court operations and administration, and to mentor and train judicial officers in addition to judicial work.[54] The job descriptions set out in these advertisements combine judicial work with development assistance, speaking to the Pacific state's need for a judge and the donor's desire to engage in 'capacity building'.

The degree to which foreign judging should encompass capacity building is a contested issue. The contest discloses different views about the rationales for the use of foreign judges, which are discussed in chapter 8. For present purposes, it is important to note two points. First, the selection criteria applying to foreign judges may be different from those for local judges, as Pacific courts seek judges with specific expertise and skills. Second, where donor organisations provide funding for foreign judges, they sometimes define the selection criteria to include qualities that go beyond simply 'being a judge', to encompass capacity building and other development-orientated outcomes.

iv. Analysis and Implications

In all cases except perhaps Tuvalu, the laws of Pacific states *permit* the appointment of foreign judges but they do not *require* it.[55] With the exception of Papua New Guinea, qualifications for appointment to judicial office are not explicitly formulated with an eye to localisation. Only in Kiribati is it expressly stated in law or policy that appointing authorities ought to give preference to qualified local candidates over foreign candidates.[56] However, in some Pacific states, the pattern of judicial appointments suggests that while there is no express policy, there is in practice a preference to fill full-time judicial positions with local candidates and look overseas only where the pool of suitably qualified local candidates willing to accept judicial appointment falls short.[57]

[54] 'Commonwealth Secretariat Vacancy: Judge of the High Court, Tarawa, Kiribati' *UNjobs* (June 2013). See also 'Puisne Judge of the High Court' *Devex* (28 November 2007); 'Puisne Judge, High Court of Solomon Islands' *Cardno Emerging Markets* (July 2019).

[55] In Tuvalu the constitutional provision is framed in such a way that, on a strict reading, it precludes the appointment of lawyers who have practised solely in Tuvalu from appointment to the High Court or Court of Appeal. A proposal to change this provision was part of a package of constitutional amendments that failed to gain the support of Tuvalu's Parliament in 2019: Constitution Amendment Bill 2019 (Tuvalu), cl 82.

[56] *High Court Judges (Salaries and Allowances) Act 2017* (Kiribati), s 4. Fiji's Constitution of 1997, which was abrogated by coup leaders in 2009, included in s 134 the principle that the composition of the judiciary should, as far as possible, reflect the ethnic and gender balance of the community. This principle seems to have been understood as primarily directed to ensuring the appointment of local judges from both the Indigenous Fijian and Indian Fijian communities, and does not appear to have restricted the appointment of foreign judges in any significant way: Reeves, Vakatora and Lal (n 11) [13.100]–[13.102]. In any event, this principle was not carried into the 2013 Constitution.

[57] See ch 2, section VI, discussing Papua New Guinea, Samoa, Solomon Islands and Vanuatu.

D. Formalities and Restrictions in the Foreign Judge's Home State

The preceding subsections focused on the laws and practices of Pacific states relating to the appointment of foreign judges. The use of foreign judges, however, means that there is an additional source of regulation, namely the judge's home state, which may impose procedural requirements or restrictions on judges serving overseas. Processes of this kind generally arise when a foreign judge is a sitting judge in his or her home jurisdiction and serves concurrently in a Pacific state, although some also apply to retired judges.

i. Seeking Approval to Serve Overseas

Generally, a serving judge will seek the agreement of the head of jurisdiction in his or her home state before accepting appointment to a Pacific court.[58] Several judges described this process as a 'formality', especially where the overseas judicial work is undertaken while the judge is on leave from his or her home court and as such does not affect its capacity.[59] Some heads of jurisdiction are more favourable than others to the judges of their courts serving overseas, which affects the take up of overseas appointments. Some heads of jurisdiction seek to limit the overseas service of judges to ensure that the court has sufficient capacity to hear its own matters. For example, the Supreme Court of Queensland adopted a general practice that only one judge might sit overseas at a time.[60] Some heads of jurisdiction appear to oppose the practice altogether.[61]

The extent of the involvement of the executive branch in acknowledging or approving the appointment of sitting judges to foreign courts varies. Some judges reported that the Chief Justice will notify the Attorney-General of a proposed overseas judicial appointment.[62] In Queensland, consultation between the Attorney-General, Chief Justice and head of the executive is required by legislation.[63] Where there are formal arrangements between courts, in which the judge's home jurisdiction provides both the judges and financial support for their service, representatives of the government agencies responsible for the administration of justice and foreign affairs may be involved. In Sri Lanka, the Judicial Services Commission was responsible for granting Sri Lankan judges leave of absence so that they could serve in Fiji.[64] Such processes largely appear

[58] Interviews F2, F3, F4, F11.

[59] Interviews F3, F10, F11.

[60] Williams (n 32) 633.

[61] Interviews F4, F10, F17.

[62] Interviews F10, F11.

[63] *Supreme Court Act 1991* (Qld), s 22 requires a judge who accepts 'another public office' to notify the Attorney-General and resign the office if the Governor in Council decides, after consultation between the Attorney-General and Chief Justice, that the office is 'inconsistent with the proper discharge of the office of a judge'.

[64] 'Fiji's Chief Justice Condemns Australian, NZ "Interference" and "Hostility"' *Pacific Scoop* (Wellington) (3 November 2009).

to be formalities, and most executive and regulatory agencies do not seek to intervene in the selections made by the donor or recipient courts.

Retired judges who engage in judicial service overseas may also have to address some procedural issues.[65] Generally these relate to the judge's pension. For example, the Constitution of Victoria provides that a judge's right to a pension ceases upon accepting appointment to any judicial office in or outside Victoria.[66] A retired judge of a Victorian court who wishes to accept appointment as a judge overseas while retaining his or her right to a pension must write to the Victorian Attorney-General and seek an order from the Governor in Council in his or her particular case.

ii. Concurrent Judicial Service

The purpose of restrictions on judges' holding another public office or outside employment not only relates to the management of resources, but also seeks to ensure that any additional positions held by judges are compatible with judicial office. There is no clear rule on whether service on a foreign court is incompatible with holding judicial office in the judge's home country. The legal issues will differ depending on the specific constitutional and legal frameworks in each state.[67] The common law rule provides that offices are incompatible

> when, from the nature or extent of the different duties and businesses attached to them, they cannot be properly and effectually executed by the same person; or when they are subordinate to, or interfere with each other, which creates a legal presumption that they will not be executed with impartiality and honesty.[68]

Under the common law rule, when an official accepts an incompatible office, he or she impliedly relinquishes the original office.[69] Concerns about this possibility led the New South Wales Parliament to legislate in 1979 to make it clear that a judge who accepted a part-time appointment to the Supreme Court of Papua New Guinea did not relinquish judicial office in New South Wales as a result of the rule of incompatible office.[70] Similarly, a model clause developed to facilitate concurrent service by Australian judges across Australian States and

[65] Interviews F1, F21.

[66] *Constitution Act 1975* (Vic), s 83(4)(i).

[67] In particular, the ability of federal judges in Australia to serve in other jurisdictions is affected by the requirements of the separation of judicial power under Chapter III of the Australian Constitution: S Murray, 'Dual Federal and State Judicial Appointments: An Australian Impossibility?' (2014) 25 *Public Law Review* 284.

[68] J Chitty, *A Treatise on the Law of the Prerogatives of the Crown* (London, J Butterworth, 1820) 87.

[69] ibid.

[70] *Judicial Office (Papua New Guinea) Act 1979* (NSW); New South Wales, *Parliamentary Debates*, Legislative Assembly, 3 November 1979, 4134 (Mr Walker, Attorney-General and Minister for Justice). A similar provision appeared in the now repealed *Conciliation and Arbitration Act 1904* (Cth), s 103A.

Territories and New Zealand expressly provides that the rule of incompatible office does not operate to prevent a judge from holding another judicial office.[71] In Queensland, legislation confers power on the executive branch to determine if an office is incompatible.[72] In New Zealand, the head of court must be satisfied that the other office is consistent with judicial office.[73] Where there is no legislation to govern the issue, the matter is left to be determined by protocol between judges, the head of jurisdiction and the executive.

Guidelines on judicial ethics do not deal expressly with concurrent judicial service overseas.[74] The practice, at least in Australia and New Zealand, suggests that service on a foreign court is not considered to be incompatible with judicial office, unless there are specific circumstances that might give rise to concerns that the judge cannot execute both offices effectively and impartially. Advice from the Solicitor General of New South Wales stated that there was no suggestion that the appointment of a judge of the New South Wales Supreme Court to a court of a Pacific state was incompatible with the proper exercise of judicial functions, particularly because the judge was to serve in the Pacific only while on leave from his or her position on the New South Wales Court.[75] The New South Wales legislation to accommodate judicial service in Papua New Guinea provided that a judge could be granted leave in order to serve as a judge in Papua New Guinea, but while on leave the judge was 'not entitled to exercise or perform any jurisdiction, powers, authorities, duties or functions' as the holder of judicial office in New South Wales.[76] However, the more recent practice of judicial secondments, in which judicial service overseas is supported financially or in kind by the judge's home court, suggests that a judge is not always required to take leave in order to sit as a judge overseas.[77] It appears that different practices and assumptions have developed in different jurisdictions over time, such that most issues are left to be resolved on a case-by-case basis rather than by a consistent, generally applicable policy.

iii. Analysis and Implications

The discussion in this section has shown how the processes for the selection of foreign judges, while formally in the hands of each individual Pacific state, are

[71] *Judicial Officers Act 1986* (NSW), s 43I; New South Wales, *Parliamentary Debates*, Legislative Council, 2 December 2009, 20395–97 (Tony Kelly).

[72] *Supreme Court Act 1991* (Qld), s 22.

[73] *Senior Courts Act 2016* (NZ), s 142, formerly *Judicature Act 1908* (NZ), s 4(2A); *District Courts Act 1947* (NZ), s 5(4).

[74] Australasian Institute of Judicial Administration, *Guide to Judicial Conduct*, 2nd edn (2007); Chief Justice New Zealand, *Protocol Containing Guidance on Extra-Judicial Employment and Offices (Senior Courts)* (2017); Judiciary of England and Wales, *Guide to Judicial Conduct* (2013).

[75] Interview F3.

[76] *Judicial Office (Papua New Guinea) Act 1979* (NSW), ss 3, 4.

[77] Interview F24.

informed in various ways by attitudes, procedures and relationships within a judge's home state and donor organisations. The multiple sites of regulation raises two important issues that are picked up later in this book. The first, discussed in chapter 6, is that the involvement of various local and foreign actors in the appointment process expands the potential sources of influence over foreign judges, and with it the risks to judicial independence. The second is that appointing authorities in Pacific states stand at a greater distance from foreign judges and, to some extent, share decisions about recruitment with a foreign judge's home state and, where used, funding organisations. In some cases, funding organisations appear to have a say in defining the role that a foreign judge is expected to perform. Such practices further attenuate the connections between a foreign judge and the Pacific state he or she serves, an issue that is explored in detail in chapter 7.

III. REMUNERATION

Arrangements for the remuneration of foreign judges vary depending on whether the foreign judge serves as a visiting court of appeal judge, or as a full-time resident judge.[78] The remuneration itself – how much foreign judges are paid – largely depends on how the judicial position is funded and whether foreign judges are paid by the Pacific state or by donor funds. As this section shows, the issue of remuneration can give rise to difficult questions of policy, balancing equal pay between local and foreign judges on the one hand, with sufficient pay to attract foreign candidates on the other.

A. Rates and Sources of Remuneration

Visiting court of appeal judges generally receive a daily sitting fee, ranging from $300 to $1,000 Australian or New Zealand dollars a day, depending on the jurisdiction and dates of service. In some jurisdictions, the sitting fees are set out in legislation or regulations.[79] In others they are set by agreement between the government and the judge. The travel, accommodation and living expenses of visiting court of appeal judges are also covered. In most cases, the government of the Pacific state provides these funds.

In contrast, foreign judges who serve as resident full-time judges are paid an annual salary. Under some contracts, judges in this category also receive benefits such as travel, accommodation and medical care. Practice varies as to who

[78] On the difference, see ch 2, section IV.

[79] eg *High Court Judges (Salaries and Allowances) Act 2017* (Kiribati); *Constitutional Offices (Terms and Conditions of Service) Act 1987* c 84 (Solomon Islands); *Judicial Services and Courts Act 2000* c 270 (Vanuatu), sch, pt 1.

pays this salary and how much it is. In some cases, the Pacific government pays entirely for the foreign judge's service.[80] In other circumstances, a donor agency might 'top up' the local salaries of foreign judges so that it is commensurate with what the person would earn as a judge in his or her home state.[81] The foreign donor might also pay an overseas living allowance and provide for tax exemptions in the judge's home state.[82] Some formal schemes entail a degree of cost sharing: for example, the donor agency might pay the judge's salary, while the Pacific state provides the judge's accommodation and transport.[83]

Some foreign judges are wholly funded by an external agency or organisation. In these cases, the rates of pay are set by the donor according to its own remuneration schedules.[84] The terms and conditions under these funding agreements vary. For example, some donor agencies prohibit the judge from receiving additional payments or benefits from the Pacific court (such as an additional sitting fee for serving on the Court of Appeal), while in other cases judges are allowed to receive additional payments of this kind.[85] Formal arrangements between courts for the provision of judges generally include terms as to remuneration and expenses. Under some such agreements, the donor court effectively subsidises the foreign judge's salary by recognising the judge's service overseas as part of his or her service in the home court.[86]

B. Analysis and Implications

The use of foreign judges places Pacific states, whose governments, by and large, have limited resources, in competition with larger, richer states. It raises a difficult question: should foreign judges be paid the same as the local judges they serve alongside, or should their pay be comparable to what they would receive in their home state? Disparities in pay between foreign and local judges, and between foreign judges paid pursuant to different funding arrangements, have given rise to concerns. Some interviewees noted that the disparity in pay could damage relationships between local and foreign judges.[87] One judge declined the offer of a salary top up from a donor agency, preferring to work on the same terms and conditions as local judges.[88] Some foreign judges negotiate the issue by using daily sitting fees to cover their expenses and returning or donating

[80] Interviews F1, F8.
[81] Interviews F4, F5, F16, F20.
[82] Interviews F13, F16, F23.
[83] Interviews F24, F26.
[84] Interview F26. Advertisements for judges of the High Court of Solomon Islands refer to the scales of pay set by the Australian Department of Foreign Affairs.
[85] Interviews F19, F26.
[86] Interviews F21, F23, F24.
[87] Interviews F6, F17, F23. In Papua New Guinea see 'Pay Disparity a Thorny Issue' *The National* (Port Moresby) (6 December 2011).
[88] Interview F6.

the balance.[89] That said, in order to attract good candidates, Pacific states and donors might need to provide salaries on a par with what a judge would earn in his or her home state.[90] Different issues arise when the Pacific state offers a significantly higher salary than a judge would earn in his or her home state, as is reportedly the case in Fiji with respect to some Sri Lankan judges. The concern is that this, combined with appointment on short, renewable contracts, might encourage judges to decide cases in a manner favourable to the government in order to secure reappointment.

Pacific governments also must consider the sustainability of continued reliance on foreign judges. Most Pacific states could not afford to pay judicial salaries at the same level as in foreign judges' home states.[91] The cost of the use of foreign judges has led some Chief Justices in the region to promote localisation. In his opening address to the Court in 2015, the Chief Justice of Solomon Islands, Sir Albert Palmer, commented that using foreign judges to fill the gaps on the High Court is too expensive and uses funds that could be utilised for other needs across the legal sector. He suggested a better approach would be to improve the salaries and conditions of local judges so that a career on the bench is more attractive to local lawyers.[92] Chief Justice Lunabek of Vanuatu has similarly called for improvements to the salaries, terms and conditions of local judges.[93]

In these ways, the competition to attract foreign judges imposes financial costs, as well as the cost of the unfairness involved when local and foreign judges receive different rates of pay. Remuneration is also critical to judicial independence: a secure income insulates judges against improper influence by the executive through control of salaries and removes incentives for judges to seek alternative corrupt sources of income. However, as will be discussed in chapter 6, the use of foreign judges requires rethinking the received wisdom about the sources of potential threats to judicial independence and how they might be addressed. As the following section shows, the security of remuneration is most often linked to security of tenure, and for foreign judges, the executive branch of the state is not the sole source of potential influence.

IV. TENURE

Secure tenure is critical to judicial independence and supports the stability of the judiciary as a whole. Across the Pacific, many foreign judges serve for fixed terms

[89] Interviews F10, F11, F17.

[90] Interview F23.

[91] Interview F18.

[92] J Kusapa, 'Expatriate Judges, Not an Answer: Chief Justice' *Island Sun* (Honiara) (21 January 2015); 'Chief Magistrate Says Foreigners No Solution to Solomons Shortage' *ABC News* (Sydney) (21 October 2013).

[93] Chief Justice Lunabek, 'Speech on the Official Opening of the Courts of Vanuatu' (Port Vila, 27 January 2012).

of weeks, months or years. While this is not a universal practice, it is commonplace. This stands in contrast to the position of judges in many other countries, and indeed the position of local judges in many (but not all) Pacific states, who are appointed for longer terms of years or until they reach a specified age of retirement. This section discusses the duration and regulation of the terms of appointment for foreign judges in the nine Pacific states. Section IV.A outlines the legal provisions that govern the tenure of foreign judges, including those in three states that expressly discriminate between citizen and non-citizen judges. Section IV.B describes how these legal provisions may be supplemented by an employment contract between the foreign judge and the state, leading in some cases to inconsistencies and disputes. Finally, section IV.C sets out the empirical findings on the duration of terms of appointment. It shows that the layers of regulation and practice in this area have produced great variation between jurisdictions and between foreign judges themselves.

A. Constitutional and Statutory Provisions

The constitutional and legislative provisions for tenure vary across the nine Pacific states and sometimes also across different courts within the same state. Table 3.1 summarises the different approaches.

Table 3.1 Tenure Provisions in the Nine Pacific States

State	Citizens	Non-citizens
PNG	10-year fixed term	Up to 3-year fixed term
Fiji	Retirement age	Up to 3-year fixed term
Samoa SC	Retirement age	May be fixed term of years
Samoa CA	Fixed term or particular matters	
Kiribati	Fixed term or particular matters	
Tuvalu	Life, fixed term or particular matters	
Tonga	On good behaviour, fixed term or particular matters	
Solomon Islands	Retirement age, fixed term if over 70 or acting judge	
Nauru	Retirement age or particular matter (but note use of acting judges)	
Vanuatu	Retirement age (but note use of acting judges)	

In Kiribati, Tonga and Tuvalu, where foreign judges far outnumber local judges, constitutional provisions permit *any* judge to be appointed for a fixed term.[94]

[94] *Constitution of Kiribati 1979*, ss 83, 91(2), 93; *Constitution of Tonga 1875*, ss 85–87; *Constitution of Tuvalu 1986*, ss 123, 126.

In these states, appointing authorities have discretion to determine the term of judges' appointments.

In three other states, the law expressly distinguishes between citizens and non-citizens for the purposes of tenure. In Papua New Guinea, non-citizen judges may be appointed for a term not exceeding three years, while citizen judges are appointed for 10-year terms.[95] The Constitutions of Fiji and Samoa expressly exempt non-citizen judges from the constitutional guarantee of tenure until the retirement age that applies to other judges. The *Constitution of Fiji 2013* provides that judges are appointed until a specified retirement age except for non-citizens, who *must* be appointed for terms of up to three years.[96] The Constitution of Samoa is less directive. It provides that non-citizens *may* be appointed to the Supreme Court for a term of years,[97] while any Court of Appeal judge (whether citizen or non-citizen) *may* be appointed for a period of time.[98]

Prior to amendments in 2009, the Constitution of Solomon Islands also distinguished between citizen and non-citizen judges for the purposes of tenure. It provided that while all judges were to be appointed until a retirement age of 60, a non-citizen over that age could be appointed for a term of years.[99] The effect of this provision was that a foreign judge of any age could be appointed for a term of years, while a citizen judge was appointed until retirement. Constitutional amendments in 2009 increased the retirement age to 70 and removed the reference to non-citizen judges.[100] The parliamentary debates indicate that the purpose of the amendment was to remove the discriminatory provision that prevented citizens over 60 from serving as judges.[101] However, the effect of the amendments is wider, because the Constitution now requires that all judges, including foreign judges, hold office until 70 years of age. While not all appointments are gazetted, those that are indicate that most foreign judges appointed after the amendments in 2009 were appointed for fixed periods, generally of two to five years. The text of the Constitution would appear to require, however, that only judges over the age of 70 (and acting judges) may now be appointed on fixed terms.[102]

[95] *Organic Law on the Terms and Conditions of Employment of Judges* (PNG), s 2.

[96] *Constitution of Fiji 2013*, s 110. The *Constitution of Fiji 1997* permitted the appointment of judges of the Supreme Court and Court of Appeal for a term of years or for sessions of the court; and judges of the High Court for a term of at least four, and no more than seven, years: s 137(2), (4). No express distinction was made between citizens and non-citizens.

[97] *Constitution of Samoa 1960*, s 68.

[98] ibid, s 75(5).

[99] *Constitution of Solomon Islands 1978*, ss 80(1), (2); 87(1), (2).

[100] *Constitution (Amendment) Act 2009* (Solomon Islands).

[101] Solomon Islands, *Parliamentary Debates*, 6 April 2009 (Hon Sikua); Solomon Islands, *Parliamentary Debates*, 7 April 2009 (Hon Tausinga, Mr Zama, Hon Lilo). Similar concerns about discrimination against local judges were raised during constitution-making discussions in Nauru: Territory of Nauru, 'Record of the Proceedings of the Constitutional Convention' (15 January 1968) 59–61.

[102] *Constitution of Solomon Islands 1978*, s 80(2).

The Constitutions of Nauru, Solomon Islands and Vanuatu fix the tenure of judges until a specified retirement age.[103] However, all three permit the appointment of acting judges on limited terms.[104] In Nauru, several foreign judges were appointed as acting judges because they were older than the specified retirement age of 65.[105] The retirement age was increased to 75 in 2009, but foreign judges, including some who are presumably younger than 75, continue to be appointed on fixed terms.[106] In Vanuatu, the gazette notices for some foreign judges expressly proclaim their appointment as 'acting judges' for specified terms.[107] However, other gazettes show the appointment of 'judges' for terms of between three months and two years.[108] The inconsistency raises questions about whether judges appointed for fixed terms are properly commissioned, or if they are in effect acting judges.

In summary, laws in the nine Pacific states permit, and some require, foreign judges to serve on short-term appointments. There are no legal restrictions on reappointment or the renewal of fixed-term appointments. In most Pacific states, local judges tend to be appointed for longer terms or until retirement, while foreign judges are appointed for short terms, even when the law does not require it.

B. Relationship between Contractual Terms and Formal Appointment

Such constitutional or legislative provisions are not, however, the only source of law governing judicial appointments. A contract might set out the term of a foreign judge's employment instead of, or in addition to, the term specified in the formal instrument of appointment. Generally, the contract is between the foreign judge and the government of the Pacific state, and covers such matters as the period of employment, remuneration and entitlements. Sometimes, these matters are set out in correspondence between the judge and the government prior to or during the judge's appointment.[109] Disputes have arisen over inconsistencies between the details of the contract and the formal appointment.

[103] *Constitution of Nauru 1968*, s 53; *Constitution of Solomon Islands 1978*, s 79; *Constitution of Vanuatu 1980*, s 47(3); *Judicial Services and Courts Act 2000* c 270 (Vanuatu), s 36(1).

[104] *Constitution of Nauru 1968*, s 53; *Constitution of Solomon Islands 1978*, s 80(2); *Constitution of Vanuatu 1980*, s 47(5); *Judicial Services and Courts Act 2000* c 270 (Vanuatu), s 35.

[105] Nauru Constitutional Review Committee, *Naoero Ituga: Report* (2007) 113.

[106] *Constitution of Nauru (Parliamentary Amendments) Act 2009* (Nauru), s 33.

[107] See instruments of appointment for Justice Coventry in Gazette 7/2000; Justice Treston in Gazettes 24/2003 and 25/2005; Justice Tuohy in Gazette 24/2006; Justices Goldsbrough and Young in Gazette 25/2007; Justice O'Regan in Gazette 26/2008; Justice MacDonald in Gazette 19/2010; Justice Heath in Gazette 29/2012; and Justice Mansfield in Gazettes 9/2007, 35/2010 and 60/2015.

[108] See instruments of appointment for Justice Dawson in Gazettes 28/2008 and 19/2010; Justice Butler in Gazette 14/2009; Justices Fatiaki and Clapham in Gazette 29/2009; Justice Sey in Gazettes 33/2012 and 63/2014; Justice Harrop in Gazette 7/2014.

[109] Interviews F1, F20.

In the early 1990s, Justice Faqir Muhammad was appointed a judge of the High Court of Kiribati. He was later appointed Chief Justice for a three-year term. This appointment was formally renewed for a further two years, to expire on 6 February 1995. The British Government had initially funded the judge's position but ceased to do so in 1994. In March 1994, the Government of Kiribati secured funding from New Zealand to cover the remainder of the judge's term. The judge and the Government of Kiribati then signed a contract, which provided that Muhammad would serve as resident judge for one year, in effect until 2 May 1995, three months after the expiry of the formal appointment. The dispute about when the judge's commission would end made its way to the High Court of Kiribati. The Court held that while the Government of Kiribati had agreed to appoint Muhammad as Chief Justice for a term ending 2 May 1995, the contract was no substitute for the formal appointment made by the President under the Constitution. While there was no way to compel the President to make the judicial appointment consistent with the contract, the Court held that if Muhammad was not formally appointed to the judicial position, he would be entitled to damages under contract.[110]

A similar case arose in Nauru in 2010, when the Supreme Court was called upon to determine a dispute between Chief Justice Millhouse and the Nauruan Government over the renewal of his contract. Before the end of his term, Chief Justice Millhouse and the responsible Minister had discussed an extension of the Chief Justice's appointment. A draft contract was prepared but no formal appointment was made. Chief Justice Millhouse in fact sat past the expiry of the term of his initial appointment and was paid at a higher rate consistent with the draft contract. However, once the Cabinet became aware that the Chief Justice's term had expired, it resolved not to renew his contract. The Supreme Court held that Millhouse was not entitled to an extension of his appointment as Chief Justice on the basis that the President's discretionary power to appoint a judge could not be curtailed by contract.[111]

A final example arose in Tonga, where, prior to 2010, the Constitution provided that judges were to be appointed by the King with the consent of the Privy Council and would hold office during good behaviour.[112] Legislation stated that the terms of judicial appointments were to be governed by employment contract, provided that the contract was not inconsistent with the Constitution.[113] While the formal instruments of appointment did not set out the term, the employment contracts of foreign judges usually specified a term of 12 months or two years. Inconsistencies between the two gave rise to

[110] *Muhammad v Attorney-General* [1995] KIHC 1.

[111] *Re President of the Republic of Nauru and in the matter of Article 53 and 55 of the Constitution of Nauru* [2010] NRSC 14; *Re President of the Republic of Nauru and in the matter of Article 53 and 55 of the Constitution of Nauru (No 2)* [2010] NRSC 15.

[112] *Constitution of Tonga 1875*, ss 85, 86.

[113] *Supreme Court Act 1903* c 10 (Tonga), s 4A(1), (2).

uncertainty about whether a judge's appointment lapsed at the expiry of the term specified in contract or continued regardless.[114] In 2010, the Constitution was amended to provide that '[t]he King in Privy Council, after receiving advice from the Judicial Appointments and Discipline Panel, shall determine the terms of appointment'.[115]

These examples illustrate the practical difficulties that have arisen in the appointment of foreign judges on short-term contracts. Such disputes between governments and judges have the potential to destabilise the judiciary, especially in small jurisdictions where there may be only the one resident judge. The legal position is that the terms specified in the formal instrument of appointment will prevail over contract, but this does not provide much security if the expiry of the contract leaves the judge without remuneration.

C. Duration of Appointments

Regardless of whether the term of appointment is stated in the contract or in the instrument of appointment, jurisdictions vary as to who determines the term of appointment and what that term is. In some states, a maximum term of appointment is set by legislation. Laws in Fiji and Papua New Guinea impose maximum three-year terms on non-citizen judges, although shorter terms are possible and used, for example, when the full term would take the appointment over the mandatory retirement age.[116] In other states, the appointing authority has discretion to decide the term of the appointment.

Data on the terms of appointment of foreign judges in the Pacific are piecemeal. The duration of the appointment may be stated in the formal instrument of appointment, but these instruments are not always published. It is sometimes noted in government announcements of new judicial appointments. Data from these sources, combined with information provided by judges themselves, yield information about the terms of appointment for just over 100 foreign judges over the case study period, from which it is possible to trace some general trends in each jurisdiction.[117] In Kiribati, Nauru, Solomon Islands, Tonga and Tuvalu, foreign judges tend to be appointed on fixed terms ranging from one to five years, although some appointments specify no term at all, in which case the

[114] Interviews F12, F20.

[115] *Act of Constitution of Tonga (Amendment) (No 3) Act 2010* (Tonga).

[116] *Constitution of Fiji 2013*, s 110(1); *Organic Law on the Terms and Conditions of Employment of Judges* (PNG), s 2.

[117] The sources of data and techniques for data collection are explained in ch 2, section II. A study on terms of appointment conducted in 2011 adopted a different methodology. Its survey of judges of the Pacific Judicial Conference yielded responses about the approaches of different courts, rather than the terms of appointment of individual judges. No responses were recorded from Fiji and Tuvalu. Its finding that non-citizen judges tend to serve on shorter appointments than citizen or resident judges is generally consistent with the more detailed data collected in this study: Ingram (n 36).

foreign judge serves indefinitely. In Samoa, judges of the Court of Appeal tend to hold indefinite appointments, while foreign judges serving on the Supreme Court are appointed for terms of years. In Vanuatu, some Judges of Appeal have no fixed term, but most are appointed for the particular sittings of the Court of Appeal, that is, a period of two weeks. Foreign judges appointed to the Supreme Court of Vanuatu are generally appointed for a term of months or years. There is therefore a great deal of variation between the duration of fixed-term appointments, even within the same state, the same court and in relation to the same judge.

A decision about the term of appointment for a foreign judge can be influenced by a number of factors. Pacific states have small budgets and governments are wary of over-committing limited financial resources.[118] Legal restrictions may indirectly lead to the appointment of judges on short terms: for example, a shortage of available judges and a relatively young retirement age led Nauru to appoint acting judges on short terms rather than permanent judges.[119] The preferences of donor states and organisations also affect the duration of the judge's term of appointment. Where a donor agency provides judicial salaries, that funding is usually limited to a fixed period, which in turn affects the term of the judicial appointment.[120] Secondment programmes are negotiated to suit both the donor court (from which the judge takes leave) and the recipient Pacific court. The secondment arrangements between the District Court of New Zealand and the Supreme Court of Vanuatu, for example, contemplate appointments of two years, which sometimes have been extended. Finally, judges themselves are in a position to negotiate the term of their appointments. There are a few instances in which foreign judges have nominated the term of their appointment[121] or negotiated clauses in the contract to protect tenure, for example to require the government to give notice of reappointment or to provide for renewal at the option of the judge.[122] The evidence gathered here suggests, however, that in most cases short-term judicial appointments reflect the preferences of Pacific states and funding organisations, rather than those of judges themselves.

Occasionally, the duration of a foreign judge's appointment is defined not by a period of time but by a particular case. The appointment of a judge to hear a specific matter is expressly permitted by law in Kiribati, Nauru, Samoa, Tonga and Tuvalu.[123] For example, Justice Muecke, a retired Australian judge, was appointed as a judge of the Supreme Court of Nauru to 'hear and dispose

[118] Interview F18.
[119] Nauru Constitutional Review Committee (n 105) 112–13.
[120] Interviews F13, F20, F23, F26.
[121] Interviews F1, F8, F12.
[122] Interviews F6, F20.
[123] *Constitution of Kiribati 1979*, s 91(2); *Supreme Court Act 2018* (Nauru), s 10(6); *Constitution of Samoa 1960*, s 75(5); *Constitution of Tonga 1875*, s 87; *Constitution of Tuvalu 1986*, s 123.

Supreme Court Case No 12 of 2017 between Republic & Mathew Batsuia & Ors'.[124] While appointments of this kind are not limited to foreign judges, they are likely to be filled by foreign judges either because of a shortage of local judges, or, as was the case in relation to Justice Muecke's appointment, to avoid perceptions of political interference or bias.[125] Limiting a foreign judge's commission in this way can give rise to practical and legal issues. In the course of hearing the named case, two constitutional issues relating to the right to a fair trial arose before Justice Muecke. Ordinarily, a judge hearing a criminal matter would have power to decide related constitutional issues, but because Justice Muecke's commission was limited to hearing the criminal matter, he did not have this constitutional jurisdiction.[126] The case had already been significantly delayed, and referring the constitutional issues to another judge would have further delayed the trial. In addition, the politically sensitive case, which involved the prosecution of a group of suspended Members of Parliament for criminal offences arising from a public protest, was overshadowed by serious allegations of executive interference and obstruction.[127] Confining the judge's commission proved to be one way in which the executive could constrain the scope of the case. Tenure defined in this way, while rare, can be problematic.

D. Analysis and Implications

The appointment of foreign judges on short renewable terms raises issues of principle and practice. The most obvious concern relates to judicial independence. Short-term appointments provide powerful executives with the opportunity to stack the court with judges who are perceived to be sympathetic to their interests. Renewability can be a lever of influence over judges, who might feel influenced to decide cases in a particular way in order to secure their reappointment. The appointment of *foreign* judges for short renewable terms raises distinctive issues for judicial independence that are discussed in chapter 6, where the empirical findings set out in this chapter are used to explain and justify the limited circumstances in which short-term appointments for foreign judges might be appropriate. The appointment of foreign judges for short periods also introduces a degree of uncertainty, which can affect the stability of the judiciary. The fact that judges serve on short terms and may not be reappointed contributes to the high number of foreign judges who have served in the region over the case study period. Inconsistencies between instruments of appointment and contracts of employment create further uncertainties and at times lead to

[124] *Nauru v Batsuia* [2018] NRSC 37, [29]–[30].
[125] 'Nauru Bringing in Australian Judge for "Riot" Trial' (n 16).
[126] *Nauru v Batsuia* (Nauru Court of Appeal, 21 June 2019) [53].
[127] M Swanson, 'Trial of the "Nauru 19"' [2018] *Bar News: Journal of the NSW Bar Association* 83.

disputes. There is a lack of clarity in the laws and practices of Nauru, Solomon Islands and Vanuatu, such that the appointments of some foreign judges may not comply with the letter of the law, or should properly be described as acting appointments. Except in states where the law prescribes a maximum term of appointment for foreign judges, there does not appear to be a consistent policy about the duration of foreign judges' appointments to guide the decisions of the appointing authorities in Pacific states as well as the organisations that provide and fund foreign judges. The ad hoc approach exacerbates the issues of uncertainty and discontinuity, but also highlights the lack of a coherent policy, informed by a consistent rationale for the use of foreign judges in the region. This broader policy question is addressed in the concluding chapter of this book.

V. REMOVAL

All Pacific constitutions set out a formal process for removing judges. In five of the nine states, the Constitution prescribes a process for removal whereby an authority, such as the judicial services commission, the executive or the parliament, can refer the question of removal to an independent tribunal, which conducts an investigation and makes recommendations to the relevant authority.[128] In Nauru and Samoa, judges may be removed only on address of the Parliament approved by two-thirds of the total number of members.[129] In Tonga and Vanuatu, the judicial services commission may recommend the removal of a judge to the King or President respectively.[130] Judges may be removed from office only for misbehaviour or inability to perform the functions of their office, although in Tonga the King retains a unilateral power to dismiss judges without cause.[131]

It is, however, rare for Pacific states to use these formal procedures to remove foreign judges.[132] Instead, governments, judiciaries and other actors have used means outside the formal process to remove foreign judges, including the non-renewal of fixed-term appointments, the cessation of invitations to sit on Courts of Appeal and the cancellation of judges' visas. The regulation of the

[128] *Constitution of Fiji 2013*, ss 111, 112; *Constitution of Kiribati 1979*, ss 83, 93; *Constitution of Papua New Guinea 1975*, ss 179–181; *Constitution of Solomon Islands 1978*, ss 80, 87; *Constitution of Tuvalu 1986*, s 127(2).

[129] *Constitution of Nauru 1968*, s 51(1); *Constitution of Samoa 1960*, s 68(5). Amendments to Samoa's Constitution passed in December 2020 mean that this procedure applies only to the removal of the Chief Justice. The procedure for removal for other judges is left to legislation, which at the time of writing, was unclear on the issue.

[130] *Constitution of Tonga 1875*, s 83C(2)(c); *Constitution of Vanuatu 1980*, s 47(3).

[131] *Constitution of Tonga 1875*, ss 85(2), 86(2).

[132] In Vanuatu in 1996, formal procedures were commenced to remove Chief Justice D'Imecourt, but the Supreme Court later held that the process was invalid: *D'Imecourt v Manatawai* [1998] VUSC 59. In Tuvalu in 2019, an independent tribunal was established to investigate allegations of misconduct by Chief Justice Sweeney.

transnational movement of judges by their home countries and, at times, by other states introduces an additional avenue for the effective removal of a foreign judge. Such extra-constitutional removal is made possible by the appointment of foreign judges on short-term contracts and the fact that, as non-citizens, foreign judges are susceptible to immigration controls that citizen judges are not.

A. Non-renewal of Contract

When a judge is appointed for a fixed term, the simplest way to effectively remove the judge is to let the term lapse and decline to renew it. In at least four Pacific states, foreign judges who have made decisions unfavourable to the government have not had their contracts renewed.[133] Such cases speak to wider concerns that the appointment of judges on short, renewable terms makes judges susceptible to executive interference, as judges might be perceived to decide cases to please the authorities responsible for their reappointment. The contractual basis for the service of foreign judges also gives external agencies who fund judicial positions a means to effectively remove a foreign judge by refusing to renew funding arrangements with the Pacific state, leaving it in the position of having to fund the judicial position itself or seek alternative funding. While there are no reports of funding agencies targeting particular judges, there are cases in which donor agencies have refused to renew funding agreements, leading in effect to the abolition of a judicial position.[134]

B. Invitations to Sit on Court of Appeal Cease

A second means to effectively remove a foreign judge is to decline to invite the judge to sit on hearings of the court of appeal. Courts of appeal in the region function on a part-time basis, with foreign judges visiting when sittings are convened. The general practice is that the Chief Justice or President of the Court of Appeal will select judges from a pool of foreign judges to constitute the bench for a particular sitting. This arrangement has practical advantages in that it accommodates part-time foreign judges who may not be available for every sitting of the Court of Appeal.[135] However, judges have been effectively removed when the Chief Justice ceases to invite them to sit on the Court.[136]

[133] Interviews F1, F8, F20, F25.

[134] Interview F20. For example in Kiribati in relation to Muhammad CJ: *Muhammad v Attorney-General* [1995] KIHC 1; in Vanuatu in relation to D'Imecourt CJ: *D'Imecourt v Manatawai* [1998] VUSC 59.

[135] Reeves, Vakatora and Lal (n 11) [13.62].

[136] Interviews F9, F12, F17.

C. Visa Cancellation

The state's power over immigration provides a third mechanism for the extra-constitutional removal of a foreign judge. As non-citizens, foreign judges enter and work in Pacific states according to the immigration laws of the state. This makes foreign judges vulnerable to removal as a result of restrictions on their travel or cancellation of their visas. There are several examples of foreign judges who have been removed in this way. In Vanuatu in 1996, the Judicial Services Commission sought to terminate the appointment of Chief Justice D'Imecourt, a British citizen, following allegations of misconduct. Before the Commission made a decision, however, the Minister for Foreign Affairs declared the Chief Justice an undesirable immigrant and prohibited him from entering Vanuatu for an indefinite period. D'Imecourt left Vanuatu, but sought judicial review of the Minister's declaration, arguing that it was tantamount to the termination of his judicial appointment outside the constitutional process for removal. The Supreme Court held that this did not make the declaration unlawful, stating that 'if any person, Chief Justice or otherwise' falls within the prohibited classes under the *Immigration Act*, 'he will become a prohibited immigrant, even if the consequence means that the person is unable to carry out … the office of Chief Justice'.[137] The Minister's declaration was held to be unlawful on other grounds.

In 2014, Nauru's Minister for Immigration revoked the visa of Chief Justice Eames, an Australian citizen. The Chief Justice had issued an injunction from Melbourne to prevent the deportation of the Resident Magistrate, also an Australian citizen, after the Magistrate had determined a case against the wishes of the Minister.[138] Unable to enter Nauru to sit on the Court, Chief Justice Eames resigned, citing the impossibility for him to perform his role remotely, his lack of confidence in the rule of law and judicial independence in Nauru, and the likelihood that his criticism of the Government's conduct would require his recusal from future cases involving the Government.[139] In 2016, it was reported that some members of the Vanuatu Government had discussed deporting Justice Mary Sey, a citizen of The Gambia, after she convicted 16 members of Vanuatu's Parliament of bribery offences, although such action was not pursued in the end.[140]

These examples show that foreign judges are vulnerable to extra-constitutional removal as a result of their non-citizenship. The fact that foreign judges depend on visa arrangements to travel to Pacific states also provides a means by which

[137] *D'Imecourt v Manatawai* [1998] VUSC 59.

[138] G Eames, 'The Rule of Law in Nauru: An Evolving Concept?', Paper presented at Law Society of South Australia Criminal Law Conference, McLaren Vale (24 October 2014).

[139] Judge's Chambers Supreme Court of Nauru, 'Geoffrey Eames Resigns as Chief Justice of Nauru' (Media Release No 5, 13 March 2014) 2–3.

[140] M Forsyth, 'The Vanuatu Judiciary: A Critical Check on Executive Power' in HP Lee and M Pittard (eds), *Asia-Pacific Judiciaries: Independence, Impartiality and Integrity* (Cambridge, Cambridge University Press, 2017) 354, 363.

other states can affect the service of foreign judges. In 2013, Chief Justice Ward, a citizen of the United Kingdom, was unable to sit in Tuvalu because the Fijian Government refused to provide him with a visa to transit in Fiji, which is the only flight route to Tuvalu.[141] Sir Gordon Ward had been President of the Court of Appeal of Fiji and had let his appointment lapse after the 2006 coup. Chief Justice Ward heard some urgent matters on the papers, while an Acting Chief Justice was appointed to preside in Tuvalu in his absence.[142] This situation continued until 2016, when Chief Justice Ward resigned and a new Chief Justice was appointed. Fijian judges were similarly affected when, following the 2006 Fiji coup and the abrogation of the Constitution in 2009, Australia and New Zealand imposed travel bans on Fijian government officials, including judges. When the travel arrangements of new Sri Lankan judges were affected, the Chief Justice of Fiji sought to 'stand up against such interference', stating that 'Fiji must have a judiciary. And it is not for Australia and New Zealand to tell us we cannot have one, or to tell us who we are to appoint.'[143] The interim Fijian Government expelled the Australian and New Zealand High Commissioners and recalled its own envoys over the issue.[144]

D. Analysis and Implications

These three categories of effective removal – non-renewal of contract, cessation of invitations and restrictions on travel – demonstrate that foreign judges are vulnerable to removal from office in ways that local judges are not. Insecure tenure, citizenship status, and their need to travel to and from Pacific states expose foreign judges to extra-constitutional removal at the hands of Pacific governments and, at times, other actors such as funding organisations and foreign states. The issue highlights points at which domestic constitutional norms interact with, and are sometimes superseded by, private contract law and the rights of sovereign states to control the entry of non-citizens. As the judgment in Chief Justice D'Imecourt's case demonstrates, constitutional protections of judicial independence have not been able to protect foreign judges from removal in these novel ways.

VI. CONDUCT OF HEARINGS

This chapter has thus far focused on the terms and conditions governing the service of foreign judges. It has shown how procedures for appointment,

[141] 'Tuvalu Judge Unable to Transit via Fiji' *Cook Islands News* (Rarotonga) (24 January 2014) 4.

[142] Office of the Attorney-General, 'Country Report of the Office of the Attorney General Tuvalu' (Report to the 34th Pacific Islands Law Officers' Network Meeting, October 2015) 7–8.

[143] 'Fiji's Chief Justice Condemns Australian, NZ "Interference" and "Hostility"' (n 64).

[144] 'Fiji Expels Envoys over Interference Claims' *ABC News* (Sydney) (4 November 2009).

remuneration, tenure and removal accommodate – and at times abuse – foreign judges. This part shifts the focus away from individual judges to the practices of Pacific courts. It shows how the long-standing use of foreign judges has affected the way in which Pacific courts conduct hearings and deliver judgments, including the language of the court; delay and speed in judicial decision making; and the place in which the court sits.

A. Language

Each of the nine Pacific states included in this study is multilingual. English is the official language of Fiji, Kiribati, Solomon Islands and Tuvalu, but in all of these states several other languages are widely spoken. In Nauru, Samoa and Tonga, the indigenous language stands alongside English as an official language. In Papua New Guinea, where there are over 800 indigenous languages, English and Tok Pisin are official languages. The three official languages of Vanuatu are English, French and Bislama. Despite this linguistic diversity, in all countries the predominant language of law is English. Legislation is drafted or translated in English. Written judgments of the higher courts are published in English. Proceedings of the superior trial court and court of appeal are generally conducted in English. One reason for this is the reliance on foreign judges recruited from anglophone common law jurisdictions. The effect is most discernible in Vanuatu, where despite colonial ties to Britain and France and constitutional recognition of English and French as official languages, the post-independence judiciary of Vanuatu has been largely anglicised as a result of the use of Australian, British and New Zealand judges and other forms of legal assistance from those countries.[145] The dominance of English across the courts of the Pacific is also a consequence of the importation of common law and statutory law from Australia, New Zealand and the United Kingdom.[146] In local and customary courts, where lay magistrates apply customary laws and procedures, proceedings are more likely to be conducted in indigenous languages.

The right to a fair trial requires that proceedings be conducted in a language that the parties understand, and if that is not possible, to have access to an interpreter.[147] Many local judges are bilingual and some resident foreign judges will learn the local language.[148] The use of foreign judges who do not speak local languages, however, often brings with it the need for court interpreters, extending both the time and costs of litigation. Sometimes, lacking an official

[145] WFS Miles, *Bridging Mental Boundaries in a Postcolonial Microcosm: Identity and Development in Vanuatu* (Honolulu, University of Hawaii Press, 1998) 166.

[146] J Corrin, 'A Question of Identity: Complexities of State Law Pluralism in the South Pacific' (2010) 61 *Journal of Legal Pluralism and Unofficial Law* 145, 147–48.

[147] S Farran, *Human Rights in the South Pacific: Challenges and Changes* (London, Routledge-Cavendish, 2009) 244.

[148] Interview F11.

interpreter, a local judge on the bench might communicate with witnesses and translate for the benefit of foreign judges.[149] The conduct of proceedings and delivery of judgments in English also limits the accessibility of the law to the wider public.[150]

B. Time

The use of foreign judges, particularly non-resident judges, affects the timing and duration of court sittings. In smaller jurisdictions where there is only a part-time foreign judge on the superior trial court, there may be difficulties hearing urgent matters.[151] Court backlogs and delays can arise when foreign judges are unable to travel into the jurisdiction,[152] or where there are gaps between departing foreign judges and their replacements.[153]

Perhaps counter-intuitively, however, the presence of foreign judges on courts of appeal has meant that these courts deliver judgments with remarkable speed. As noted previously, courts of appeal in the region sit part time, and foreign judges visit for a week or two for the sittings period. In the majority of cases, courts of appeal hand down their judgments in the same sittings in which the case is heard. It is rare for courts of appeal comprising foreign judges to reserve judgment beyond the sittings period, although they will do so in complex cases or where judges have different opinions on the outcome.[154] The general practice of courts of appeal is that each judge will be allocated cases to prepare the first draft. Draft judgments are circulated to the panel of judges and discussed and amended, before being handed down as judgments of the court. Judges sitting on courts of appeal in the Pacific therefore take on a high workload in sitting weeks. Many also undertake significant preparatory work before the sittings to take advantage of the library resources and research services available in their home jurisdictions.[155]

The presence of foreign judges is a key reason for the speedy delivery of appellate decisions. Part-time foreign judges seek to contain their work in the

[149] Interview F3.

[150] TLS Mulitalo Seumanutafa, *Law Reform in Plural Societies* (Cham, Springer, 2018) 132.

[151] Nauru Constitutional Review Committee (n 105) 116.

[152] Government of Tuvalu, 'Te Kakeega III: National Strategy for Sustainable Development 2016 to 2020' (March 2016) 12; Office of the Attorney-General (n 142) 7–8; 'Tuvalu Judge Unable to Transit via Fiji' (n 141).

[153] 'The Political Scene: More Supreme Court Judges Resign' *The Economist Intelligence Unit* (London) (1 October 2010).

[154] Interviews F5, F14, F24; see also Lord Cooke of Thorndon, 'Final Appeal Courts: Some Comparisons', *Occasional Paper No 7* (New Zealand Centre for Public Law, 2001) 10. The Supreme Court of Papua New Guinea is an exception that might confirm the trend, in that it is more likely to be composed of local judges and resident foreign judges, and separate concurrences and dissents are relatively common.

[155] Interviews F2, F12.

sittings period. This is especially important for foreign judges who also sit concurrently on a court in their home jurisdiction, who must take care to ensure that their service in the Pacific does not interfere with their work on their home court.[156] The practice also has historical roots, deriving from a time when communications between judges in different countries was more difficult than it is today.[157] Even now, judges tend to prefer discussing and finalising judgments when together in person, rather than coordinating conferences across different countries and time zones.[158] The practice has the advantage of improving the efficiency of the courts and access to justice. In circumstances where a court of appeal sits only once or twice a year, there is often a delay between the time that an appeal is lodged and heard, and judges are keen not to further delay the resolution of the case more than necessary.[159]

C. Place

Where a court consists of foreign judges, there may be times when it sits outside its physical jurisdiction. In the smaller states, where a foreign judge is, at times, the only judge, he or she might be called upon to issue orders remotely or sit in a court outside the state in order to take evidence.[160] There is a strong argument, developed in other common law jurisdictions, that such arrangements are authorised as part of the inherent powers of the court.[161] Kiribati and Tuvalu make express legislative provision for their courts to sit outside the state,[162] and their Courts of Appeal, which predominantly comprise foreign judges from New Zealand, have sat in Auckland on occasion.[163] Such arrangements may be necessary to ensure that a properly constituted court can sit in a timely way. They do, however, raise questions about the ease with which the parties, the public and local media can access the court.[164] For these reasons, most courts sit in the country of jurisdiction, even when they are entirely composed of foreign judges.

Although the legacies of the use of foreign judges on the conduct of proceedings before Pacific courts are likely to remain, new technologies and new

[156] Interviews F3, F24.

[157] A Mason, 'Reflections of an Itinerant Judge in the Asia-Pacific Region' (2000) 28 *International Journal of Legal Information* 311, 318.

[158] Interviews F3, F24.

[159] Interview F12.

[160] In Nauru and Tuvalu see Eames (n 138) 2; Office of the Attorney-General (n 142) 8.

[161] *Endean v Canadian Red Cross Society* [2014] CarswellBC 363 [79]–[82]; *Attorney-General of the Turks and Caicos Islands v Misick* [2020] UKPC 30 [66].

[162] *Court of Appeal Act 1980* (Kiribati), s 6; *Superior Courts Act 1987* c 7.68 (Tuvalu), ss 6(3)(b), 12(2)(b).

[163] eg *Tokataake v Attorney-General* [2003] KICA 4; *Ielemia v R* (Court of Appeal of Tuvalu, 18 September 2017).

[164] V Black and SGA Pitel, 'Out of Bounds: Can a Court Sit Outside Its Home Jurisdiction?' (2013) 41 *Advocates' Quarterly* 503.

circumstances will prompt change. The Covid-19 pandemic that commenced in 2020 required Pacific courts reliant on visiting foreign judges to quickly adapt. In order to limit the spread of the Covid-19 virus, all Pacific states imposed strict controls over the entry of foreign citizens. Foreign judges' home states likewise restricted international travel. With foreign judges unable to easily travel to conduct hearings, courts of appeal in particular had to modify their procedures. In 2020, the Courts of Appeal of Samoa, Tonga and Vanuatu conducted hearings by video to enable foreign judges to participate.[165] Other states are expected to follow this lead: in 2020, Nauru amended its law to permit the Court of Appeal to conduct proceedings by video in 'urgent or exceptional circumstances'[166] and Australia gifted video-conferencing equipment to the Solomon Islands judiciary.[167] The long-term effects of the changes required to mitigate the disruptions caused by the pandemic remain to be seen. Adaptation to virtual court proceedings has the potential to change how foreign judges participate and the timing and duration of sittings. Potentially, it might also affect the cohort of foreign judges itself, as Pacific states rely more heavily on local or resident judges present in the jurisdiction. It is even possible to imagine that virtual proceedings might facilitate greater participation by judges from outside the region's traditional donor states.

VII. CONCLUSION

This chapter shows that distinctive issues arise in relation to the appointment, remuneration, tenure and removal of foreign judges in the Pacific. It also shows how legal frameworks have been adapted, and in some cases circumscribed and bypassed, as courts, government authorities and donor organisations negotiate the challenges presented by the use of foreign judges.

While these processes are largely effective in securing the services of foreign judges, there is a degree of irregularity and uncertainty that affects the appointment of foreign judges and the terms of their service and, as a consequence, Pacific courts. Foreign judges are recruited in the main by informal means. Even where more formal recruitment measures are used, appointing authorities face the challenge of assessing candidates for judicial appointment from a distance. The tenure of foreign judges' service is insecure, affected by short-term appointments and their vulnerability to removal by extra-constitutional means. The use of foreign judges, in combination with other factors, has meant that

[165] 'Tonga's Appeal Court Proceeds via Teleconference' *Matangi Tonga* (Nuku'alofa) (24 March 2020); Republic of Vanuatu Chief Justice's Chambers, 'Guidance Note for Remote Hearings – Vanuatu Court of Appeal' (28 April 2020).

[166] *Nauru Court of Appeal (Amendment) Act 2020* (Nauru).

[167] J Kusapa, 'High Court Receives Video Conferencing Equipment' *Island Sun News* (Honiara) (2 October 2020).

the language, timing and place of judicial proceedings are not fully tailored to the needs of litigants and the people, an issue foreign judges themselves have sought to address in the conduct of hearings. Meanwhile, judges' home courts and donor organisations add a layer of their own, largely ad hoc, procedures and requirements, affecting in some cases the availability, the selection criteria, remuneration and tenure of foreign judges. The legal frameworks do not cover the range of issues that arise, leaving Pacific judiciaries, donor courts and organisations, and foreign judges themselves, to negotiate appropriate practices, often on a case-by-case basis.

In chapter 8, this book draws on the comparative insights gained from the different experiences across the Pacific to suggest a range of initiatives that Pacific courts and governments, donor organisations and foreign judges themselves might adopt to address these issues.

4

The Significance of Nationality

I. INTRODUCTION

THE GLOBAL NORM is that the judges who sit on courts of constitutional jurisdiction will be citizens. In over 100 states, constitutional or statutory provisions require judges of the constitutional or apex court to be citizens or nationals of the state.[1] Even where there is no express legal requirement of citizenship, the dictates of politics or convention may make the appointment of a non-citizen to the highest court inconceivable. In these states, citizenship is a primary and non-negotiable requirement for judicial appointment. Where the law requires judges to be citizens, citizenship trumps merit in the sense that a non-citizen with expertise and experience in the state's legal system could not be appointed to judicial office.

This citizenship norm is also reflected in international principles and standards. Since the 1980s, international organisations have developed minimum standards of judicial independence and conduct capable of operating within the different domestic constitutional frameworks across the world. While no international standards *require* citizenship, several expressly exempt nationality from the prohibited grounds of discrimination in judicial appointments. For example, the *Basic Principles on the Independence of the Judiciary* provide that a requirement that a candidate for judicial office must be a national of the country is not equivalent to impermissible discrimination on the grounds of 'race, colour, sex, religion, political or other opinion, national or social origin, property, birth or status'.[2]

[1] Audit of national laws relating to the qualifications for judicial appointment to the constitutional or highest national courts in all countries as at 1 July 2017.

[2] *Basic Principles on the Independence of the Judiciary* adopted by the Seventh UN Congress on the Prevention of Crime and the Treatment of Offenders, Milan, 26 August–6 September 1985, endorsed by the UN General Assembly Resolutions 40/32 and 40/146 of 1985, art 10. See also International Project of Judicial Independence of the International Association of Judicial Independence and World Peace, *Mt Scopus International Standards on Judicial Independence* (19 March 2008) art 21.15.1; *Beijing Statement of Principles of the Independence of the Judiciary in the Law Asia Region* adopted by the Sixth Conference of the Chief Justices of Asia and the Pacific, Beijing (August 1997) art 13.

Legal theoretical scholarship has largely not considered the nationality of the judges on constitutional courts, whether to justify the requirement of citizenship or to challenge the exceptional use of foreign judges.[3] This chapter draws attention to significant theoretical issues that merit examination, by setting out the ways in which citizenship, informed by the thicker notion of nationality, can be significant to the role of the judges who sit on courts of constitutional jurisdiction. It does so by identifying, in section II, three qualities that are understood to accompany nationality – knowledge, membership and identity – and assessing the significance of each to the role of the judge.

The resulting analysis covers three aspects of judging. The first, considered in section III, relates to the task of adjudication. For this, nationality might indicate a technical knowledge of the national law, which is necessary to the judge's core duty to resolve disputes according to law. Nationality also implies a broader, contextual knowledge of the national community, which can assume significance when judges come to engage in constitutional interpretation. The second aspect of judging relates the qualities of judicial office, in particular allegiance, responsibility, impartiality and independence. Section IV considers how a judge's membership of the national community provides avenues for judicial responsibility to the state and its people; and conversely, how a foreign judge's distance from the national community might provide a kind of judicial independence. The third and final aspect is connections between the judge and the state and its people. Section V shows how the identity of the judges who sit on a state's courts gives expression to the relationship between the people, the state and the law.

The purpose of this analysis is not to make a case for or against the use of foreign judges on courts of constitutional jurisdiction. Rather, the aim is to identify aspects of judging in which the nationality or citizenship of the judges on a court of constitutional jurisdiction is relevant. The concepts of nationality and citizenship are capable of different manifestations and interpretations. There are also different understandings of the nature of judging and the qualities deemed desirable in judges. Because legal systems differ in their understandings of both nationality and the role of the judge, the extent to which the nationality of judges is significant will also differ across legal systems. Notwithstanding this variation, the analysis presented in this chapter shows that nationality and citizenship are significant to constitutional adjudication, judicial independence, and connecting judges and judiciaries to the wider constitutional system in which they operate. These three aspects of judging form the framework for assessing the implications of the use of foreign judges in the Pacific in the subsequent chapters of this book.

[3] A notable exception, discussed later in this chapter, is P Kahn, 'Independence and Responsibility in the Judicial Role' in IP Stotzky (ed), *Transition to Democracy in Latin America: The Role of the Judiciary* (Boulder, CO, Westview Press, 1993) 73.

II. NATIONALITY, CITIZENSHIP AND FOREIGNNESS

Foreignness is commonly defined against nationality or citizenship. Foreignness is therefore defined relatively: no one is inherently foreign, and a foreigner in one place is at home in another.[4] Foreignness is also defined negatively by what a person is not: relevantly for this discussion, a foreigner is a non-national or non-citizen.[5] As such, the meaning of foreignness and the values associated with it will depend on the meanings and values attached to nationality and citizenship. The task of understanding the significance of foreignness is further complicated by the differences between nationality on the one hand and citizenship on the other. This section navigates the complexities of nationality, citizenship and foreignness to identify the qualities that are thought to accompany nationality and citizenship and that are relevant to the role of the judges on courts of constitutional jurisdiction, namely, knowledge, membership and identity.

The statuses of nationality and citizenship derive from a person's connection with a nation-state. The concepts are burdened by the complexities of the relationships between people, place, the culturally and socially 'imagined' community of the nation, and the legal and political conception of the state. Part of this complexity arises from the distinction between the nation and nationality on the one hand, and the state and citizenship on the other. A nation is a community bound by beliefs about and connections to people, place and history. The state is a self-governing political entity, comprising a population, territory, government and capacity to enter relations with other states. Nationality, which is characterised by qualities of belonging and attachment, is distinct from citizenship, which is a formal legal and political status conferred on an individual by the state.[6] Nationality is a thicker concept than citizenship, and may not necessarily align to citizenship.

Although they are conceptually distinct, the nation is commonly seen as coterminous with the state, which is defined by territorial boundaries and the limits of political authority. As such, the term 'citizenship' is often used interchangeably with 'nationality'. The diversity of peoples within states on the one hand and conditions of globalisation on the other challenge the equation of nation and nationality with the state and citizenship. State borders are arbitrary: it is possible for there to be several nations within the one state and for there to be one nation across several states.[7] The global movement of peoples has 'scrambled' national identities, such that a person's nationality may not match

[4] R Saunders, *The Concept of the Foreign: An Interdisciplinary Dialogue* (Lanham, MD, Lexington Books, 2003) ch 1.

[5] ibid.

[6] C Gans, 'Citizenship and Nationhood' in A Shachar et al (eds), *The Oxford Handbook of Citizenship* (Oxford, Oxford University Press, 2017) 107; D McCrone and R Kiely, 'Nationalism and Citizenship' (2000) 34(1) *Sociology* 19.

[7] S Tierney, *Constitutional Law and National Pluralism* (Oxford, Oxford University Press, 2004).

his or her state of citizenship or residence.[8] A person may hold more than one citizenship. Nevertheless, a state-centred notion of nationality continues to have salience, especially in the areas of politics and law in which judges function.[9] Domestic law begins and ends within the boundaries of the state and is made pursuant to the state's constitution. The idea of sovereignty, in which a defined polity (sometimes described as the nation) is understood to make and legitimate state law, serves to further connect the nation and the state.[10] Even in conditions of legal pluralism characterised by the coexistence of state and non-state legal systems, state law occupies an important, even central, place.[11] For these reasons, in this chapter nationality is presumed to primarily relate to a nation-state and, as it does in many other contexts, citizenship stands as the proxy for the thicker notion of nationality. I take the standard case to be one where the citizenship of judges indicates their nationality, putting to one side those cases where this equation fails to properly capture differences or conflicts between nationality and citizenship.

While the relationships between individuals, communities, nations and states will vary, it is possible to identify some of the qualities of nationality at an abstract level.[12] First, nationality implies knowledge of a nation and national community. Shared experience creates an 'insider view' of national sensibilities, cultures and beliefs. Miller calls this 'a common public culture', which might include shared political principles, cultural ideals, religion and language.[13] This culture is inscribed and communicated in the media of the 'imagined' national community, through education, discourse, history and values.[14] Members of the nation are assumed to know their common public culture, even as they might resist it, seek to change it or define themselves in opposition to it.[15] Such knowledge can be acquired through study and experience, but it is presumed to be more readily accessible to those who are part of the national community.

Second, nationality implies membership. The qualities of membership can include affective ties of belonging, a sense of solidarity with fellow members,

[8] S Benhabib, *The Rights of Others: Aliens, Residents, and Citizens* (Cambridge, Cambridge University Press, 2004) 174. On the movement of peoples across what are now the states and territories of the Pacific, see E Hau'ofa, 'Our Sea of Islands' in E Hau'ofa, E Waddell and V Naidu (eds), *A New Oceania: Rediscovering our Sea of Islands* (Suva, University of the South Pacific in association with Beake House, 1993) 2; T Banivanua-Mar, *Decolonisation and the Pacific: Indigenous Globalisation and the Ends of Empire* (Cambridge, Cambridge University Press, 2016) esp ch 1; S Lilomaiava-Doktor, 'Beyond "Migration": Samoan Population Movement (Malaga) and the Geography of Social Space (Vā)' (2009) 21(1) *Contemporary Pacific* 1.

[9] Gans (n 6) 109–10; W Kymlicka, 'Citizenship in an Era of Globalization' in I Shapiro and C Hacker-Cordón (eds), *Democracy's Edges* (Cambridge, Cambridge University Press) 112, 114–15.

[10] D Miller, *On Nationality* (Oxford, Oxford University Press, 1997) 30.

[11] W Twining, *General Jurisprudence: Understanding Law from a Global Perspective* (Cambridge, Cambridge University Press, 2009) 364.

[12] Miller (n 10) 13.

[13] ibid 26–27.

[14] B Anderson, *Imagined Communities: Reflections on the Origin and Spread of Nationalism* (London, Verso, rev edn, 2006).

[15] Miller (n 10) 42.

mutual obligations, and shared values and interests.[16] These qualities of membership give content to the concept of 'effective nationality' in international law, which understands nationality not simply as the status of citizenship conferred on an individual by the laws of a state but as a matter of 'social fact', evidenced by a 'genuine connection' between individual and nation.[17] The concept of allegiance captures a further dimension of nationality as membership, implying both personal attachment and formal obligations of loyalty to the nation and its people.[18]

Third, nationality is an aspect of personal identity.[19] A person's identity may be framed around multiple characteristics, such as gender, race, religion and language, as well as nationality. The extent to which nationality is core to one's identity varies, and, like all identity characteristics, might assume less or more importance for some individuals and in specific circumstances. Along with other identity characteristics, nationality influences the way in which a person experiences the world. This is not to ascribe to stereotyped national traits, or to say that the peoples of a nation are homogeneous. The point is rather that the peoples of a nation share in an identity informed by common history, place, customs and languages, which affects how they see and are seen in the world.

The qualities of knowledge, membership and identity are not unique to nationality. They arise in many kinds of communities.[20] The nation is just one of several, overlapping communities to which a person may belong. However, nationality carries distinctive features arising from the nation as an 'imagined community'. Unlike other kinds of community, members of a national community will never personally know all other members; nor are they bound to them by ties of kinship or formal membership rituals.[21] Nations are instead 'imagined' and bound together by shared identity, common culture, historical continuity, collective action and law.[22] As such, a nation can be conceived in many different ways. A nation might be defined by the distinctive ethnicity or culture of its peoples, or by the civic engagement of all citizens in shared political institutions.[23] It is not necessary here to decide between these different imaginings but only to note that they will affect how nationality and the qualities of knowledge, membership and identity are understood and practised in particular contexts.

[16] R Cotterrell, *Law, Culture and Society: Legal Ideas in the Mirror of Social Theory* (Aldershot, Ashgate, 2006) 76.

[17] *Nottebohm Case (Liechtenstein v Guatemala) (second phase)* [1955] ICJ Rep 4, 26.

[18] E Arcioni, 'Identity at the Edge of the Constitutional Community' in F Jenkins, M Nolan and K Rubenstein (eds), *Allegiance and Identity in a Globalised World* (Cambridge, Cambridge University Press, 2014) 31, 36–37.

[19] L Jamieson, 'Theorising Identity, Nationality and Citizenship: Implications for European Citizenship Identity' (2002) 34(6) *Sociologia* 507.

[20] Cotterrell (n 16) ch 4.

[21] Anderson (n 14) 6.

[22] Miller (n 10) 22–26; Cotterrell (n 16) 165–66.

[23] Gans (n 6) 110–11.

Nationality and foreignness speak to ways of seeing the world that are shaped by a national identity informed by history and culture, and by membership in and exclusion from defined national communities. The concepts of nationality and foreignness can be filled with various kinds of significance and meaning, with both positive and negative connotations. As a result, the quality of foreignness can be put to different functions. One is the process of othering, by which the boundaries of the nation are established and maintained by defining what is foreign, that is, what the nation is not. In classical political thought, foreignness was seen as a threat to national identity and the stability of the national community.[24] The fear that diversity might undermine or corrupt the ties of membership and belonging between the peoples of a nation persists in some theoretical work and in nationalist discourses.[25] Foreignness can also be understood to serve more positive values. Honig explores some of these in her work on the function of the foreigner in stories of democratic founding, which shows how foreigners can symbolise the novelty, externality and impartiality crucial to the imagined project of nation-building and state-building.[26] In this way, foreignness and nationality are given content in the 'imaginings' – as expressed in various media, including the laws and legal systems – of particular national communities. A national practice that judges must be citizens, or alternatively that judges may be foreign, is informed by these meanings and speaks to the qualities of knowledge, membership and identity in ways that are outlined in each of the following sections of this chapter.

III. KNOWLEDGE

Nationality is assumed to carry with it a particular knowledge and way of seeing the world that is distinctive to that national community. The nationality of a judge may be important because it implies knowledge of two kinds: a technical knowledge of the national law and legal system; and a broader knowledge of the national, social and cultural context in which that law operates.

Judges require technical knowledge of the law. A judge's knowledge of law is usually measured by legal qualifications, examination and professional experience.[27] Usually, these qualifications and experience relate to the jurisdiction in which the judge sits. Even in the United Kingdom, where judges may be from Ireland or any Commonwealth country, candidates for judicial appointment must still have a minimum number of years of professional practice in the

[24] B Honig, *Democracy and the Foreigner* (Princeton, NJ, Princeton University Press, 2001) 1–3.
[25] ibid; Saunders (n 4) ch 3.
[26] Honig (n 24).
[27] On the different qualifications for judicial office in civil law and common law systems, see PH Russell, 'Judicial Recruitment, Training and Careers' in P Cane and HM Kritzer (eds), *The Oxford Handbook of Empirical Legal Research* (Oxford, Oxford University Press, 2010).

United Kingdom.[28] Foreign judges are an exception, as they are eligible for judicial appointment on the basis of qualifications and experience obtained outside the jurisdiction. This means, however, that, all other things being equal, foreign judges are less likely to have the same level of knowledge of the national law than a person who has trained and practised in that legal system.

The emphasis placed on a judge's prior and direct knowledge of national law varies across national contexts, legal systems and areas of law. National or state law is not completely closed and isolated, in origin or in application.[29] Connections across national legal systems can make foreignness a matter of degree. Two examples of such connections, which resonate in the Pacific and beyond, are the continuity of the common law tradition and the use of legal transplants. The common law is typically understood as a continuous tradition of adjudication, based on values and principles that originated in English law but which have evolved over time across different jurisdictions.[30] Common law legal systems share a method of legal reasoning to resolve disputes and develop judge-made law. They also share foundational doctrines and principles, even as the details are developed to suit local circumstances.[31] The institutions and procedures of the common law are also similar; indeed some common law states continue to share a final court of appeal in the Judicial Committee of the Privy Council. The result is a form of law that is recognisable across different national jurisdictions, facilitating not only engagement with foreign legal precedents,[32] but also the movement of judges across jurisdictional boundaries within the common law world.[33] The use of legal transplants can also connect the laws of different legal systems. Sometimes, states directly adopt codes or statutes from another state, as a transitional or permanent measure.[34] Laws enacted locally might be heavily based on an overseas precedent. Many recently enacted constitutional provisions are based on 'archetypes' drawn from other constitutions or from international human rights instruments.[35] The resulting similarities can make such laws familiar and accessible to judges trained in the laws of the 'donor' jurisdiction or fellow recipient jurisdictions.

[28] *Constitutional Reform Act 2005* (UK), s 25.

[29] HP Glenn, 'Transnational Common Laws' (2005) 29(3) *Fordham International Law Journal* 457.

[30] T Poole, 'Back to the Future? Unearthing the Theory of Common Law Constitutionalism' (2003) 23(3) *OJLS* 435.

[31] C Saunders, 'Common Law Public Law: Some Comparative Reflections' in J Bell et al (eds), *Public Law Adjudication in Common Law Systems: Process and Substance* (Oxford, Hart Publishing, 2015) 353.

[32] C Saunders, 'Judicial Engagement with Comparative Law' in T Ginsburg and R Dixon (eds), *Comparative Constitutional Law* (Northampton, Edward Elgar, 2011) 571, 575–77.

[33] Lord Cooke of Thorndon, 'The Dream of an International Common Law' in C Saunders (ed), *Courts of Final Jurisdiction: The Mason Court in Australia* (Annandale, Federation Press, 1996) 138, 142–45.

[34] eg in the Pacific, J Corrin Care, 'Discarding Relics of the Past: Patriation of Laws in the South Pacific' (2009) 39(4) *Victoria University of Wellington Law Review* 635.

[35] VC Jackson, *Constitutional Engagement in a Transnational Era* (Oxford, Oxford University Press, 2010) 40.

Despite the similarities across certain legal systems, national law may still be distinctive and specialised. Transplanted law, including the common law, can come to assume different meanings and functions as it is adapted to new contexts marked by different language, culture, institutions and history.[36] Transplanted laws interact with pre-existing laws, each influencing the other, and in some cases generating plural legal orders.[37] Despite globalisation and some convergence of laws, knowledge of the national legal system – understood broadly to include not just positive law, but also the social context, history, values and beliefs that inform those laws – remains important. For this reason, a requirement that a judge must be a citizen might function *in addition to* formal legal qualifications because it implies a broader kind of knowledge of how the law works in the particular national context.

The extent to which this kind of broader contextual knowledge is regarded as valuable or essential depends on conceptions of the role of the judge. The following discussion focuses on constitutional interpretation to illustrate how knowledge of the nation and national community can be relevant, to varying degrees, to the role of a constitutional judge. The text of a written constitution can be indeterminate. Constitutional provisions may be vague, ambiguous or inadequate to address developments unforeseen at the time the constitution was made. Such cases can present difficult questions regarding the meaning and application of constitutional provisions. Nevertheless, judges must carry out their duty to interpret and apply constitutional provisions to resolve the issues before them.[38] Accordingly, questions invariably arise about interpretive practices (that is, *how* judges reason) and their legitimacy (that is, whether and to what extent a given practice is permitted within the relevant conception of the judicial role).[39] Comparative constitutional practice and constitutional theory provide a range of possible answers. One typology, developed by Goldsworthy, organises approaches to constitutional reasoning across two spectrums.[40] The first spectrum ranges from textualism, in which the constitution comprises the

[36] A phenomenon described as 'no transportation without transformation': W Twining, 'Diffusion of Law: A Global Perspective' (2004) 49 *Journal of Legal Pluralism and Unofficial Law* 1, 24.

[37] W Menski, *Comparative Law in a Global Context: The Legal Systems of Asia and Africa*, 2nd edn (Cambridge, Cambridge University Press, 2006) 120; BZ Tamanaha, 'Understanding Legal Pluralism: Past to Present, Local to Global' (2008) 30(3) *Sydney Law Review* 375.

[38] M Cappelletti, *The Judicial Process in Comparative Perspective* (Oxford, Clarendon Press, 1989) 5; J Goldsworthy, 'Constitutional Interpretation' in M Rosenfeld and A Sajó (eds), *The Oxford Handbook of Comparative Constitutional Law* (Oxford, Oxford University Press, 2012) 689, 689; D Grimm, *Constitutionalism* (Oxford, Oxford University Press, 2016) 205.

[39] The characterisation of judicial decision making as a mechanical task with no scope for interpretation is no longer regarded as an accurate description of the judge's task, if it ever was: MH McHugh, 'The Judicial Method' (1999) 73 *Australian Law Journal* 37, 38–39; Lord Reid, 'The Judge as Lawmaker' (1972) 12 *Journal of the Society of Public Teachers of Law* 22.

[40] Goldsworthy (n 38). Other typologies relate to interpretation in particular constitutional systems and cover comparable ground: eg P Bobbitt, *Constitutional Fate: A Theory of the Constitution* (New York, Oxford University Press, 1982).

written text; through legalism, in which the constitutional text is supplemented by other legal sources; to what Goldsworthy terms 'normativism', in which the constitution is understood to encompass or express deeper abstract principles. The second spectrum ranges between originalism and non-originalism, indicating the degree to which the constitutional text is to be interpreted by reference to the intentions of the constitutional founders or to the values of contemporary society.[41] The choice between various combinations is informed by the judge's personal philosophies about the judicial role, legal and political culture, and the institutional structure of the court.[42] It might also be guided by the text of the constitution itself, which may include, for example, an express direction to interpret constitutional provisions by reference to values or principles.[43]

The importance of a judge's contextual knowledge of the nation and the national community will vary depending on the approach taken to constitutional interpretation. Textualism requires judges to interpret the constitution by reference to its words. Legalism requires judges to look to the constitutional text in the context of its purpose and history, as well as other legal sources such as precedent.[44] All else being equal, on these approaches to constitutional interpretation, contextual knowledge of the nation and national community would appear to matter less, provided that the judge can understand the language of the constitution and other legal sources sufficient to interpret their meaning. Similarly, originalism, in which constitutional interpretation is to be guided by the purposes and objectives of the constitutional drafters, requires historical knowledge of the framing of the constitution, rather than contextual knowledge of the contemporary society of the kind that national judges are assumed to gain through their own experience.

Moving towards the other ends of each spectrum, however, judges' contextual knowledge of the nation and national community assumes greater importance. One variation of non-originalism is the idea that the constitution should be capable of development and adjustment to changing societal needs and contemporary values.[45] The adaptation of law to social context through constitutional interpretation requires that judges have knowledge of the contemporary society[46] of a kind that nationals who are a part of that society are assumed to have. A related claim, made in political science literature, is that a constitutional court seeking to engage in legal change must behave strategically, for fear that a court that develops the law in a way that is out of step with the elected branches of

[41] Goldsworthy (n 38) 691–92.

[42] ibid 707–16.

[43] GJ Jacobsohn, 'Constitutional Values and Principles' in Rosenfeld and Sajó (eds) (n 38) 777, 779–80.

[44] A Stone, 'Judicial Reasoning' in C Saunders and A Stone (eds), *Oxford Handbook of the Australian Constitution* (Oxford, Oxford University Press, 2018) 472.

[45] Goldsworthy (n 38) 699.

[46] Grimm (n 38) 209.

government or the community will overstep its role and suffer backlash, or alternatively will underperform in its role and become irrelevant.[47] Strategic judicial behaviour requires that judges have knowledge of the wider political context and the interests and likely reactions of other actors. Foreign judges unfamiliar with local politics and legal culture might therefore be poorly situated strategic actors.[48]

Constitutions often encompass or express values and principles on which the constitution and the nation are built. These values and principles may be set out in the text of the constitution – for example in the preamble, directive principles or provisions on interpretation[49] – or they may be implicit in constitutional, political and social norms.[50] Jacobsohn posits a distinction between constitutional *values*, which derive from the culture, history and traditions of the particular nation, and constitutional *principles*, which give expression to the constitutional order and political morality of the state. Values then have a contextually specific, culturally determined meaning, while principles might be more transnational or cross-cultural because they draw on shared political values such as democracy, equality and justice.[51] While values and principles are often likely to overlap, the distinction is salient, because the nationality of the judge might assume greater importance when a constitution is informed by national values, and less importance where it is informed by transnational constitutional principles.

Where the constitution requires judges to give effect to specific national values, judges who interpret and apply the constitution must have a plausible claim to know those national self-understandings and values. Nationality is presumed to provide judges with the knowledge and experience necessary to undertake this kind of constitutional interpretation. Aharon Barak – the former President of the Supreme Court of Israel, who ascribes to a philosophy of constitutional interpretation as necessarily driven by the basic values of the legal system – makes this connection between interpretation and nationality explicit:

> The judge learns about basic values from the fundamental documents, such as the constitution itself. … The judge learns about basic values from statutes and precedents. Above all – he learns about them from the national experience, from the

[47] G Vanberg, 'Constitutional Courts in Comparative Perspective: A Theoretical Assessment' (2015) 18 *Annual Review of Political Science* 167, 179–81; L Epstein, J Knight and O Shvetsova, 'The Role of Constitutional Courts in the Establishment and Maintenance of Democratic Systems of Government' (2001) 35(1) *Law and Society Review* 117.

[48] A Schwartz, 'International Judges on Constitutional Courts: Cautionary Evidence from Post-Conflict Bosnia' (2019) 44 *Law and Social Inquiry* 1, 5, 19, 25.

[49] In the Pacific, for example, all nine states' constitutions include preambles. For directive principles, see *Constitution of Fiji 1997*, s 6; *Constitution of Papua New Guinea 1975*, preamble; *Constitution of Tuvalu 1986*, preamble. For interpretative provisions, see *Constitution of Fiji 2013*, s 3; *Constitution of Fiji 1997*, s 3; *Constitution of Papua New Guinea 1975*, s 8 and sch 1; *Constitution of Tuvalu 1986*, s 4.

[50] Goldsworthy (n 38) 702; Grimm (n 38) 209.

[51] Jacobsohn (n 43).

> nature of the political system as a democracy, and from his understanding of the basic conceptions of the nation.[52]

For Barak, in rare cases judges are left to decide cases by reference to their subjective beliefs, as shaped by their life experience and their own judicial philosophy. This subjectivity is, however, constrained by nationality:

> Every judge is part of his people. At times he lives in an ivory tower, but my tower is on the hills of Jerusalem, not on Mt Olympus. As a judge, I am conscious of what is taking place in my nation, I am a part of it.[53]

All else being equal, it is much more difficult for foreign judges to draw upon the fundamental values of the national community when interpreting a constitution, in part because they lack intimate knowledge and connection with the nation's history, culture and political system.[54] To take one example, British judges when sitting on the Judicial Committee of the Privy Council display more caution when interpreting a foreign constitution in an expressive manner than those same judges do when determining matters arising in their British jurisdictions.[55]

While some constitutions might be understood to express or derive from peculiarly national values, others might be understood as expressing shared common, or even universal, principles. This might be reflected in the constitutional text. For example, interpretation provisions may require constitutional rights to be interpreted and applied to promote the values of a democratic society, human dignity and equality, and might expressly permit courts to consider international law on the protection of human rights.[56] The idea that there are common constitutional principles shared across national borders has led to transnational engagement with foreign law as judges look to the decisions of foreign courts when interpreting their own constitutions, not as binding precedent but as a source of knowledge to inform their decision making. Where legal principles are understood to be shared across jurisdictions, judges' knowledge of local context might become less important. Indeed, a transnational perspective might be particularly valuable where the domestic court interprets and applies laws that have a foundation in international law, such as human rights, or where the court draws upon transnational principles such as constitutionalism or democracy.[57] Similarly, shared common law principles can provide a resource

[52] A Barak, 'The Role of the Supreme Court in a Democracy' in MT Andenæs, Lord Slynn of Hadley and D Fairgrieve (eds), *Judicial Review in International Perspective* (The Hague, Kluwer Law International, 2000) 121, 122–23.

[53] ibid 128–29.

[54] R Dworkin, 'Discussion: International Criminal Justice' in R Badinter and S Breyer (eds), *Judges in Contemporary Democracy: An International Conversation* (New York, New York University Press, 2004) 189, 252–53.

[55] T Robinson and A Bulkan, 'Constitutional Comparisons by a Supranational Court in Flux: The Privy Council and Caribbean Bills of Rights' (2017) 80 *MLR* 379, 410.

[56] Again, taking examples from the Pacific, see, eg, *Constitution of Fiji 2013*, s 7; *Constitution of Fiji 1997*, s 43; *Constitution of Papua New Guinea 1975*, s 39.

[57] Jackson (n 35) ch 3.

for interpreting and applying national laws. As Lord Haldane, a member of the Judicial Committee of the Privy Council in the early part of the twentieth century, wrote:

> The Judges try to look for the common principle underlying systems of jurisprudence of differing kinds. … We are constantly finding that, where great broad principles of justice are concerned you find – veiled, but still there, and only distinguished by technicalities – the same substance as belongs to other systems. The human mind is much the same all the world over.[58]

Where constitutional interpretation draws on constitutional and legal principles that transcend national boundaries, contextual knowledge of the national law and legal system may be less critical to the judge's task.

There are, however, two caveats to any claim that common constitutional principles might loosen the ties between judges and nationality. First, the convergence of constitutional ideas should not be overstated: differences between national constitutions persist, including differences that might be obscured by apparently similar legal language.[59] Second, shared or universal principles must be adapted to the circumstances of the nation, which requires an understanding of the national context and legal culture,[60] returning once again to the significance of contextual knowledge that is presumed to accompany nationality.

In summary, nationality is thought to provide judges with knowledge of national culture and values, which informs how they interpret the constitution and develop the law. Such knowledge does not necessarily follow from nationality – some national judges might be out of touch with the values and aspirations of the national community, while some foreign judges might gain knowledge and local insight through experience and study. As a generalisation, however, nationality is presumed to provide judges with the contextual knowledge required to understand the distinctive cultural, social and political values of the national community and how they inform the law. The relevance of knowledge of this kind to the task of adjudication varies depending on theories of constitutional interpretation and understandings of law. All else being equal, nationality assumes more importance where the constitution is understood to express (whether implicitly or explicitly) distinctive national values or customs, and less importance where constitutional interpretation is understood as primarily based on reading the text of the constitution. Knowledge of the national context in which the law operates also assumes less significance where constitutions are understood to give expression to shared transnational constitutional principles, or where constitutional provisions have been influenced by or

[58] P Mitchell, 'The Privy Council and the Difficulty of Distance' (2016) 36(1) *OJLS* 26, 48 quoting Lord Haldane, 'The Work for the Empire of the Judicial Committee of the Privy Council' (1923) 1 *CLJ* 143, 154.

[59] C Saunders, 'Towards a Global Constitutional Gene Pool' (2009) 4(3) *National Taiwan University Law Review* 1, 22.

[60] Jacobsohn (n 43) 786.

'transplanted' from other states. In such cases, not only might nationality matter less, but the comparative or transnational knowledge of foreign judges might be particularly valuable.

IV. MEMBERSHIP

Membership captures the relationships and ties of belonging between people that arise from living together in a community. This section considers how membership of the national community informs the role of judges on courts of constitutional jurisdiction. It suggests that the ties of national membership manifest in two qualities associated with judging. The first is allegiance, which captures a sense of loyalty and commitment to the nation-state. The second is the concept of responsibility, which affects how judges approach the task of constitutional adjudication and how the national community perceives judges in that role. The sense that foreign judges lack such ties can be characterised as a deficit and reason to object to their presence on courts of constitutional jurisdiction. It can also, however, be cast as a virtue, in that foreign judges who are not invested in the nation bring impartiality and objectivity to the adjudication of disputes.

Membership of a nation is formally expressed in the concept of allegiance. Allegiance was historically understood as a pledge of obedience in exchange for the sovereign's protection, but now refers to both a personal attachment and an obligation of loyalty to the nation.[61] The feelings of attachment and loyalty denoted by the idea of allegiance are sometimes understood to affect the impartiality of judges. This issue is taken seriously in international courts and tribunals. Dannenbaum argues that the rules and procedures of international courts exhibit a 'deep anxiety about the capacity of international judges to be impartial to and independent from their state of nationality'.[62] As a result, international courts might allow only one judge of each nationality on the court,[63] or permit state parties to appoint an ad hoc judge of their own nationality,[64] or require judges to recuse themselves from cases involving their state of nationality.[65] Meanwhile, parties to international commercial arbitration will

[61] Arcioni (n 18) 37.

[62] T Dannenbaum, 'Nationality and the International Judge: The Nationalist Presumption Governing the International Judiciary and Why it Must be Reversed' (2012) 45(1) *Cornell International Law Journal* 77, 112.

[63] eg *Statute of the International Court of Justice*, art 3; *Statute of the Inter-American Court of Human Rights*, art 4; *Rome Statute of the International Criminal Court*, art 35(7).

[64] eg *Statute of the International Court of Justice*, art 31(2); *Statute of the Inter-American Court of Human Rights*, art 10.

[65] eg *Protocol to the African Charter on Human and Peoples' Rights on the Establishment of an African Court on Human and Peoples' Rights*, art 22. See also M Markovic, 'International Criminal Trials and the Disqualification of Judges on the Basis of Nationality' (2014) 13 *Washington University Global Studies Law Review* 1.

often seek an arbitrator of a nationality different from that of the parties.[66] These practices are motivated by the assumption that a judge or arbitrator will, consciously or unconsciously, be influenced in favour of his or her state of nationality, in part because of his or her sense of allegiance.

In contrast to the position on international courts, judges on national courts are expected to have allegiance to the state. For example, the judicial oath often includes a commitment to uphold the laws and constitution of the state. In some legal systems, judges also swear an oath of allegiance, making both a personal promise and a public commitment of loyalty and service to the state. Judges who are citizens are thought to have an undivided allegiance to the nation.[67] In contrast, a foreign judge will have an allegiance to his or her home state, but also swear an allegiance (at least to the point contemplated in the judicial oath) to the state in which he or she serves as a foreign judge. As such, foreign judges are members of more than one national community, but they are presumed to have stronger ties of belonging and a deeper interest in and sense of obligation to their home state.

The sense of commitment to the nation and the national community suggested by the concept of allegiance also informs how judges engage in the task of constitutional adjudication. In his theoretical exploration of the relevance of nationality to the role of the judge, Kahn identifies *judicial responsibility* as the key reason why states reject staffing their courts with foreign judges.[68] For Kahn, a judge's responsibility to the state and its people is particularly significant in constitutional adjudication. Adjudication is not simply the resolution of a private dispute; it is the resolution of a dispute according to the public standards and values expressed in the law. In constitutional litigation, a private citizen assumes a public role. He or she becomes an 'agent' of the public order and presents a vision of the constitution that might, through judicial decision, become law. In this respect, judicial decisions are not simply the application of law to facts but are rather a narrative of the legal order: judges 'speak for' the whole society when they decide which vision of the constitution prevails.[69] For Kahn, only a national judge can produce this kind of public narrative, because a national judge – as a citizen and as part of the political structure – shares in the people's responsibility for the law as it is and as it may become.[70] In contrast, a foreign judge is able to make a judicial decision, but cannot take responsibility for the laws of the past or the future. To use an analogy employed by Miller in his discussion of nationality, the 'people of a nation are not in a lifeboat, randomly thrown together'. Rather they are bound by ties of custom

[66] I Lee, 'Practice and Predicament: The Nationality of the International Arbitrator (With Survey Results)' (2008) 31 *Fordham International Law Journal* 603.

[67] D Terris, C Romano and L Swigart, *The International Judge: An Introduction to the Men and Women Who Decide the World's Cases* (Waltham, MA, Brandeis University Press, 2007) 151.

[68] Kahn (n 3).

[69] ibid 77.

[70] ibid 82.

and practice that stem from historic identity, in ways that the people in a life boat, who share a common immediate purpose but not a common past, are not.[71]

The concept of responsibility presented by Kahn focuses on the task of adjudication. A similar sense of responsibility is also relevant to how judges understand their role in the constitutional order. Philip Bird, a citizen of the United States, was appointed Chief Justice of the Marshall Islands in the late 1980s. His appointment came after several judges were removed or had resigned in protest at interference by the political branches in the judiciary. The Marshall Islands Parliament enacted a law that effectively ordered the High Court to dismiss a long-running legal dispute over a chiefly title. When Chief Justice Bird refused to uphold that legislation, the Parliament passed a resolution to dismiss him for his failure to faithfully discharge the duties of his office. The Chief Justice resigned, stating that he did so in order to 'alleviate the growing constitutional crisis', but added 'were this my country I would have seen the matter through to the end'.[72] Here, the Chief Justice articulates a deeper commitment to core constitutional principles in his own state, which would incline him to act differently if the same situation arose there. As a foreign judge, however, he did not feel it was his place to play a central role in the constitutional crisis of a foreign country.

The responsibilities of membership that are presumed to motivate citizen judges can serve to alleviate some of the concerns about the legitimacy of constitutional review. The democratic objection to constitutional review, broadly put, is that courts, which are not democratically accountable, should not have the final say on the constitutionality of legislative and executive action.[73] Scholars have sought to counter the democratic objection in a variety of ways. One line of defence claims that judges should have a share in the determination of constitutional questions and review the exercise of power by the political branches of government because they too are 'of the people'. For example, Sir John Muria, the first Solomon Islander to serve his country as a Judge and Chief Justice, dismisses the objection to constitutional review

> for one basic reason, that is, the Courts and those who preside over them belong to the particular society or community; they understand the aspirations of the country and its people; they are therefore in the best position to envision the path that the country needs to travel to fulfil that vision.[74]

[71] Miller (n 10) 41–42.

[72] JM Van Dyke, 'The Pacific Judicial Conference: Strengthening the Independent Judiciary and the Rule of Law in the Pacific' (2011) 22(1–2) *Western Legal History* 127, 153–55.

[73] J Waldron, *Law and Disagreement* (Oxford, Clarendon Press, 1999) 213; R Bellamy, *Political Constitutionalism: A Republican Defence of the Constitutionality of Democracy* (Cambridge, Cambridge University Press, 2007) ch 1.

[74] J Muria, 'The Role of the Courts and Legal Profession in Constitutional and Political Disputes in the Pacific Islands Nations' (2002) 6 *Journal of South Pacific Law*, available at www.informit.org/doi/abs/10.3316/agispt.20031163. See also C Palley, 'Rethinking the Judicial Role: The Judiciary and Good Government' (1969) 1 *Zambia Law Journal* 1, 31–32.

In other words, judges, by virtue of their knowledge and their membership, have a legitimate role in the determination of constitutional issues.

In contrast, it might be easier for governments and others to object to the legitimacy of judicial review when it is conducted by foreign judges.[75] There are occasions when governments have rejected the decisions of foreign judges as corrupt, ill-informed or serving outside interests, resulting in the resignation of those judges or their forcible removal.[76] Such cases illustrate the risk that government actors will refuse to engage with the 'vision' of the constitution offered in a foreign judge's decision and instead make the foreign judge a scapegoat, expelling him or her from the jurisdiction along with the rejected constitutional vision.[77] The fact that a judge is a foreign judge makes the physical act of expulsion easier: as a non-citizen, a foreign judge requires the government's permission to enter and stay in the country, and is vulnerable to removal pursuant to a change in his or her immigration status.[78] Of course, governments also criticise national judges who make unfavourable decisions. There is, however, a stronger imperative for institutional dialogue about the meaning of the constitution and the visions and aspirations of the country when the key actors are all themselves of the people.[79]

The ties of nationality that arise from membership facilitate responsibility because judges, as citizens, are invested in their community, their government and their constitution. Citizen judges live in the community and are themselves subject to the laws that they have a hand in shaping. Judges, as much as members of the other branches of government and the public, are affected by the constitutional decisions they make.[80] While foreign judges might act in the best interests of the community they serve, they are not invested in the fate of the community and the nation in the same way that national judges are.[81] The ties of membership mean that citizen judges cannot simply leave; they are a part of the national community and responsible to it for their decisions.

The fact that a foreign judge is not invested in the community and the constitutional order may, however, be cast as a virtue. A common justification for the use of foreign judges is that they are not enmeshed in the political and social

[75] RE Howard, 'Legitimacy and Class Rule in Commonwealth Africa: Constitutionalism and the Rule of Law' (1985) 7(2) *Third World Quarterly* 323, 331.

[76] In the Pacific, ch 3, section V; in Timor Leste, D Cohen and L-A Lipscomb, 'Justice at the Crossroads in Timor-Leste', *Report No 22* (Institute for Policy Analysis of Conflict, 7 September 2015); in Eswatini, M Langwenya, *Swaziland Justice Sector and the Rule of Law: A Review by AfriMAP and the Open Society Initiative for Southern Africa* (Johannesburg, Open Society Initiative, 2013) 98, 101.

[77] On the foreigner as scapegoat, see Honig (n 24) 32–34.

[78] See ch 3, section V.

[79] On dialogue as a common endeavour between equals (and its limits), see A Kavanagh, 'The Lure and the Limits of Dialogue' (2016) 66(1) *University of Toronto Law Journal* 83, 86–87, 120.

[80] Jackson (n 35) 174–75; D Pannick, *Judges* (Oxford, Oxford University Press, 1987) 43, 53–54.

[81] On nation-states as 'communities of fate', see Kymlicka (n 9) 115.

intrigues of the nation and so bring impartiality and objectivity.[82] Honig identifies a range of constitutional values that, symbolically, can be served by foreign entities, including foreign judges.[83] Standing outside the community and its politics, the foreign judge can adjudicate according to the constitution alone, independent and uninfluenced by extraneous considerations. As an entity external to 'the people', the foreign judge can impose the law without disturbing the sense that all members of the people are equal before the law.[84] Finally, a foreign judge does not threaten the other branches of government or the wider constitutional order, because he or she arrives when called upon to determine a dispute and leaves having performed his or her task, intervening in democratic politics without self-interest.[85]

In summary, membership of the national community is relevant to the way in which judges understand and perform their role and, in turn, how the community perceives judges and courts. The qualities of membership speak to the personal relationships and commitments that judges make to the nation-state and its laws, formally through allegiance and in practice through judicial responsibility. In this sense, nationality can function as an indicator for some of the desirable personal qualities or virtues of a judge.[86]

V. IDENTITY

Nationality as an aspect of identity focuses attention on the value of appearances. This function of identity is explored in the literature on 'reflective judiciaries', which refers to the sense in which the composition of the judiciary ought to reflect the community it serves, and in particular gender, ethnic and other kinds of identities within the community. It is claimed that only a judiciary that reflects the diversity of identity characteristics will have the confidence of all communities within the state and will express democratic values of inclusiveness and participation.[87] In this way, the personal identity of each individual judge contributes to the identity of the judiciary as an institution. This section

[82] In the Pacific, see ch 6, section III. This idea also informs the idea of 'neutral' foreign judges on courts in post-conflict states: J Marko, 'Foreign Judges: A European Perspective' in Y Ghai and SNM Young (eds), *Hong Kong's Court of Final Appeal* (Cambridge, Cambridge University Press, 2013) 637, 640.

[83] Honig (n 24) ch 2.

[84] ibid 21.

[85] ibid 23.

[86] RA MacDonald, 'Exercising Judgement' in *Which Judge for Which Society? Proceedings of the 2008 Judges' Conference* (Québec City, 2008) 51.

[87] L Barmes and K Malleson, 'Lifting the Judicial Identity Blackout' (2018) 38(2) *OJLS* 357, 376; E Rackley, *Women, Judging and the Judiciary: From Difference to Diversity* (Abingdon, Routledge, 2013) 23–24; PH Russell and K Malleson, 'Conclusion' in PH Russell and K Malleson (eds), *Appointing Judges in an Age of Judicial Power: Critical Perspectives from around the World* (Toronto, University of Toronto Press, 2006) 434.

explores how the national identity of judges expresses values associated with sovereignty. In doing so, it suggests that the nationality of the judge performs a representative or symbolic function.

The preference for citizen judges and the rejection of non-citizen judges is often framed as a matter of sovereignty. In the United States, for example, the citation of foreign judgments was criticised as an illegitimate practice that 'dramatically undermines sovereignty',[88] and it is not difficult to imagine that foreign judges would be received in the same vein. Writing in Europe, Marko states that the doctrine of state sovereignty makes it 'almost inconceivable that a foreign citizen should serve on the bench of a national supreme court or separate constitutional court of another country with the power to review legislation'.[89] Lord Cooke of Thorndon argued in favour of replacing the Privy Council with a local New Zealand court of final appeal on the ground that 'it is inconsistent with nationhood to submit our legal issues to the adjudication of those, whoever they may be, who happen at any one time and in any particular case to comprise a majority of Judges of another country'.[90]

'Sovereignty' has a range of different meanings.[91] Two are relevant to the nationality of judges on constitutional courts. The first is an international meaning of sovereignty. In international law, sovereign states are equal, have the power to enter international relations and are protected against intervention by other states in their domestic affairs. However, where foreign judges are appointed to a domestic court by a domestic state authority according to the laws of the state, the state's sovereignty is not infringed. States can consent to relinquish some aspects of their sovereignty, for example to submit to the jurisdiction of an international court. The use of foreign judges would infringe state sovereignty in the international sense only if imposed on the state from outside.

The second is a domestic meaning of sovereignty. Here, sovereignty refers to the ultimate political authority and source of law within the state. In western nation-states, the sovereign has been conceived in many institutional forms: the monarch, the nation, the people.[92] In modern constitutional democracies the sovereign is conceived as the people ruling through a body of national law. The functions of courts – which include resolving disputes according to the laws made by the sovereign, communicating that law and at times developing the law – associate judging with sovereignty.[93] In interpreting, applying and enforcing the laws made by the sovereign, the court is understood to act on behalf

[88] AL Parrish, 'Storm in a Teacup: The US Supreme Court's Use of Foreign Law' [2007] *University of Illinois Law Review* 637, 660.
[89] Marko (n 82) 637.
[90] Lord Cooke of Thorndon, 'Final Appeal Courts: Some Comparisons', *Occasional Paper No 7* (New Zealand Centre for Public Law, 2001) 18.
[91] M Troper, 'Sovereignty' in Rosenfeld and Sajó (eds) (n 38) 1304.
[92] ibid 354; MM Shapiro, *Courts: A Comparative and Political Analysis* (Chicago, IL, University of Chicago Press, 1981) 100.
[93] Shapiro (n 92) 26, 34; D Smilov, 'The Judiciary: The Least Dangerous Branch?' in Rosenfeld and Sajó (eds) (n 38) 859, 869.

of the sovereign. In some European states, this is made explicit when the court expressly delivers every judgment 'in the name of the people'.[94]

The use of foreign judges can be reconciled with domestic sovereignty when the sovereign through its own law authorises foreign judges to determine legal disputes. However, a preference for national judges can serve as a powerful expression of sovereignty. Democratic constitutions seek to promote a sense that the people create and own the laws that bind them. A judiciary composed only of citizen judges expresses the sovereignty of the people, because a court comprised of members of the people *is* a court of the people.[95] In contrast, judges from outside the nation might express a sense that the law is imposed from outside, an experience particularly pertinent in post-colonial states in which the constitution reflects (and in some cases is a product of) an externally imposed legal system.[96] However, a diversity of nationalities on the bench might, in other contexts, express a state's openness to international influence and the value placed on comparative legal experience, institutionally and in the court's jurisprudence.[97]

In this way, the nationality of the judges on a state's courts of constitutional jurisdiction might express different values in different contexts. Although these values might differ, the sense in which those values are expressed through the identity of the judge and the composition of the court is the same. The identity of judges as national or foreign serves a representative or symbolic function, which informs and is informed by how people perceive the court and its role in the wider community.

VI. CONCLUSION

Citizenship is not an essential prerequisite for the judges of constitutional courts. The global norm, however, is that judges will be citizens of the state on whose courts they serve. This chapter set out a range of reasons for the preference for national judges on courts of constitutional jurisdiction. National judges might be thought to bring the kind of knowledge of national laws and the context in which they operate that is necessary to the task of constitutional adjudication and interpretation. National judges are bound by ties of membership to the nation and its people, which are thought to affect how they decide cases and behave in judicial office. Finally, national judges can serve as a visible expression of sovereignty.

[94] A von Bogdandy and I Venzke, *In Whose Name? A Public Law Theory of International Adjudication* (Oxford, Oxford University Press, 2014) 20.

[95] Kahn (n 3) 85.

[96] Honig (n 24) 29; SE Merry, *Colonizing Hawai'i: The Cultural Power of Law* (Princeton, NJ, Princeton University Press, 2000) 47, 89.

[97] J Resnik, 'Law as Affiliation: Foreign Law, Democratic Federalism, and the Sovereigntism of the Nation-State' (2008) 6 *International Journal of Constitutional Law* 33.

Different legal systems emphasise different values associated with judging, which might make these qualities associated with nationality less or more important in different contexts. A theory of constitutional interpretation that focuses on the meaning of the text and other legal sources, rather than underlying values or principles, might make the knowledge of community values deemed to accompany nationality less important. The responsibilities of judicial office traced by Kahn might be distinctive to the experience of the United States and not directly transferrable to other legal and political traditions. In contemporary circumstances of globalisation, some legal systems might more openly embrace transnational constitutional principles and so be more receptive to foreign law and foreign judges. In short, the significance of nationality to judging depends on how understandings of nationality, law, adjudication and the role of the court align in a particular context.

Although the importance of a judge's nationality might vary across different contexts, the focus on the significance of nationality to the role of the constitutional judge highlights the importance of *personal* qualities to judging and judicial office. Knowledge of the law and the wider context in which it operates, the sense of allegiance and responsibility that derive from membership, and the expressiveness of identity are all relevant to the role of the judge but are not explicitly captured in the formal qualifications for judicial office or guaranteed through institutional means. Nationality is no sure guarantee of these qualities either. Rather, paying attention to the nationality of the judge highlights these aspects of judicial office that are often assumed rather than expressly stated, and as a result under-theorised.

The purpose of this chapter has been to identify the points of connection between nationality and judging in order to develop a framework for assessing the use of foreign judges in the particular context of the Pacific. It has shown how national knowledge, national membership and national identity might, to varying degrees and in different ways, be significant to three aspects of judging, namely, constitutional adjudication, judicial independence, and the connection of judges and judiciaries to the wider constitutional system and society. These three aspects of judging, and how, in the Pacific, they might be affected by the use of foreign judges, are the focus of the following three chapters. Chapter 5 considers the kinds of knowledge that foreign judges bring to the Pacific and the influence that this might have on the constitutional jurisprudence and the role of judges in the region. Chapter 6 assesses a prevalent claim made about foreign judges arising from their non-membership of the state: that foreign judges, by virtue of their distance from the community, bring a degree of impartiality to Pacific courts that they otherwise lack. Finally, chapter 7 considers issues relating to the allegiance and responsibility of foreign judges and the 'reflectiveness' of courts in the Pacific, using the lens of representation as a means to examine the connections between foreign judges and the state and its people.

5

Constitutional Adjudication

I. INTRODUCTION

CHAPTER 4 SET out a range of ways in which nationality is relevant to the role and function of judges on courts of constitutional jurisdiction. One quality associated with nationality is knowledge, both of the law and the national context in which it operates. Foreign judges bring a different degree of knowledge to bear on constitutional adjudication. Foreign judges have a knowledge *reach*, in that their knowledge extends beyond local circumstances to encompass direct knowledge and experience of their home jurisdiction. They also face a knowledge *gap*, in that foreign judges generally will not have the same depth of knowledge about the national legal, social and political context as local judges.

In chapter 4 I suggested that the degree to which the kinds of knowledge associated with nationality might be important depends on the distinctiveness of the national law and legal system and the approach that judges take to constitutional interpretation. This chapter examines the connection between the dimensions of knowledge that foreign judges bring to Pacific courts and the approach that those courts take to constitutional adjudication. It suggests that prevalent features of constitutional adjudication across the Pacific states are at least partly explicable by reference to the kinds of knowledge brought by foreign judges.

From a reading of over 80 constitutional cases from the nine Pacific states, I identify three general features of constitutional adjudication across the region: the influence of the common law; the limited integration of custom and constitutional law; and a predominantly textualist approach to constitutional interpretation. There are of course differences in the approaches taken by courts in different states and by individual judges. These three features, however, recur across the nine states, indicating that they are predominant characteristics of Pacific constitutional adjudication. Drawing on an analysis of these cases as well as curial and extra-curial statements by judges and interviews with foreign judges serving in the Pacific,[1] this chapter shows how each of these features has some degree of fit with the kinds of knowledge that foreign judges bring to the task of constitutional adjudication. Section II explains in greater detail the

[1] The methodology for the interviews is set out in ch 2, section II.

two dimensions of knowledge foreign judges bring, namely a knowledge reach and a knowledge gap. Section III considers the transnational reach of foreign judges' knowledge, which in the Pacific is most notable in the continued influence of common law concepts in constitutional interpretation, reflecting the shared common law foundations and consequent similarities between Pacific states and the jurisdictions from which foreign judges are recruited. Section IV turns to explore the implications arising from the limits of foreign judges' knowledge of the national law and the context in which it operates. It deals first with the knowledge gap in relation to the customary elements of Pacific legal systems, examining the claim that the use of foreign judges is one reason for the limited integration of custom and constitutional law. It then considers a second knowledge gap, in relation to the community values and cultural context of each Pacific state. This section posits that this knowledge gap is one reason why foreign judges might prefer to adopt a textualist approach to constitutional interpretation, rather than approaches that draw on national values and principles that might be thought, and are sometimes expressed, to underlie and inform the constitutions of Pacific states. Finally, section V considers ways in which local judges serve to bridge the real or perceived distance between the law as it is interpreted and applied by foreign judges and the national community.

This chapter does not make definitive causal claims that foreign judges *always* approach constitutional adjudication in a particular way, or that the contours of constitutional adjudication in the Pacific region are *solely* attributable to foreign judges. Claims of this kind face a range of methodological challenges. Different judges and different courts employ a variety of approaches to constitutional reasoning. These approaches are influenced by a wide range of factors, including directives in the constitutional text; conceptualisations of the separation of powers and rule of law; the social and political context in which constitutional questions arise; and the attributes of individual judges, such as their professional qualifications, social and intellectual backgrounds, and legal education.[2] The diversity of approaches and influences means that an attempt to demonstrate that foreign judges adopt a particular approach *because they are foreign* would be difficult.[3] This chapter instead describes a degree of fit, by

[2] J Goldsworthy, 'Constitutional Interpretation' in M Rosenfeld and A Sajó (eds), *The Oxford Handbook of Comparative Constitutional Law* (Oxford, Oxford University Press, 2012) 689, 706–17.

[3] One possibility would be to compare the approach of the same judges in their home country with their approach in a foreign jurisdiction: eg T Robinson and A Bulkan, 'Constitutional Comparisons by a Supranational Court in Flux: The Privy Council and Caribbean Bills of Rights' (2017) 80 *MLR* 379. However, it is difficult to control for all explanatory factors, such as the factual and legal contexts giving rise to the constitutional issue and differences in constitutional texts. A second possibility would be to compare the approaches of local and foreign judges in the same matter. Again, however, other dimensions of adjudication are likely to contribute. Citizen judges on national courts often disagree on questions of method, and it is rarely possible to attribute such differences to a single causal factor.

which I mean that prevalent features of constitutional adjudication are understandable in light of the kinds of knowledge that foreign judges bring to the task of adjudication. The analysis identifies the potential ways in which the use of foreign judges might, at least in part, have a bearing on interpretative method, in turn affecting judicial decisions in particular cases and the development of law in the Pacific.

II. TWO DIMENSIONS OF KNOWLEDGE

Judges are expected to have technical knowledge of the law, as well as a broader knowledge of the social and political context in which the law operates. However, all judges – foreign and local – will have gaps in their knowledge. The range and complexity of the issues that come before any court mean that judges are called upon to determine issues outside their personal knowledge and experience. Sir David Baragwanath, a judge of the New Zealand Court of Appeal who also served as a foreign judge in Samoa, reflected on the challenges of adjudication at home and abroad:

> It is a real problem, of which my first serious experience was as counsel before the Waitangi Tribunal in the Muriwhenua fishing case. When the enormity of the case dawned upon me – deprivation of the five tribes' access to fishing rights, from being the wealthiest tribes in New Zealand to the poorest – I lost a stone in a week. It was my task to get inside their minds and look out through their eyes in order to equip myself to represent them. I was looking across a cultural and racial divide at what my people had done to theirs. I have had a similar challenge presiding in the Court of Appeal of Samoa – parachuting into others' society, with responsibility for interpreting their Constitution and administering justice according to their culture and their values. It is burdensome and impossible to achieve completely. But one's task is to try.[4]

In this way, foreign judges, as well as local judges in a diverse society, must confront the limits of their knowledge of the law and the community. However, even if they lack specific knowledge of the issue, local judges are likely to have a greater degree of knowledge about the legal, social and political context of the place in which they sit as judges, acquired by virtue of their experience as members of the national community. In contrast, foreign judges, who lack this experience, are not, generally speaking, able to claim the same depth of knowledge of the local context.[5] There are of course exceptions. In particular, foreign judges who have lived and worked in the Pacific state for some time might claim a high degree of local knowledge. Other foreign judges admit to having little

[4] D Baragwanath, 'Judging: A Butterfly View' (2010) 16 *Canterbury Law Review* 243, 246.

[5] M Pulea, 'Pacific Courts and Personnel' in G Powles and M Pulea (eds), *Pacific Courts and Legal Systems* (Suva and Clayton, University of the South Pacific and Monash University, 1988) 37, 39; G Hassall and C Saunders, *Asia-Pacific Constitutional Systems* (Cambridge, Cambridge University Press, 2002) 187.

to no prior knowledge of the country in which they serve as judges.[6] Speaking generally, foreign judges face a *knowledge gap* in relation to the laws of the Pacific state and the social and political context in which those laws operate.

Foreign judges do, however, have knowledge that reaches beyond local legal circumstances, based on their direct knowledge and experience of their home jurisdiction and, potentially, other national and international jurisdictions.[7] They are therefore in a position to bring comparative knowledge to bear on adjudication.[8] This *knowledge reach* raises issues familiar in comparative constitutional law about the transfer of constitutional concepts and doctrines from one context to another.[9]

Judges, whether sitting on courts of constitutional jurisdiction at home or abroad, face a weighty task. The challenges are magnified when judges rule 'in and sometimes on' the constitutions of another state.[10] In the early years of Papua New Guinea's independence, Sir William Prentice, an Australian who at that time was Deputy Chief Justice of the Supreme Court of Papua New Guinea, reflected on the responsibilities placed upon foreign judges:

> The task of commencing the interpretation of the striking document that now forms the Constitution of the Independent State of Papua New Guinea and purports to express in noble sentiments the ambitions devised and entertained by the indigenous people for their own future government and well-being, comes now somewhat invidiously to be performed by the Supreme Court comprised still, as it was initially, by expatriate judges. One can only shoulder the responsibility with all due humility, conscious that the Constitution makers deliberately thrust it upon this Court exclusively, knowing … that its members would for some time be expatriates.[11]

The 'somewhat invidious' nature of the task of constitutional adjudication arises from features of written constitutions. Constitutions structure and regulate the exercise of public power by distributing responsibilities between institutions of government and regulating the relationship between government and the people. Constitutions might also have an expressive function, reflecting national identity, values and commitments. Constitutions are superior to legislation, such that a court exercising powers of constitutional review can invalidate legislation that is inconsistent with the constitution. Procedures for making formal amendments

[6] Interview F8.

[7] As noted in ch 2, section III, 34 of the 225 foreign judges serving during the period 2000 to 2019 sat in more than one Pacific state. Some foreign judges have also served as judges on domestic, regional or international courts outside the Pacific region.

[8] R Dixon and V Jackson, 'Hybrid Constitutional Courts: Foreign Judges on National Constitutional Courts' [2019] *Columbia Journal of Transnational Law* 283, 311–13.

[9] W Twining, 'Diffusion of Law: A Global Perspective' (2004) 49 *Journal of Legal Pluralism and Unofficial Law* 1; V Perju, 'Constitutional Transplants, Borrowing, and Migrations' in Rosenfeld and Sajó (eds) (n 2) 1304.

[10] N Baird, 'Judges as Cultural Outsiders: Exploring the Expatriate Model of Judging in the Pacific' (2013) 19 *Canterbury Law Review* 80, 93.

[11] *Constitutional Reference No 1 of 1977 Re Rights of Person Arrested or Detained* [1977] PGSC 15.

to a constitution are often more onerous than amendments to ordinary legislation, which may mean that the court, in effect, has the last word on the meaning of a constitutional provision. Judicial decisions have a significant influence on the law, particularly in legal systems where the doctrine of precedent means that earlier judicial opinions are influential into the future. Constitutions are written in general, abstract language, and require interpretation to clarify vague provisions, resolve ambiguities and, at times, develop the law to cover developments unforeseen at the time the constitution was made. Constitutional interpretation can therefore require judges to act creatively to determine the meaning of the constitution. Views differ about what does – and what should – guide this element of judicial creativity.[12]

These features of constitutional adjudication mean that the work of judges can shade into judicial law making. This has led to concerns about the democratic legitimacy of constitutional review in states with courts composed entirely of citizen judges,[13] concerns that are amplified when the judges are not only unelected but foreign.[14] Many foreign judges are aware of the complexities of their role as constitutional adjudicators in Pacific states. The analysis in this chapter explores the ways in which these complexities play out as foreign judges undertake the challenging task of adjudicating constitutional disputes outside of their home jurisdiction.

III. TRANSNATIONAL KNOWLEDGE REACH

Judges require knowledge of the laws they are to apply to determine legal disputes. In most countries, judges must have legal qualifications and professional experience in the jurisdiction in which they are appointed, which effectively serves as a measure of knowledge of the local law. In contrast, Pacific states recognise legal qualifications and experience obtained outside the jurisdiction.[15] As discussed in chapter 4, however, similarities across legal systems can make foreignness a matter of degree, and it is notable that all foreign judges serving on Pacific courts are recruited from other common law jurisdictions. Transnational sources of law, such as the common law and international law, can provide foreign judges with familiar doctrines and principles to apply when adjudicating constitutional matters in Pacific states. The knowledge reach of foreign judges into these areas of law can be demonstrated by the way in which foreign judges cite foreign law

[12] Goldsworthy (n 2); A Jakab, A Dyevre and G Itzcovich, *Comparative Constitutional Reasoning* (Cambridge, Cambridge University Press, 2017) 17.

[13] J Waldron, *Law and Disagreement* (Oxford, Clarendon Press, 1999) 213; R Bellamy, *Political Constitutionalism: A Republican Defence of the Constitutionality of Democracy* (Cambridge, Cambridge University Press, 2007) ch 1.

[14] For similar concerns in relation to the citation of foreign judgments, see RP Alford, 'In Search of a Theory for Constitutional Comparativism' (2005) 52(3) *UCLA Law Review* 639, 709–10.

[15] The relevant provisions are detailed in ch 3, section II.C.

and import understandings from their own legal systems when interpreting the provisions of Pacific constitutions.

A. Shared Sources of Law

The idea of a transnational common law provides one way in which foreign judges can claim knowledge of the laws and legal systems of the Pacific. In interviews, several judges cited the shared common law as a factor that enabled them to adjudicate in the Pacific.[16] Pacific constitutions recognise and continue the common law as source of law.[17] Local lawyers and judges are educated in the common law tradition.[18] The common law, and other points of similarity such as Westminster-style parliamentary systems, provides judges from common law jurisdictions with familiar concepts and points of reference to assist them in constitutional adjudication in the Pacific.

The common law was transplanted from England to polities across the globe as part of the process of colonisation. The imperial history of the common law shows how law is mobile across different peoples and, later, across national borders. The Judicial Committee of the Privy Council, as the court of final appeal for British colonies and later some independent states, served to homogenise, to a degree, the common law standards that were applied across empire.[19] A colonial bureaucracy was created to administer the laws in each colony, including judges who moved across the colonies to take up judicial appointments.[20] After independence, the national courts of former colonies began to develop distinctive national systems of common law, in some cases departing significantly from the English common law that was originally applied. Despite some divergence, the common law remains a shared foundation that shapes the ways in which common law jurisdictions approach constitutional adjudication.[21] The understanding of the common law as a transnational legal tradition means that both legal expertise and legal personnel are readily transferable between jurisdictions.

[16] Interviews F4, F5, F8, F10, F12, F23.

[17] G Powles, 'The Common Law as a Source of Law in the South Pacific: Experiences in Western Polynesia' (1988) 10 *University of Hawaii Law Review* 105, 107–12.

[18] J Corrin Care, 'Finding the Right Balance in Plural Systems: Training Lawyers in the South Pacific' (2006) 4(2) *Journal of Commonwealth Law and Legal Education* 171.

[19] R De, '"A Peripatetic World Court" Cosmopolitan Courts, Nationalist Judges and the Indian Appeal to the Privy Council' (2014) 32 *Law and History Review* 821, 824; B Ibhawoh, *Imperial Justice: Africans in Empire's Court* (Oxford, Oxford University Press, 2014) esp ch 1.

[20] ER Feingold, *Colonial Justice and Decolonization in the High Court of Tanzania, 1920–1971* (Cham, Palgrave Macmillan, 2018) ch 2; C Jeffries, *The Colonial Empire and Its Civil Service* (Cambridge, The University Press, 1938) ch XI.

[21] C Saunders, 'Common Law Public Law: Some Comparative Reflections' in J Bell et al (eds), *Public Law Adjudication in Common Law Systems: Process and Substance* (Oxford, Hart Publishing, 2015) 353.

Judges on Pacific courts frequently draw on the common law in the course of constitutional interpretation. Words in Pacific constitutions are often interpreted to correspond to their common law meaning. For example, Justice Pratt, when determining the meaning of the words 'unlimited original jurisdiction' in the Constitution of Solomon Islands, noted that while courts should not slavishly follow concepts of English law, there was no reason to think that the constitutional drafters intended to give the phrase a meaning other than that familiar to common law lawyers.[22] The common law has been used to import particular understandings of concepts such as prerogative power,[23] parliamentary privilege,[24] elections[25] and due process,[26] although recourse to common law definitions is sometimes tempered by making it subject to the written constitution.[27] An example of a different kind arises in the decision of Chief Justice Webster in *Taione v Tonga*, in which the Supreme Court of Tonga considered the validity of amendments to the constitutional provision protecting freedom of speech.[28] The original provision provided that 'no law shall ever be enacted' to restrict freedom of speech, but also provided that this clause should not be held to outweigh the law of slander or laws for the protection of the King and Royal Family.[29] Amendments in 2003 permitted the enactment of laws considered necessary for national security, public order, morality, cultural traditions, the privileges of the legislative assembly, contempt and to regulate the media. Chief Justice Webster held that some elements of the newly amended provision were unconstitutional because they were inconsistent with the guarantee of freedom of speech. In order to interpret the scope of the freedom of speech, Chief Justice Webster looked to the English common law and the principles in the European Convention on Human Rights, which he considered to be substantively the same. The preference for using common law to give content to constitutional rights and freedoms was justified by reference to the context in which Tonga's Constitution was made. Chief Justice Webster concluded that

[22] *Kenilorea v Attorney-General* [1984] SBCA 3, taking cues from the decision of Lord Diplock in *Hinds v The Queen* [1977] AC 195, 211–12.

[23] eg *Lali Media Group Ltd v Lavaka Ata* [2003] TOSC 27; *Qarase v Bainimarama* [2008] FJHC 241, [132]; *Qarase v Bainimarama* [2009] FJCA 67, [78]–[79].

[24] *Fotofili v Siale* [1987] TOPC 2; *Harris v Adeang* [1998] NRSC 1; *Keke v Scotty* [2014] NRSC 7; *State v Social Democratic Liberal Party, Ex parte Tikoca* [2017] FJHC 654. For decisions that take the view that the written constitution modifies or displaces common law rules on the privileges of parliament, see *Huniehu v Attorney-General* [1997] SBCA 9; *Constitutional Reference No 1 of 2008* [2009] 1 LRC 453; *Attorney-General v Jimmy* [1996] VUCA 1; *Natapei v Tari (No 2)* [2001] VUSC 38.

[25] *Tatireta v Tong* [2003] KIHC 1.

[26] *Qalo v Qaloboe* [2004] SBCA 5. On the continuing influence of common law rights in Pacific jurisdictions, see S Farran, *Human Rights in the South Pacific: Challenges and Changes* (London, Routledge-Cavendish, 2009) 77–83.

[27] Compare, for example, the reasons for decision of Kidu CJ and Kapi J with those of Greville Smith J on the issue of standing in *Re Somare* [1981] PGSC 23. See also *Huniehu v Attorney-General* [1997] SBCA 9.

[28] *Taione v Tonga* [2004] TOSC 47.

[29] *Constitution of Tonga 1875*, s 7.

'it is undisputed that when the Constitution was adopted in 1875 it was done to reassure the Western powers and prevent them colonising Tonga. In which it succeeded. I therefore consider that the [constitutional] freedoms … have to be understood in a western sense and not in the Tongan sense.'[30] The result was that the newly inserted exceptions that were consistent with common law understandings of freedom of speech (namely laws to protect national security, public order, morality, privileges of parliament and contempt of court) were upheld, while those deemed inconsistent with the English common law (namely laws to uphold cultural traditions and regulate the media) were not. The case demonstrates how reliance on a shared common law can work to displace efforts to develop a constitutional jurisprudence grounded in local circumstances.

A second shared system of law and values might be found in human rights that are protected in both international law and the domestic constitutions of all Pacific states.[31] Although some constitutions expressly permit courts to refer to international human rights law when interpreting constitutional rights provisions,[32] Pacific courts tend to look instead to the common law.[33] Chief Justice Webster's decision in *Taione v Tonga* referred to the European Convention on Human Rights on the basis that it reflected standards of the common law.[34] In *Fiji v Prasad*, the Fiji Court of Appeal had to determine the legality of actions by the military to abrogate the Constitution and assume executive power following the civilian coup in 2000, during which Members of Parliament were held hostage.[35] The Court of Appeal, composed of judges from Australia, New Zealand, Papua New Guinea and the United Kingdom, held that while the abrogation of the Constitution was justified in the immediate hostage situation, it could not continue after that crisis was resolved. The Court also considered whether, despite the illegality of the military's actions, it had in effect created a new legal order. In doing so, the Court developed a test for the 'efficacy' of a new legal order as part of the common law of Fiji. The Court rejected submissions from foreign counsel to add a criterion to the test that would require the new regime to acknowledge international human rights, stating that the Constitution, which was 'made in Fiji for Fiji by the Parliament and people of Fiji', already contained many rights. The Court instead drew upon decisions of the courts of other common law jurisdictions, although with the caveat that 'in formulating our understanding of the common law of Fiji … we are conscious

[30] *Taione v Tonga* [2004] TOSC 47.

[31] Farran (n 26) ch 2.

[32] *Constitution of Fiji 1997*, s 43(2); *Constitution of Fiji 2013*, s 7(1)(b); *Constitution of Papua New Guinea 1975*, s 39(3)(b)–(e); *Constitution of Tuvalu 1986*, s 15(5)(c).

[33] For rare examples of constitutional interpretation – from both foreign and local judges – that proceed from the basis of universal human rights principles, see *Naba v Fiji* [2001] FJHC 127, Prakash J; *Ali v State* [2001] FJHC 169, Prakesh J; *State v Pickering* [2001] FJHC 51, Shameem J; *Singh v Prasad* [2002] FJSC 2, Elias J; *McCoskar v State* [2005] FJHC 500, Winter J; *Teonea v Pule o Kaupule of Nanumaga* [2009] TVCA 2, Paterson JA.

[34] *Taione v Tonga* [2004] TOSC 47.

[35] *Fiji v Prasad* [2001] FJCA 2.

that we are sitting as Judges of a Fiji Court, [and] consequently, statements by judges which may have been appropriate for other countries … need not be adopted here.'[36] There are several reasons why foreign judges might tend to overlook international human rights law in favour of the common law. One is that it reflects the orthodoxies of constitutional interpretation in judges' home states of Australia, New Zealand and the United Kingdom, where there are no written constitutional bills of rights and legislative bills of rights are relatively recent introductions.[37] Another, suggested by the reasoning in *Fiji v Prasad*, is that judges might be concerned that international human rights law will be perceived as a foreign import, rather than grounded in local law.[38]

While it may be possible to characterise the common law as more local than international law, for some it was and continues to be foreign.[39] *Taione v Tonga* represents how reliance on the common law to give content to constitutional provisions can serve to entrench both the colonial common law and dimensions of pre-independence external influence in constitutional interpretation. In this, the preference for common law meanings in constitutional interpretation sits uneasily with efforts taken in some Pacific states to establish an autochthonous constitution representing a break with the colonial legal system.[40]

B. Legal Borrowing

The transnational knowledge reach of foreign judges facilitates the 'borrowing' of legal concepts and doctrines from other countries in order to interpret, develop or apply constitutional law. One way in which transnational ties between jurisdictions are manifest in judicial decisions is the citation of foreign judgments.[41] The use of foreign judges facilitates the citation of foreign judgments, which might be particularly valuable in small jurisdictions where local precedents may not always be available. In a study of citations in the decisions of foreign judges on Pacific courts across all areas of law, Smith found that foreign judges from Australia, New Zealand and the United Kingdom were each more likely to cite

[36] ibid.

[37] *New Zealand Bill of Rights Act 1990* (NZ); *Human Rights Act 1998* (UK); *Human Rights Act 2004* (ACT); *Charter of Human Rights and Responsibilities Act 2006* (Vic).

[38] Interview F4.

[39] B Narokobi, *Lo Bilong Yumi Yet: Law and Custom in Melanesia* (Papua New Guinea, Melanesian Institute for Pastoral and Socio-Economic Service University of the South Pacific, 1989) ch 11; M Pulea, 'A Regional Court of Appeal for the Pacific' (1980) 9(2) *Pacific Perspective* 1, 9; A Amet, 'Severing the Umbilical Cord from the Common Law' in J Rannells and J Aleck (eds), *Custom at the Crossroads* (Faculty of Law, University of Papua New Guinea, 1995) 62, 64.

[40] P Bayne, 'The Constitution and the Franchise in Western Samoa' (1985) 1 *Queensland Institute of Technology Law Journal* 201, 213.

[41] VC Jackson, *Constitutional Engagement in a Transnational Era* (Oxford, Oxford University Press, 2010); T Groppi and M-C Ponthoreau (eds), *The Use of Foreign Precedents by Constitutional Judges* (Oxford, Hart Publishing, 2013).

cases from their own jurisdictions.[42] However, some judges interviewed for this project described a more careful approach, in which they sought to cite cases from across common law jurisdictions rather than their home country, as a diplomatic gesture to foreign judges from other jurisdictions on the court or in recognition of constitutional provisions on the reception of laws from a particular jurisdiction.[43] My own study of citations in constitutional judgments across the nine Pacific states found that while foreign judges are more likely than local judges to cite foreign judgments local and foreign judges both tend to cite judgments from the same set of common law jurisdictions.[44] The citation of foreign law is thus one manifestation of the knowledge reach of foreign judges.

Foreign judges come to Pacific courts with not only their own legal precedents and citations, but also their own understandings of constitutional concepts and institutions. The case of *Afeau v Judicial and Legal Services Commission* from Solomon Islands provides a striking illustration.[45] The Court of Appeal had to determine whether the Prime Minister had the power to direct the Judicial and Legal Services Commission to remove the Attorney-General from office. The Solomon Islands Constitution established the office of the Attorney-General and set out the nature and functions of the office, but did not expressly provide for the removal of the Attorney-General. The gap in the law was to be filled by the Court of Appeal by way of constitutional interpretation. The two judges in the majority, Lord Slynn of Hadley (from the United Kingdom) and Justice Salmon (from New Zealand), held that the Prime Minister had an implied power to dismiss the Attorney-General. Both judges drew on the comparable position of the Attorney-General in 'Solomon Islands and London' and common law rules relating to prerogative appointments. The dissenting judgment of Justice Adams (an Australian) tied its conclusions more closely to the text of the Constitution. Justice Adams emphasised that in Solomon Islands the Attorney-General is a public official who serves as the principal legal adviser to government, a position that differs from the political role of the Attorney-General in Australia, New Zealand and the United Kingdom. He concluded that the removal of the Attorney-General was governed by constitutional provisions relating to the removal of public officers and was not vested in the Prime Minister.

A second example shows how approaches to constitutional adjudication in a judge's home state may also be carried into the Pacific jurisdiction. In *Namah v Pato*, the Supreme Court of Papua New Guinea held that the detention of asylum seekers transferred by Australia to Manus Island was contrary to their

[42] SE Smith, 'The Way We Do Things Back Home: Do Expatriate Judges Preferentially Cite the Jurisprudence of Their Home Countries?' (2013) 13(2) *Oxford University Commonwealth Law Journal* 331.

[43] Interviews F3, F12.

[44] A Dziedzic, 'Foreign Judges of the Pacific as Agents of Global Constitutionalism' (2021) 10(2) *Global Constitutionalism* (forthcoming).

[45] *Afeau v Judicial and Legal Services Commission* [2007] SBCA 19.

right to personal liberty under Papua New Guinea's Constitution.[46] While all five judges agreed on the result, only two judges gave reasons for their decisions: Justice Kandakasi, a Papua New Guinean judge, and Justice Higgins, a judge from Australia. In his reasons, Justice Higgins read into the general limitations clause in the bill of rights a principle derived from Australian administrative law that detention must be limited to what is reasonably capable of being seen as necessary and incidental to the purpose of the detention.[47] In contrast, Justice Kandakasi held that restrictions on rights must be necessary and justified in all the circumstances having regard to the reasons for the proposed restriction, citing the words of the Constitution and precedents from the human rights case law of Papua New Guinea.[48] While both judges arrived at the same result, the different approaches illustrate how the law and judicial method of a foreign judge's home state, informed in Australia by the absence of a constitutional bill of rights, may be carried into the very different legal context of the Pacific state.

Afeau v Judicial and Legal Services Commission and *Namah v Pato* demonstrate how foreign judges might bring understandings of constitutional doctrine and institutions from their home jurisdictions to bear on their interpretation of Pacific constitutions. This can be problematic where those understandings are informed by the different constitutional context of the foreign judge's home state, be it informed by the lack of a single written constitution (as in New Zealand and the United Kingdom),[49] the lack of a constitutional bill of rights (as in Australia) or the absence of the power of post-enactment constitutional review of legislation (as in Sri Lanka). The danger is that concepts and institutions that appear familiar on the surface are in fact very different in the particular Pacific constitutional system. It is difficult, if not impossible, to shed the deeply ingrained assumptions, practices and understandings of one's own legal system when coming to consider another.[50] One judge interviewed for this project commented that the biggest difficulty judges face when moving across jurisdictions is that judges see a familiar law and assume that it is the same in the Pacific as it is at home, and warned that foreign judges needed to guard against this assumption.[51] Even where institutions or concepts have been directly transplanted, their meanings are likely to change as they adapt to the different legal and social context of a Pacific state and the constitutional order established by a new written constitution upon independence.[52]

[46] *Namah v Pato* [2016] PGSC 13.

[47] ibid [81], citing *Plaintiff S4/2014 v Minister for Immigration and Border Protection* (2014) 243 CLR 219.

[48] ibid [52].

[49] M Casey, 'New Zealand Judges in Overseas Courts' in I Barker and G Wear (eds), *Law Stories: Essays on the New Zealand Legal Profession 1969–2003* (Wellington, LexisNexis NZ, 2003) 89, 91.

[50] G Frankenberg, 'Critical Comparisons: Re-Thinking Comparative Law' (1985) 26 *Harvard International Law Journal* 411.

[51] Interview F23. Two other judges interviewed emphasised that there is no 'pan Pacific' common law: Interviews F4, F17.

[52] Twining (n 9).

Finally, these transnational dimensions of foreign judging serve to expand the potential audience of judicial decisions. The primary audience of a constitutional judgment is the litigants and officials within the Pacific state itself. In some cases, however, foreign judges write with an eye to the reception of the judgment in their home state. This is not only evident in cases such as *Namah v Pato*, where the litigation directly affected political interests in the foreign judge's home state, but also manifest in more subtle choices about judicial method. For example, Sir Kenneth Keith, a New Zealand judge who served in Samoa, notes the cautious approach taken by the foreign judges on the Samoan Court of Appeal when referring to debates of the Samoan Constitutional Convention.[53] In *Attorney-General v Olomalu*, decided in 1982, the Court made it clear that the drafting history was used 'only to confirm the interpretation already reached' on the text of the Constitution.[54] In this it seems that the judges were speaking not only to a Samoan audience, but also to their home jurisdiction of New Zealand, where the common law rules of statutory interpretation did not permit reference to parliamentary materials. This position changed four years later, when Lord Cooke, who was a member of the Court of Appeal in *Olomalu*, relaxed the prohibition on the use of *Hansard* as an aid to statutory interpretation while sitting as a judge in his home state of New Zealand.[55]

In summary, it is understandable that foreign judges turn to the common law to interpret the constitutions of Pacific states. The similarities between common law jurisdictions serve to minimise the significance of foreign judges' limited knowledge of the local legal system and maximise the significance of their knowledge of comparative foreign jurisdictions. Appeal to shared, familiar laws and principles is one way in which foreign judges can minimise the gap between their expertise in their own legal systems and those of the Pacific.[56] This transnational approach can, however, be self-reinforcing. The effect is seen most dramatically in Vanuatu, where, despite combined colonial legal influences from the British common law and the French civil law, the post-independence law of Vanuatu has been largely anglicised as a result of the use of Australian, British and New Zealand judges and other forms of assistance from those countries.[57] In this we see that foreign judges do not merely *utilise* similarities between their home jurisdiction and the Pacific legal systems in which they serve, but also *create* similarities in the course of adjudication.

[53] K Keith, 'Reflections on Some Pacific Constitutions' (2012) 18 *New Zealand Association for Comparative Law Yearbook* 133, 142–43.

[54] *Attorney-General v Olomalu* [1982] WSCA 1. Cf the position in Papua New Guinea, where s 24 of the Constitution expressly authorises courts to use such materials to aid interpretation; and Nauru, where from the earliest days the Supreme Court has accepted references to Convention debates to aid constitutional interpretation: *Jeremiah v Nauru Local Government Council* [1971] NRSC 5.

[55] *Marac Life Assurance Ltd v Commissioner of Inland Revenue* [1986] 1 NZLR 694, 701.

[56] P Mitchell, 'The Privy Council and the Difficulty of Distance' (2016) 36(1) *OJLS* 26, 47–50.

[57] WFS Miles, *Bridging Mental Boundaries in a Postcolonial Microcosm: Identity and Development in Vanuatu* (Honolulu, University of Hawaii Press, 1998) 166.

IV. LOCAL KNOWLEDGE GAPS

Although it has a transnational dimension, the common law proceeds on a view of law as the expression of the shared values of the community, capable of change as the aspirations, values and social institutions of the community evolve.[58] With limited direct contextual knowledge, foreign judges face the challenge of adjudicating according to the 'customs, conditions and way of life of the people they are judging'.[59] The result is reflected in two features of constitutional adjudication in the Pacific: first, the limited integration of custom and constitutional law; and, second, the predominantly textual approach to constitutional interpretation.

A. Custom

The readiness of Pacific courts to turn to common law understandings to support constitutional interpretation contrasts with their reticence to draw on an alternative source of law, namely, custom. Custom refers to the codes of behaviour and values that constituted the legal systems of Indigenous peoples of the Pacific islands prior to colonisation and which continue today. In some Pacific states, custom is formally recognised as a source of law by the constitution and in legislation.[60] In all nine states there are specialised courts or tribunals to deal with customary matters such as land and titles.[61] In addition, local authorities may have jurisdiction to adjudicate disputes according to custom.[62] Whether formally recognised or not, for many Pacific Indigenous peoples, custom operates alongside common law, statute and constitutional law, interacting in different ways in each national legal system. Custom is part of the legal and social context in which Pacific constitutions operate. Legal recognition and the continuing role of custom in Pacific societies provide grounds for judges to take custom into account in constitutional interpretation. Some scholars go further and argue that not only is it permissible for judges to consider custom, but also that they ought to do so.[63]

[58] T Etherton, 'Liberty, the Archetype and Diversity: A Philosophy of Judging' [2010] *Public Law* 727, 733.

[59] Pulea (n 39) 9. See also Baragwanath (n 4) 246.

[60] J Corrin Care and D Paterson, *Introduction to South Pacific Law*, 2nd edn (London, Routledge-Cavendish, 2008) ch 3; New Zealand Law Commission, 'Converging Currents: Custom and Human Rights in the Pacific', *Study Paper SP17* (2006) 35–36, app 4.

[61] *Native Lands Act 1905* c 133 (Fiji); *Magistrates Court Ordinance 1977* c 52 (Kiribati), pt VI; *Nauru Lands Committee Act 1956* (Nauru); *Land Disputes Settlement Act 1975* (PNG), pt IV; *Land and Titles Act 1981* (Samoa), pt 6; *Land and Titles Act 1968* c 133 (SI), s 255; *Land Act 1927* c 132 (Tonga), pt X; *Native Lands Act 1956* c 46.20 (Tuvalu); *Customary Land Tribunal Act 2001* c 271 (Vanuatu).

[62] eg *Village Courts Act 1989* (PNG); *Village Fono Act 1990* (Samoa); *Local Courts Act 1942* c 19 (Solomon Islands); *Island Courts Act 1965* c 7.32 (Tuvalu); *Island Courts Act 1983* c 167 (Vanuatu).

[63] J Aleck, 'Beyond Recognition: Contemporary Jurisprudence in the Pacific Islands and Common Law Tradition' (1991) 7 *Queensland University of Technology Law Journal* 137, 143; B Narokobi, 'In

Custom represents an obvious knowledge gap for most foreign judges serving on Pacific courts. Custom derives from the worldviews of Indigenous peoples of the Pacific,[64] which differ fundamentally from those that inform the legal systems of western democracies with which most foreign judges are familiar. As a very broad generalisation, Pacific cultures and customs are obligation-based or 'other-orientated' and place the individual, in complex ways, within the context of community. This understanding is often contrasted with western legal understandings of communities as comprising autonomous, rights-bearing individuals.[65] In the contemporary conditions of legal pluralism, custom operates and influences many areas of law and social relations, but is particularly significant in personal matters such as marriage and adoption, the ownership and management of land, and local-level governance, which in many states includes authority to deal with some criminal and civil matters. Custom is generally uncodified and changes over time and in response to new circumstances, presenting additional challenges for courts seeking to apply or incorporate custom into their legal decisions. There is a great diversity of custom across Pacific states, and often also across different groups within states, such that in diverse countries like Papua New Guinea and Solomon Islands, citizen judges may well lack knowledge of the customs of groups other than their own.[66]

Conscious of the limitations of their knowledge, foreign judges are understandably hesitant to deal too closely with custom.[67] The use of foreign judges is cited as one reason why Pacific courts have been slow to develop an Indigenous jurisprudence that draws on both custom and common law.[68] While there are examples of judicial decisions in which judges have read constitutions by reference to the customs of the society,[69] such instances are rare and courts generally prefer to resolve the issue on either the text or the common law.[70]

Search of a Melanesian Jurisprudence' in P Sack and E Minchin (eds), *Legal Pluralism: Proceedings of the Canberra Law Workshop VII* (Canberra, Australian National University, 1986) 215, 227.

[64] As a non-Indigenous person, I do not seek to speak to uniquely Indigenous ways of knowing and experiencing Indigenous custom. For scholarship by Indigenous writers, see eg Narokobi (n 39) ch 2, 4; Tui Atua Tupua Tamasese Efi, *Su'esu'e Manogi In Search of Fragrance: Tui Atua Tupua Tamasese Ta'isi and the Samoan Indigenous Reference* (Apia, Centre for Samoan Studies, National University of Samoa, 2008) esp chs 14, 29.

[65] Farran (n 26) 102–03; TLS Mulitalo Seumanutafa, *Law Reform in Plural Societies* (Cham, Springer, 2018) 50–51; I Salevao, *Rule of Law, Legitimate Governance and Development in the Pacific* (Canberra, ANU Press, 2005) 122–25.

[66] eg *To'ofilu v Oimae* [1997] SBHC 33, Palmer J; *In re Miriam Willingal* [1997] PGNC 7, Injia J; New Zealand Law Commission (n 60) 205.

[67] Baird (n 10) 87; J Zorn, 'Custom Then and Now: The Changing Melanesian Family' in A Jowitt and T Newton Cain (eds), *Passage of Change: Law, Society and Governance in the Pacific* (Canberra, Pandanus Books, 2003) 95, 97.

[68] P MacFarlane, 'Some Challenges Facing Legal Strengthening Projects in Small Pacific Island States' (2006) 4(1) *Journal of Commonwealth Law and Legal Education* 103, 108; FM Sapolu, 'Adjudicators in Western Samoa' in G Powles and M Pulea (eds), *Pacific Courts and Legal Systems* (Suva and Clayton, University of the South Pacific and Monash University, 1988) 60, 61–62.

[69] *Taamale v Attorney-General* [1995] WSCA 1; *Teonea v Kaupule* [2005] TVHC 5.

[70] Examples of constitutional cases in which custom was raised by counsel and considered by courts but rejected or held not to be decisive include: *Taione v Tonga* [2004] TOSC 47; *Pita v Attorney-General* [1995] WSCA 6; *Attorney-General v Olomalu* [1982] WSCA 1; *Re Somare* [1981] PGSC 23.

Some scholars have been critical of foreign judges' reticence to draw on custom. Bernard Narokobi writes:

> Expatriate judges often say that they are not nationals and cannot pronounce on custom. If they are serious about such views, they should not have accepted appointment. … On being appointed a judge, a lawyer assumes the duty of facilitating the development of the law of the people. If the expatriate judges are shy about developing indigenous law, they may be excused. But what of judges who are citizens? Perhaps they too can be excused on the grounds they do not know the different laws of the people. But at least they can take more interest in encouraging practising lawyers to present material on the people's laws.[71]

The use of foreign judges is not the only reason for the slow integration of custom through judicial development of the law. As Narokobi indicates, in Papua New Guinea local judges have also been slow to use custom. Tamanaha, writing about Micronesia, suggests that the failure of the law to become more Micronesian is not because of the use of foreign judges, but because of differences between the 'internal legal attitudes' of lawyers and non-lawyers in a legal system comprising both transplanted western law and local customary law.[72] Other factors include the lack of legislative rules for pleading custom, the failure by advocates to raise issues of custom in their submissions to the court, difficulties in ascertaining custom and a lack of attention to custom in legal education.[73]

Another reason why judges on Pacific courts rarely use custom in the course of constitutional adjudication may be that customary concepts are not expressly included in the constitutional text. In some states, customary principles, institutions and laws were marginalised in the written constitution, reflecting tensions between western constitutionalism and customary governance.[74] Even where references to customary values or institutions were included, written constitutions did not purport to resolve the tensions between custom and western models of constitutionalism.[75] As a result, Pacific courts and judges have struggled to resolve difficult questions on the relationship between custom

[71] Narokobi (n 39) 158–59.

[72] BZ Tamanaha, *Understanding Law in Micronesia: An Interpretive Approach to Transplanted Law* (Leiden, EJ Brill, 1993) 56.

[73] M Forsyth, 'Beyond Case Law: Kastom and Courts in Vanuatu' (2004) 35 *Victoria University of Wellington Law Review* 427, 438–43; Mulitalo Seumanutafa (n 65) 78; J Nonggorr, 'Development of an "Indigenous Jurisprudence" in Papua New Guinea: The Past Record and Future Prospects' in Rannells and Aleck (eds), (n 39) 68; Zorn (n 67) 97–98.

[74] eg G Nimbtik, 'The Struggles of Adoption and Adaptation in the Governance Space of Vanuatu: The Incorporation of Jifly Authority and Kastom Governance into the Legal-Rational System' in JI Lahai and H Ware (eds), *Governance and Societal Adaptation in Fragile States* (Cham, Palgrave Macmillan, 2020) 237; A Va'ai, 'The Idea of Law: A Pacific Perspective' (1997) 21 *Journal of Pacific Studies* 225, 243.

[75] G Powles, 'Traditional Institutions in Pacific Constitutional Systems: Better Late or Never?' in PG Sack (ed), *Pacific Constitutions: Proceedings of the Canberra Law Workshop VI* (Canberra, Australian National University, 1982) 345, 346.

and constitutionalism, a struggle that is most visibly manifest in cases concerning custom and constitutionally protected human rights.[76] In something of a self-fulfilling prophecy, there is evidence in two states that customary law and institutions were deliberately excluded from the constitutional text, partly out of concern that they would fall to be interpreted by foreign judges. In response to a question from a member of the Constitutional Convention of Nauru about whether a judge's responsibility to uphold the law should include a duty to uphold custom, the Australian constitutional adviser stated that

> I think that it would be dangerous to give a Judge of the Supreme Court, particularly for so long as the judge of the Supreme Court is not Nauruan, the power of interpreting custom. He, first of all, wouldn't have the same deep understanding of the custom; and, secondly, he would be bound to interpret it, I think, according to the precedents and procedures of the judicial system within which he worked.[77]

In Samoa, members of the Constitutional Convention and the Constitution Drafting Committee discussed at length ways to reflect the traditional position of the *tama-a-aiga* (paramount chiefs) in the Constitution. The aspiration to require that only *tama-a-aiga* may hold the office of head of state quickly become complicated by many factors and in the end was abandoned. One of the arguments put against the idea was that matters written in the Constitution would fall to be interpreted by a court (which was likely to be composed of foreign judges for the foreseeable future) rather than the Parliament whose members, as *matai* (chiefs), would have knowledge of custom.[78]

In contrast to the position taken at the time of constitution making, there is now a trend to encourage or require courts to consider custom when interpreting the Constitution.[79] Tuvalu's Constitution of 1986 departed, in innovative ways, from the Constitution made under imperial law for its independence in 1978. It sets out seven constitutional principles, many of which emphasise the importance of Tuvaluan custom and tradition, which are expressed to form the 'basis of this Constitution' and are to be 'observed in its interpretation and application'.[80]

[76] eg J Corrin Care, 'Negotiating the Constitutional Conundrum: Balancing Cultural Identity with Principles of Gender Equality in Post-Colonial South Pacific Societies' (2006) 5 *Indigenous Law Journal* 51.

[77] Territory of Nauru, 'Record of Proceedings of the Constitutional Convention' (15 January 1968) 78.

[78] L Meti, *Samoa: The Making of the Constitution* (Apia, National University of Samoa, 2002) ch 8, esp 105, 107; JW Davidson, *Samoa Mo Samoa: The Emergence of the Independent State of Western Samoa* (Melbourne, Oxford University Press, 1967) 373. The constitutional adviser in Nauru and Samoa was JW Davidson, a historian from Australia. In Samoa, only *matai* are eligible to stand for election to the Parliament.

[79] The early precedent in the wider Pacific region is art XI, s 11 of the *Constitution of the Federated States of Micronesia*, which provides that 'Court decisions shall be consistent with this Constitution, Micronesian customs and traditions and the social and geographical configuration of Micronesia'.

[80] *Constitution of Tuvalu 1986*, preamble.

A specific provision on constitutional interpretation requires the Constitution to be interpreted and applied consistently with the principles and in 'such a way as to achieve the aims of fair and democratic government, in the light of reason and experience and of Tuvaluan values'.[81] These provisions were included to prevent the judiciary, which has always comprised foreign judges, from 'imprinting their own particular philosophies on constitutional language'.[82] In 2020, both Samoa and Tonga amended their Constitutions to insert 'judicial guidance' clauses that permit judges on all courts to take account of custom.[83] The amendments sought to address the concern that the Constitution and the courts too heavily favour western legal values over custom, which in both cases was seen to result, at least in part, from the use of foreign judges.[84] Whether such guidance will overcome the difficulties that courts face in identifying, ascertaining and applying unwritten custom, and in practice effect the greater integration of custom and constitutional law, remains to be seen.

There is a variety of procedures that foreign judges can use to obtain information on custom. The Court of Appeal of Samoa has acknowledged that

> [t]he judiciary are deemed to be familiar with the laws of the state in which they sit and to take judicial notice of them; to the extent they lack such knowledge, as is sometimes the case with expatriate judges, they must take care with the assistance of counsel to educate themselves in such matters.[85]

Prior to independence, some courts in the Pacific region sat with assessors to provide judges with insights into local conditions. The practices of colonial courts varied: in some, the assessors were European settlers; in others they were chiefs or senior members of the Indigenous community.[86] Some aspects of this practice continued into independence, although today assessors generally sit only on criminal cases as a substitute for a jury,[87] or to advise judges on customary land matters.[88] Although legislation in some states permits appellate courts to appoint an assessor where it appears that special knowledge is required for

[81] ibid s 4(2) and (3).

[82] S Levine, 'Constitutional Change in Tuvalu' (1992) 27(3) *Australian Journal of Political Science* 492, 502.

[83] *Constitution Amendment Act 2020* (Samoa), cl 4, inserting new s 71; *Act of Constitution (Amendment) Bill 2020* (Tonga) inserting new s 89A.

[84] Samoa Law Reform Commission, 'Samoa Mo Samoa: Fetuunai Muniao' *Research Report* vol 1, Samoa Law Reform Commission, (2020); P Fonua, 'Controversial Bill to Amend Constitution' *Matangi Tonga* (Nuku'alofa) (22 September 2020); P Fonua, 'Parliament Amends Tongan Constitution to Include Unwritten "Customs"' *Matangi Tonga* (Nuku'alofa) (17 October 2020).

[85] *Ali'i and Faipule of Siumu District v Attorney-General* [2010] WSCA 5.

[86] JM Van Dyke, 'The Pacific Judicial Conference: Strengthening the Independent Judiciary and the Rule of Law in the Pacific' (2011) 22(1–2) *Western Legal History* 127, 208.

[87] E Colvin, 'Criminal Procedure in the South Pacific' (2004) 8(1) *Journal of South Pacific Law*, available at www.usp.ac.fj/index.php?id=13266, 18–20; P Duff, 'The Evolution of Trial by Judge and Assessors in Fiji' (1997) 21 *Journal of Pacific Studies* 189.

[88] eg *Land and Titles Act 1981* (Samoa), pt XI; *Land Act 1927* c 132 (Tonga), s 147(1).

the proper determination of the case,[89] it is rare for judges hearing a constitutional matter to sit with assessors.

There are some examples of constitutional cases in which a foreign judge has heard evidence of custom to establish, for example, the authority of customary chiefs in a particular subnational community[90] or the nature of customary norms of gifting and reciprocity in a case concerning electoral treating.[91] Alternatively, judges might seek submissions from counsel. There are limitations to both approaches. Evidence is a useful way for judges to obtain knowledge of custom in a transparent manner in open court. However, this approach does risk treating custom in the same way as foreign law – that is, as a matter of fact to be determined on expert evidence – rather than as a matter of law, resonating with wider questions about the extent to which Pacific legal systems accommodate legal pluralism.[92] Second, the practicalities of foreign judging in the Pacific mitigate against taking detailed evidence, particularly in appellate courts constituted predominantly or solely by foreign judges. As explained in chapter 2, Pacific courts of appeal sit part time, with foreign judges visiting for sittings of one to two weeks, during which they hear and usually determine several appeal cases. In very small states, the superior trial courts constituted by foreign judges also sit part time. While courts can adjourn a hearing to receive evidence or submissions, it is a rare occurrence, and can be avoided, for example, by determining the case on other grounds.[93] Finally, the extent to which courts can rely on counsel to provide information on custom is limited by the knowledge and experience of the advocates before the court. Counsel appearing in constitutional matters are sometimes themselves foreign, briefed because of a shortage of local lawyers or in an effort to obtain advocates with specialist legal expertise. It has also been suggested that foreign counsel might be engaged because the judges of the court are foreign.[94] While local advocates may be in a better position to make submissions on custom, the ability of individual lawyers to do so depends on their own experience and will be informed by their legal training, which focuses predominantly on the common law.[95]

The reticence of Pacific courts to directly draw upon custom in constitutional adjudication is consonant with the knowledge gap faced by foreign judges serving in Pacific jurisdictions. While not the only explanatory factor, the use of

[89] *Court of Appeal Act 1980* (Kiribati), s 27(e); *Court of Appeal Act 1978* c 6 (SI), s 28(e); *Court of Appeal Act 1966* c 9 (Tonga), s 22(e).

[90] *Teonea v Kaupule* [2005] TVHC 5.

[91] Keith (n 53) 137–38.

[92] JG Zorn and J Corrin Care, 'Barava Tru: Judicial Approaches to the Pleading and Proof of Custom in the South Pacific' (2002) 51 *International and Comparative Law Quarterly* 611.

[93] As in *Ali'i and Faipule of Siumu District v Attorney-General* [2010] WSCA 5.

[94] A Mason, 'Reflections of an Itinerant Judge in the Asia-Pacific Region' (2000) 28 *International Journal of Legal Information* 311, 316–17.

[95] M Forsyth, *A Bird That Flies with Two Wings: The Kastom and State Justice Systems in Vanuatu* (Canberra, ANU Press, 2009) 146–47.

foreign judges who do not have direct knowledge of custom in Pacific societies has inhibited the judicial development of a Pacific jurisprudence drawing upon custom.

B. Constitutional Interpretation

In the Pacific, as elsewhere, written constitutions are framed in general language. Judges tasked with interpreting the constitution are sometimes faced with a choice about the application and meaning of constitutional provisions. Building on scholarship first undertaken by Baird in her study of foreign judging in the Pacific,[96] this section examines the factors that potentially guide foreign judges in that choice. It first demonstrates the predominance of a textual approach to constitutional interpretation in the region, even where constitutional provisions encourage recourse to constitutional principles. It then considers how this approach has a degree of fit with the gaps in the knowledge generally held by foreign judges.

On the whole, Pacific courts generally take a textual approach to constitutional interpretation. Textualism refers to methods of interpretation that draw primarily on the meaning of the words of the constitution. Textualism is manifest in the rules of constitutional interpretation most commonly cited by Pacific courts. The first and foremost of these is that the meaning of a constitutional provision is to be ascertained by applying the ordinary and clear meaning of the words of the text, permitting courts to go beyond the text only where the words are unclear or ambiguous. As a result, constitutional interpretation begins, and in many cases ends, with the text alone. Where the court determines that the words of the constitution are plain, the court has no need or authority to consider preambles,[97] constitutional principles,[98] 'spirit and intent',[99] implications[100] or common law rules of statutory interpretation.[101]

[96] Baird (n 10).

[97] *Mulitalo v Attorney-General of Samoa* [2001] WSCA 8; *Minister for Provincial Government v Guadalcanal Provincial Assembly* [1997] SBCA 1, Goldsbrough JA; *Folotalu v Attorney-General* [2001] SBHC 149; *Premdas v The State* [1979] PGSC 20, Wilson J; *President v Speaker of Parliament* [2008] VUSC 77. See also K Brown and J Corrin Care, 'More on Democratic Fundamentals in Solomon Islands: Minister for Provincial Government v Guadalcanal Provincial Assembly' (2001) 32 *Victoria University of Wellington Law Review* 653, 655–59.

[98] *Reference by HE the President* [2002] FJSC 1, Tuivaga P, Tikaram, Eichelbaum and Sapolu JJ; *Chaudhry v Qarase* [2002] FJCA 1, although on appeal the Supreme Court took a different approach to constitutional interpretation: *Qarase v Chaudhry* [2003] FJSC 1.

[99] *In the matter of Articles 55 and 45 (and Articles 36 and 40) of the Constitution* [2008] NRSC 7; *Speaker v Attorney-General* [1987] KIHC 1.

[100] *Constitutional Reference No 1 of 1977 Re Rights of Person Arrested or Detained* [1977] PGSC 15, Prentice DCJ; *Chaudhry v Qarase* [2002] FJCA 1.

[101] *Vaikona v Fuko (No 2)* [1990] TOSC 11; *In the Matter of the Constitution and in the Matter of the Dissolution of the Eighteenth Parliament* [2010] NRSC 16, in which Von Doussa J noted that 'ritualistic adherence to established rules of statutory interpretation may be too limiting to ensure a

Where the meaning of the words of the constitution is unclear or ambiguous, Pacific courts tend to follow one of two interpretative paths. The first is to interpret the words of the constitution 'generously'. This approach has its origins in decisions of the Judicial Committee of the Privy Council, which sought to distinguish the interpretation of constitutions from that of ordinary statutes. An oft-cited dictum is that constitutional provisions 'call for a generous interpretation avoiding what has been called "the austerity of tabulated legalism"'.[102] This requires that the words of a constitutional provision are read in light of the character and purpose of a constitution in protecting human rights and regulating the powers of government.[103] Where constitutional rights are involved, a 'generous' interpretation tends to mean that the protected right is to be given a wide application.[104] For other constitutional provisions, the call for a 'generous' interpretation does not, in itself, provide much guidance, especially when interpretation involves balancing competing constitutional rights or principles: as Frame points out, it is not clear to whom or to what an interpretation is to be generous.[105] In these cases, a 'generous' interpretation tends to mean a purposive approach, in which the ordinary meaning of the words is read in light of the character and purpose of the constitution.[106]

The second approach is to interpret the words of the provision in the context of the *particular* constitution. For this, judges might look to indications in the constitutional text, such as the values set out in the preamble, principles or interpretation provisions. Sometimes, judges will use these resources only where the meaning of the text is unclear,[107] or in order to confirm an interpretation that is primarily supported by the text.[108] In Fiji and Papua New Guinea, however, some judges, guided by the Constitution, have advocated for a different approach, in which a judge is to look *first* to constitutional values or principles to inform the reading of the constitutional provisions. This approach is worth exploring in detail here, because it demonstrates the persistence of textualism, even where express constitutional directives promote a different approach.

constitution is properly understood and applied', but held it was neither helpful nor necessary to go beyond the words of the text.

[102] *Home Affairs v Fisher* [1980] AC 319, 328.

[103] *Hinds v The Queen* [1977] AC 195; *Attorney-General (Fiji) v Director of Public Prosecutions* [1983] AC 672.

[104] eg *Attorney-General v Olomalu* [1982] WSCA 1; *Bohn v Vanuatu* [2013] VUSC 42; *Lyndon v Legal Aid Commission* [2003] FJHC 323; *Malifa v Sapolu* [1999] WSSC 47; *Korman v Natapei* [1997] VUSC 46.

[105] A Frame, 'The Tahitian Pomare Code of 1819: First Steps to Written Law in the Pacific', Paper presented at the Pacific Judicial Conference, Auckland (9–12 March 2014) 20–21.

[106] eg *Prime Minister v Governor General* [1999] SBCA 6; *Application by Attorney-General re Interpretation of Section 32(2) of the Constitution* [2020] KIHC 14; *Attorney-General v Electoral Commission* [2015] FJHC 420; *Speaker v Philip* [1991] SBCA 1; *Huniehu v Attorney-General* [1997] SBCA 9.

[107] See cases cited nn 97–99.

[108] eg *Minister for Provincial Government v Guadalcanal Provincial Assembly* [1997] SBCA 1, Kapi P; *Attorney-General v Olomalu* [1982] WSCA 1; *Pita v Attorney-General* [1995] WSCA 6; *Attorney-General v Speaker to Parliament* (High Court of Tuvalu, 2 November 2016).

Constitution makers in Fiji and Papua New Guinea directed judges towards a principles-based approach by setting out constitutional principles and expressly providing that they guide constitutional interpretation.[109] The preamble to the Constitution of Papua New Guinea contains the National Goals and Directive Principles, which cover human development and freedom; equality and participation; national sovereignty and economic self-reliance; the use of natural resources; and Papua New Guinean forms of social, political and economic organisation. The National Goals and Directive Principles are non-justiciable, but the Constitution provides that laws should be applied in such a way as to give effect to the Principles, or at least not derogate from them, where doing so is reasonable and consistent with the intention of Parliament and the Constitution.[110] There is some evidence that these provisions were included in the Constitution to counter what the Constitutional Planning Committee characterised as a judicial tendency to textualism. In canvassing arguments against judicial enforcement of the Constitution, the Committee noted:

> The courts tend to be formalistic and legalistic. While it is true that the Constitution is law, it is a special kind of law. All too often the courts approach the Constitution as if it were like ordinary law. They adopt a literal approach and sacrifice the spirit for the letter of the Constitution.[111]

Against this, the Committee was concerned to ensure that judges take full account of the social goals and values set out in the Constitution, and take an active and progressive approach to the development of Papua New Guinean law.[112]

The 1997 Constitution of Fiji included a 'Compact', which, while expressed to be non-justiciable, was to inform the interpretation of constitutional provisions where relevant.[113] The Compact set out principles for the conduct of government in Fiji, including respect for the rights of individuals and communities, special protections for Indigenous Fijian custom, and the equitable sharing of political, economic and commercial power amongst all communities in Fiji.[114] A separate provision directed courts to interpret the Constitution in a way that promoted the spirit, purpose and objects of the Constitution as a whole.[115] As in Papua New Guinea, the inclusion of an express provision on the approach to constitutional interpretation in the 1997 Constitution arose from concerns that 'courts have sometimes placed too much stress on what appeared to be the literal

[109] The *Constitution of Tuvalu 1986* also sets out principles to guide its interpretation and application. The use of these principles in constitutional rights cases is discussed in ch 7, section IV.

[110] *Constitution of Papua New Guinea 1975*, ss 25(1), 25(3), 63(3).

[111] Constitutional Planning Committee Papua New Guinea, *Final Report of the Constitutional Planning Committee* (1974) ch 8, [144].

[112] ibid ch 8, [5]–[6]; B Kama, *Reconceptualising the Role of the Judiciary in Papua New Guinea's 'Home-Grown' Constitution*, PhD Thesis (Canberra, Australian National University, 2019) ch 5.

[113] *Constitution of Fiji 1997*, s 7.

[114] ibid s 6.

[115] ibid s 3(a).

meaning of the words used, without looking at the provision in its context and in light of its purpose and in the spirit of the Constitution as a whole'.[116] The interpretation provision was intended to serve as a reminder to judges to take account of factors beyond the immediate text.

Despite constitutional directives of this kind, some judges nevertheless prefer a textualist approach to constitutional interpretation. In Fiji, the use of the Compact was considered in two cases concerning the power-sharing arrangements in the 1997 Constitution. The first case sought an Advisory Opinion from the Supreme Court on the application of section 64 of the Constitution, which set out the mechanism by which members of the opposition were to be appointed to the Senate. Opposition parties that held at least 10 per cent of the seats in the House of Representatives were entitled to nominate persons as Senators. The Leader of the Opposition was required to ensure that the eight Senate seats reserved for opposition parties were filled in proportion to the representation of each opposition party in the House of Representatives.[117] Following the 2002 election, only one opposition party, the Fiji Labour Party, held more than 10 per cent of the seats in the House of Representatives. The question was whether all eight seats were to be filled by members of the Fiji Labour Party, or if the other minor parties must also be represented. A majority of judges of the Supreme Court – which was composed of two local judges and judges from New Zealand and Samoa – held that on a plain reading of the provisions of the Constitution, no question of proportional representation arose where only one opposition party held the requisite 10 per cent of seats in the House of Representatives. Because it reached this conclusion on the text, the majority did not have recourse to the principles relating to power sharing set out in the Compact.[118] Justice Amet, a judge from Papua New Guinea, dissented. He held that the proper starting point for interpreting an autochthonous constitution is the specific guidelines for interpretation set out in that constitution. He held that the principles of power sharing, together with the spirit of the Constitution and the context in which it was drafted, directed judges to the true interpretation, which was that the eight Senate seats were to be shared amongst all opposition parties.[119]

The second case, *Qarase v Chaudhry*, concerned whether the Prime Minister had followed the constitutional requirements to secure a multiparty cabinet.[120] The Court of Appeal (composed of three judges from New Zealand and judges from Australia and the United Kingdom) held that the meaning of the text was clear, so there was no scope to consider the principle of equitable power

[116] P Reeves, TR Vakatora and BV Lal, 'The Fiji Islands: Towards a United Future Report of the Fiji Constitution Review Commission' (Fiji, Parliamentary Paper No 34 of 1996) [5.67].

[117] *Constitution of Fiji 1997*, ss 64, 99.

[118] *Reference by HE the President* [2002] FJSC 1, Tuivaga P, Tikaram, Eichelbaum and Sapolu JJ.

[119] ibid, Amet J.

[120] *Constitution of Fiji 1997*, s 99.

sharing set out in the Compact.[121] The Supreme Court (composed of the Fijian Chief Justice, three judges from Australia and one judge from New Zealand) disagreed on this interpretive method, stating that it was not appropriate to approach a constitutional text on the basis that the court must find an ambiguity before it can seek guidance from the interpretation provision and statements of principle.[122] Even so, it agreed with the Court of Appeal in the result.

A similar tension is evident in judgments of the Supreme Court of Papua New Guinea, with some judges turning to the National Goals and Directive Principles only in cases of doubt, while others have developed a 'principles first' approach. The different approaches emerged early in the court's jurisprudence. In the 1979 case of *Premdas v Papua New Guinea*, Justice Wilson, an Australian, adopted the orthodox textual approach that where there is no doubt as to the meaning of a constitutional provision, it is unnecessary and inappropriate to refer to the Principles.[123] The contrasting approach was explained by Justice Barnett, also an Australian, albeit one who had worked as a lawyer in Papua New Guinea:

> It seems to me that the Constituent Assembly gave a clear direction to courts interpreting constitutional laws. That direction is to reverse the previous conservative approach to statutory interpretation which tends to commence the task by a detailed and literal study of the words used, turning to some 'deemed' intention of the legislature only in cases of verbal ambiguity or internal conflict. That direction is to enlighten the judicial mind first and then examine the actual words used from the viewpoint of that enlightened mind. It must be a mind striving to give effect to the National Goals and Directive Principles.[124]

Vergil Narokobi has traced how the differences in approach have persisted, with the textual approach prevailing in most cases. The result, in his view, is that the court has failed to fulfil its duty to implement the National Goals and Directive Principles.[125]

This study of cases from Fiji and Papua New Guinea shows that the methods of constitutional interpretation adopted by individual judges vary. Some are tightly tied to the text, while others expressly draw on constitutional principles and values. It also shows that there is no neat distinction between foreign judges and local judges in their approaches to constitutional interpretation. There are differences within and across each cohort, with examples of local and

[121] *Chaudhry v Qarase* [2002] FJCA 1.

[122] *Qarase v Chaudhry* [2003] FJSC 1.

[123] *Premdas v Papua New Guinea* [1979] PGSC 20, Wilson J.

[124] *Constitutional Reference No 3 of 1987, Reference by Simbu Provincial Executive* [1987] PGSC 17. See also *State v Independent Leadership Tribunal; Ex Parte Sasakila* [1976] PNGLR 491, Kearney J.

[125] V Narokobi, *The Implementation of Papua New Guinea's National Goals and Directive Principles and Basic Social Obligations*, PhD thesis (Wellington, Victoria University of Wellington, 2016) 68–81. See also PJ Bayne, 'Judicial Method and the Interpretation of Papua New Guinea's Constitution' (1980) 11 *Federal Law Review* 121.

foreign judges taking strongly textual approaches, and local and foreign judges taking 'principle-first' approaches. Despite the variation, the generally accepted approach is clearly textualist, with only a few judges taking a principles-first approach, and then usually in dissent.[126]

There are of course examples of cases across the region where judges have drawn on approaches to interpretation that reach beyond the words of a constitutional provision. Occasionally, judges have given constitutional directives a 'workable' rather than strict interpretation in order to resolve issues that were not anticipated when the constitution was drafted.[127] Some judges frame an unconstitutional law as inconsistent with the 'spirit' and 'intent' of the constitution.[128] Others characterise the constitution as a living document, which develops in line with the changing social and political context.[129] As discussed, judges might look to the common law or (more rarely) to custom to determine constitutional meaning. My claim is that these approaches are relatively uncommon and that the predominate orthodox approaches to constitutional interpretation across the Pacific region are tightly tied to the text of constitutional provisions.

The textualist approach to constitutional interpretation taken by Pacific courts 'fits' with the knowledge gap that foreign judges face. Textual approaches are motivated in part by distrust of judicial law making.[130] They seek to limit judicial discretion in interpretation out of concern that a judge's subjective views will come to displace the intentions of the legislature or the constitutional drafters. Textualism casts the judge's role as a technical one, such that the judge's personal views – and the judge's background and nationality (to the extent they are thought to influence those views) – do not matter. Textualism, and its relationship to a judge's nationality, is illustrated by comments made by Chief Justice Ward in the Tongan case of *Attorney-General v Namoa*. A member of the Tongan Parliament and an academic had publicly criticised a decision made by two foreign judges on Tonga's Supreme Court. They said that the case should have been heard in the Land Court, where an assessor could have 'clarified matters to the [judges] pertaining to how we live as Tongans, our culture and our connection to the land'. They suggested the King should intervene, because 'this King does not accept a Chief Justice or a foreigner to come here and want to make decisions concerning the land of this country'. Chief Justice Ward ruled

[126] *Reference by HE the President* [2002] FJSC 1, Amet J; *Constitutional Reference No 3 of 1987, Reference by Simbu Provincial Executive* [1987] PGSC 17, Barnett J. See also *Guadalcanal Provincial Assembly v Speaker of National Parliament* [1997] SBHC 5.

[127] eg *Application by Attorney-General re Interpretation of Section 32(2) of the Constitution* [2020] KIHC 14; *Nori v Attorney-General* [2006] SBHC 134.

[128] For cases outside Fiji (where the Constitutions of 1997 and 2013 direct judges to have regard to the 'spirit' of the Constitution), see eg: *Reference by the Ombudsman Commission* [2010] PGSC 10, Injia CJ [68], Kirriwom J [158], [169], Gavara-Nanu J [205]; *Nukufetau v Metia* [2012] TVHC 8; *Sefo v Attorney-General* [2000] WSSC 18.

[129] eg *Wells v Taga Tarikarea* [2003] VUSC 103; *Naba v Fiji* [2001] FJHC; *Jackson v Attorney-General* [2009] WSSC 73.

[130] Goldsworthy (n 2) 690.

that this second comment amounted to a contempt of court, because there was a real risk that it would diminish the Court's authority. He stated:

> The judges are here to apply the law as it stands and, if that law is such that it is necessary to be Tongan to understand its true meaning, I would venture to suggest it is poorly worded. If the law is clear in its terminology, the nationality of the judge will have no effect upon his interpretation.[131]

In this way, textualism purports to offer a technical, value-free method of constitutional interpretation: if the language of the law is clear, it should make no difference whether a local or foreign judge interprets it. In this, textualism supports a characterisation of the foreign judge as a legal expert, skilled in interpreting legal texts, regardless of the jurisdiction in which those texts are made and applied. One criticism, however, is that reference only to the text serves to conceal, rather than eliminate, the choices that judges inevitably make when determining the meaning and application of a constitutional provision.[132] It allows judges to 'escape from the somewhat awful responsibility of interpreting the community to itself, a responsibility which [common law] judges … have always had'.[133] Although the idea of the law as a reflection of the community's values is strong in the common law tradition,[134] foreign judges might understandably be reluctant to take on this role. How can judges who are not part of the community have knowledge of the nation's history, culture, legal system and political morality sufficient to 'interpret the community to itself'? The difficulty is apparent even where constitutions provide guidance in the text, partly in order to assist foreign judges who may be 'hampered in their attempt to contextualise [constitutional] rights by lack of knowledge of cultural nuance'.[135]

V. THE ROLE OF LOCAL JUDGES IN BRIDGING THE NATIONAL AND TRANSNATIONAL

This chapter has identified characteristics of constitutional adjudication in the Pacific that are explicable, in part, by the extensive use of foreign judges on courts of constitutional jurisdiction. It is difficult to say whether Pacific judiciaries wholly composed of local judges would have led to significant differences in approach. Styles of constitutional adjudication are influenced by too great a variety of factors to pinpoint a single cause. It is possible, however, to identify a sense that local judges are understood to have different knowledge and authority because they are *local* judges.

[131] *Attorney-General v Namoa* [2000] TOSC 13.

[132] F Schauer, 'Formalism' (1987) 97 *Yale Law Journal* 509, 511–17.

[133] Bayne (n 40) 219, 221, citing KS Jacobs, 'Lawyers' Reasonings: Some Extra-Judicial Reflections' (1965) 5 *Sydney Law Review* 425, 428.

[134] Etherton (n 58) 733.

[135] J Corrin, 'Breaking the Mould: Constitutional Review in Solomon Islands' (2007) 13 *Revue Juridique Polynésienne* 143, 149.

Several judges interviewed noted the benefits of sitting with local judges on panels of the courts of appeal. Local judges were seen to provide the court with a better understanding of custom[136] and to foster a sense of the court as belonging to the nation and its people.[137] These potential benefits are, however, limited by practice. In states where there are few or no local judges, it is often not possible to include local judges on panels of the court of appeal. In Fiji, Samoa, Solomon Islands and Vanuatu, mixed panels of local and foreign judges are becoming more common on courts of appeal. In Papua New Guinea, the extent of localisation means that foreign judges now sit on constitutional cases in smaller numbers and always with local judges, and sometimes not at all.[138] Amendments made to Samoa's Constitution in 2020 introduced a requirement that a bench of the Court of Appeal include only one 'overseas non-Samoan Court of Appeal judge'.[139] This amendment was introduced as part of a package of reforms to Samoa's judiciary that aimed to better reflect Samoan custom and values in the Constitution. It is the only attempt in the Pacific region to control, by law, the proportion of foreign and local judges on a court.[140]

Another way in which the knowledge of local judges is recognised arises when foreign judges defer to or expressly endorse the decisions of local judges. As a general rule in common law systems, judges in appeal cases will defer to courts below on issues of fact and evaluative judgment, on the basis that the primary decision maker has had the benefit of hearing the evidence first hand. In some cases, judges on Pacific courts have added the circumstances of foreign judging as a reason to respect the findings of a court below. One example is a decision of the Court of Appeal of Kiribati, constituted by a bench of two judges from New Zealand and one from Australia, concerning a dispute about land boundaries. The Court of Appeal upheld the decisions of two magistrates at first instance and of the Chief Justice, assisted by local magistrates, on appeal. In doing so, the Court of Appeal noted that 'it would be a rare case indeed where expatriate judges could reverse such concurrent findings, and this is manifestly not such a case'.[141] This approach reflects the 'double concurrence principle' developed by the Privy Council when considering appeals from India and other dominions, which held that the court would not depart from concurrent findings of fact from local courts below without strong grounds.[142]

[136] Interviews F1, F2, F7, F12, F20.

[137] Interviews F1, F7.

[138] Ch 2, section VI.

[139] *Constitution Amendment Act 2020* (Samoa), cl 4, inserting new s 74(1).

[140] Examples from outside the region include the Court of Final Appeal in Hong Kong, which permits only one overseas non-permanent judge on the bench of five (*Hong Kong Court of Final Appeal Ordinance 1995* c 484, s 16), and the Constitutional Court of Liechtenstein, which requires that a majority of judges on the bench be citizens (*Constitution of the Principality of Liechtenstein 1921*, s 105).

[141] *Temarewe v Tekautu* [2017] KICA 1. For similar sentiment, see also *Teonea v Pule o Kaupule of Nanumaga* [2009] TVCA 2 [34], Tompkins JA.

[142] *Devi v Roy* [1946] AC 508 [13]; Dixon and Jackson (n 8) 345–46.

In Samoa, the Court of Appeal, which until very recently was composed only of foreign judges, has given weight to local Samoan judges of the Supreme Court in cases on the sensitive issue of banishment. Banishment is a customary punishment in which village authorities order a person and his or her family to leave the village. In a series of cases, Samoan courts have considered whether banishment offends the constitutionally protected right to freedom of movement.[143] In *Taamale v Attorney-General*, the Court of Appeal, comprised of three judges from New Zealand, held that the power to order banishment, now exercised by the Land and Titles Court, was constitutional.[144] In its decision, the Court of Appeal extracted long quotations from the decision of Chief Justice Sapolu, a Samoan, in the Supreme Court below, which set out the role and function of banishment in Samoan society. The Court of Appeal agreed with the Chief Justice that banishment was a reasonable restriction on freedom of movement imposed by law in the interests of public order. The extensive quotation of Chief Justice Sapolu's findings and analysis assisted the Court of Appeal to speak with authority on the place of banishment in contemporary Samoan society and law, matters otherwise outside the three judges' direct knowledge and experience. It stands in contrast to the approach of former foreign judges, one of whom issued a unilateral practice direction that banishment was unconstitutional.[145]

The Court of Appeal in *Taamale* explicitly left open the prospect for future change, noting that 'like the Chief Justice, we by no means exclude the prospect that as … Samoan society continues to develop the time may come when banishment will no longer be justifiable'.[146] Ten years later, the Court of Appeal revisited the issue, this time to consider whether village councils themselves could order banishment. This time, Justice Va'ai, a Samoan judge of the Supreme Court, had decided that village councils did not have authority to order banishment, under either legislation or custom, leaving the power solely in the hands of the Land and Titles Court.[147] The Court of Appeal upheld that decision, stating:

> We agree with Va'ai J that to go further by holding that a village council also ha[s] the power [of banishment], would be 'tantamount to winding back the clock of progress'. And we are fortified in our ruling by noting that it is one of Samoa's own indigenous Supreme Court Judges who has said as such.[148]

The Samoan Court of Appeal has tended to take a cautious approach to constitutional adjudication, confining its role to the determination of legal issues and

[143] *Constitution of Samoa 1960*, s 13.
[144] *Taamale v Attorney-General* [1995] WSCA 1.
[145] M Meleisea, *The Making of Modern Samoa: Traditional Authority and Colonial Administration in the History of Western Samoa* (Suva, University of the South Pacific, 1995) 231.
[146] *Taamale v Attorney-General* [1995] WSCA 1.
[147] *Leituala v Mauga* [2004] WSSC 9.
[148] *Mauga v Leituala* (Samoa Court of Appeal, March 2005) extracted in Leulua'iali'i Tasi Malifa, 'Village Fono Act Reforms: Paper Presented at Samoa Law Society Biennial Law Symposium' *Samoa Observer* (Apia, Samoa) (20 December 2015). See also *Punitia v Tutuila* [2014] WSCA 1.

leaving policy changes, especially those affecting custom, to the legislature.[149] These cases fit that trend. However, they also show how the Court of Appeal used the findings of local judges to more confidently uphold developments in constitutional law as reflective of changing social attitudes. As members of the local community and as judges with legal qualifications and professional experience, local judges can serve to bridge the real or perceived distance between the law, as it is interpreted and applied by foreign judges, and the national community.

VI. CONCLUSION

Constitutional adjudication in the Pacific is characterised by three general features: first, the reliance on the common law to inform understandings of constitutional concepts and institutions; second, the limited integration of custom and constitutional law; and, third, a predominantly textualist approach to constitutional interpretation.

This chapter has shown how each of these characteristics is consistent with the extensive use of foreign judges on courts of constitutional jurisdiction in the region. Emphasising the common law foundations shared between foreign judges' home jurisdictions and the Pacific states in which they sit, serves to close the gap between foreign judges' expert knowledge of their home legal systems and more limited knowledge of Pacific legal systems. It minimises the significance of foreign judges' knowledge gap and maximises the significance of their knowledge reach into comparative foreign jurisdictions.

The minimal recourse to custom in constitutional adjudication also reflects the use of foreign judges. Foreign judges, particularly those drawn from outside the Pacific region, are unlikely to have close knowledge of customary rules and institutions and the values on which they are based. Without this knowledge, foreign judges are understandably reticent to directly draw upon custom in constitutional adjudication, or to make assumptions about its continuing influence in the community and in law. Recognising this, constitution makers and judges themselves have developed understandings of the constitution as separate from custom. The potential risk of this approach is that it gives rise to a mismatch between law and society, in which the values and norms of the law are different from those of the people.[150]

Finally, the predominantly textual approach to constitutional interpretation fosters an understanding of constitutional adjudication as a largely technical

[149] AH Angelo, '"Steady as She Goes": The Constitution and Court of Appeal of Samoa' (2012) 18 *New Zealand Association for Comparative Law Yearbook* 145. The implications of this approach for the representative function of the court are discussed in ch 7, section IV.

[150] BZ Tamanaha, 'Battle between Law and Society in Micronesia' in DJ Galligan and M Versteeg (eds), *Social and Political Foundations of Constitutions* (Cambridge, Cambridge University Press, 2013) 584, 585.

activity, in which the task of the judge is to interpret and apply the text of the constitution. This minimises the sense that judges might create new legal understandings by drawing on national aspirations, community values or social context – all of which are unlikely to be within the direct knowledge and experience of foreign judges. The strength of textualism can be seen in its persistence even in states where the text of the constitution expressly sets out principles and values to guide constitutional interpretation. An emphasis on the technicalities of constitutional interpretation also fosters a sense of the judge as an expert, proficient in legal skills and techniques that are transferable across national borders.

None of these features of constitutional adjudication is unique to courts composed of foreign judges. Courts in common law jurisdictions regularly refer to doctrines and precedents from other common law states. Many courts around the world adopt a form of textualism as the preferred method of constitutional interpretation. The use of these techniques by Pacific courts arises not only because the judges on those courts are outsiders, but also because foreign judges bring their knowledge of the law (as well as underlying assumptions about how to interpret it) from their home jurisdictions. These approaches are then reinforced through the operation of precedent and in legal education.

It is not the case that foreign judges consciously and consistently take a deliberately different approach to constitutional adjudication when they sit in the Pacific than they would if sitting in their home states. Only occasionally, when judges expressly situate themselves as foreign or expatriate judges or emphasise the views of a local judge, are there hints that judges themselves tailor their role around their foreignness. Regardless of whether the approaches traced here are a conscious strategy or a less deliberate trend, the use of foreign judges has had an effect on the contours of constitutional adjudication and the development of constitutional law in the Pacific.

6

Judicial Impartiality and Independence

I. INTRODUCTION

THE USE OF foreign judges raises distinctive issues for the impartiality and independence of Pacific judiciaries. Some of these issues arise as a consequence of attributes of foreignness, such as the claim that foreign judges, as outsiders, are impartial. Others stem from the practice of foreign judging in the Pacific, such as the appointment of foreign judges for short renewable terms. Some of these issues are unique to judiciaries that use foreign judges, while others resonate with issues encountered by judiciaries elsewhere.

The courts of Pacific states are often overlooked in global studies of judicial independence.[1] The conditions in which Pacific courts operate, including the circumstances of small island developing states, post-colonialism and the use of foreign judges, are rarely accounted for in the global standards on judicial independence developed over the last 35 years. This chapter begins, in section II, by developing an understanding of judicial impartiality and independence that accommodates the circumstances of Pacific island states. The use of foreign judges opens judiciaries up to a range of potential sources of influence beyond the government of the Pacific state in which the judges serve. It also highlights the ways in which the personal attributes of individual judges, including their nationality, interact with institutional and legal structures for judicial independence in the Pacific state and in judges' home states. An assessment of the implications of foreign judging in the Pacific therefore requires adapting global standards of impartiality and independence to the context of Pacific states.

Sections III and IV assess the effect that the use of foreign judges has on the impartiality and independence of Pacific judiciaries using the legal standards, guidelines for judicial conduct and principles identified and developed in section II. A common justification for the use of foreign judges is that they are, or are seen to be, more impartial than local judges. In section III, I contest the assumptions underlying this claim and argue that the impartiality of local judges is not compromised by their membership of the small Pacific communities they serve and that foreign judges, as a class, should not

[1] An exception is HP Lee and M Pittard (eds), *Asia-Pacific Judiciaries: Independence, Impartiality and Integrity* (Cambridge, Cambridge University Press, 2017), which includes chapters on Fiji and Vanuatu.

be considered more impartial than local judges by virtue only of their distance from the local community.

Section IV assesses how the use of foreign judges can affect the independence of Pacific judiciaries. It considers, first, whether the appointment of foreign judges for short renewable terms is justified, and whether the risks to judicial independence are ameliorated by mitigating factors such as the professional backgrounds of foreign judges and the independence of the authority responsible for renewing judicial appointments. Second, section IV examines the vulnerability of foreign judges to arbitrary removal from office. The appointment of judges for short renewable terms and the potential for arbitrary removal both pose a risk to judicial independence because they expose foreign judges to undue influence from the governments of Pacific states, as well as from external entities that recruit, fund or provide foreign judges.

The analysis in this chapter suggests that there has been a tendency to overstate the impartiality that foreign judges bring to Pacific judiciaries and understate the risks to judicial independence, with implications for policy and for perceptions of foreign judges in the region.

II. ASSESSING JUDICIAL IMPARTIALITY AND INDEPENDENCE

Theories of judicial impartiality and independence, and the ways in which these qualities are met in practice, are anchored in particular contexts and legal systems. This section defines judicial impartiality and independence, and outlines how these concepts ought to be understood in the context of Pacific states.

A. Components

Judicial impartiality and independence are overlapping but distinguishable concepts. Judicial impartiality requires that a judge is not biased towards a party or the outcome of the case before him or her. It is generally measured by reference to the conduct, attitudes and beliefs of individual judges in relation to a particular case before the court. Judicial independence refers to the relationship between the judiciary as an institution and other social and political actors. It seeks to ensure that judges are not subject to improper influences from social actors such as the media or lobby groups and, most significantly, from the political branches of government.

Judicial impartiality and independence can be measured by reference to institutional structures and judges' behaviour.[2] Institutional structures

[2] PH Russell, 'Toward a General Theory of Judicial Independence' in DM O'Brien and PH Russell (eds), *Judicial Independence in the Age of Democracy: Critical Perspectives from around the World* (Charlottesville, VA, University Press of Virginia, 2001) 6.

include the legal frameworks, court procedures and the formal conditions of judicial service that seek to insulate individual judges and the judiciary as a whole from improper influences. These frameworks relate to the methods for appointing and removing judges, the terms of judicial service, and the extent to which a judiciary controls its own budget, administration and procedures. In contrast, behavioural elements focus on the conduct of judges that demonstrates their impartiality and independence. It is measured by the personal qualities and actions of individual judges that show that they are in fact free from undue influence and capable of making impartial decisions.[3]

Structural and behavioural understandings of judicial impartiality and independence interact in particular ways for foreign judges. Foreignness is thought to bring with it particular behavioural qualities, including, most relevantly here, impartiality. In addition, weaknesses in the structural safeguards for judicial independence in Pacific states, such as the appointment of foreign judges for short renewable terms, are sometimes thought to be ameliorated by the strength of structural independence in foreign judges' home states. An analysis of the impartiality and independence of foreign judges must therefore encompass both structural and behavioural measures.

B. Purpose

Judicial impartiality and independence support three core attributes of judiciaries: the function of determining disputes according to law; the separation of powers; and public confidence in the courts.

The judge's position as an impartial and independent adjudicator is central to the 'logic' of courts: people will entrust courts to resolve their disputes only if they are assured that the judge is not partial to one party over the other and has no interest in the outcome of the case.[4] The independence of courts seeks to ensure that judges determine disputes based only on the law and the facts of the case, such that all people are treated equally before the law and the law is applied in a consistent way.

Judicial independence is also important to the separation of powers, which seeks to ensure that the branches of government – the legislature, executive and judiciary – do not abuse or exceed the constitutional limits of their powers. Courts of constitutional jurisdiction in all nine Pacific states have the power of

[3] RA MacDonald and H Kong, 'Judicial Independence as a Constitutional Virtue' in M Rosenfeld and A Sajó (eds), *The Oxford Handbook of Comparative Constitutional Law* (Oxford, Oxford University Press, 2012) 833. See also D Pimental, 'Reframing the Independence v Accountability Debate: Defining Judicial Structure in Light of Judges' Courage and Integrity' (2009) 57 *Cleveland State Law Review* 1.

[4] M Cappelletti, *The Judicial Process in Comparative Perspective* (Oxford, Clarendon Press, 1989) 31; MM Shapiro, *Courts: A Comparative and Political Analysis* (Chicago, IL, University of Chicago Press, 1981) 8.

judicial review, by which the court can declare legislation and executive actions invalid on the ground that they are inconsistent with the constitution. In order to perform this constitutional role effectively, the judiciary must have an appropriate degree of independence from the other branches of government. Without an independent arbiter, there is a risk that conflicts about constitutionality will be decided in accordance with the political inclinations of elected representatives, rather than in accordance with the constitution.[5]

Finally, judicial independence and impartiality are necessary to public confidence in the judiciary. People are unlikely to seek to resolve disputes, including constitutional disputes, through the court or accept a court's decision where they are concerned that the court will not give them a fair and impartial hearing. As such, judicial independence is a prerequisite for effective legal regulation. On this basis, judicial independence is sometimes also characterised as instrumental to the achievement of other outcomes. For example, the literature on rule of law development often characterises judicial independence as instrumental to the economic growth of developing states, because investors require confidence in the systems of legal regulation.[6]

C. Standards

While judicial impartiality and independence are universally recognised as important, there is no single, uniform standard by which to measure them. There are different views on the ends to which judicial impartiality and independence are directed and how those ends might be achieved.[7] In addition, judicial impartiality and independence are to be balanced against other values that serve the ends of the rule of law and separation of powers, including the need for consistency in adjudication and some form of judicial accountability. The rules and structures that support an impartial and independent judiciary vary across different constitutional systems, informed by the practical realities in which courts operate, including the size and wealth of the state, its history and understandings of the court's role in the constitutional system.[8]

The legal rules, institutional arrangements and conduct required to support judicial impartiality and independence can be derived from constitutional

[5] D Grimm, *Constitutionalism* (Oxford, Oxford University Press, 2016) ch 9, 220.

[6] KW Dam, *The Law-Growth Nexus: The Rule of Law and Economic Development* (Washington, DC, Brookings Institution Press, 2006) ch 5; IFI Shihata, *The World Bank in a Changing World* (Dordrecht, M Nijhoff Publishers, 1991).

[7] L Heuschling, 'Why Should Judges Be Independent? Reflections on Coke, Montesquieu and the French Tradition of Judicial Dependence' in KS Ziegler, D Baranger and AW Bradley (eds), *Constitutionalism and the Role of Parliaments* (Oxford, Hart Publishing, 2006) 220.

[8] A Allott, 'The Independence of the Judiciary in Commonwealth Countries: Problems and Provisions' (1994) 20(4) *Commonwealth Law Bulletin* 1428, 1431; D Smilov, 'The Judiciary: The Least Dangerous Branch?' in Rosenfeld and Sajó (eds) (n 3) 859, 860–62.

texts, the common law and scholarship. In an effort to identify universal minimum standards, several international associations have developed guidelines for judicial impartiality and independence. This section sets out the general standards before explaining how they ought to be adapted to the context of the Pacific states.

The written constitutions of each of the nine Pacific states reflect the values of judicial impartiality and independence. They all contain express guarantees that criminal matters, and sometimes also civil disputes, will be heard by an impartial and independent tribunal,[9] drawing on the right to a fair trial enshrined in international human rights instruments.[10] These constitutional guarantees emphasise the value of an impartial adjudicator for the fair resolution of disputes. In addition, two written constitutions expressly provide for the independence of the judiciary from other branches of government. The Constitution of Fiji states that 'all judicial officers are independent of the legislative and executive branches of government and subject only to the Constitution and the law'.[11] The Constitution of Papua New Guinea states that no person or authority, other than the Parliament through legislation, has power to give directions to the court in respect of the exercise of judicial powers or functions.[12] Even where the written constitution contains no express language of this kind, the independence of the judicial branch from the political branches is held to be 'an essential part' of constitutional government.[13]

The principles of judicial impartiality and independence enshrined in the constitutions are given greater content in international guidelines. Four such guidelines have particular relevance to the Pacific, two because of their global acceptance and two because they arose from regional or international processes that included Pacific states.

The *Basic Principles on the Independence of the Judiciary* were developed by United Nations bodies in the early 1980s.[14] They set out the duty of judges to decide cases impartially according to law, and proscribe improper interference in judicial decision-making by state and private entities. The principles themselves deal mainly with matters of structural independence, covering critical

[9] *Constitution of Fiji 2013*, s 15; *Constitution of Kiribati 1979*, s 10(1), (8); *Constitution of Nauru 1968*, s 10(2), (9); *Constitution of Papua New Guinea 1975*, ss 37(3), 59(2); *Constitution of Samoa 1960*, s 9(1); *Constitution of Solomon Islands 1978*, s 10(1); *Constitution of Tonga 1875*, s 15; *Constitution of Tuvalu 1986*, s 22(2), (11); *Constitution of Vanuatu 1980*, s 5(2).

[10] Universal Declaration of Human Rights (1948) art 10; International Covenant on Civil and Political Rights (1966) art 14. The exception is the *Constitution of Tonga 1875*, s 15, which requires that courts and judges be 'unbiased'.

[11] *Constitution of Fiji 2013*, s 97(2).

[12] *Constitution of Papua New Guinea 1975*, s 157.

[13] *Kenilorea v Attorney-General* [1984] SBCA 3.

[14] *Basic Principles on the Independence of the Judiciary*, adopted by the Seventh United Nations Congress on the Prevention of Crime and the Treatment of Offenders held at Milan from 26 August to 6 September 1985 and endorsed by General Assembly Resolutions 40/32 of 29 November 1985 and 40/146 of 13 December 1985.

aspects of the selection, appointment, discipline, remuneration, tenure and removal of judges. The *Basic Principles* have become a standard reference point for international and regional human rights bodies, and for those engaged in reviewing and reforming national judiciaries.

The *Bangalore Principles of Judicial Conduct* were developed in 2002 by an international group of judges.[15] In contrast to the *Basic Principles*, the *Bangalore Principles* emphasise behavioural independence. The document identifies six values of judicial conduct – independence, impartiality, integrity, propriety, equality, and competence and diligence – and sets out ways to support each. The *Bangalore Principles* were endorsed by the United Nations Economic and Social Council in 2006 as complementary to the *Basic Principles*.[16] They have been affirmed by nine Chief Justices in the Pacific region and have been used in several states as the basis for guidelines for judicial conduct.[17]

The *Latimer House Principles on the Accountability of and the Relationship between the Three Branches of Government* were adopted by Commonwealth heads of government, including each of the nine Pacific states, in 2003.[18] The *Latimer House Principles* and supplementary Guidelines define the roles of each of the three branches of government in Commonwealth countries. In doing so, they set out structural requirements to secure judicial independence, covering the appointment, tenure and removal of judges, the adequate resourcing of courts, and interactions between the parliament, executive and the judiciary.

The *Beijing Statement of Principles of the Independence of the Judiciary in the Law Asia Region* were adopted in 1997 and signed by 32 Chief Justices from the Asia-Pacific region, including Chief Justices of the nine Pacific states.[19] The *Beijing Statement* covers similar ground to the *Basic Principles*, but with some recognition of the different contexts in which judiciaries in the Asia-Pacific operate, acknowledging, for example, different approaches to appointing and removing judges.

These international documents do not prescribe institutional arrangements or rules for judges and judiciaries. Rather, they operate as checklists as to the kinds of issues that might affect the impartiality of judges and the independence of judiciaries. In this way they seek to accommodate the variety of ways in which states organise and regulate their judiciaries. However, the international standards have been informed predominantly by the laws and practices of select

[15] *Bangalore Principles of Judicial Conduct*, Judicial Group on Strengthening Judicial Integrity, The Hague, 25–26 November 2002.

[16] United Nations Economic and Social Committee, Resolution 2006/23 of 2006.

[17] Pacific Judicial Development Programme, *Toolkit for Review of Guidance on Judicial Conduct* (Federal Court of Australia and New Zealand Ministry of Foreign Affairs and Trade, 2014) 13.

[18] *Commonwealth (Latimer House) Principles on the Three Branches of Government*, agreed by Law Ministers and endorsed by the Commonwealth Heads of Government Meeting, Abuja, Nigeria, 2003 ('*Latimer House Principles*').

[19] *Beijing Statement of Principles of the Independence of the Judiciary in the LAWASIA Region*, 19 August 1995 ('*Beijing Statement*').

established national legal systems, with the result that they rest on assumptions that do not necessarily capture the circumstances of judiciaries in Pacific states and the phenomenon of foreign judging. Two examples illustrate the point.

First, international standards tend to assume that the greatest source of influence over the judiciary is the political branches of the state. This is likely to be the case in many countries, where the political branches select and appoint judges and are responsible for remunerating judges and the costs of maintaining the judicial system. While international guidelines acknowledge the possibility that litigants, media and others can influence judges, they are mostly directed at insulating judges and judiciaries from interference by the state's political branches. The political branches of Pacific governments, however, do not necessarily hold all of these levers of influence over foreign judges. As the findings in chapter 3 show, while the final decisions about judicial appointments rest with the relevant authority in the Pacific state, donor states and organisations have a role in the selection of foreign judges. Some foreign judges serving in the Pacific are paid not by the state but directly or indirectly by external organisations or subsidised by their home courts. Laws and policies in the judge's home state can affect foreign judges' abilities to travel, work and receive remuneration in Pacific states. While donor states and organisations take care to ensure that they respect both the independence of the judiciary and state sovereignty, their involvement in key areas of judicial administration means that they are also a potential source of influence over Pacific judiciaries.

A second example relates to the relationship between judges and the wider community. The *Bangalore Principles* state that 'a judge shall be independent in relation to society in general and in relation to the particular parties to a dispute which the judge has to adjudicate'.[20] Judges in the Pacific work in small, isolated communities where they have family and community connections to many people. Noting that international guidelines on judicial independence were not necessarily drafted with the distinctive circumstances of small island states in mind, the *Pacific Toolkit on Judicial Conduct* recognises that Pacific judiciaries might need to adapt the *Bangalore Principles* to suit the Pacific context.[21] For example, as discussed in section III, several Pacific jurisdictions, in developing their own guidelines on judicial conduct, have come to their own understandings of the appropriate distance to be maintained between judges and the community.

Although the need to adapt international standards and comparative models to the circumstances of small island states and the use of foreign judges has been acknowledged,[22] there is little guidance as to what these adaptations should involve. For example, the *Latimer House Principles* note that in

[20] *Bangalore Principles of Judicial Conduct* (n 15) art 1.2.
[21] Pacific Judicial Development Programme (n 17) 13.
[22] Allott (n 8) 1431–32.

small jurisdictions, the appointment of judges on fixed-term contracts may be 'inevitable'.[23] However, there is limited guidance on the justifications for such appointments, their duration and protections for tenure.[24] The phenomenon of foreign judging, although prevalent in the Commonwealth, is not explicitly addressed by the *Latimer House Principles*, nor in any other international guidelines.

Standards that serve to protect judicial impartiality and independence in one context may not be practical or appropriate in another. Rather than characterise departures from these standards as deficiencies in judicial impartiality and independence, this chapter considers whether the standards themselves might require adaptation to the context of Pacific states, before being applied to assess the practice of foreign judging. The chapter therefore examines points at which the practice of foreign judging, as it arises in the Pacific, poses a risk to judicial impartiality and independence or, alternatively, enhances it, by reference to its purpose in supporting the adjudication of disputes according to law, the separation of powers and public confidence.[25] This examination necessarily covers the interacting components of judicial impartiality and independence, in both their structural and behavioural aspects.

III. IMPARTIALITY

Chapter 4 outlined the significance of nationality to the role and functions of judges on courts of constitutional jurisdiction. It suggested that one reason why states might require their judges to be citizens is because of the value placed on their allegiance to the state. Not only do foreign judges lack ties of membership to the nation, but they also hold such ties to a foreign state. In some contexts, a discussion of foreign judges would question whether a foreign judge's allegiance to his or her home state *compromised* his or her impartiality. For example, concerns about the perception of bias due to the ties of nationality have led international courts and tribunals to develop a range of procedures to remove or counterbalance judges adjudicating cases that involve parties from their home state.[26] The issue of whether an international judge's allegiance to his or her home state constitutes an influence sufficient to compromise

[23] *Latimer House Principles* (n 18) pt II, para 1.

[24] J van Zyl Smit, *The Appointment, Tenure and Removal of Judges under Commonwealth Principles: A Compendium and Analysis of Best Practice* (London, Commonwealth Secretariat, 2015) [2.2.15] outlines some justifications for short renewable appointments for foreign judges, but places this issue outside the scope of the *Compendium*.

[25] Following the approach to assessing judicial independence advocated by J Ferejohn, 'Independent Judges, Dependent Judiciary: Explaining Judicial Independence' (1999) 72 *Southern California Law Review* 353, 370; CM Larkins, 'Judicial Independence and Democratization: A Theoretical and Conceptual Analysis' (1996) 44(4) *American Journal of Comparative Law* 605, 618; Russell (n 2) 12.

[26] Such as the appointment of an ad hoc judge by a state not otherwise represented on the bench.

impartiality is the subject of judicial decisions and scholarship.[27] Issues of this kind, however, rarely arise in relation to the use of foreign judges on Pacific courts, even where foreign judges hear cases affecting fellow nationals or the interests of their home state.[28] Instead, foreign judges are widely regarded as impartial because they are *not* members of the Pacific community they serve. In this, the emphasis is less on foreign judges as nationals of their home states, and more on foreign judges as *non-nationals* of the Pacific state.

A common argument in favour of using foreign judges is that they provide impartiality to Pacific judiciaries. As outsiders, foreign judges are distanced from the personal, political and professional connections that are regarded as inevitable in small communities.[29] In the Pacific, this argument is reinforced by cultural values of reciprocity and communal harmony, the hierarchical structure of some Pacific societies, and the extended kinship or 'wantok' ties embedded in community relations.[30] These social values are regarded by several external commentators,[31] as well as by some in Pacific communities,[32] as a burden on local judges' impartiality. Foreign judges, free from these social connections and cultural demands, are thought to provide greater impartiality and in turn support public confidence in the judiciary.[33] There has, however, been no empirical study

[27] T Dannenbaum, 'Nationality and the International Judge: The Nationalist Presumption Governing the International Judiciary and Why It Must Be Reversed' (2012) 45(1) *Cornell International Law Journal* 77; M Markovic, 'International Criminal Trials and the Disqualification of Judges on the Basis of Nationality' (2014) 13 *Washington University Global Studies Law Review* 1.

[28] While rare, such cases do arise: eg *Namah v Pato* [2016] PGSC 13, in which a five-member bench of the Papua New Guinea Supreme Court, including an Australian judge, was required to determine the constitutionality of arrangements made by the Australian and Papua New Guinean Governments for the detention of asylum seekers.

[29] D Schofield, 'Maintaining Judicial Independence in a Small Jurisdiction' in J Hatchard and P Slinn (eds), *Parliamentary Supremacy and Judicial Independence: A Commonwealth Approach* (London, Cavendish Publishing, 1999) 73, 73–74; W Veenendaal, *Politics and Democracy in Microstates* (Abingdon, Routledge, 2015) 187.

[30] Wantok (one-talk) means, broadly, a member of the same group, and indicates the reciprocal ties within and between tribal, filial or kinship groups: J Nonggorr, 'The Maintenance of Judicial Independence and Integrity in Papua New Guinea: Some Recent Developments' (1992) 18(3) *Commonwealth Law Bulletin* 1181, 1188.

[31] S Boyd, 'Australian Judges at Work Internationally: Treason, Assassinations, Coups, Legitimacy of Government, Human Rights, Poverty and Development' (2003) 77 *Australian Law Journal* 303, 306; K King, 'Order from the Court: Judiciaries as a Bulwark Against Legislative Corruption in Vanuatu' *The Global Anticorruption Blog* (18 December 2015); T Mellor and J Jabes, *Governance in the Pacific: Focus for Action, 2005–2009* (Manila, Asian Development Bank, 2004) 37; WFS Miles, *Bridging Mental Boundaries in a Postcolonial Microcosm: Identity and Development in Vanuatu* (Honolulu, University of Hawaii Press, 1998) 167–68.

[32] RL Kautoke, 'The Jury System in Tonga' (2009) 13(1) *Journal of South Pacific Law* 8, 18; JA Keniapisia, 'Judges from Other Commonwealth Jurisdictions Serving in the High Court and Court of Appeal of Solomon Islands', Paper presented at the 20th Commonwealth Law Conference, Melbourne (22 March 2017) 6; PF Sapolu et al, 'Law and Custom' in M Meleisea, P Schoeffel Meleisea and E Meleisea (eds), *Samoa's Journey 1962–2012: Aspects of History* (Wellington, Victoria University Press, 2012) 18, 25–26.

[33] This view was expressed by some judges interviewed (Interviews F3, F4, F7, F26) but refuted by others (Interviews F11, F23).

of whether local judges are in fact partial to particular groups or interests, and no social scientific studies that seek to gauge public opinion.

This book does not provide empirical data of this kind. Rather, I contest the claim that local judges lack impartiality by applying legal standards and guidelines of judicial conduct. I argue that the impartiality of local judges is not compromised by their membership of the small Pacific communities they serve, but is at issue only where judges have personal connections to the parties or a direct interest in the case. Where local judges meet the legal and ethical standards of impartiality, the assumption that foreign judges are, as a class, more impartial than local judges does not provide a principled rationale for the general use of foreign judges as a matter of course. Further, while it is a common claim, the idea that foreign judges bring an impartiality to adjudication that local judges lack, risks diminishing public confidence in local Pacific judges.

Judicial impartiality requires that a judge must not be biased towards or against a party or the outcome of the case. Two kinds of processes seek to ensure that judges are impartial. The first is the rule against bias, which requires that a judge who is, or might appear to be, biased in a particular case must not hear that case. There are various formulations of the legal test for bias across common law jurisdictions. The test is framed around whether the court, or alternatively a fair-minded and informed observer, having considered the facts, would conclude there is a danger or real possibility that the decision-maker was biased. Different versions of this test have been adopted in the law of Pacific states.[34] The second method for ensuring judicial impartiality focuses on the behaviour and integrity of judges. All judges take an oath of office in which they swear to impartially discharge their judicial duties and do right to all manner of people according to law, without fear or favour, affection or ill will.[35] Conventions of judicial conduct, which in some states have been set out in written guidelines,[36] seek to ensure that a judge's conduct, in court and outside it, maintains public confidence in the judge's impartiality and minimises the occasions on which it will be necessary for a judge to disqualify himself or herself.[37] These conventions restrain the ways in which a judge may associate with people in government and politics, publicly comment upon contentious matters, and engage in other employment or activities.

[34] *Koya v State* [1998] FJSC 2; *PNG Pipes Pty Ltd and Sankaran Venugopal v Mujo Sefa* [1998] PGSC 52; *Peniamina v Land and Titles Court* [2004] WSCA 1; *SMM Solomon Ltd v Axiom KB Ltd* [2017] SBCA 12; *Latu v Lavulavu* [2015] TOSC 46; *Matarave v Talivo* [2010] VUCA 3.

[35] *Constitution of Fiji 2013*, s 109; *Constitution of Kiribati 1979*, s 82; *Constitution of Nauru 1968*, s 52; *Constitution of Papua New Guinea 1975*, s 249; *Constitution of Samoa 1960*, s 67; *Constitution of Solomon Islands 1978*, s 141; *Constitution of Tonga 1875*, s 95; *Oaths and Statutory Declarations Act 1979* c 7.48 (Tuvalu), s 3; *Oaths Act 1964* c 37 (Vanuatu), s 4.

[36] Judicial Department of Fiji, *Judicial Code of Conduct* (2005); *Code of Conduct for Judicial Officers of the Republic of Kiribati* (2011); *Judicial Code of Conduct Rules 2010* (Tonga); *Code of Judicial Conduct for Tuvalu* (2011). See generally Pacific Judicial Development Programme (n 17).

[37] *Bangalore Principles of Judicial Conduct* (n 15) arts 2.2, 2.3.

The common law rules and guidance on judicial conduct do not seek to insulate judges from *all* influences but only certain kinds. Cultural or community ties that might cause a judge to identify with one party more than another may well give rise to a kind of partiality, but such ties are not considered to be grounds to challenge judicial impartiality in either the laws relating to disqualification for bias or guidelines on judicial conduct. The legal tests for bias narrow the grounds down to a direct and personal connection to a party or interest in the outcome of the case. In the English case of *Locabail v Bayfield Properties*, the High Court considered it *inconceivable* that an objection to a judge could be based on the judge's community ties, expressed in the form of religion, ethnic or national origin, gender, age or class; and *unlikely* based on the judge's social, educational or professional background.[38]

The legal tests of bias reflect the nature of the judge's role.[39] Court procedures and the methodologies of judicial reasoning encourage judges to set aside irrelevant biases and decide cases only on the relevant law and facts. On this view, membership of a community is irrelevant to the task of judging and will be put aside by all judges. Those critical of the possibility of such objectivity might reframe a judge's identity and life experience as an asset to the judicial role. On this view, judges necessarily bring their own values to bear on judicial decision making, particularly when called upon to apply community standards (such as reasonableness or fairness) and when developing the law through interpretation. On this view, the appropriate response is not to seek to suppress such influences but to ensure that judges understand and reflect the diversity of community values.[40] There are also policy reasons why the law of bias and judicial guidelines do not characterise community ties as prohibited impartiality. The necessity for there to be a judge requires that judges should not be disqualified for reason of their race, ethnicity, religion or cultural affiliations. Every judge has these attributes, and the claim that a judge might be partial to a party who shares those attributes would serve to disqualify most judges from most cases.[41]

For these reasons, there is no principled basis on which to claim that the impartiality of local Pacific judges, as a class, is compromised in all cases by virtue of membership of their own Pacific communities. If the impartiality of local judges is not at issue then the use of foreign judges on the basis that they provide an impartiality that is otherwise lacking is difficult, without more, to justify. The claim also does not reflect the practice of foreign judging in the Pacific. The judges most likely to have personal connections to parties or a direct interest in the case are the lay judges and magistrates serving on lower courts,

[38] *Locabail (UK) Ltd v Bayfield Properties Ltd* [2000] QB 451, 480.

[39] J Leubsdorf, 'Theories of Judging and Judge Disqualification' (1987) 62 *New York University Law Review* 237, 237.

[40] T Etherton, 'Liberty, the Archetype and Diversity: A Philosophy of Judging' [2010] *Public Law* 727, 740; E Rackley, *Women, Judging and the Judiciary: From Difference to Diversity* (Abingdon, Routledge, 2013) 28, 131.

[41] Leubsdorf (n 39) 241.

who are members of the small communities they serve. However, foreign judges serve mainly on higher national courts, which are already at a greater distance from the local community.[42]

In the Pacific states, it is well established that where a judge has a close family or other connection to a party or an interest in the outcome, the judge should not sit on that case. Local and foreign judges will recuse themselves in appropriate circumstances and failure to recuse is a ground for appeal.[43] However, the appropriate circumstances for recusal in small island communities are sometimes different from those in larger jurisdictions. Some Pacific states have expressly adapted the requirements of recusal and guidelines for judicial conduct to meet the practical realities of being a judge in the Pacific. The *Code of Conduct for Judicial Officers of Kiribati* states:

> Kiribati is a small country and the island jurisdictions are very small. If Judicial Officers were to disqualify themselves in every case where they know one or other participant, the hearing of minor matters might be considerably delayed. Undue delay can, in itself, constitute a denial of justice. Therefore, the interest of justice requires that Judicial Officers are careful not to disqualify themselves too readily. Inevitably Judicial Officers will hear cases where they know something of the parties. In every case it should be clear to all observers that the trial is conducted fairly. The Judicial Officers should explain their decision clearly giving their full reasoning. The reasons should leave no doubt that the decision was based on the law as applied only to those facts established by evidence in open court.[44]

The *Niue Code of Judicial Conduct* suggests that people in small island communities understand better than most the separation of the person from the office, noting that 'the Niuean people are used to the idea that individuals may "wear a number of different hats" and the judges must make it clear from the way they conduct themselves, that with the judicial hat comes impartiality'.[45]

These guidelines emphasise impartiality as a personal and professional quality, rather than as something to be guaranteed only through legal rules and institutional structures. They suggest that the challenges of impartial judging in small jurisdictions are addressed most effectively by the behaviour of individual judges. Indeed, the integrity of senior local judges has gone a long way to secure the reputations of the judiciary in Papua New Guinea and Vanuatu.[46] This has been achieved in different ways, including strategies

[42] Interview F23.

[43] P MacFarlane, 'Some Challenges Facing Legal Strengthening Projects in Small Pacific Island States' (2006) 4(1) *Journal of Commonwealth Law and Legal Education* 103, 106.

[44] *Code of Conduct for Judicial Officers of the Republic of Kiribati* (2011), art 2.6. *The Code of Judicial Conduct for Tuvalu* (2011), art 2 is in similar terms.

[45] *Code of Judicial Conduct for Niue* (2011), extracted in Pacific Judicial Development Programme (n 17), Additional Documents A-18. While Niue is not one of the nine Pacific states compared in this book, it shares with them the challenges of smallness.

[46] In Papua New Guinea: Nonggorr (n 30) 1187; in Vanuatu: M Forsyth, 'Understanding Judicial Independence in Vanuatu', *Discussion Paper 2015/9, State, Society and Governance in Melanesia* (Australian National University, 2015) 10–12.

of social isolation to avoid conflicts of interest, and the professionalism of judges as demonstrated through transparent and consistent judicial decision making.[47]

It is not only misleading to justify the use of foreign judges on the basis that they provide an impartiality that is otherwise lacking, it is also potentially damaging, as it diminishes the reputation of, and public confidence in, local judges. The story of localisation in Samoa illustrates the point. Following independence in 1962, there was 'continuing public uncertainty as to whether Samoans would be able to resist pressure from their families and apply the law impartially'.[48] The appointment of Samoans to a presidential position in the Land and Titles Court and the magistracy in 1966 succeeded in 'breaking through public attitudes to Samoan judges'.[49] The perception of local judges has changed with localisation. In 2018, the Supreme Court of Samoa refused a request from the Attorney-General for a foreign judge to be appointed to hear a criminal case involving a judge of the Land and Titles Court. Chief Justice Sapolu stated that '[i]t would be taking a retrograde step for Samoa if we are to engage an overseas Judge because all the local Judges are said to be disqualified from hearing a case on the ground of apparent or perceived bias'. It would be 'an unnecessary surrender of our judicial sovereignty to an outsider when we have our own Judges to deal with these cases'.[50]

The potential for an individual judge to be, or appear to be, biased in a particular case should not be given wide and general application to all local judges. Claims about the impartiality provided by foreign judges should be narrowed down to better reflect the legal rule against bias and the challenges of smallness. In a small community it is likely that a local judge will encounter situations in which he or she has a direct and personal connection with parties in the case, by way of family relationships, close friendships or business connections, or a personal interest in the outcome. This, combined with limited numbers of judges, means that a foreign judge might need to be recruited to hear a specific case or class of cases. Pacific judiciaries have occasionally sought foreign judges on this basis. For example, in 2006 two Australian judges were appointed to the Supreme Court of Samoa to hear election petitions over a three-month period. This arrangement was made at the request of the Chief Justice, who was concerned that as many of Samoa's senior judges had family or social connections with election candidates, perceived conflicts of interest might arise.[51] In Vanuatu, a judge from New Zealand was appointed to hear a

[47] G Donne, 'Introduction' in G Powles and M Pulea (eds), *Pacific Courts and Legal Systems* (Suva and Clayton, University of the South Pacific and Monash University, 1988) 3, 4–5; Forsyth (n 46) 11; Schofield (n 29) 79; Veenendaal (n 29) 188–9.

[48] Sapolu et al (n 32) 25.

[49] ibid 26.

[50] *Police v Ropati* [2018] WSSC 85, [11].

[51] Supreme Court of Tasmania, *Report of the Chief Justice of the Supreme Court of Tasmania: Annual Report 2005–2006* (2006) 11.

defamation case brought by a former magistrate against the Chief Justice and Chief Magistrate.[52] In Kiribati, Chief Justice Millhouse, an Australian citizen, disqualified himself from hearing an electoral petition on the basis that he had prior knowledge of the parties and witnesses, and an acting judge from Australia was appointed to hear the case.[53] These examples have parallels with practices in larger states. For example in Australia, instead of recruiting foreign judges, judges from other State and Territory jurisdictions have been appointed on a temporary basis to hear cases to which local judges are, or would appear to be, too closely connected.[54]

Foreign judges therefore support the impartiality of Pacific judiciaries where they stand in for judges who must recuse themselves from hearing a particular case or cases, in circumstances where an alternative local judge is unavailable. Putting the argument for foreign judges' impartiality on this more precise basis better reflects the legal requirements of impartiality and the realities of judging in Pacific states.

IV. INDEPENDENCE

Chapter 3 outlined the processes for the appointment, remuneration, tenure and removal of foreign judges in the Pacific. International guidelines tend to focus on these processes as objective conditions of judicial independence.[55] However, these guidelines require adaptation to meet the needs of Pacific island states and the practicalities of foreign judging. This section considers each of these aspects of judicial service by focusing on the two issues of greatest concern for judicial independence, that is, the insecurity of tenure arising from the appointment of foreign judges for short renewable terms and the vulnerability of foreign judges to arbitrary removal from office.

A. Short Renewable Appointments

Many foreign judges serve on Pacific courts on short renewable appointments. In some states, the law requires that foreign judges may only be appointed for a specified maximum term. Other states permit flexible arrangements, which allow the appointing body to determine the duration of a judge's appointment on an ad hoc basis. As discussed in chapter 3, the duration of short-term appointments varies across Pacific states, and courts within them, but ranges from a period of

[52] *Waltersai Ahelmhalahlah v Vanuatu* [2018] VUSC 24.

[53] *Tatireta v Tong* [2003] KIHC 1.

[54] R French, 'Judicial Exchange: Debalkanising the Courts' (2006) 15 *Journal of Judicial Administration* 142.

[55] *Basic Principles on the Independence of the Judiciary* (n 14); *Latimer House Principles* (n 18); *Beijing Statement* (n 19).

weeks or months to one to five years. There are no legal or procedural limits on the renewal of judges' appointments. While some foreign judges are appointed until retirement or for no specified term, this occurs as a result of the exercise of discretion by the appointing authority, rather than because it is mandated by law. Even where constitutions provide for all judges to serve until a specified age of retirement, Pacific states may avoid this requirement by appointing foreign judges as acting judges.

International principles on judicial independence generally insist on tenure – whether for life, for a fixed term, or until the judge reaches retirement age – that is secure against executive interference.[56] It is the *renewability* of appointments that poses a risk to judicial independence. It raises the concern that judges will be influenced to decide cases in the interests of those responsible for renewing their appointment, rather than independently on the law and facts of each case. For foreign judges in the Pacific, those responsible for renewal might include the executive government, members of the judicial services commission, the Chief Justice or external organisations that fund the judge's position.

A study of judicial decisions in Namibia, where foreign judges are also appointed for short renewable terms, found that foreign judges were slightly more likely to decide in favour of the Government.[57] Although there has been no similar empirical study of Pacific courts, there are concerns that short-term appointments provide an avenue for the executive and others to exert pressure on foreign judges.[58] Several judges interviewed for this study provided examples of judges who made decisions unfavourable to the government and did not have their contracts renewed.[59] Instances of this kind have been reported in Fiji,[60] Nauru[61] and Tonga,[62] although any malpractice was denied by the respective governments. There are, however, examples where foreign judges' appointments have been renewed, despite the unpopularity of their past decisions.[63]

[56] *Latimer House Principles* (n 18) II(1); *Beijing Statement* (n 19) art 20; International Bar Association, *Minimum Standards of Judicial Independence* (New Delhi, 22 October 1982) art 22. Cf *Basic Principles on the Independence of the Judiciary* (n 14) art 12, which provides for guaranteed tenure until judges' retirement age or the expiry of their term of office. See also *Valente v R* [1985] SCR 673 [31].

[57] P VonDoepp, 'Context-Sensitive Inquiry in Comparative Judicial Research: Lessons from the Namibian Judiciary' (2008) 41(11) *Comparative Political Studies* 1515.

[58] CB Ingram, 'The Length of Terms of Judges in the Pacific and Its Impact on Judicial Independence' in *Land Law and Judicial Governance in the South Pacific: Comparative Studies* (Wellington, New Zealand Association for Comparative Law, 2011) 375, 377; G Powles, 'Law, Courts and Legal Services in Pacific Societies' in Powles and Pulea (eds) (n 47) 6, 27; B Robertson, 'Judicial Independence in the Pacific' in *Land Law and Judicial Governance in the South Pacific: Comparative Studies* (Wellington, New Zealand Association for Comparative Law, 2011) 267, 272.

[59] Interviews F1, F8, F20, F25.

[60] J Pratihba, 'Judiciary Independent: Chief Justice' *Fiji Sun* (Suva) (28 August 2018).

[61] 'Nauru Magistrate Departs after Contract Non Renewed' *Radio New Zealand* (Wellington) (12 December 2016).

[62] 'The Political Scene: More Supreme Court Judges Resign' *The Economist Intelligence Unit* (London) (1 October 2010).

[63] Kautoke (n 32) 18.

There is also a risk that the extensive use of short renewable appointments creates a perception that the government is filling the judiciary with compliant judges, impairing public confidence in judicial independence. In an early decision, a judge of the Papua New Guinea Supreme Court considered that public criticisms of the Court by the Minister for Justice amounted to a contemptuous attempt to influence the court because, amongst other factors, they occurred in a context in which judges are appointed for short terms.[64] In Fiji, the appointment of large numbers of foreign judges on short renewable terms has been criticised as a means by which a strong executive can create a 'compliant judiciary'.[65] Similar concerns have been raised in some African countries that also use foreign judges.[66]

The appointment of judges for short renewable terms clearly poses a risk to judicial independence. In some countries outside the Pacific, short renewable appointments have been found to be incompatible with judicial independence,[67] while in others they have been upheld.[68] Much depends on the context in which renewable appointments are used, including the extent of the practice, the reasons for their use and mitigating factors such as the kinds of persons appointed and the independence of the authority responsible for renewing judicial appointments. The following sections consider each of these factors in order to assess the effect that the appointment of foreign judges for short renewable terms has on judicial independence in Pacific states.

i. Reasons for Short Renewable Appointments

The appointment of foreign judges for short renewable terms has become accepted practice in the Pacific. It resonates with earlier colonial practices. The judges appointed to colonial courts were employees of the Colonial Legal Service and generally served on a court for a short period before being transferred

[64] *Public Prosecutor v Rooney (No 2)* [1979] PNGLR 448, 497, Wilson J; cf ibid 488, Kearney J. For discussion of the Rooney affair, see ch 7, section V.A.

[65] BV Lal, *Historical Dictionary of Fiji* (Lanham, MD, Rowman & Littlefield, 2016) 24. See also V Iyer, 'The Judiciary in Fiji: A Broken Reed?' in Lee and Pittard (eds) (n 1) 109, 115. In *Fiji v Citizens' Constitutional Forum Limited* [2013] FJHC 220, the High Court of Fiji held that the statement that 'the independence of the judiciary cannot be relied on' was in contempt of court. In rejecting a defence of honest and fair comment or justification, the court noted, among other issues, that fixed renewable appointments have long featured in Fiji as well as Australia: ibid [85].

[66] M Mutua, 'Justice under Siege: The Rule of Law and Judicial Subservience in Kenya' (2001) 23(1) *Human Rights Quarterly* 96; International Bar Association, *Under Pressure: A Report on the Rule of Law in The Gambia* (August 2006).

[67] *Justice Alliance of South Africa v President* 2011 (5) SA 388; *Decision regarding the appeal of Judge Ivo Rosa against the non-renewal of his Contract by the Superior Council for the Judiciary* (Timor Leste Court of Appeal, 31 December 2008).

[68] *Bar Association of Belize v Attorney-General* [2017] CCJ 4 (AJ), *Attorney-General v Bar Association of Belize* (Belize Court of Appeal, 14 October 2015); *President v National Amalgamated Local Central Government and Parastatal Workers Union* (Botswana Court of Appeal, June 2017).

across jurisdictions.[69] They were appointed 'at pleasure', but by convention would not be removed except in the event of proven misconduct.[70]

The *Latimer House Principles* state that the circumstances of small jurisdictions may make the appointment of judges on short-term contracts 'inevitable',[71] an assertion that has been cited in case law in the Pacific and other Commonwealth countries.[72] Some authors characterise short renewable appointments as a 'necessary evil' in small jurisdictions,[73] where 'for reasons of size and geography' there is 'no alternative but to seek judges prepared to serve … for a fixed term of years'.[74] However, it is not always made clear *why* short-term appointments are necessary or inevitable in all circumstances in which foreign judges are used in small jurisdictions.

Several explanations have been offered. A Commonwealth-wide study suggested that fixed-term appointments are more attractive to individual judges willing to serve on a part-time and non-residential basis, but this claim was not supported by empirical evidence.[75] The information collected in interviews suggests that individual judges hold a range of views but generally defer to the terms proposed by the appointing authority and, where relevant, external funders.[76] The evidence in the Pacific suggests that short-term appointments reflect the preferences of states and external donor organisations, rather than those of judges themselves.

One significant reason for the appointment of foreign judges on short renewable terms is the financial constraints on many small states. In small states, the institutions and functions of government are particularly expensive on a per capita basis.[77] The appointment of judges for long terms imposes significant costs on states, particularly where there is uncertainty about whether the need for that judicial position will be sustained over time. Short appointments can be used flexibly to meet demand. In addition, small developing states rely on foreign aid, including to support the institutions of law and justice. External donors recruit foreign judges on a contractual basis, usually for terms of one to two years, after which the funding arrangement, and with it the judge's appointment, is reconsidered. While valid, these financial constraints really only

[69] Allott (n 8) 1431.

[70] C Jeffries, *The Colonial Empire and Its Civil Service* (Cambridge, The University Press, 1938) 147–48.

[71] *Latimer House Principles* (n 18) II(1).

[72] eg *Tu'ifua v Public Service Tribunal* [2014] TOSC 14, [19]; *Bar Association of Belize v Attorney-General* [2017] CCJ 4 (AJ), [52].

[73] Schofield (n 29) 76. See also Y Vyas, 'The Independence of the Judiciary: A Third World Perspective' (1992) 11 *Third World Legal Studies* 127, 144.

[74] Zyl Smit (n 24) [2.2.15].

[75] ibid. See also Territory of Nauru, 'Record of the Proceedings of the Constitutional Convention' (15 January 1968) 59.

[76] Ch 3, section IV.

[77] L Briguglio, 'Small Island Developing States and Their Economic Vulnerabilities' (1995) 23 *World Development* 1615, 1617.

apply to the appointment of full-time, resident judges. Visiting judges on courts of appeal, whatever the term of their appointment, sit only when invited to constitute a panel of the court. They do not draw a fixed salary or pension but instead receive a daily sitting fee. As a result, in some Pacific states foreign judges of appeal are appointed without any specified term, or for significantly longer periods than foreign judges appointed to the courts below.[78]

Other reasons for short-term appointments are pragmatically orientated to the perceived realities of foreign judging. One author suggests that Pacific states prefer to appoint retired judges on a short-term basis due to concerns over their age and potential healthcare needs.[79] Short-term appointments are sometimes seen as a way to redress shortcomings in the recruitment process, by providing an opportunity for both the judge and the appointing authority to assess whether the judge is suited to local conditions.[80] These justifications point to problems that are better met by other processes that avoid burdening judicial independence. Concerns about a judge's suitability for appointment are more appropriately addressed through the appointment process, while concerns about a judge's healthcare needs can be addressed through specific contractual arrangements.

A compendium of best practices for the appointment, tenure and removal of judges across the Commonwealth notes that it is 'difficult to justify the appointment of judges for a fixed period of years to serve alongside judges holding permanent appointments in the same courts'.[81] This, however, is commonly the case in the Pacific, where foreign judges (who are usually appointed for short terms) sit alongside local judges (who are usually appointed until a specified retirement age).[82] There is, however, a principled justification for the different treatment of foreign judges and citizen judges. Where the use of foreign judges is understood as a transitional measure pending localisation, the appointment of foreign judges on short terms means that there will be a judicial position readily available when a qualified citizen becomes eligible for appointment.[83] The appointment of a judge (foreign or local) for a short term is also justified where the appointment seeks to address a temporary shortage of judges, for example because a permanent judge is conflicted out of hearing particular cases (as discussed in section III) or to address a backlog of cases.

This analysis suggests that the most compelling justifications for the appointment of foreign judges for short renewable terms relate, first, to the recruitment

[78] This is the case for the Courts of Appeal of Samoa and Tuvalu, for example.

[79] Ingram (n 58) 376.

[80] ibid; Schofield (n 29) 77; P Reeves, TR Vakatora and BV Lal, 'The Fiji Islands: Towards a United Future Report of the Fiji Constitution Review Commission' (Fiji, Parliamentary Paper No 34 of 1996) [13.108].

[81] Zyl Smit (n 24) [2.2.16].

[82] Ch 3, section IV.

[83] Schofield (n 29) 76; Constitutional Planning Committee Papua New Guinea, *Final Report of the Constitutional Planning Committee* (1974) ch 8, [90].

of foreign judges to sit as acting judges where permanent judges are not available; and, second, to localisation, to ensure that there is space on the bench for suitably qualified local candidates. These justifications fit with the predominant rationale for the use of foreign judges in Pacific states, in which foreign judges are used because there are insufficient numbers of qualified citizens willing and able to take up judicial office. These two justifications provide a principled basis for assessing whether a short-term appointment is indeed appropriate. For example, in circumstances where localisation is slow or unlikely, there is less justification for appointing a foreign judge for a short term, and consideration ought to be given to longer-term appointments. Where these justifications do not apply, there is a risk that the appointment of foreign judges for short renewable terms compromises judicial independence.

ii. The Relevance of Professional Background

It may be argued that the risk of undue influence associated with short renewable appointments does not arise as sharply for some categories of foreign judge. Foreign judges who are sitting judges in their own state or retired judges with a judicial pension are less dependent on reappointment to the Pacific court for personal financial or career security.[84] As such, they are considered to be relatively immune to the implied threat to independence that arises from short renewable appointments.[85] Assumptions of this kind underlie some of the case law in other Commonwealth countries. In *Bolkiah v Brunei Darussalam*, the Judicial Committee of the Privy Council considered whether the fact that a foreign judge was appointed on a short-term contract renewable at the discretion of the Sultan of Brunei created a perception of bias. In holding that it did not, the Privy Council emphasised the position and reputation of the judge in question, noting that he was 'a judge of unblemished reputation, nearing the end of a long and distinguished judicial career in more than one jurisdiction, … and already enjoying what he described as "reasonably adequate" pension provision'.[86] The Privy Council considered that a fair-minded observer would 'dismiss as fanciful the notion that such a judge would break his judicial oath and jeopardise his reputation in order to curry favour with the Sultan and secure a relatively brief extension to his contract'.[87]

[84] JM Van Dyke, 'The Pacific Judicial Conference: Strengthening the Independent Judiciary and the Rule of Law in the Pacific' (2011) 22(1–2) *Western Legal History* 127, 161.

[85] G Appleby et al, *Temporary Judicial Officers in Australia: A Report Commissioned by the Judicial Conference of Australia* (2017) 28; PH Russell and K Malleson, 'Introduction' in PH Russell and K Malleson (eds), *Appointing Judges in an Age of Judicial Power: Critical Perspectives from around the World* (Toronto, University of Toronto Press, 2006) 5.

[86] *Bolkiah v Brunei Darussalam* [2007] UKPC 62 [21].

[87] ibid. See also *Misick v The Queen (Turks and Caicos)* [2015] UKPC 31, [27]–[28]; *Bar Association of Belize v Attorney-General* [2017] CCJ 4 (AJ), [39].

Arguments of this kind place faith in the integrity of individual foreign judges and the institutional safeguards for structural judicial independence in their home countries (such as a guaranteed judicial pension), rather than the constitutional structures in the jurisdictions in which foreign judges serve. Some Pacific states, as a matter of practice, recruit only persons with judicial experience in their home states to be foreign judges. In Kiribati, Samoa and Vanuatu this is the case for both the superior trial court and court of appeal; and in Solomon Islands, Tonga and Tuvalu for courts of appeal. However, not all foreign judges serving on Pacific courts are sitting or retired judges. Over the period from 2000 to the end of 2019, roughly a third of the foreign judges serving in the Pacific were recruited from the legal profession or public service in their home state or abroad.[88] For these individuals, judicial appointment in the Pacific might be a promotion, bringing better pay, prestige and conditions, such that they are in a position where they may be influenced by the prospect of the renewal of their appointment. Further, as Iyer notes in his assessment of the Fijian judiciary, foreign judges in Fiji have proved just as prone as their local counterparts to factionalism in the wake of constitutional crisis.[89] While the status and reputation of individual foreign judges can be relevant, it should not be assumed to apply across the board so as to compensate for the weaknesses in structural judicial independence arising from short renewable appointments.

iii. The Nature of the Appointing Authority

Finally, concerns about undue influence over the renewal of judicial appointments might be addressed by ensuring that renewal is in the hands of a body independent of the executive.[90]

In some states, there may be concerns about cronyism or favouritism on the part of the executive appointing body when it comes to making judicial appointments,[91] raising concerns about the extent to which judges are independent from the government. In some such states, the use of foreign judges is seen as a way to address such concerns. However, it is important to distinguish between arrangements in the Pacific states and elsewhere. For example, it has been suggested that the judges of the Eastern Caribbean Supreme Court are perceived to be free from domestic political influence because they are appointed by a regional body, rather than by national political elites.[92] Similar arguments

[88] Ch 2, section V.B.

[89] Iyer (n 65) 130. See also R Naidu, 'Coup and Crisis: Comments on the Fiji Experience', Paper presented at the 20th Annual Conference of the Australian Institute of Judicial Administration, Brisbane (13 July 2002).

[90] *Bar Association of Belize v Attorney-General* [2017] CCJ 4 (AJ), [34]–[35], [53]; *Misick v The Queen (Turks and Caicos)* [2015] UKPC 31 [24].

[91] Briguglio (n 77) 1617; Ingram (n 58) 377.

[92] Veenendaal (n 29) 120.

are made in support of the independence of the Judicial Committee of the Privy Council, which is composed of judges appointed by a foreign government.[93] In these circumstances, the processes for the appointment of foreign judges are removed from the hands of domestic political actors and placed in a regional or foreign body.

Pacific states follow a different model, in which responsibility for the appointment of foreign judges rests with the state concerned. Even where foreign judges are recruited by external organisations or their home courts, the final decision is made by the relevant authority in the Pacific state. As a result, no more than local judges can foreign judges avoid the risks associated with an executive-controlled appointment process. As described in chapter 3, Pacific states vest the power of judicial appointment in the head of state acting on the advice of government or a judicial services commission. The use of judicial services commissions is one way in which Pacific states seek to ensure the integrity of the processes for the appointment of local and foreign judges alike.

The smallness of Pacific legal communities creates conditions in which judges deal directly with those responsible for renewing their appointments. This opens up a range of potential avenues for influence or the appearance of it. A case from the Supreme Court of Tonga, in which a litigant sought to prevent the Lord Chancellor from appearing as a barrister for the opposing party, illustrates the point. The litigant argued that because the Lord Chancellor was the chair of the Judicial Appointments and Discipline Panel (JADP) and involved in decisions about the appointment, remuneration and discipline of judges, there was a risk that the judge might favour, or be seen to favour, the party represented by the Lord Chancellor.[94] In his judgment, the Chief Justice noted that other officials involved in the administration of the judiciary, including the Attorney-General, the Minister for Justice and a Law Lord who was also a member of the JADP, regularly appeared as legal representatives before the Court. He dismissed the concerns for impartiality as having little regard to the realities of legal practice in Tonga.[95] The case shows that it should not be assumed that the executive is the only source of potential influence over reappointment and that, in small states, other appointing authorities might also be directly involved in litigation before the court. When foreign judges are funded by organisations outside the state, donors may also have a role in the renewal of a foreign judge's appointment. On one hand, diversity of influences might work to protect independence by ensuring that no one source of influence can prevail. On the other hand, it might also serve to obscure sources of influences beyond the executive, which is the usual focus of attention.

[93] S Voigt, M Ebeling and L Blume, 'Improving Credibility by Delegating Judicial Competence: The Case of the Judicial Committee of the Privy Council' (2007) 82(2) *Journal of Development Economics* 348, 350.

[94] *Tu'ifua v Public Service Tribunal* [2014] TOSC 14.

[95] ibid [21]–[23].

iv. Addressing the Risk to Judicial Independence

This discussion suggests that the appointment of foreign judges on short renewable terms does not in itself necessarily undermine the independence of Pacific judiciaries, but there are circumstances in which it might combine with other dimensions of foreign judging to do so. One such circumstance is where there is limited localisation such that most, if not all, judges serve on short renewable terms. The appointment of a few foreign judges on a temporary basis to supplement judges with longer tenure does not raise the same concerns about independence as a judiciary composed predominantly or entirely of judges on short renewable appointments. Concerns for independence might also arise where judicial service in the Pacific supports the judge's career progression and provides greater pay and benefits than opportunities in the judge's home state, increasing the sense in which a foreign judge is dependent on reappointment. Finally, judicial independence might be compromised where executives or other appointing authorities have demonstrated that they will not renew the appointments of judges who make decisions that are perceived to be against their interests.

Chapter 8 sets out some good practice initiatives to support the legitimacy and effectiveness of foreign judging in the Pacific, including a range of solutions to prevent the use of short renewable appointments compromising the independence of Pacific judiciaries. Not all such measures would be necessary or suitable in each Pacific state or for all instances of foreign judging. In light of the widespread and almost automatic use of short renewable appointments in the Pacific, I suggest that the most significant reform would consist of a general requirement that states that use foreign judges, and the organisations that provide and fund them, confine the use of short renewable appointments to circumstances in which they can be justified. These are the appointment of acting judges to meet a temporary need and to support localisation. Confining short-term renewable appointments to these circumstances would require states, donor organisations and judges themselves to more carefully consider and justify short-term appointments. It would reduce the number and proportion of foreign judges serving for short renewable terms and minimise the risks that it poses to the independence of the judiciary as a whole.

B. Arbitrary Removal

Foreign judges are susceptible to removal by means other than the formal constitutional process. The formal removal processes advocated by international guidelines ensure that judges are subject to removal only for reasons of incapacity or misbehaviour, and that procedures for removal are fair and set out in law.[96] They seek to protect judges from arbitrary removal and the improper

[96] *Basic Principles on the Independence of the Judiciary* (n 14) arts 17–20; *Latimer House Principles* (n 18) art VI 1(a); *Beijing Statement* (n 19) arts 22–26.

influence that the threat of arbitrary removal entails. Pacific constitutions establish formal procedures for the removal of judges. They are rarely used, however. Instead, states and other actors have used means outside the formal processes to remove foreign judges, including non-renewal or termination of a judge's contract, the cessation of invitations to visit to sit on the court of appeal, and the cancellation of a foreign judge's visa.[97] Unlike the formal procedures for removal, these processes are not transparent. No reasons are required, and as the case law discussed in chapter 3 indicates, legal remedies are more likely to arise in private law (such as damages for breach of contract) than constitutional law. These kinds of extra-constitutional removal are made possible by the ad hoc, part-time nature of foreign judges' service and the fact that as non-citizens, foreign judges are subject to immigration regulations.

The removal of foreign judges by cessation of invitations to sit on the court of appeal raises similar kinds of concerns for judicial independence as the use of short renewable appointments. Just as there is a risk that a judge on a short-term contract might feel beholden to the authority responsible for his or her reappointment, there is a risk that visiting judges of appeal might similarly feel beholden to the Chief Justice to continue in service. This concern may be particularly acute in circumstances where the court of appeal hears appeals from decisions of the Chief Justice.[98] International standards on judicial independence recognise that the judiciary itself, and ultimately the Chief Justice, ought to be responsible for the administration of the court, including the assignment of cases to judges.[99] However, where the exercise of this responsibility can, in effect, result in the removal of a judge, there may be concerns about 'internal judicial independence' – that is, the ability of individual judges to decide cases without undue pressure from their fellow judges.[100] In *Rees v Crane*, the Privy Council held that while the Chief Justice is responsible for controlling the administrative arrangements of the court, a decision by the Chief Justice that a judge was not to sit went beyond administration and was tantamount to suspension.[101] There are some practical ways in which these concerns might be allayed. One is to place the responsibility for inviting judges of appeal in the hands of the President of the Court of Appeal, rather than the Chief Justice.[102] Another is to prepare panels for the court of appeal well in advance of each sittings, although the unpredictability of the court's caseload may make this difficult. A third option is to cap the number of judges of appeal. Smaller, more settled pools reduce the risk of 'judge shopping' when it comes to determining the composition of the bench in particular cases. For example, for a time in

[97] Instances of all three are described in ch 3, section V.

[98] Interview F12.

[99] eg *Beijing Statement* (n 19) art 35.

[100] S Shetreet, 'The Challenge of Judicial Independence in the Twenty-First Century' (2000) 8(2) *Asia Pacific Law Review* 153, 156–57.

[101] *Rees v Crane* [1994] 1 All ER 833; Allott (n 8) 1439.

[102] As is the case in Samoa and Solomon Islands.

Tonga, only three judges held commissions for the Court of Appeal and would visit for each sitting, although this process has changed since 2013.

Decisions about the status and immigration of non-citizens provide a way in which executive governments can directly interfere in the judiciary. The powers of the executive to control the entry and presence of non-citizens have been held to override considerations of judicial independence. In its review of the executive decision to revoke the visa of Chief Justice D'Imecourt, the Supreme Court of Vanuatu held that the Chief Justice could be declared a prohibited immigrant, even though it was tantamount to removal of a judge outside the constitutional processes.[103] The vulnerability of foreign judges to removal by cancellation of their visas constitutes a significant threat to judicial independence in states that use foreign judges. Claims about the right of sovereign states to determine the entry of non-citizens are difficult to counter. One small, but potentially significant counterpoint is that the removal of a foreign judge in this way is likely to garner international attention, in the judge's home state and beyond.[104] For example, the removal of Australian Geoffrey Eames as Chief Justice of Nauru was met with condemnation from regional and international bodies,[105] although not by the Australian Government, which stated that it was a 'domestic matter' for the Nauruan Government to resolve.[106]

V. CONCLUSION

It is commonly claimed that foreign judges support impartiality and independence because as outsiders they are removed from the personal, political and professional connections that arise in small communities. This notion is often taken for granted. When it is countered, it is by contrasting the social distance that foreign judges provide with the local knowledge that comes from living within the community.[107] This chapter has sought to assess the impartiality and independence of foreign judges in the Pacific on its own merits according to widely accepted legal standards and principles.

This chapter challenges the received wisdom on the impartiality and independence of foreign judges. The analysis in section III demonstrates that the claim that foreign judges provide an impartiality otherwise lacking in local judges does not provide a principled justification for the use of foreign judges, except in cases where local judges must recuse themselves under the established

[103] *D'Imecourt v Manatawai* [1998] VUSC 59.

[104] R Dixon and V Jackson, 'Hybrid Constitutional Courts: Foreign Judges on National Constitutional Courts' [2019] *Columbia Journal of Transnational Law* 283, 315.

[105] G Eames, 'The Rule of Law in Nauru: An Evolving Concept?', Paper presented at Law Society of South Australia Criminal Law Conference, McLaren Vale (24 October 2014) 4; Commonwealth Magistrates' and Judges' Association, 'Judicial Independence and Human Rights Issues: Nauru' (2014) 35 *CMJA News* 3–4.

[106] Eames (n 105) 4, 7.

[107] Powles (n 58) 27–28; Van Dyke (n 84) 180–83.

legal tests for bias. The discussion in section IV shows that foreign judges are vulnerable to particular forms of influence from a variety of sources, including the government, authorities responsible for their appointment and, in some cases, the organisations that fund them. These vulnerabilities arise primarily as a result of insecure tenure: first, the prevalent and entrenched use of short renewable appointments for foreign judges; and, second, the removal of foreign judges by extra-constitutional means, taking advantage of their status as part-time judges and as non-citizens.

Impartiality and independence are critical to the legitimacy and effectiveness of Pacific judiciaries. Not every point of dependence identified in this chapter will, in and of itself, be fatal to judicial impartiality and independence. They may be mitigated by the behaviour of judges and by demonstrations of respect for judicial independence by governments and, where relevant, external actors such as funding organisations. However, taken together and in combination, the structural shortcomings identified here can put both the practice and the perception of judicial independence at risk. Chapter 8 outlines some good practice initiatives, including to reduce short renewable appointments, that would assist Pacific states, funding organisations and judges themselves to identify and address the potential risks to judicial independence.

The findings of this chapter suggest that there has been a tendency to overstate the benefits and understate the risks of foreign judging to the impartiality and independence of Pacific judiciaries. Scholars have made a similar finding in the analogous context of hybrid tribunals, in which local and foreign judges sit together to try criminal offences committed during conflict. They have observed a dynamic on these tribunals in which the local is overly personalised and contextualised to the point that local judges are presumed to be partial, while international judges are regarded as neutral experts.[108] 'Over-valorising the international' in this way risks overlooking the various sources of influence that foreign judges face,[109] while the implication that local judges are not, and cannot be, impartial can damage public confidence in localised judiciaries.

Despite this, the perception that foreign judges are more impartial and independent is persistent. In chapter 5, I suggested that emphasising the technical legal expertise of foreign judges facilitates the movement of judges across national borders. The emphasis on impartiality performs a similar function, in that it casts foreign judges as independent professionals who can readily assume a role of the impartial adjudicator in any jurisdiction. Impartiality, like expertise, is a feature of the *transferable* judge.

[108] EM Bruch, 'Hybrid Courts: Examining Hybridity through a Post-Colonial Lens' (2010) 28(1) *Boston University International Law Journal* 1, 35–36; H Hobbs, 'Hybrid Tribunals and the Composition of the Court: In Search of Sociological Legitimacy' (2016) 16(2) *Chicago Journal of International Law* 482, 487.

[109] Bruch (n 108) 35–36. On this issue in the different context of Bosnia Herzegovina, see D Feldman, 'The Independence of International Judges in National Courts: Lessons from Bosnia Herzegovina' in CF Forsyth and S Shetreet (eds), *The Culture of Judicial Independence: Conceptual Foundations and Practical Challenges* (Boston, MA, Martinus Nijhoff Publishers, 2011) 215.

7

Representation

I. INTRODUCTION

SPECIALIST LEGAL KNOWLEDGE and impartiality are core attributes of judicial office. There is, however, more to the judicial role, that attention to the nationality of judges helps to draw out. Chapter 4 surveyed a range of reasons for the global norm that only citizens serve as judges on national courts of constitutional jurisdiction. It found that nationality was potentially relevant to a judge's knowledge of national law and the national community and could, on some understandings, affect impartiality. The nationality of a judge was, however, far more significant to other qualities associated with judicial office, namely allegiance and judicial responsibility, and the expressive function of the judiciary as a national institution. These qualities all relate to the relationship between judges, the state and the people. They all point to the sense that the attributes of judicial office extend beyond the core judicial function of the impartial adjudication of disputes according to law, to encompass the virtues, agency and identity of the individuals who hold judicial office. In other words, the significance of nationality suggests that *who* a judge is, and not just what he or she does, matters.

What follows when foreign citizens hold judicial office? It is likely that the use of foreign judges will attenuate or diminish the significance placed on a judge's allegiance to the state; his or her sense of membership of, and responsibility to, the people; and the extent to which the judiciary, as an institution, is seen to be 'of the people'. If this is so, what alternative loyalties, responsibilities and expressive values might arise in their place? This chapter examines the different ways in which the foreign individuals who hold judicial office are connected to that office, the state and its people, using the lens of representation. While there are other possible lenses through which to examine such connections, the concept of representation is apt for several reasons.

In some respects, describing the judiciary in terms of representation is incongruent because it seems inconsistent with judicial impartiality.[1] A judge cannot represent a particular constituency or stakeholder in the same way a Member of

[1] A Phillips, *The Politics of Presence* (Oxford, Clarendon Press, 1995) 186.

Parliament represents his or her electorate. Judges are, however, representative in other ways. As public officials, they act on behalf of the state, and, in democracies, the people. As adjudicators, judges speak for the community when they pronounce judgment and state the law, and so might be said to represent the law or justice. In this, judges illustrate how the concept of representation takes on different meanings that each, in Pitkin's terms, become part of 'an incomplete jigsaw puzzle'.[2] Pitkin's approach to understanding representation by identifying various 'views' of representation is helpful when it comes to examining the different ways in which judges may be characterised as representative. It allows us to understand judges as representatives in some contexts and in certain ways, without having to say that representation is their only or even predominant function or characteristic.

The concept of representation is also capable of capturing the range of potential relationships between an individual, his or her office, and more abstract notions such as the law, the state or the people. At its most general, representation means making present, in some sense, something that is not literally present.[3] This definition implies first, a representor, the person or thing who is making something present; second, something or someone being represented; and third, an audience to whom the representation is communicated.[4] In this chapter, the representor is the foreign judge, but it will be shown that the something or someone being represented might be the law, the people or the state; while the audience might be the litigants before the court, the judge's professional peers, or wider communities in and beyond the state. The concept of representation provides a way to disaggregate these various connections, without privileging one kind of connection, such as between judges and the people (as an analysis from the standpoint of democratic legitimacy might tend to do), or judges and the state (as might be foregrounded in an analysis based on sovereignty), or between judges themselves (as in a study of judicial culture or ethics). Finally, representation deals in appearances, expression and perceptions, all of which can be understood only in their context. As such, the concept of representation directs attention to contextual, rather than global, understandings of the role of judges in a particular constitutional system.

Section II explains the ways in which a judiciary is – and is not – representative. It identifies three senses in which judges might be understood as representative: as formal representatives; as 'acting for' or 'speaking for' representatives; and as descriptive representatives. Each of these three understandings of representation is used in sections III, IV and V respectively to examine the implications of foreign judging as it arises in the Pacific. Section III examines the formalities of representation, that is the procedures by which a person is given authority to act

[2] HF Pitkin, *The Concept of Representation* (Berkeley, CA, University of California Press, 1967) 10, 59.

[3] ibid 8.

[4] A Rehfeld, 'Towards a General Theory of Representation' (2006) 68(1) *Journal of Politics* 1, 4.

as a judge and is held accountable in that position. Section IV considers how judges, in the course of constitutional adjudication, act or speak for particular ideas. Finally, the descriptive or expressive function of the judiciary as an institution is examined in section V by considering the value placed on a judiciary that represents – in the sense of reflecting or resembling – the society it serves. In each case, the circumstances of foreign judging limit the extent to which foreign judges are understood to be authorised by, accountable to, speaking for, or reflective of the people or the state. As such, any sense that foreign judges represent the nation or the community, which might feature in other constitutional systems, is downplayed. In its place, an understanding emerges of foreign judges as representatives of a *profession*, with duties and responsibilities arising primarily from their professional commitments.

II. HOW ARE JUDGES AND JUDICIARIES REPRESENTATIVE?

It is important to be clear first about the ways in which judges and judiciaries are *not* representative. One understanding of representation involves a relationship where the representative acts on behalf of another person or group.[5] For example, a member of the legislature might represent his or her constituency or political party by presenting its views in the legislature. In an agent–principal relationship, the agent represents the principal by acting as the principal directs. Pettit characterises these examples as 'responsive representation' because the elected representative or agent must track and respond to the wishes of those he or she represents or risk being removed.[6] Judges are not representative in this responsive sense. They do not act on behalf of a particular person, group or interest, because to do so would compromise their impartiality. Nor are they held to account for being 'unresponsive' to the wishes of others: judicial independence requires that judges cannot be removed from office except in very narrow circumstances, and certainly not for making a decision that is unpopular or contrary to the wishes of the government or anyone else.[7] There is, however, a range of other categories of representation, three of which accord with aspects of the judicial role.[8]

First, a representative can be understood as someone who has been authorised to act and who will be held accountable for his or her actions. Pitkin characterises

[5] Pitkin (n 2) 113.

[6] P Pettit, 'Varieties of Public Representation' in I Shapiro et al (eds), *Political Representation* (Cambridge, Cambridge University Press, 2009) 61, 65.

[7] M Tushnet, 'Judicial Accountability in Comparative Perspective' in N Bamforth and P Leyland (eds), *Accountability in the Contemporary Constitution* (Oxford, Oxford University Press, 2013) 57, 60. The grounds for the removal of judges by political process are generally confined to capacity and misbehaviour.

[8] I draw primarily on Pitkin (n 2) and Pettit (n 6), as their accounts focus on the representative functions of public officials and not just political representatives.

this as a 'formalistic' view of representation, because it focuses on the transactions that take place prior to or after the representing occurs, rather than the substance of what the representative does.[9] This formal view of representation captures the sense in which public officials, including judges, are authorised to perform functions and exercise powers on behalf of the state, such that the decisions judges make are not private opinions but are attributed to the state and binding upon it.[10] The 'transactions' of representation encompass the conferral and acceptance of public office. For judges, this includes the means by which individuals are selected to become judges, the processes of appointment and the ritual of the oath of office. These formalities distinguish public officials from employees of the state or the government.[11] They reflect the distinctive commitment that judges make to the state and its people, and provide avenues by which judges are held accountable, or at least made responsive, to the public.

A second sense of representation relevant to the judiciary conceives a representative as someone who *acts for* or *speaks for* others. On this understanding, a person represents what guides his or her actions. The focus is therefore on the *activity* of representation, that is, what a representative actually does.[12] Judges are guided in their decisions by a range of different values and considerations.[13] Judges make decisions based on the law, and so might be said to represent the law.[14] Where a judge is faced with a law that is unclear or that leads to an unjust outcome, or a question of law that has wide social or political ramifications, he or she might be guided by a range of values not strictly contained within the law. A judge might understand the law to be a 'reflection of the community's values'[15] and so be guided by – and speak for – those values. Alternatively, a judge might seek to represent more abstract ideals, such as justice or fairness.[16] An example of a different kind of representation emerges from scholarship that seeks to reconcile constitutional review with democracy. Constitutional review is sometimes characterised as a counterbalance to or check on the popular pressures on the elected branches of government, in which judges use their 'representative judgment to bring these pressures to balance'.[17] In these circumstances, judges may represent – 'speak for' – the range of social and political considerations in issue, filtering them through distinctively judicial modes of deliberation and

[9] Pitkin (n 2) 58–59.
[10] ibid 40–41, 116–17.
[11] N Roughan, 'The Legitimacy of Whom?' in K Walton, W Sadurski and M Sevel (eds), *Legitimacy: The State and Beyond* (Oxford, Oxford University Press, 2019) 82, 92–93; MR Rutgers, 'The Oath of Office as Public Value Guardian' (2010) 40(4) *American Review of Public Administration* 428.
[12] Pitkin (n 2) 113–19.
[13] ibid 116–19.
[14] P Hamburger, 'Judicial Office' (2011) 6 *Journal of Law, Philosophy and Culture* 53.
[15] T Etherton, 'Liberty, the Archetype and Diversity: A Philosophy of Judging' [2010] *Public Law* 727, 733.
[16] Pitkin (n 2) 117–18.
[17] ibid 117.

reasoning.[18] The point here is not to decide between these different understandings of judicial decision making, but rather to show that they share in common a sense that judicial decisions are guided by values or interests that judges might then be said to represent.

The third relevant category is descriptive representation, which is the idea that the representative person or institution *stands for* or *resembles* that which it represents.[19] Examples of descriptive representation include the legislature as the 'mirror' of the people[20] and the jury as a cross-section of the community.[21] The idea of the judiciary as descriptively representative has been most fully developed in the literature on a 'reflective judiciary'. While there are many ways in which a judiciary might be said to be reflective,[22] the predominant understanding is a judiciary whose *composition* reflects that of the community. In most cases, a reflective judiciary requires that diverse identity groups within the citizenry, in terms of gender, ethnicity, territorial origin, religion or linguistic affiliation, are included in the composition of the judiciary. It is claimed that a reflective judiciary supports public confidence because people are more likely to respect and trust a judiciary in which they can 'see themselves'.[23] In this, descriptive representation focuses on appearances: it is about what the judiciary looks like, rather than how it speaks or acts. There is, however, some degree of overlap between descriptive representation and 'speaking for' representation. Judges with diverse identities and experiences will be a source of information and contribute to the way in which courts understand and develop the law.[24] The reflectiveness of the judiciary can also function as a justification in support of the claim that judiciaries 'speak for' the whole of society.[25]

The remainder of this chapter explains how the use of foreign judges in the Pacific affects each of these three representative functions of the judiciary and who or what foreign judges might be thought to represent. In relation to formal and 'speaking for' representation, the focus is on the connections between individual foreign judges and who or what they represent. In relation to descriptive representation, the focus broadens to the composition of the judiciary as a whole.

[18] eg R Alexy, 'Balancing, Constitutional Review, and Representation' (2005) 3(4) *International Journal of Constitutional Law* 572; D Dyzenhaus, 'Are Legislatures Good at Morality? Or Better at It than the Courts?' (2009) 7(1) *International Journal of Constitutional Law* 46, 51–52.

[19] Pitkin (n 2) ch 4.

[20] ibid 62.

[21] Pettit (n 6) 67.

[22] S Turenne, *Fair Reflection of Society in Judicial Systems: A Comparative Study* (Cham, Springer, 2015) 3–12.

[23] L Barmes and K Malleson, 'Lifting the Judicial Identity Blackout' (2018) 38(2) *OJLS* 357; E Rackley, *Women, Judging and the Judiciary: From Difference to Diversity* (Abingdon, Routledge, 2013) 23–24; PH Russell and K Malleson, 'Conclusion' in PH Russell and K Malleson (eds), *Appointing Judges in an Age of Judicial Power: Critical Perspectives from around the World* (Toronto, University of Toronto Press, 2006) 434.

[24] RJ Cahill-O'Callaghan, 'Reframing the Judicial Diversity Debate: Personal Values and Tacit Diversity' (2015) 35(1) *Legal Studies* 1, 5–7; Pitkin (n 2) 81.

[25] Barmes and Malleson (n 23) 376–78; Pitkin (n 2) 82.

III. FORMAL REPRESENTATION: AUTHORISATION AND ACCOUNTABILITY

Judges, by virtue of holding public office, are representatives in the formal sense: they are authorised to act on behalf of the state and to exercise the judicial powers of the state. Accounts of judges as formal representatives seek to explain how the state and its people ensure that judges act in their interests. Garoupa and Ginsburg employ an agent–principal model in which the principal – in their account the people or society – hires judges as its agents to provide the service of judging. They seek to explain how a society might manage what they characterise as the 'agency costs' that arise when the preferences of the judiciary do not match those of the society, or when judges do not perform well in their role.[26] Pettit suggests that judges are 'indicative representers' or 'proxies' of the public. They are 'professionally constrained and motivated to implement' the public's objective in having a judiciary, that is the impartial adjudication of disputes according to law. As independent office holders who are not subject to removal or reappointment, judges are motivated by 'professional reputation to act reliably in a manner that answers to the interest of the people as a whole'.[27]

There are various mechanisms that seek to ensure that judges will properly represent the state and the people. One is processes for the selection and appointment of judges that involve or are responsive to the people. A second is the oath of office and allegiance, by which an individual commits to perform the duties of judicial office and to be loyal to the state. These mechanisms are *ex ante* formalities that authorise an individual to hold judicial office. However, they also function as means of accountability by defining the mandate of judicial office and constraining judges to act within it.[28] This section shows how the processes for the selection and appointment of judges and the oath of office and allegiance operate differently as mechanisms for accountability for local and foreign judges in the Pacific, in practice and sometimes also in law.

A. Selection and Appointment

The processes for the selection and appointment of judges provide an avenue to connect judges to the people they serve. In the Pacific, judges are appointed by the head of state on the advice of the executive government or a judicial services commission. As such, the authorities responsible for selecting judges are generally elected representatives of the people (as members of the executive)

[26] N Garoupa and T Ginsburg, *Judicial Reputation: A Comparative Theory* (Chicago, IL, University of Chicago Press, 2015) 59–65.

[27] Pettit (n 6) 70.

[28] Russell and Malleson (n 23) 427–30; Tushnet (n 7).

and/or representatives of constituencies within the community such as the legal profession (as members of a judicial services commission). The formal procedures for appointing both local and foreign judges thereby maintain links to the people.

The primary, and in most cases only, criterion for judicial appointment is a minimum period of years of judicial or legal experience.[29] However, in addition to professional experience, there are many other qualities that are highly valued in a judge, such as impartiality, integrity, fairness and loyalty to law.[30] In Vanuatu, the Judicial Service Commission is directed by law to consider the candidate's experience, abilities, character and standing in the community.[31] Appointing authorities in other states presumably also consider such qualities when making or recommending judicial appointments. It is only by assessing these qualities that selectors can be confident that candidates will be desirable representatives of the state and its people in judicial office.

It is at this point that the selection processes for local and foreign judges diverge in practice. As in many other common law countries, the local judges on Pacific courts are generally recruited from the local legal profession. Those responsible for selecting candidates for appointment are likely to have ready access to information about local candidates, either from their own knowledge or by consulting judges and members of the legal profession, to enable them to assess whether a person will fulfil the mandate of judicial office. When appointing foreign judges, however, the local appointing body is generally at much greater distance from potential candidates,[32] presenting challenges in identifying and assessing their suitability for judicial appointment. Chapter 3 discussed the different methods of recruiting foreign judges, including through advertisements, recommendations of other judges, the networks developed at international judicial conferences, and donor organisations. In all cases, local appointing authorities are at a disadvantage when assessing a candidate's suitability for judicial appointment in the particular legal and social context of the Pacific state. Appointing authorities are unlikely to have direct knowledge of the candidate and must rely instead on recommendations from people in the candidate's home state and their professional qualifications on paper. This can have serious implications. Where a foreign judge does not meet the standards expected of a judge, collegial relations within the court and the standing of the court in the eyes of the community are at risk.

The difficulties associated with assessing the personal qualities of foreign candidates for judicial appointment result in an emphasis on their professional qualifications and experience, which are likely to have been gained in the

[29] Ch 3, section II.C.

[30] RA MacDonald, 'Exercising Judgement' in *Which Judge for Which Society? Proceedings of the 2008 Judges' Conference* (Québec City, 2008) 51, 62–63.

[31] *Judicial Services and Courts Act 2000* c 270 (Vanuatu), s 33(3).

[32] While this is often the case, a notable exception would be those judges who, although non-citizens, have practised as lawyers in the Pacific state. See ch 2, sections II and V.

judge's home state. Professional qualifications are mandated and recognised by the legal profession in each jurisdiction. Tushnet suggests that the predominance of professional, rather than political, standards in judicial appointment processes can nevertheless provide a form of political accountability on the basis that there is a rough correlation between wider social values and the values of the legal profession that inform professional standards.[33] However, this connection to the people of the state is weakened when the assessment of professional standards is predominantly formed in a foreign legal context.

B. Oath of Office and Allegiance

Before a foreign judge commences judicial service in a Pacific state, he or she will take the judicial oath. The precise words of the judicial oath vary across jurisdictions but generally include a commitment to 'well and truly' serve the sovereign or the state, to act in accordance with the constitution and the law, and to 'do right to all manner of people, without fear or favour, affection or ill will'.[34] The oath is a personal commitment and public promise to fulfil the obligations of judicial office. Traditionally, it was made to a divine witness. Today the significance of the oath rests on oath-takers' sense of honour, that is, their desire to think well of themselves and to be thought of well by others.[35] The judicial oath is also a statement of the values of judicial office, which include service and fidelity to the people, impartiality, loyalty to law and the attainment of justice.[36] The oath is often used as the touchstone for determining whether an individual's conduct is consistent with judicial office. The oath therefore operates to define a profession and commits its members to upholding the standards of that profession.

The judicial oath includes a commitment to serve the sovereign or the state. In five Pacific states, judges also make an additional oath of allegiance, in which the judge swears to 'bear true allegiance' to the state or sovereign.[37] The concept of allegiance was historically understood as an obligation of

[33] Tushnet (n 7) 64.

[34] *Constitution of Fiji 2013*, s 109, sch; *Constitution of Fiji 1997*, s 135, sch; *Constitution of Kiribati 1979*, ss 82, 92, sch 1; *Constitution of Nauru 1968*, s 52, sch 4; *Constitution of Papua New Guinea 1975*, s 249, sch 4; *Constitution of Samoa 1960*, s 67, sch 3; *Official Oaths Act 1978* c 24 (Solomon Islands), s 3; *Constitution of Tonga 1875*, s 95; *Oaths and Statutory Declarations Act 1979* c 7.48 (Tuvalu), s 3, sch 1; *Oaths Act 1964* c 37 (Vanuatu), s 6(2).

[35] P Horwitz, 'The Constitutional Marriage of Personality and Impersonality: Office, Honor, and the Oath' (2018) 33 *Constitutional Commentary* 101, 106–07.

[36] G Brennan, 'Speech on Swearing in as a Chief Justice' (1995) 183 *CLR* ix, x.

[37] *Constitution of Fiji 2013*, s 109, sch; *Official Oaths Act 1978* c 24 (Solomon Islands), s 3; *Oaths and Statutory Declarations Act 1979* c 7.48 (Tuvalu), s 3; *Oaths Act 1964* c 37 (Vanuatu), s 6(2). Judges in Papua New Guinea take a 'Declaration of Loyalty' to the state and its people: *Constitution of Papua New Guinea 1975*, ss 6, 249.

fidelity and obedience to the sovereign. Now it might describe personal feelings of attachment to the nation, or denote a formal legal relationship between the state and its citizens.[38] New citizens take an oath of allegiance to their new country, and public officials are required to swear or affirm their allegiance to the state they serve. The reason to require public officials to do so goes to their formal representative function. Appointment to public office authorises an individual to exercise the powers of the state, vesting in him or her special status and authority. As a representative, a public official is obliged to act in the public interest. The oath of allegiance serves to make this obligation not only a public duty, but also a personal moral commitment.[39]

There is sometimes hesitation about the taking of an oath of allegiance by foreign judges. The Constitution of Tonga sets out a separate oath of office for judges who are not Tongan subjects that excludes the pledge of loyalty to the King of Tonga.[40] Laws in Papua New Guinea and Tuvalu exempt non-citizens from swearing loyalty or allegiance where doing so might adversely affect their nationality or citizenship status.[41] Outside the Pacific, some foreign judges have expressed discomfort about taking an oath of allegiance to a foreign state. Lord Millett, a citizen of the United Kingdom, served as a non-permanent judge of the Hong Kong Court of Final Appeal, as well as on the House of Lords. To allay his concerns about taking an oath of allegiance to the Hong Kong Special Administrative Region of the People's Republic of China, he says he 'carefully put my British passport in my breast pocket and took the oath in the American manner with my right hand over my heart and, more importantly, over my passport'.[42] The concern that a judge who swears allegiance to different jurisdictions will have divided loyalties animates much of the discussion about the motivations of national judges on international courts.[43]

Most foreign judges serving in the Pacific seem comfortable swearing allegiance to the relevant Pacific state, either as part of the judicial oath or in a separate oath of allegiance. This is because the oath is understood as a commitment not directly to the state but to the *laws* of the state. This is not unique to foreign judges: the oath of allegiance does not impose a duty to be obedient to a particular government or individual but an abstract and higher loyalty to

[38] E Arcioni, 'Identity at the Edge of the Constitutional Community' in F Jenkins, M Nolan and K Rubenstein (eds), *Allegiance and Identity in a Globalised World* (Cambridge, Cambridge University Press, 2014) 31, 38.

[39] Rutgers (n 11) 430.

[40] *Constitution of Tonga 1875*, s 95.

[41] *Constitution of Papua New Guinea 1975*, s 251; *Oaths (Non-Citizens) Act 1985* c 7.44 (Tuvalu).

[42] P Millett, *As in Memory Long* (London, Wildy, Simmonds & Hill Publishing, 2015) 191.

[43] T Dannenbaum, 'Nationality and the International Judge: The Nationalist Presumption Governing the International Judiciary and Why it Must be Reversed' (2012) 45(1) *Cornell International Law Journal* 77, 112–13; Y Shany, 'Dédoublement Fonctionnel and the Mixed Loyalties of National and International Judges' in F Fontanelli, G Martinico and P Carrozza (eds), *Shaping Rule of Law through Dialogue: International and Supranational Experiences* (Groningen, Europa, 2010) 27.

the public interest.[44] When taken by a judge, the oath is understood to mean allegiance to law. As one foreign judge serving in the Pacific explained, because his home jurisdiction and the Pacific state he served both shared a commitment to the rule of law, he could be faithful to his judicial oath by supporting the rule of law in both countries.[45]

Taking an oath to serve the state and uphold its laws has special significance for foreign judges because it expresses a commitment to a state in which they do not hold the ties of identity and membership implicit in citizenship. The oath, along with responsibility for appointment in the hands of the Pacific state, are the clearest points of connection between a foreign judge and the Pacific state he or she serves. This connection is, however, attenuated. In both cases, the emphasis is on the professional qualifications and responsibilities of the foreign judge, rather than a sense that the foreign judge commits to the specific social values of the Pacific state. In other words, the foreign judge represents the state by fulfilling the professional requirements of judicial office.

C. Accepting and Resigning Judicial Office

Oaths of office and allegiance formalise not only the *conferral* of public authority, but also the *acceptance* of that authority by the individual office holder.[46] The acceptance of judicial office by foreign judges has special significance. In her work on representations of the foreigner in stories of democratic founding, Honig explains that one symbolic function of the foreigner is to reassure citizens of the 'choice-worthiness' of their social and political regime.[47] For example, immigrants who voluntarily swear allegiance to the state symbolically affirm the legitimacy of the legal, social and political regime of the state for all citizens.[48]

There is a similar sense in which the use of foreign judges is seen to bestow legitimacy on courts and legal systems. This affirmative function comes to the fore not only in the act of accepting judicial office, but also in resigning from it. There have been several instances in the Pacific where foreign judges have resigned on principle. In Papua New Guinea in 1979, five foreign judges resigned in protest at what they saw as executive interference in judicial independence.[49] Geoffrey Eames resigned as Chief Justice of Nauru following the summary deportation of the Resident Magistrate and the cancellation by the Government of his own visa.[50] In Fiji, several foreign and local judges resigned following the coups of 1987, 2000 and 2006.

[44] Rutgers (n 11) 435.
[45] Interview F24.
[46] Roughan (n 11) 101.
[47] B Honig, *Democracy and the Foreigner* (Princeton, NJ, Princeton University Press, 2001) 75, 109.
[48] ibid 92–95.
[49] The 'Rooney affair' is discussed in section V.
[50] G Eames, 'The Rule of Law in Nauru: An Evolving Concept?', Paper presented at Law Society of South Australia Criminal Law Conference, McLaren Vale (24 October 2014).

The Fiji coup of 2006, and subsequent abrogation of the Constitution in 2009, raised particularly difficult questions for foreign judges. Over 2007 and 2008, eight foreign judges serving on the Fijian courts resigned, citing concerns about judicial independence and the administration of the court,[51] while others stayed for the duration of their existing commissions but did not seek reappointment.[52] Whether to accept or continue judicial appointment from a government of questionable legality was regarded ultimately as a question for the conscience of individual judges.[53] On one hand, Fiji needed judges so that the judiciary could continue to operate despite the political crisis. On the other hand, by accepting appointment, judges might be seen to acquiesce in or accept an unlawful regime.[54] One foreign judge framed this issue using the language of allegiance, stating that 'any expat now thinking of taking a position will effectively be swearing allegiance to an illegal dictator'.[55] Justice French, an Australian judge who was appointed to the Supreme Court of Fiji prior to the coup, outlined the dilemma as follows:

> Australian judges involved in the Supreme Court of Fiji after the coup have had to consider the benefits gained from their continued contribution to the rule of law against the risk that they may be perceived to have made an implicit bargain with a government whose legality is in question.[56]

Both views emphasise the degree of choice that individuals have in accepting judicial appointment. In making that choice, individuals confer a degree of legitimacy on the court and the state in which they accept appointment by demonstrating, in Honig's terms, its 'choice-worthiness'.[57] Foreign judges, by virtue of their foreignness, are in a special position to do this. As visiting non-citizens, the personal costs of leaving are often less than those for citizen judges, especially where the foreign judge is not reliant on judicial service in the

[51] Six judges of appeal resigned on 3 September 2007: 'Aust, NZ Judges Quit Fiji's Appeal Court' *ABC News* (Sydney) (4 September 2007). Sir John Steele Henry resigned early in 2007 and Roger Coventry resigned in January 2009: 'Fiji Judge Urges Lawyers to Speak Out' *FijiLive* (Suva) (25 January 2008).

[52] G Leung, 'The Erosion of Judicial Independence' in J Fraenkel, S Firth and BV Lal (eds), *The 2006 Military Takeover in Fiji: A Coup to End All Coups?* (Canberra, ANU Press, 2009) 301, 303; R Smellie, *Few Regrets: Reflections on a Life in the Law* (Auckland District Law Society, 2008) 90–91, 126. Interviews F3, F4, F23.

[53] R French, 'Judges in Fiji Face "Interim" Problem' *The Australian* (Canberra) (2 May 2008) 29. Interviews F3, F4, F23.

[54] J Corrin, 'Judge or Be Judged: Accepting Judicial Appointment in an Unlawful Regime' (2009) 16(2–3) *International Journal of the Legal Profession* 191, 197–98; G Leung, 'Some Challenges to the Rule of Law in Fiji', Paper presented at the 36th Australian Legal Convention, Perth (18 September 2009) 4. See also *Qarase v Bainimarama* [2009] FJCA 67, [168]–[169].

[55] C Merritt, 'Sacked Fiji Judges Warn Expats on Treason' *The Australian* (Canberra) (13 April 2009) 1.

[56] French (n 53).

[57] Acceptance of appointment can also be seen to support the terms and conditions of judicial office. In *Fiji v Citizens' Constitutional Forum Limited* [2013] FJHC 220, a Fijian non-governmental organisation (NGO) was held to have scandalised the court when it stated that 'the independence of the judiciary cannot be relied on'. Amongst the evidence that the NGO provided in justification was a document written by former Justice Marshall, which set out how short-term appointments were

Pacific for his or her livelihood.[58] Foreign judges bring with them an international audience in their home state and perhaps beyond, such that acceptance, but particularly resignation, of judicial office can garner international attention.[59] So, for example, a representative of the Australian Government commented that 'the state of the Fijian judiciary is a matter of concern, as evidenced by the fact that most expatriate judges, including a number of Australian nationals, have resigned or have refused to renew their contracts'.[60] Resignations can signal, intentionally or not, that there is something wrong.

D. Accountability

Finally, the obligations of office also provide a framework for judicial accountability. Discussions of judicial accountability often focus on formal mechanisms, such as procedures for the discipline and removal of judges, and the scrutiny and review of judicial decision making. However, judges are also subject to informal mechanisms of accountability. Judges are concerned for their personal reputation amongst their peers and the legal profession, and for the reputation of the judiciary as a whole in the eyes of the community.[61] This concern for relationships and reputation can motivate judges to act with integrity. They work, however, because judges are situated within a wider legal and social context.[62] The experience in post-coup Fiji demonstrates how these lines of informal accountability for foreign judges lead predominantly to professional peers in the judges' home state, rather than in the state in which they serve. While local bodies such as the Fiji Law Society and NGOs criticised the erosion of judicial independence,[63] pressure from peers in their home states seemed most likely to dissuade foreign judges from accepting appointment in Fiji. The Australian and

a threat to judicial independence. The presiding judge dismissed the significance of these claims, noting that Justice Marshall was himself seeking such an appointment, prompting him to ask 'why did Mr Marshall not resign his appointment during the course of his contract if the independence of the judiciary had been so compromised'? (ibid [21]–[24]).

[58] Some foreign judges hold full-time employment in their home state. Foreign judges who are retired judges in their home state receive pensions.

[59] R Dixon and V Jackson, 'Hybrid Constitutional Courts: Foreign Judges on National Constitutional Courts' [2019] *Columbia Journal of Transnational Law* 283, 315–16. See, eg, the support that Eames CJ received from the Commonwealth and foreign lawyers associations: Eames (n 50) 4.

[60] N Berkovic, 'Judge Criticised over Fiji Posting' *The Australian* (Canberra) (10 March 2008) 4.

[61] Garoupa and Ginsburg (n 26) ch 1.

[62] J McIntyre, *The Judicial Function: Fundamental Principles of Contemporary Judging* (Singapore, Springer, 2019) 267–69; S Shetreet, 'Judicial Accountability: A Comparative Analysis of the Models and the Recent Trends' (1986) 11(2) *International Legal Practitioner* 38.

[63] T Draunidalo, 'The Rule of Law and Judicial Independence amidst the Coups and Attempted Coups in Fiji since 1987' in Fraenkel, Firth and Lal (eds) (n 52) 311; Fiji Women's Rights Movement, *Herstory: Celebrating 25 Years of Balancing the Scales 1986–2011* (Suva, 2011) 34.

New Zealand Bar Associations advised their members against accepting 'tainted' judicial appointments from the military government.[64] In Sri Lanka, criticisms of the appointment of Sri Lankans to the Fijian courts were framed in terms of the negative effect that judges serving an overseas 'military dictatorship' would have on the integrity of the Sri Lankan judiciary.[65] Such arguments centred the interests and reputation of foreign judges in their home state, rather than in Fiji.

This dynamic, and its limitations, can be illustrated by the challenge to appointment of Jocelynne Scutt, an Australian barrister practising in the state of Victoria, as a judge of the High Court of Fiji. Following her appointment, the Pacific Centre for Public Integrity, an NGO based in Suva, made a complaint to the Legal Services Commission of Victoria, accusing Scutt of professional misconduct. The NGO alleged that by accepting judicial appointment from the 'constitutionally unlawful regime' in post-coup Fiji, Scutt had undermined the integrity and independence of Fiji's judiciary. It argued that the Australian legal profession had a duty to regulate the activities of Australian lawyers overseas, especially in countries such as Fiji, 'where the national legal processes are politically and legally not able to address these issues'.[66] The Victorian Legal Services Commissioner rejected these arguments and held that Scutt had not engaged in professional misconduct. She said that the acceptance of judicial appointment was not conduct in connection with the practice of law; and in the circumstances would not, in itself, 'be regarded as disgraceful or dishonourable by members of the legal profession'.[67] In this, the Commissioner's decision is very much tied to her own territorial jurisdiction. She seems to have considered only how the conduct was connected to the practice of law in *Victoria* and how it would be regarded by members of the *Victorian* legal profession, even though, as Corrin points out, there was no legal requirement to confine her considerations in such a way.[68]

The complaint and the reasons for its dismissal highlight the way in which foreign judges are, first and foremost, members of and accountable to, the legal community in their home state. As the NGO noted, there was no practical way to challenge the judicial appointment in Fiji. By bringing a complaint in Victoria, the NGO recognised that it is amongst their peers in their home states

[64] C Merritt, 'When Backlogs Lead to Payback' *The Australian* (Canberra) (1 May 2009) 27; 'NZ Lawyers Should Not Work for Fiji Regime, Law Society Says' *NZ Herald* (Auckland) (21 April 2009).

[65] U Kurukulasuriya, 'Can We Expect Justice and Independence from Servants of Military Dictators?' *Colombo Telegraph* (Colombo) (30 October 2011).

[66] C Merritt and N Berkovic, 'Fiji's Democracy Lobby Tries to Scuttle Scutt Appointment' *The Australian* (Canberra) (14 March 2008) 33.

[67] The decision of the Legal Services Commissioner is not publicly available. The findings were reported in C Merritt, 'Jocelynne Scutt Cleared of Misconduct' *The Australian* (Canberra) (8 August 2008) 33.

[68] Corrin (n 54) 203, noting precedents where Legal Services Commissioners considered conduct occurring overseas.

that foreign judges' reputations are forged, maintained and of greatest professional importance. Indeed, the Legal Services Commissioner assessed Scutt's conduct in accepting judicial appointment in Fiji only by reference to how it was perceived in Victoria. The case shows how, once again, the conditions of foreign judging mean that the sense in which a judge represents and is responsible to the people of the state in which he or she serves, is mediated through channels of professional, rather than political, accountability. Importantly, however, those professional obligations and the judge's professional reputation are more tightly connected to the foreign judge's home state than to the Pacific state in which he or she serves.

In summary, the formalities of representation highlight two ways in which foreign judges are connected to the state and its people. First, the procedures by which individuals are authorised to hold judicial office are in the hands of the Pacific state, and so provide an important point of connection between foreign judges and the state they serve. There is no sense, for example, that a foreign judge is a representative of his or her home state, in the way that judges on some international courts are regarded.[69] Second, the judge's acceptance of judicial office and the commitments made in the judicial oath provide a framework of accountability to a judge's peers, the legal profession and the community. The practicalities of foreign judging, however, distance foreign judges from the legal profession and community in the Pacific state and import the judge's home state and its legal profession and community into the processes of authorisation and accountability. Channels for the recruitment of judges and lines of professional accountability tend to lead back to the foreign judge's home state, attenuating the connection between foreign judges and the Pacific state and its people.

IV. 'ACTING FOR' REPRESENTATION: WHAT GUIDES FOREIGN JUDGES' DECISIONS?

'Acting for' representation captures the sense in which judges are guided in their decisions by certain values and interests. As explained in section II, there are different views about the kinds of values and interests that judges do, and ought to, represent. This section considers what *foreign* judges might be understood to represent and the effect this might have on how they approach constitutional adjudication.

Foreign judges who serve in the Pacific are themselves fairly clear that they represent the law and the judicial qualities of impartiality and expertise. When asked about their role on Pacific courts, several judges interviewed stated that they were there to be judges, with no expectation or encouragement to take

[69] R Mackenzie et al, *Selecting International Judges: Principle, Process, and Politics* (Oxford, Oxford University Press, 2010) 31.

on additional roles.[70] On occasion, however, there was a sense, shared in a few interviews, in which foreign judges were understood to represent what might be more broadly characterised as the rule of law. Foreign judges, especially those funded by development programmes, are sometimes seen as part of and complementary to wider efforts to strengthen law and justice systems, and promote good governance and the rule of law in Pacific states.[71]

The analysis of constitutional cases across the nine Pacific states set out in chapter 5 supports the idea that foreign judges tend to speak for the law and minimise or avoid overt claims to speak for the people or the community. Chapter 5 examined this issue in light of the kinds of knowledge that foreign judges bring to bear on constitutional adjudication. It suggested that foreign judges, generally speaking, will have gaps in their knowledge regarding custom and the social values of Pacific communities. As a result, foreign judges tend to turn to legalistic methods, such as textualist approaches to constitutional interpretation, rather than attempt to 'speak for' the place of social values and custom in (what is to them) a foreign jurisdiction.

The preference for textualism may not only be a consequence of the kinds of knowledge that foreign judges bring to the task of constitutional adjudication in the Pacific. It might also arise as a result of perceptions about the legitimacy of judges, and foreign judges in particular, to represent the people or the community. Writing in the context of the United States, Kahn argues that the authority of a court depends on the ability of its audience – the people – to identify with the narrative that the court constructs about the constitutional order. For Kahn, a foreign judge would undermine this sense of identification between speaker and audience, breaking the relationship between the judge, the law and the people.[72] Barmes and Malleson make a similar connection when they argue that judicial office must be open to all groups within society so as to 'give voice' to different perspectives.[73] We might expect foreign judges to be hesitant about leading social change or developing the law in light of changing social values because, as outsiders, they lack the authority to speak for the people in this way. This section examines this intuition by comparing the way in which courts in Fiji, Samoa and Tuvalu have approached politically and socially sensitive constitutional cases.

In her study of the reasoning of foreign judges on Pacific courts, Baird discusses judicial deference as a potential way in which foreign judges might deal with contentious cases with cultural or customary elements.[74] Deference

[70] Interviews F4, F5, F8, F9.

[71] J Logan, 'Law and Justice in Papua New Guinea', Paper presented at the Australian Institute of International Affairs, Brisbane (23 June 2015) 48–50. Interviews F1, F7, F11, F20, F24.

[72] P Kahn, 'Independence and Responsibility in the Judicial Role' in IP Stotzky (ed), *Transition to Democracy in Latin America: The Role of the Judiciary* (Boulder, CO, Westview Press, 1993) 73, 82–83.

[73] Barmes and Malleson (n 23) 376–79.

[74] N Baird, 'Judges as Cultural Outsiders: Exploring the Expatriate Model of Judging in the Pacific' (2013) 19 *Canterbury Law Review* 80, 93–95.

occurs when courts openly accord weight to the judgement of another decision maker.[75] There are two main rationales for deference.[76] The first is that the other decision maker has greater institutional competence or knowledge to determine the issue. An example, discussed in chapter 5, is deference to a local judge on a court below on the grounds he or she has greater knowledge of custom and local conditions. The second rationale for deference arises from the recognition that the other decision maker has greater legitimacy to determine the issue. On this basis, courts composed of foreign judges might defer, to some extent, to the decisions of local authorities composed of members who are 'of the people', such as legislatures or village councils.

The Samoan Court of Appeal, which until very recently comprised only foreign judges, provides an example of this second kind of deference, which may be illustrated by its approach to electoral matters. In Samoa the franchise was initially restricted to *matai* (chiefs). The first case ever heard by the Court of Appeal, *Attorney-General v Olomalu*, challenged this restricted franchise.[77] The plaintiff argued that the constitutional guarantee of equality required universal suffrage. The Samoan Government, however, argued that the unique nature of Samoan culture should weigh in favour of the preservation of *matai*-only suffrage. The Court of Appeal held that *matai*-only suffrage was constitutional. Its decision was primarily based on the text of the Constitution. However, the Court also looked to the debates of the Constitutional Convention, which had expressly considered and rejected a provision for universal suffrage and had decided not to entrench *matai* suffrage so that the Parliament might revisit the question in the future. In 1990, the Parliament did amend the *Electoral Act* to provide for universal suffrage, following a plebiscite on the issue. Once again, the Court of Appeal upheld this amendment, refusing to find that the Constitution entrenched either universal or *matai*-only suffrage.[78] Finally, in *Samoa Party v Attorney-General*, the Court of Appeal upheld the validity of legislation that restricted the right to bring a petition to challenge an election result to candidates who had received more than a certain number of votes.[79]

The picture that emerges from these cases is of a court that seeks to follow changes in the community's views rather than lead such change.[80] The Court of Appeal has defined its role narrowly in relation to the Parliament. In *Olomalu*, the Court stated that its decision to uphold the constitutionality of the restricted

[75] P Horwitz, 'Three Faces of Deference' (2008) 83 *Notre Dame Law Review* 1061, 1072; A Kavanagh, 'Defending Deference in Public Law and Constitutional Theory' (2010) 126 *LQR* 222, 223.

[76] Horwitz (n 75) 1078–90.

[77] *Attorney-General v Olomalu* [1982] WSCA 1.

[78] *Pita v Attorney-General* [1995] WSCA 6.

[79] *Samoa Party v Attorney-General* [2010] WSCA 4. Only *matai* are eligible to stand for election to the Samoan Parliament.

[80] AH Angelo, '"Steady as She Goes": The Constitution and Court of Appeal of Samoa' (2012) 18 *New Zealand Association for Comparative Law Yearbook* 145, 157–58; Baird (n 74) 90.

franchise should not be read to 'imply any view of the Court about whether continuing with *matai* voting is in the long term interest of Samoa – this a question of social and political philosophy determined by parliament'.[81] Similarly, in the *Samoa Party* case, the Court expressly confined its role to determining whether the Constitution had been infringed; it was not to 'impose its own ideas'.[82] It recognised Parliament, 'with its double legitimacy as the chosen representatives of the people and as composed of *matai* who are versed in both Christian principles and Samoan tradition', as the appropriate body to determine the rights of electoral petitioners.[83] While an expansive right to bring electoral petitions would provide greater protection of free and fair elections, the Court noted that parliamentarians are answerable to the community for the allocation of resources, stating that 'for a court to rule otherwise would place it, not the parliament, in breach of the Constitution, unless that course was essential to achieve the standards required by the Constitution'.[84] The deferential approach of the Court of Appeal of Samoa is not necessarily replicated in other Pacific jurisdictions, nor is it unique to courts that comprise foreign judges. It has, however, been suggested that the Court's cautious approach is a model for how a court comprising foreign judges might contribute to the stable development of the law.[85]

The approach of the Samoan Court of Appeal may be compared to the approach of the Tuvalu Court of Appeal in *Teonea v Pule of Kaupule of Nanumaga*. This case concerned whether the *Falekaupule* (the customary island authority) had the power to ban the establishment of new churches on its island. The *Falekaupule* of Nanumaga resolved to prohibit new churches out of concern that it would cause division and conflict within the community. Tuvalu's Constitution, anticipating such concerns, included express limitations on the freedom of religion and the freedom of expression, to permit laws that restrict the right to spread beliefs or communicate ideas that might be divisive, unsettling or offensive to the people or directly threaten Tuvaluan values and culture.[86] In addition, the Constitution sets out principles that form 'part of the basic law of Tuvalu, from which human rights and freedoms derive and on which they are based'.[87] Several of the principles emphasise the importance of Tuvaluan values. For example, the third principle states that

> the stability of Tuvaluan society and the happiness and welfare of the people of Tuvalu, both present and future, depend very largely on the maintenance of Tuvaluan values, culture and tradition, including the vitality and the sense of identity of island

[81] *Attorney-General v Olomalu* [1982] WSCA 1.
[82] *Samoa Party v Attorney-General* [2010] WSCA 4, [45].
[83] ibid [10]; Baird (n 74) 89–90.
[84] *Samoa Party v Attorney-General* [2010] WSCA 4, [55].
[85] Angelo (n 80) 164–65. For discussion, see Baird (n 74) 93–95.
[86] *Constitution of Tuvalu 1986*, s 19(4), (5).
[87] ibid s 13.

> communities and attitudes of cooperation, self-help and unity within and amongst those communities.[88]

At first instance, Chief Justice Ward, a citizen of the United Kingdom with long judicial experience in several Pacific states, held that the *Falekaupule* was entitled to impose the ban on new churches, in essence deferring to the local customary decision maker.[89] The Court of Appeal, composed of three judges from New Zealand, overturned this decision by majority and held the ban was unconstitutional. Justice Tompkins in dissent upheld the *Falekaupule's* decision as a valid exercise of its traditional decision-making powers and held that, under Tuvalu's Constitution, the protection of Tuvaluan values and customs was the dominant consideration.[90] The two judges in the majority, however, held that the *Falekaupule's* decision to ban the new church violated the constitutional protection of the freedom of religion. Justice Fisher did not accept that once it was shown that there was a threat to Tuvaluan values, the Court should defer to the *Falekaupule* or that Tuvaluan values should automatically prevail. Rather, it is for the Court to determine whether the *Falekaupule's* decision is consistent with the Constitution.[91] He stated:

> I can well understand the view that the threat to Nanumaga stability, culture and unity is a high price to pay for permitting the introduction of another religion on the island. However in the end I have concluded that the time has come to allow the people of Nanumaga their constitutional freedoms.[92]

Justice Paterson framed the issue for determination as 'the extent to which universally accepted human rights can be modified or restricted by the customs and traditions of Tuvalu'.[93] For Justice Paterson, the starting point was Tuvalu's international obligation to protect and promote all human rights and fundamental freedoms.[94] He emphasised the desire, expressed in the constitutional principles, 'that Tuvalu must take its rightful place amongst the community of nations',[95] and the recognition that the principles on which the Constitution is based are subject to change over time.[96] Like Justice Fisher, Justice Paterson determined that 'the time has come' to recognise – and indeed to effect – a change in the value that Tuvalu placed on the freedom of religion.

The two judges in the majority came to their decision by balancing the values, both enshrined in the Constitution, of respect for traditional authority and freedom of religion. The decision to favour freedom of religion over traditional

[88] ibid preamble.
[89] *Teonea v Kaupule* [2005] TVHC 5.
[90] *Teonea v Pule o Kaupule of Nanumaga* [2009] TVCA 2 [35].
[91] ibid [125]–[127], [134].
[92] ibid [158].
[93] ibid [167].
[94] ibid [211].
[95] ibid [217] referring to Principle 3 of the *Constitution of Tuvalu 1986*.
[96] ibid [215] referring to Principle 7 of the *Constitution of Tuvalu 1986*.

authority caused social unrest and division. Many people of Nanumaga did not accept the decision, to the point where police on the island could not or would not enforce the Court's ruling.[97] The Tuvaluan Parliament quickly passed a constitutional amendment that further emphasised traditional values and expressly permitted restrictions on freedom of religion of the kind at issue in *Teonea*.[98] This might be read positively, as an engagement by the Court and the Parliament in 'dialogue' over the meaning and scope of constitutional rights, a dialogue that was made possible only because the Court did not defer but rather dealt with the rights claim before it. However, the events can also be read as a case in which foreign judges on the Court of Appeal misread the significance placed by the Tuvaluan people and the Constitution on the maintenance and protection of Tuvaluan values, which was met by backlash and non-compliance as a result. Angelo has criticised the case as one where the Court of Appeal sought to impose a radical constitutional development, rather than allow constitutional change to 'occur organically at the instigation of the people of Tuvalu and their elected representatives' after the approach modelled by the Samoan Court of Appeal.[99]

This is not to say that foreign judges sitting on Pacific courts cannot contribute to, or even lead, social and legal change. The case of *McCoskar v Fiji* is in many ways analogous to the *Teonea* case in Tuvalu. In *McCoskar*, Justice Winter, a resident judge from New Zealand, held that laws criminalising private consensual sexual conduct between adult men were an unconstitutional interference with the rights to privacy and equality.[100] The decision inflamed an already intense public debate about the rights of sexual minorities in Fiji, in which conservative politicians and religious leaders condemned homosexuality as a threat to the social morality of Fiji.[101] Following the High Court's decision, some Christian leaders called for public marches protesting homosexuality, while the Prime Minister said that homosexual conduct would remain a crime in Fiji, despite the Court's ruling. Justice Winter's reasons for decision in *McCoskar* acknowledged this context, stating that the 'genuine and sincere conviction shared by a large number of responsible members of the Fijian community that any change in the law to decriminalize homosexual conduct would seriously damage the moral fabric of society' was 'relevant for the purposes of interpretation of the Constitution'. Justice Winter referred also to the slow trend to decriminalise homosexual conduct across the Commonwealth, noting that the cautious approach of legislatures and courts reflected the 'deep religious and

[97] Angelo (n 80) 164.

[98] *Constitution (Recognition of Traditional Standards, Values and Practices) Amendment Act 2010* (Tuvalu).

[99] Angelo (n 80) 164–65. See also Baird (n 74) 93.

[100] *McCoskar v Fiji* [2005] FJHC 500.

[101] For a detailed discussion situating this debate in context, see N George, 'Contending Masculinities and the Limits of Tolerance: Sexual Minorities in Fiji' (2008) 20(1) *The Contemporary Pacific* 163.

moral beliefs involved'. He held, however, that such beliefs could not on their own justify the unconstitutional interference with the right to privacy enshrined in Fiji's Constitution. In this way, different community views were represented in Justice Winter's reasons for decision, assisted by the amicus briefs from the Attorney-General and the Human Rights Commission. The judgment echoed the strategic approach of Fijian advocates for the rights of sexual minorities, which sought to avoid confronting powerful figures of authority and focused instead on the law and Fiji's human rights record and international reputation.[102] Justice Winter in *McCoskar* and the majority judges in *Teonea* therefore approached a contentious constitutional rights issue in much the same way, acknowledging the social context and the importance of religion and custom but ultimately upholding the rights of the minority group. In Fiji, however, the outcome was accepted despite the rhetoric: the impugned provisions were formally removed from the criminal code in 2009 and the new Constitution of 2013 retained the prohibition on discrimination on the grounds of sexual orientation. The differences mostly relate to the constitutional context, which in Fiji were informed by greater judicial engagement with constitutional rights, sustained civil society advocacy and, in complex ways, by the intervening coup in 2006.[103]

Teonea is a case in which the constitutional understandings about the authority of the *Falekaupule* and the balance between rights and customary values expressed by the court did not reflect those of the wider society.[104] In Kahn's terms, the constitutional narrative offered by the court, although guided by law, was not one in which the people could 'see themselves'.[105] This is not a problem that arises only for foreign judges: all courts face the challenge of keeping in step with social change, especially when there are deeply-held conflicting views within the society. Foreign judges, however, face particular difficulties. Many foreign judges, particularly on courts of appeal, visit the Pacific state only occasionally for short periods, and so have limited opportunity to experience and understand public sentiment. Only in a few Pacific states do foreign judges sit on panels with local judges, again limiting the opportunities to fully appreciate local perspectives on constitutional questions before the court. While these difficulties relate to access to knowledge, they compound the problem of legitimacy that arises from the sense that it is not appropriate for foreign judges, as outsiders, to speak for local values or sentiments.

It is not surprising, therefore, that foreign judges on courts of constitutional jurisdiction are seen, and see themselves, as representatives of the law. Just as foreign judges understand the oath of allegiance as an allegiance to *law*, they understand their role in constitutional adjudication as serving the people by

[102] ibid 168–69.
[103] ibid.
[104] E Apinelu, 'Societal Culture and Constitutions: The Case of Tuvalu' in *Implications of Culture for Constitution Building* (International IDEA and Constitution Transformation Network, 2018).
[105] Kahn (n 72) 82.

being guided by their laws. As *Teonea* illustrates, however, difficulties arise when the constitution seeks to enshrine a plurality of values, derived from customary and western constitutional traditions. It is difficult for any judge to resolve such tensions within the constitutional text and communicate that resolution to the community, but perhaps more so for a foreign judge, who is not a member of that community and who does not share in its indigenous customary values.

V. DESCRIPTIVE REPRESENTATION: FOREIGN JUDGES AND A REFLECTIVE JUDICIARY

The use of foreign judges means that the judiciaries of the Pacific are not reflective of the communities they serve, although variations in the proportion of foreign judges vis-à-vis local judges makes this unreflectiveness more prominent in some states than others. Where foreign judges predominate, the court is composed, at least by majority, of judges of a different nationality, and generally also of a different ethnic and cultural identity from that of the community. The practice of foreign judging, at least to date, has also contributed to the fact that Pacific courts are composed mostly of *male* judges. Women are underrepresented in judicial office across the region, including in the cohort of foreign judges who have served in the Pacific over the past two decades. So while the use of foreign judges gives Pacific states access to a wider and potentially more gender-diverse pool of candidates for judicial appointment, it has not in practice enhanced gender balance on Pacific courts.[106]

The use of foreign judges, and the increasing use of local judges, affects public perceptions of the judiciary. This is illustrated by the 'Rooney affair' in Papua New Guinea, where a constitutional contest between the executive and the judiciary tested public confidence in a court composed of foreign judges. Aside from the Rooney affair, however, the use of foreign judges has not, by and large, threatened public confidence in Pacific judiciaries. Instead, the idea of judges as descriptive representatives directs attention to the different audiences that foreign judges speak to, both within and outside the state.

A. Public Confidence

The value of a reflective judiciary is generally framed in terms of public confidence. Because this focuses on public perceptions of the judiciary, it takes different forms in different contexts. In the United Kingdom, for example, it

[106] Of the 225 foreign judges who served in the nine Pacific states over the period from 2000 to 2019, only 16, or 7%, were women: ch 2, section V.C. See further A Dziedzic, '"To Join the Bench and Be Decision-Makers": Women Judges in Pacific Island Judiciaries' in M Crouch (ed), *Women and the Judiciary in the Asia-Pacific* (Cambridge, Cambridge University Press, 2021) 29.

is claimed that public confidence is undermined when people see judges as distant, elite or 'other'.[107] In countries where certain groups have historically been excluded from the judiciary and legal profession, the presence of persons from those groups on the courts signals equal rights and inclusion.[108] In both cases, the claim is that people are more likely to respect and trust a judiciary in which they can 'see themselves'[109] and which, collectively, has greater and wider knowledge of the community it serves.[110]

In some countries, a judiciary predominantly composed of foreign judges would be regarded unfavourably by the public. This has not generally been the case in the Pacific. While there is no comprehensive empirical study of public confidence in Pacific judiciaries, the superior courts in most of the nine Pacific states – all of which include foreign judges – are generally well-respected. Two exceptions are Nauru and Fiji, where interference by the executive or military government in the courts has compromised public confidence. In these cases, however, the concern is not so much that the judges are foreign, but rather that foreign judges have been particularly susceptible to influence by a powerful executive.[111]

It is in Papua New Guinea that the use of foreign judges tested the confidence of the public and other branches of government in the judiciary, in what is known as the 'Rooney affair'.[112] Nahau Rooney was the Minister for Justice. In July 1979, she wrote a letter to the Chief Justice, following a decision by another judge to grant an injunction to prevent the executive from deporting a non-citizen. Expressing 'the feelings of the Nation', the Minister accused the Court of intervening in matters properly left to the executive. She urged the judges to 'make a greater effort to use their discretion effectively to develop the National legal system in the context of a proud and growing National consciousness'. In reply, the Chief Justice accused the Minister of an 'unconstitutional attempt to interfere with the Judiciary in its duty' and asserted that judges would not

[107] Cahill-O'Callaghan (n 24) 4; Etherton (n 15) 744.

[108] eg in the United States, EM Chen, 'The Judiciary, Diversity, and Justice for All' (2003) 91(4) *California Law Review* 1109, 1117; in South Africa, F Du Bois, 'Judicial Selection in Post-Apartheid South Africa' in Russell and Malleson (eds) (n 23) 280, 283–84.

[109] P Hoster, 'Understanding the Value of Judicial Diversity through the Native American Lens' (2011) 36 *American Indian Law Review* 457, 459–61; Rackley (n 23) 23–24; Russell and Malleson (n 23) 434.

[110] Framed in this way, arguments for judicial diversity can avoid a sense that judges 'represent' a particular identity group, as well as the essentialist implication that all persons of a particular identity group share the same experience and speak with one voice: Cahill-O'Callaghan (n 24); Etherton (n 15) 745.

[111] Eames (n 50); Leung (n 54).

[112] This description of events is drawn from accounts in B Narokobi, 'How Independent Are the Courts in Papua New Guinea? The Somare/Rooney Affair' (1980) 9(2) *Pacific Perspective* 12; J Nonggorr, 'The Maintenance of Judicial Independence and Integrity in Papua New Guinea: Some Recent Developments' (1992) 18(3) *Commonwealth Law Bulletin* 1181; D Weisbrot, 'Judges and Politicians' (1979) 4 *Legal Service Bulletin* 240.

accept directions or pressure from a Minister or anyone else. Rooney responded with an apology, stating she did not intend to interfere in a particular decision but rather sought to identify some 'grey areas' of potential conflict between the executive and the judiciary. The Chief Justice, in a special sitting of the Supreme Court, revealed the correspondence. Rooney also went public, stating on radio that she had 'no confidence in the Chief Justice and the other Judges' because 'it appears that the foreign judges on the bench are only interested in the administration of foreign laws, and not the feelings and aspirations of the Nation's political leaders'.[113]

The State Prosecutor charged Rooney with contempt, alleging that her letter to the Chief Justice was an attempt to influence the judges hearing the deportation case and that her comments on radio had scandalised the Court, because there was a real risk that her comments would impair public confidence in the judiciary. A majority of the Supreme Court found Rooney guilty of contempt and sentenced her to eight months' imprisonment with light labour.[114] One day into her sentence, the Prime Minister appointed himself the new Minister for Justice and exercised that Minister's powers to release Rooney. By the end of the affair, five foreign judges had resigned in protest at what they characterised as executive interference in judicial independence. In the aftermath, the Government appointed the first Papua New Guinean judges to the National and Supreme Courts, beginning an early and distinctive trend to localisation that Papua New Guinea has sustained ever since.[115]

It is not necessary here to determine whether Minister Rooney was justified in her criticisms, or whether the Court was right to convict her of contempt. What is relevant is the way in which the composition of the Court, which consisted entirely of foreign judges, affected how the dispute was perceived by the Government, the public and the Court itself. Rooney's trial was a dramatic illustration of a non-reflective judiciary. In the Supreme Court on the day of the trial, the only Papua New Guinean present was Rooney herself: 'she was prosecuted by foreigners, defended by foreigners and judged by foreigners according to foreign law which [Papua New Guinea] has adopted under its Constitution'.[116] The Court refused Rooney's offer of a customary apology.[117] As Minister for Justice, Rooney had worked towards nationalising the judiciary and had earlier clashed with the Chief Justice, when he, as a member of the Judicial and Legal Services Commission, had blocked the appointment

[113] The letters and interviews are extracted in *Public Prosecutor v Rooney (No 2)* [1979] PNGLR 448, 453–57.

[114] ibid. Four judges held that a sentence of imprisonment was warranted on the more serious charge of attempting to influence the court in a pending case. Justice Kearney dissented, dismissing this charge on the grounds that there was no pending case at the time Rooney made her comments. He would have imposed a fine for the lesser offence of scandalising the court.

[115] See ch 2, section VI.A.

[116] Narokobi (n 112) 18.

[117] ibid 17.

of a senior Papua New Guinean lawyer to the judiciary.[118] The Minister was also a former member of the Law Reform Commission, which at that time was promoting the development of a jurisprudence based on custom and the localisation of the judiciary.[119] A court of foreign judges was sitting in judgment on a Minister who had advocated for localisation and had criticised foreign judges for failing to develop the law to suit the conditions of Papua New Guinea.

The judgment shows how the unreflective nature of the bench affected how the Court perceived its own authority. Some judges expressly recognised that, in a contest between the judiciary and the executive, they could not rely on the support of the public. In his reasons for decision, Justice Wilson acknowledged that it remained to be seen whether the judiciary had the 'support and confidence of the community at large' and 'whether its independence from government is not only known to exist but, more importantly, is valued'. He acknowledged that the Court's 'show of strength' against the executive might cause short-term damage, but hoped 'in the long term that will be seen as being in the interests of the people'.[120] It has been suggested that the Court's invocation of the outdated offence of scandalising the court revealed the Court's own lack of confidence in the community's respect for it.[121] As in other contexts, the resignation of the judges communicated concerns for the integrity of the constitutional system.

Foreign judges can be an easy scapegoat for governments and others to discredit judicial decisions, by representing them, as Rooney did, as foreigners applying foreign laws, or neo-colonial agents promoting external interests. In Samoa and Tonga, foreign judges have been criticised for failing to fully understand the local context.[122] In Nauru, government ministers criticised Australian judges who decided cases against the Government's interests, labelling them 'white ears' (a disparaging term for white people) with values different from those of the people of Nauru,[123] and accusing them of 'conflicts of interest and disregard for the laws of our nation'.[124]

In *Rooney*, the judges characterised the Minister's comments not as criticisms of the practice of foreign judging, but as attacks on judicial independence

[118] Weisbrot (n 112) 244.

[119] A connection that informed the language of her criticism of the Court, as recognised by Kearney J: *Public Prosecutor v Rooney (No 2)* [1979] PNGLR 448, 487. See Law Reform Commission of Papua New Guinea, 'Declaration and Development of Underlying Law', *Working Paper No 4* (1976); B Narokobi, 'The System of Selecting Judges of the National and Supreme Courts: A Proposal', *Occasional Paper No 7* (Law Reform Commission of Papua New Guinea, 1978).

[120] *Public Prosecutor v Rooney (No 2)* [1979] PNGLR 448, 506–07. See also ibid 469, Raine DCJ.

[121] D Brown, 'Judicial Independence: An Examination' (1986) 58(4) *The Australian Quarterly* 348, 349–50.

[122] *Attorney-General v Namoa* [2000] TOSC 13; M Casey, 'New Zealand Judges in Overseas Courts' in I Barker and G Wear (eds), *Law Stories: Essays on the New Zealand Legal Profession 1969–2003* (Wellington, LexisNexis NZ, 2003) 89, 100.

[123] 'Nauru Justice Minister Attacks Nauru 19 Lawyers' *Radio New Zealand* (Wellington) (15 August 2018).

[124] Government of Nauru, 'Nauru Government Sets the Record Straight' *Media Release* (24 February 2014).

and therefore on the Constitution. One judge characterised Rooney as daring 'to pit her puny might, not against unimportant foreign judges administering insignificant foreign laws, but against the majesty of law and justice which the people of this country had freely adopted as their own'.[125] The judges chose to insist on the authority of the court rather than demonstrate 'sensitivity to the special cultural conditions and jurisprudential traditions of Papua New Guinea'.[126] Much has changed across the Pacific since 1979, including the temperament and attitudes of individual foreign judges, the best of whom are described as acting with humility and sensitivity to local conditions.[127] Nevertheless, the Rooney affair illustrates how foreign judges might rely on the 'majesty' of law[128] and a conception of the judge as the bearer of that law to shield themselves from criticisms of the wider practice of foreign judging.

The Rooney affair shows how the use of foreign judges can contribute to a sense that the court is out of step with the government and the people. This, combined with other circumstances, might diminish the confidence of the government, the people, and of the judges themselves, in the judiciary. Papua New Guinea recovered from the Rooney affair. It continues to use foreign judges, although in much smaller proportions than any other Pacific state. The judiciary is highly respected for its independence.[129] As in other Pacific states, public confidence in the judiciary has not suffered because of the use of foreign judges: indeed, it is more commonly claimed that foreign judges enhance public confidence because of popular perceptions about their impartiality and expertise.[130] It seems, therefore, that while the use of foreign judges *risks* compromising public confidence in the courts, in the Pacific it has not actually done so.

B. External Audiences and the Sovereignty Paradox

Claims about public confidence usually centre on the perception of the judiciary in the eyes of the national community. Scholarship on the idea of a reflective judiciary similarly proceeds on the assumption that the judiciary ought to resemble the national community. Courts, however, have other audiences. The use of foreign judges can be understood as one way to support the confidence of those outside the state, because it speaks to external audiences.

[125] *Public Prosecutor v Rooney (No 2)* [1979] PNGLR 448, 483, Saldanha J.
[126] Weisbrot (n 112) 243.
[127] Interviews F14, F23, F24.
[128] Brown (n 121).
[129] S Dorney, *The Embarrassed Colonialist* (Melbourne, Penguin Group Australia, 2016) 40.
[130] eg M Forsyth, 'Understanding Judicial Independence in Vanuatu', *Discussion Paper 2015/9, State, Society and Governance in Melanesia* (Canberra, Australian National University, 2015) 11–12; V Iyer, 'The Judiciary in Fiji: A Broken Reed?' in HP Lee and M Pittard (eds), *Asia-Pacific Judiciaries: Independence, Impartiality and Integrity* (Cambridge, Cambridge University Press, 2017) 109, 128–29.

The independence, expertise and credibility of the judiciary have been characterised by the World Bank and others as critical conditions for foreign investment and economic growth in developing countries.[131] Foreign judges are sometimes seen as a way to provide specialist expertise, for example in complex commercial matters, to a Pacific court.[132] Even where they do not have specialist expertise, foreign judges, particularly when they are recruited from among the sitting or retired judges of 'trusted' courts of developed countries, are seen to assure foreign investors. Iyer writes that foreign judges in Fiji have brought a 'wealth of talent, expertise, prestige, trustworthiness, old-world courtesy, sound judgment, robust common sense and a broad outlook which inspires confidence in the general public and the world of international business alike'.[133] Lin Feng identifies a similar dynamic in Hong Kong, where the presence of foreign judges serves to 'preserve the image' of an impartial and corruption-free judiciary for foreign investors.[134] This 'image' is a function of descriptive representation: foreign investors who 'see themselves', or at least a judge associated with their own or a more familiar national jurisdiction, are thought to have greater confidence in both the judiciary and the legal system.

A similar idea is also apparent in the use of foreign judges to enhance the authority of constitutional decisions made by Pacific courts. Boyd writes that foreign judges on Pacific courts of appeal are valuable because

> it is vitally important, if the review judgment is to be respected by all parties, and to be worthy of serving as precedent for future judgments in a wider range of jurisdictions, that the judges are seen to be impartial, experienced, respected and wiser than the judges who brought down the original judgment.[135]

One judge interviewed noted that sometimes Pacific courts of appeal hearing contentious constitutional cases are deliberately composed of judges from a diverse range of jurisdictions.[136] Again, the value of foreign judges is, at least in part, understood to lie in the way that they reflect an external audience – in these cases the regional or international community – which is thought to bolster the credibility of the decision.

[131] KW Dam, *The Law-Growth Nexus: The Rule of Law and Economic Development* (Washington, DC, Brookings Institution Press, 2006) ch 5; IF Shihata, *The World Bank in a Changing World* (Dordrecht, M Nijhoff Publishers, 1991).

[132] Interviews F9, F11, F22, F24.

[133] Iyer (n 130) 128–29.

[134] F Lin, 'The Expatriate Judges and Rule of Law in Hong Kong: Its Past, Present and Future' in S Shetreet and W McCormack (eds), *The Culture of Judicial Independence in a Globalised World* (Leiden, Brill Nijhoff, 2016) 279, 304.

[135] S Boyd, 'Australian Judges at Work Internationally: Treason, Assassinations, Coups, Legitimacy of Government, Human Rights, Poverty and Development' (2003) 77 *Australian Law Journal* 303, 307.

[136] Interview F4. Cases in this category might include *Fiji v Prasad* [2001] FJCA 2, concerning the legality of the purported abrogation of the Constitution during the 2000 coup, heard by a panel of five judges from Australia, New Zealand, Papua New Guinea and the United Kingdom; and *Reference by HE the President* [2002] FJSC 1, concerning the allocation of seats in the Fiji Senate, heard by a panel of five judges from Fiji, New Zealand, Papua New Guinea and Samoa.

The colonial resonances of such ideas are difficult to ignore. Colonial narratives characterised the Indigenous peoples of the Pacific as uncivilised and incapable of self-government.[137] Some Indigenous leaders established written constitutions drawing on western precedents in the hope that establishing systems of government familiar to western eyes would demonstrate self-government and ward off colonisation.[138] European settlers, however, were generally hostile to the idea of submitting to courts presided over by Indigenous judges and demanded instead their own judges.[139] A similar dynamic played out as Pacific colonies obtained independence over the years between 1962 and 1980. Independent Pacific states chose to continue the systems of government introduced by colonial administrations in part to signal their capacity for self-government to the departing colonial regime and the international community.[140] The result is described by Merry as the 'sovereignty paradox', whereby Pacific nations adopted western forms of governance in order to gain international recognition as sovereign states, but required skilled foreigners to administer the very institutions of government that marked their independence.[141] MacFarlane's critique of foreign judges in the Pacific is compelling in light of this history, when he writes that the continued use of foreign judges, particularly where there are local judges available, is 'akin to saying that these independent states are not ready or able to be self-governing'.[142] These tensions lie deep in colonialism and in modern international development assistance and rule of law initiatives.[143] For newly independent states, localisation across government and the private sector was, and continues to be, a visible and achievable expression of nationalism.[144] The appointment of local judges, particularly to the highest courts, is 'a symbol of independence' and one way in which Pacific states express their sovereignty and self-sufficiency.[145]

[137] T Banivanua-Mar, *Decolonisation and the Pacific: Indigenous Globalisation and the Ends of Empire* (Cambridge, Cambridge University Press, 2016) ch 5; AM Healy, 'Colonial Law and Metropolitan Defence: The Curious Case of Australia in New Guinea' in H Hiery and JM MacKenzie (eds), *European Impact and Pacific Influence: British and German Colonial Policy in the Pacific Islands and the Indigenous Response* (London, Tauris Academic Studies, 1997) 214, 221–25.

[138] S Lātūkefu, 'Constitution-Making in the Pacific Islands in the Nineteenth Century' in PG Sack (ed), *Pacific Constitutions: Proceedings of the Canberra Law Workshop VI* (Canberra, Australian National University, 1982) 21.

[139] In Fiji: T Banivanua-Mar, 'Frontier Space and the Reification of the Rule of Law: Colonial Negotiations in the Western Pacific, 1870–74' (2009) 30 *Australian Feminist Law Journal* 23, 30–32; in Tonga: G Powles, 'The Common Law as a Source of Law in the South Pacific: Experiences in Western Polynesia' (1988) 10 *University of Hawaii Law Review* 105, 120–21.

[140] A Anghie, *Imperialism, Sovereignty and the Making of International Law* (Cambridge, Cambridge University Press, 2005) 107–08; Banivanua-Mar (n 137) 146.

[141] SE Merry, *Colonizing Hawai'i: The Cultural Power of Law* (Princeton, NJ, Princeton University Press, 2000) 47, 89.

[142] P MacFarlane, 'Some Challenges Facing Legal Strengthening Projects in Small Pacific Island States' (2006) 4(1) *Journal of Commonwealth Law and Legal Education* 103, 105–06.

[143] M Brown, '"An Unqualified Human Good"? On Rule of Law, Globalization, and Imperialism' (2018) 43(4) *Law and Social Inquiry* 1391.

[144] Weisbrot (n 112) 243.

[145] MacFarlane (n 142) 105; Narokobi (n 119) 3–4, 6.

Another way in which sovereignty is expressed and maintained is through control over *who* is selected to sit on the courts of Pacific states. Upon independence, several African states that relied on foreign judges undertook to 'Africanise' their judiciaries, recruiting black judges from other African countries and the Caribbean in preference to white judges from the former colonial power as a way to break the racial hierarchies inherent in colonialism.[146] Pacific island states did not adopt a similar strategy. The empirical study in chapter 2 shows that the majority of foreign judges were, and still are, recruited from the former colonial powers of Australia, New Zealand and the United Kingdom. Only 15 of the 225 foreign judges serving in the Pacific between 2000 and 2019 were from other Pacific states. There are, however, signs that some states are increasingly looking to appoint Pacific Islander judges as foreign judges. One notable example is Nauru, which since 2014 has appointed three Fijian judges to the office of Chief Justice[147] and in 2018 created a new Court of Appeal, whose inaugural members were all senior judges from other Pacific states.[148] Sir John Muria, a Solomon Islander and former Chief Justice in his own country, served as Chief Justice of Kiribati from 2011 to 2020. Papua New Guinea, which has a larger local legal profession and judiciary than other Pacific states, has a long history of providing judges to Solomon Islands, Vanuatu and now Nauru.[149] Recruiting judges from within the region and from other post-colonial states in the Global South[150] changes the appearance of the judiciary, and with it the way in which internal and external audiences perceive it. It is possible to read a variety of meanings into this development: an affirmation of regional self-sufficiency and solidarity; the potential for greater integration of customary values into Pacific legal systems; and a rejection of colonial assumptions about Indigenous peoples and a recognition of the expertise, independence and integrity of Pacific Islander judges.

C. Internal Audiences and Legal Pluralism

Democratic political theory rests on the idea that the people are the authors of their own law. A judiciary composed of foreign judges raises questions about the

[146] R Ellett, *Pathways to Judicial Power in Transitional States: Perspectives from African Courts* (Abingdon, Routledge, 2013) 56. Although leaders in some states, such as Tanganyika, rejected Africanisation as racially discriminatory: ER Feingold, *Colonial Justice and Decolonization in the High Court of Tanzania, 1920–1971* (Cham, Palgrave Macmillan, 2018) 168–69.

[147] Joni Madraiwiwi (2014), Filimone Jitoko (2018) and Daniel Fatiaki (2021).

[148] Vincent Lunabek (Vanuatu); Sir Albert Palmer and Sir John Muria (Solomon Islands).

[149] These include Kubulan Los (Solomon Islands); Reggett Maram (Vanuatu) and Sir Arnold Amet (Fiji and Vanuatu). In 2018, Justice Nicholas Kirriwom was sworn in as a judge of the Nauru Court of Appeal, pursuant to an MOU: 'Senior PNG Judge Sworn in as Nauru Judge' *Loop PNG* (18 November 2018).

[150] Over the period 2000 to 2019, six African judges have served on courts in Kiribati, Papua New Guinea, Solomon Islands and Vanuatu. Since 2009, 47 Sri Lankans have served on courts of constitutional jurisdiction in Fiji.

extent to which the judiciary that applies and sometimes develops laws should be composed of members 'of the people'.

The circumstances of legal pluralism that pertain in Pacific states complicate democratic theories about the connection between law, people and judges. Legal pluralism in the Pacific entails the coexistence of transplanted laws and indigenous custom. The interaction between these legal systems differs across states, areas of law and institutions, giving rise to a great deal of complexity. Sometimes the systems mix, in that statutes or common law might recognise or incorporate custom; or custom might operate within a statutory framework.[151] Sometimes, the interaction is at the point of legal or constitutional values, in that customary values are used to inform the interpretation of constitutional law and institutions.[152] Other times, the legal systems are regarded as separate and exclusive spheres of jurisdiction, as a result of law or practice.[153]

Both the western-derived constitutional system and indigenous legal systems are laws of the people, but in different ways, and potentially with different degrees of ownership. Writing in the context of Fiji, Kaplan argues that coup leaders and chiefs have understood their actions as justified by values of Fijian society that are more fundamental than constitutions and courts.[154] Nanau suggests that Solomon Islanders see government institutions as alien and turn instead to cultural structures and allegiances.[155] Tamanaha, in his study of law in Micronesia, develops a theory to explain these dynamics in situations of transplanted law.[156] For Tamanaha, understanding law requires an inquiry not into the substantive legal rules, but into how different communities think and act about law. He identifies four such communities in Micronesia: expatriate lawyers and judges; Micronesian lawyers; lay Micronesian judges; and the wider population. These groups each have a different internal understanding of what law means, which emerges in the different ways they view, for example, the authority of a judge or the function of the constitution. For the wider community of Micronesian citizens, law is important but exists apart from community life: law is a source of rules and powers, but not the only, or even central, source. The assumption animating theories about the democratic legitimacy of law is that the community generates the social norms enforced by legal institutions. In Micronesia, however, the different ways of thinking

[151] J Corrin, 'Moving beyond the Hierarchical Approach to Legal Pluralism in the South Pacific' (2009) 59 *Journal of Legal Pluralism and Unofficial Law* 29.

[152] But see ch 5, section IV.A.

[153] M Forsyth, *A Bird That Flies with Two Wings: The Kastom and State Justice Systems in Vanuatu* (Canberra, ANU Press, 2009) ch 4.

[154] M Kaplan, 'Promised Lands: From Colonial Lawgiving to Postcolonial Takeovers in Fiji' in SE Merry and DL Brenneis (eds), *Law and Empire in the Pacific: Fiji and Hawaii* (Santa Fe, NM, School of American Research Press, 2004) 153, 182.

[155] GL Nanau, 'Solomon Islands' in SI Levine (ed), *Pacific Ways: Government and Politics in the Pacific Islands*, 2nd edn (Wellington, Victoria University Press, 2016) 291, 297.

[156] BZ Tamanaha, *Understanding Law in Micronesia: An Interpretive Approach to Transplanted Law* (Leiden, EJ Brill, 1993).

about law within each community mean that there is no shared community understanding, with the result that law is 'autonomous' and detached from community life.[157]

Tamanaha's theory of transplanted law helps to explain, at least in part, why the use of foreign judges on national courts is accepted practice in the Pacific. The use of imported, technical experts to administer transplanted laws seems appropriate, because in one sense the laws are as foreign as the judges. Recruiting an outsider to determine disputes according to custom, would, in contrast, disrupt the internal logic of the customary legal system. Because the two legal systems are not completely separate, tensions are most likely to arise when formal courts and foreign judges are required to determine matters that affect custom, as illustrated in Tuvalu by the *Teonea* case. This is not to suggest that one or other of the component bodies of law in a pluralist legal system is illegitimate or irrelevant. The point is rather that they are understood in different ways and directed to different purposes, and that this affects the degree to which it matters that the judiciary reflects the people.

D. Accounting for Public Confidence in Foreign Judges

Why do courts comprising foreign judges retain public confidence in the Pacific, when they would not do so in other countries? One answer relates to the context in which Pacific legal systems operate, the realities of small developing states and the continuing effects of colonisation. The intricacies of the internal and external audiences described here provide an explanation – albeit partial – for how the use of foreign judges shapes perceptions of Pacific courts in ways that do not diminish public confidence. Writing in the context of the United Kingdom, Barmes and Malleson pose a similar question: why, despite 'its grossly unreflective composition' over many years, does the United Kingdom judiciary continue to enjoy public confidence? Their answer is that, in the absence of any serious crisis of confidence, the authority of courts might be secured by maintaining the traditional view of judges as technicians, applying the law impartially in allegiance to law alone.[158] A similar dynamic is at play in the Pacific: any sense that the judiciary ought to be a descriptive representative of the society it serves is overshadowed by the perception of the foreign judge as an impartial professional, skilled in adjudicating disputes according to law, and in particular those laws derived from the transplanted western legal system.

[157] ibid 29, 160, 170.
[158] Barmes and Malleson (eds) (n 23) 374–75.

VI. CONCLUSION

Benhabib describes how the movement of people across national borders requires individuals to develop and sustain multiple allegiances.[159] The movement of judges across national boundaries has a similar effect. It multiplies the allegiances that a judge – as an individual and a public official – holds, as well as the audiences of his or her actions, blurring the lines of authorisation and accountability. Foreign judges serving on courts of constitutional jurisdiction in the Pacific are not regarded as representatives of their home state, guided by patriotic or nationalist feelings. But neither are they able to 'act for' the Pacific state in the same way that they might 'act for' their home jurisdiction, for example by proactively leading social or legal reforms when the occasion arises.

The experience of foreign judging in the Pacific suggests that the way that states, communities and judges themselves deal with this is to focus, as much as possible, on the sense that judges are professionals, authorised by, acting for and representative of the law. Foreign judges might swear allegiance to the state and its people, but they also swear a judicial oath of professional performance. While some lines of accountability for the appointment of foreign judges lead to the political institutions and people of the Pacific state, reputational and professional ties connect foreign judges more securely to their peers and constituencies in their home states. Foreign judges might not feel that they are legitimate representatives of the nation and its people, but they are qualified representatives of the law. Rather than speak for the community or the state, foreign judges much more readily adopt a role in which they act on, and thus represent, the law. The presence of foreign judges means that the composition of the judiciary is not reflective of the community it serves, but resemblance to constituencies outside the state fosters a view of judges as transnational legal experts, as skilled at adjudication overseas as in their own country. Emphasising these professional and technical aspects of judging requires glosses and omissions that result in some tensions, particularly in constitutional cases where a court reviews the laws or conduct of the elected branches of government, or where courts must engage matters of custom. By and large, however, it is this understanding of foreign judges as professionals for hire that underwrites the practice of foreign judges in the Pacific.

[159] S Benhabib, *The Rights of Others: Aliens, Residents, and Citizens* (Cambridge, Cambridge University Press, 2004) 174.

8

A Transnational Profession and Practice

I. INTRODUCTION

THE USE OF foreign judges is a long-standing and familiar practice across the Pacific states of Fiji, Kiribati, Nauru, Papua New Guinea, Samoa, Solomon Islands, Tonga, Tuvalu and Vanuatu. It reaches back to a colonial past in which judges were recruited by colonial administrators from outside these polities and courts of appeal were located in regional or metropolitan centres. Aspects of these arrangements continued into independence, the difference being that the governments of independent Pacific states now exercised the authority to appoint the judges and to opt in or out of the jurisdiction of external courts of appeal. The practices surrounding the use of foreign judges continue to evolve with the changing circumstances of the Pacific states that use foreign judges and the countries and organisations that provide them. The countries of origin and professional backgrounds of foreign judges, the rationales for their use and the expectations placed upon them, have all changed in response to the appointment of local judges in greater number, the pressures of political crises of the kinds seen in Fiji and Solomon Islands, and the nature of law and justice development assistance as it is provided by donors and received by states. There are signs that in the future the practice may change again, as more foreign judges are recruited from within the Pacific region and other states of the Global South. Although the practice is evolving, Pacific states are likely to continue to use foreign judges for the foreseeable future.

Despite its entrenchment, foreign judging is a somewhat precarious practice for both foreign judges and Pacific judiciaries. It is subject to limited regulation both in the Pacific states and in judges' home states and donor organisations. For judges, appointments tend to be ad hoc and tenure insecure. For judiciaries, the practice introduces an element of instability, as judicial positions are filled by a succession of foreign judges rather than by a single permanent judge. The challenges in recruiting foreign judges have led, in some cases, to shortcomings in the assessment of candidates, insecure conditions of employment, and the use of incentives that create disparities in the treatment of local and foreign judges. In other cases, however, the appointment of foreign judges who have a commitment to the Pacific state and an approach appropriate to the context in which Pacific courts operate has provided Pacific judiciaries with expertise and enhanced their independence and reputation.

This book has shown that foreign judges are subject to conditions of service different from those of local judges, sometimes by express legal provision and inevitably in practice. This different treatment can be justified because foreign judges *are*, in certain ways, different from local judges. Foreign judges bring different dimensions of knowledge to bear on constitutional adjudication. They face distinctive burdens on their independence, deriving not only from the insecurities of tenure but also from their commitments to their home countries and the diverse institutions involved in their recruitment. Finally, foreign judges have a different relationship with the people and the state, such that they are most readily understood as representatives of a profession, while citizen judges are capable of also representing the state and its people.

The empirical description and critical analysis of the implications of the use of foreign judges presented in this book provide the evidence necessary to understand the rationales for the use of foreign judges and the legitimacy of the practice, and to suggest improvements for the future. These are the tasks taken up in this concluding chapter. In section II, I set out four rationales for the use of foreign judges in the Pacific and assess the extent to which the practice meets its own objectives. I suggest that greater clarity about the rationales for using foreign judges would provide a more secure foundation for some of the distinctive and problematic features of foreign judging. In section III, I examine the challenges that the use of foreign judges poses to the legitimacy of courts of constitutional jurisdiction. I show that the legitimacy of foreign judges is tested when the role of the judge is seen to move beyond the adjudication of disputes according to law, as may be the case when judges must attend to an unfamiliar law such as custom, or to the social and political effects of a constitutional decision. On the basis of these assessments, in section IV I propose five good practice initiatives to better support the rationales and address the challenges of foreign judging, which might be used to inform the regulation of foreign judges by Pacific states, judges' home states and donor organisations. I conclude with some observations about the global significance of this study, as the use of foreign judges takes different forms in new contexts across the world.

II. RATIONALE

Constitution makers, legislators, executive governments, courts, donors and judges have offered a range of rationales for the use of foreign judges in the Pacific. The legal frameworks and the practices of foreign judging disclose further, and sometimes different, understandings of the function that foreign judges are to perform. This points to the existence of several rationales, which may be invoked to suit different audiences and to serve different purposes.

This section discusses the four rationales commonly offered for the use of foreign judges in the Pacific: as a transitional measure pending localisation; to develop local capacity; to enhance the reputation of the court; and to provide impartiality.[1] It assesses whether the Pacific practice of foreign judging meets each rationale, by analysing the concurrence between the rationale, the conception of the role of foreign judges, and the legal frameworks and practices regulating the service of foreign judges.

A. Transition

Transition, albeit over a long period, provides a compelling rationale for the use of foreign judges in the Pacific. Where there is a shortage of qualified citizens willing and able to take up judicial office, foreign judges can temporarily take the place of local judges. In development assistance parlance, this practice is known as 'gap filling'. Foreign experts are recruited to fill gaps in government agencies to ensure that essential government services, including judicial services, are delivered.[2]

Under the transition rationale, foreign judges provide necessary judicial services for Pacific polities until a local judge becomes available. This rationale accords with the predominant understanding that foreign judges in the Pacific are there, first and foremost, to sit *as judges*. Foreign judges have the same status, powers and duties as local judges. In most cases, the terms of their commissions are not limited to hearing particular kinds of cases, or to performing particular judicial and non-judicial tasks. Quotas to require that a certain number or proportion of the judges on the bench must be either local or foreign are rare.

While foreign judges perform the same functions as local judges, they are treated differently, most notably in relation to tenure. Foreign judges tend to be appointed on short renewable contracts, while local judges generally have tenure to a specified age of retirement. I argue in chapter 6 that the most compelling justification for the appointment of foreign judges on short renewable terms is to assist the state to transition to local judges. The short-term appointment of foreign judges means that a judicial position will be available when a qualified citizen becomes eligible for appointment. The transition rationale therefore justifies short-term appointments for foreign judges. It could also justify mandatory term limits for non-citizen judges, as is the case in Fiji and Papua New Guinea.[3]

[1] These rationales are set out in ch 1, section II.

[2] M Cox, E Duituturaga and E Scheye, 'Solomon Islands Case Study: Evaluation of Australian Law and Justice Assistance' (Australian Government Office of Development Effectiveness, Ausaid, 2012) 21.

[3] Ch 6, section III.

However, the transition rationale does not properly justify short-term appointments for foreign judges in circumstances unaccompanied by efforts towards localisation. This appears to be the case in Fiji, where the number of local judges appointed to courts of constitutional jurisdiction has decreased since 2009, to the point that in 2019 there was only one more Fijian judge on the relevant courts than in 2000.[4] Indeed, the Fijian Government expresses an entirely different rationale for the use of foreign judges. The understanding, or at least rhetoric, in Fiji post-2009 is that there is no difference between foreign and local judges, and that all judges are assessed on merit against the same criteria.[5] The problem is then a disconnect between the merit-based rationale for the use of foreign judges and the practice of short-term appointments. The mandatory requirement that non-citizen judges be appointed on renewable terms of up to three years[6] lacks justification in the absence of efforts at localisation. This, and the high number of foreign judges on short-term appointments, opens the Fijian judiciary to claims that judicial independence is compromised.[7] In contrast, Papua New Guinea, which also has a mandatory three-year term for non-citizen judges, is not subject to the same criticism because of the efforts it has taken towards localisation and the high proportion of local judges who serve for longer terms.

Another concern raised by the transition rationale, particularly where the period of transition is as lengthy as it is in the Pacific, relates to the stability of the judiciary. Where foreign judges temporarily stand in for local judges, membership of the judiciary is potentially very fluid. Part-time service and the use of short-term appointments contribute to the high number and turnover of foreign judges. This has implications for the expertise of the judges, because it means that foreign judges have limited opportunity to gain both detailed knowledge of the law and a broader knowledge of the context in which it operates. Some states have benefited from having a core group of foreign judges who return to sit on the same court for many years, even without the security of long-term appointments, providing a continuity that bolsters public confidence.[8]

Finally, there is a risk that the use of foreign judges to 'fill gaps' makes Pacific judiciaries overly dependent on external assistance. This was acknowledged in an assessment of the Regional Assistance Mission to Solomon Islands (RAMSI),

[4] Ch 2, section VI.B.

[5] Letter from AHCT Gates, Chief Justice of Fiji, to Anna Dziedzic, 6 October 2016; Fiji, *Parliamentary Debates*, 10 February 2016, 1063–65 (Aiyaz Sayed-Khaiyum, Attorney-General).

[6] *Constitution of Fiji 2013*, s 110.

[7] V Iyer, 'The Judiciary in Fiji: A Broken Reed?' in HP Lee and M Pittard (eds), *Asia-Pacific Judiciaries: Independence, Impartiality and Integrity* (Cambridge, Cambridge University Press, 2017) 109, 115; BV Lal, *Historical Dictionary of Fiji* (Lanham, MD, Rowman & Littlefield, 2016) 24.

[8] eg in Vanuatu: M Forsyth, 'Understanding Judicial Independence in Vanuatu', *Discussion Paper 2015/9, State, Society and Governance in Melanesia* (Canberra, Australian National University, 2015) 12.

which found that 'the practice of inserting foreigners into line positions in … law and justice institutions and agencies is not a sustainable development activity, unless Australia makes an undertaking to fund an open-ended commitment to maintain [Solomon Islands'] law and justice operations'.[9] Reliance on foreign judges without promoting localisation is not sustainable for Pacific judiciaries.[10]

B. Capacity Building

Foreign judges can be understood as part of and complementary to wider efforts to strengthen law and justice systems and promote good governance and the rule of law in Pacific states.[11] To again adopt the language of development assistance, foreign judges support 'capacity building'. This may be cast as building the capacity of the judiciary as an institution, or the capacities of personnel, such as judges, court staff and the local legal profession.

Foreign judges might contribute to the *institutional* capacity of a Pacific judiciary by providing specific expertise that the judiciary otherwise lacks. Papua New Guinea provides an example. The emphasis on localisation since the 1979 Rooney affair means that the National and Supreme Courts are predominantly composed of Papua New Guinean judges. The renewed use of visiting foreign judges on the Supreme Court since 2011 is not, therefore, readily justified by the transition rationale.[12] Instead, the appointment of part-time foreign judges was seen as a way to build the expertise of the Court, by providing judges experienced in dealing with commercial matters of the kind increasingly before Papua New Guinean courts.[13] An example of a different kind occurred in Samoa, where two judges of the District Court of New Zealand were appointed judges in Samoa for approximately a year each, to assist in the establishment of a new family court and a drug and alcohol court.[14] This sense of capacity building is similar to the 'gap-filling' rationale previously described, only instead of filling gaps arising from insufficient numbers of judges, foreign judges fill gaps in specialist areas of judicial expertise.

This understanding of capacity building stands in contrast to the idea that foreign judges help to build the capacity of *personnel* in Pacific judiciaries, which

[9] Cox, Duituturaga and Scheye (n 2) 33.

[10] B Narokobi, 'The System of Selecting Judges of the National and Supreme Courts: A Proposal', *Occasional Paper No 7* (Law Reform Commission of Papua New Guinea, 1978) 6.

[11] J Logan, 'Law and Justice in Papua New Guinea', Paper presented at the Australian Institute of International Affairs, Brisbane (23 June 2015) 48–50.

[12] These developments are discussed in ch 2, section VI.A.

[13] Logan (n 11) 41–42.

[14] 'NZ Judge Praised for Work Samoa' *Radio New Zealand* (Wellington) (27 June 2014); Lanuola Tusani Tupufia, 'Court Tackles Drugs and Alcohol Abuse' *Samoa Observer* (Apia) (28 February 2016).

is most apparent when foreign judges are recruited and paid for by a donor organisation. As noted in chapter 3, advertisements for judges from organisations such as RAMSI or the Commonwealth Fund for Technical Cooperation tend to include in the foreign judge's job description tasks such as improving judicial systems; transferring knowledge and skills to the national judiciary, government staff and practitioners; and mentoring and training court staff and judicial officers.[15] Aid agencies tend to regard this kind of capacity building as part of the work of foreign judges, or at least as a desirable outcome of their service. These advertisements tend to seek a full-time resident foreign judge, to serve for a period of years – conditions of service that provide the continuity and presence to support this kind of capacity building. The capacity-building rationale does not, however, easily justify the use of part-time foreign judges who visit only occasionally to conduct hearings, and who therefore have limited opportunity to identify knowledge gaps or build relationships with judicial colleagues, court staff or the profession in the Pacific state.

The degree to which foreign judging should be linked to foreign aid and development outcomes is a contested and sensitive issue. The idea of the foreign judge as an expert who teaches local judges and lawyers about the law and judicial administration carries overtones of paternalism and imperialism. It risks creating the perception – internally within the state and externally – that local judges and lawyers are not sufficiently qualified and able in their roles. Concerns of this kind are canvassed in the literature on hybrid tribunals, where, in some instances, the 'unstated assumption that the role of the international judge is to impart her wisdom on lesser local counterparts' has undermined the collegiality of the court and opportunities for mutual learning.[16]

Much depends on the attitudes of foreign judges, local judges and the heads of jurisdiction who shape the role of foreign judges within Pacific judiciaries. Several foreign judges interviewed stated that there was no need or expectation that they take on any capacity-building functions.[17] Some acknowledged the sensitivities of taking on such a role, and did so only at the request or with the agreement of the Chief Justice of the Pacific state. These judges tended to regard their contributions to legal education and court reforms and their engagement with local judges and lawyers as incidental to their role rather than as a core purpose, akin to the position they would take in their home jurisdictions.[18] A few noted that foreign judges were in a position to connect Pacific courts and legal professions with experts and donors in their home states, facilitating for example, training for the legal profession, research

[15] Ch 3, section II.C.

[16] H Hobbs, 'Hybrid Tribunals and the Composition of the Court: In Search of Sociological Legitimacy' (2016) 16(2) *Chicago Journal of International Law* 482, 519.

[17] Interviews F4, F5, F8.

[18] Interviews F9, F10.

assistance from law students, or donations of library and other resources.[19] This approach implicitly acknowledges that other programmes and providers may be more appropriate avenues for personal capacity building than foreign judges themselves.[20]

The capacity-building rationale for the use of foreign judges is therefore best confined to institutional capacity building by providing specific and sought-after expertise, or as complementary to other programmes that seek to build the personal capacity of local judges, court staff and legal professions. This rationale for foreign judges ought only to apply in circumstances where capacity-building activities (such as training, mentoring or administrative reforms) are needed, have the support of the head of jurisdiction, and where the full-time residential nature of the foreign judge's service supports it.

C. Reputation

A third rationale sometimes offered is that the presence of foreign judges enhances the reputation of Pacific courts.[21] In contrast to capacity building, in which foreign judges provide specific expertise and engage in activities directed to education or reform, reputational benefits are fulfilled by the mere presence of foreign judges on the bench. This rationale thus draws predominantly on the representative role of a foreign judge. It exploits the status of the foreign judge and the judge's home jurisdiction in order to express the 'choice-worthiness' of the Pacific court.[22]

This rationale is only sometimes reflected in the Pacific practice of foreign judging. It fits most easily when foreign judges are (or were) judges of courts in their home countries that themselves have a high reputation. However, as the data presented in chapter 2 show, the cohort of foreign judges is far more diverse. In particular, approximately 25 per cent of the foreign judges serving in the Pacific over the case study period were practising lawyers at the time of their appointment as judges in the Pacific.[23] While such appointments can and do bring valued expertise to Pacific judiciaries, they do not carry the kind of reputational value that this rationale relies upon.

Another disconnect between the reputation rationale and the practice of foreign judging in the Pacific arises, once again, from the smallness of

[19] Interviews F1, F7, F11, F13, F19, F20, F24.

[20] eg Pacific Judicial Strengthening Initiative funded by the New Zealand Government and implemented by the Federal Court of Australia.

[21] eg S Boyd, 'Australian Judges at Work Internationally: Treason, Assassinations, Coups, Legitimacy of Government, Human Rights, Poverty and Development' (2003) 77 *Australian Law Journal* 303, 307; Iyer (n 7) 128–29.

[22] Ch 7, section III.B.

[23] Ch 2, section V.B.

Pacific island states. The small developing states of the Pacific have limited resources to fund judiciaries and remunerate judges. They are sometimes isolated and difficult places in which to work. Pacific states have benefited from judicial service from eminent and highly regarded jurists, some who take up judicial office in the Pacific out of a sense of service,[24] others who are supported in various ways by their home jurisdictions or donor organisations.[25] However, it is to be expected that, with limited resources, Pacific states will struggle to compete in the global marketplace for judges. The costs of attracting good foreign judges can also lead to their own problems, such as disparity in pay between local and foreign judges.

Because this rationale deals in reputation and appearances, it also risks reinforcing colonial assumptions about the qualities and capacities of foreign and local judges. Foreign judges in the Pacific tend to be citizens of the Global North, with the social and economic capital to work transnationally.[26] There are, however, some signs of change, such as the appointment of judges from Africa;[27] Fiji's turn to Sri Lanka;[28] the appointment of eminent Pacific islander judges to the newly created Nauru Court of Appeal;[29] and the emphasis on south–south collaborations by the Commonwealth Fund for Technical Cooperation.[30] These examples aside, reputation – rightly or wrongly – like the majority of foreign judges, is seen to travel from developed western states to developing Pacific island states.

D. Impartiality

A fourth rationale for the use of foreign judges is that, as outsiders, foreign judges are distanced from small Pacific communities and are thus able to provide a degree of impartiality not available to local judges. In chapter 6, I argued that while this view is prevalent, it does not provide a coherent rationale for the widespread use of foreign judges. Judges on Pacific courts who are, or appear to be, partial in a particular case will recuse themselves or be disqualified

[24] Interviews F3, F8, F9, F11, F12, F24. Sir Salamo Injia, Chief Justice of Papua New Guinea, has paid tribute to foreign judges, commenting on their 'deeply felt desire and conviction to help those in need of their professional expertise. The undertaking is purely voluntary and comes with personal sacrifices … knowing full well the nature of their calling': M Arnold, 'PNG Judiciary Honors Late Justice Foulds' *Post Courier* (Port Moresby) (8 October 2018).

[25] Ch 3, sections II.B, III.

[26] EM Bruch, 'Hybrid Courts: Examining Hybridity through a Post-Colonial Lens' (2010) 28(1) *Boston University International Law Journal* 1, 14, identifies a similar dynamic on hybrid tribunals.

[27] eg the appointment of distinguished Botswanan judge Oagile Key Dingake to the National and Supreme Courts of Papua New Guinea in late 2017.

[28] Ch 2, section V.A.

[29] Ch 7, section V.B.

[30] Commonwealth Secretariat, *Report of the Commonwealth Secretary-General 2011–2013* (London, Commonwealth Secretariat, 2013) 21.

according to the common law test for bias. Membership of the community, and ethnic, religious or cultural affiliations do not, in and of themselves, give rise to impermissible conflicts of interest or bias. The Pacific practice of foreign judging presents a further problem for justifications based on impartiality. The local judges most likely to have personal connections to parties or an interest in the outcome would be lay judges and magistrates serving on lower courts, but foreign judges tend to serve on higher courts that are at a greater distance from the community.[31] For these reasons, impartiality does not provide a sound rationale for the widespread use of foreign judges. In the conditions of smallness that pertain in most Pacific jurisdictions, however, the impartiality rationale does support the use of foreign judges in more confined circumstances, that is, where they stand in for local judges who must recuse themselves from hearing a particular case.

E. The Means and the Ends of Foreign Judging

The four rationales outlined here are not mutually exclusive and often overlap. They are worth disaggregating, however, in order to determine which rationales are supported by practice and which rationales predominate in what circumstances. In the Pacific, transition is the predominant rationale for the use of foreign judges. Until such time as there are sufficient numbers of qualified local candidates willing to take up judicial appointment in the conditions in which Pacific judiciaries operate, Pacific states will continue to rely on foreign judges. As Pacific courts develop specialist jurisdictions, such as commercial, family and youth courts, foreign judges might also be used to provide expertise to Pacific courts for the same 'gap-filling' reasons. The capacity-building and impartiality rationales, when properly circumscribed, are supplementary in that they justify the use of foreign judges for particular purposes, which might, over time and with localisation, be met by citizen judges. The idea that the use of foreign judges enhances the reputation of the court is the most problematic justification for their use. While it may be true in instances where individual foreign judges have a strong personal reputation, the idea that foreign judges, as a class, bestow credibility on a national judiciary is not sustainable and risks damaging the esteem in which local judges are held.

Being clear about the rationale for the use of foreign judges affects the justifications available for some of the distinctive features of foreign judging, such as short-term appointments, funding and payment arrangements, and the involvement of entities outside the Pacific state. Rationales for the use of foreign judges will differ across jurisdictions and change over time, including as prospects for the appointment of local judges increase. Rationales might also differ

[31] Ch 6, section III.

across the courts within a state, for example between full-time superior courts, part-time courts of appeal and emerging specialist courts. In all cases, clarity about the rationale for using foreign judges ought to inform the laws and policies that regulate the use of foreign judges, both in Pacific states themselves and in the external state agencies and organisations that recruit and fund foreign judges.

On all four rationales, the use of foreign judges is understood as an exception. Each rationale takes the preference and the goal to be that Pacific courts should be composed of local judges when the circumstances of Pacific states support it.[32] Although the practice is conceived as exceptional, the period of transition has been, and is likely to continue to be, long. As such, it is important to also understand the effect that the sustained use of foreign judges has on the legitimacy of Pacific courts and address the concerns that arise.

III. LEGITIMACY

The legitimacy of judges, judiciaries and the decisions they make is open to challenge in all constitutional systems. This section considers the distinctive challenges posed by the use of foreign judges to the legitimacy of courts of constitutional jurisdiction, and identifies the points at which pressures on the legitimacy of foreign judges are likely to arise.

Legitimacy is the quality that explains why the decisions of a court (or other authority) are morally binding and why people and governments obey them.[33] To investigate the challenges posed to legitimacy by the use of foreign judges, two major accounts of legitimacy are considered here: the service conception of authority articulated by Raz;[34] and a democratic account of legitimacy. On both accounts, whether or not foreign judges pose a challenge to the legitimacy of courts depends on the view one takes on what judges do, and ought to do, in constitutional adjudication.

A. The Service Conception of Authority

On the service conception, an authority (in this case, a court) is legitimate to the extent its directives promote greater conformity to right reason than if its

[32] N Baird, 'Judges as Cultural Outsiders: Exploring the Expatriate Model of Judging in the Pacific' (2013) 19 *Canterbury Law Review* 80, 96.

[33] This is a normative conception of legitimacy, rather than a social or descriptive account: F Peter, 'Political Legitimacy' in EN Zalta (ed), *Stanford Encyclopedia of Philosophy* (Stanford, CA, Stanford University, 2010) pt 1.

[34] J Raz, 'The Problem of Authority: Revisiting the Service Conception of Authority' (2006) 90 *Minnesota Law Review* 1003.

subjects tried to undertake their own assessment of the reasons that apply to them.[35] Judges have legitimate authority when they are better placed, or more likely, than those subject to their authority to determine the right reasons for action. Judges might be in this position because of their impartiality, their expertise about the facts and law, and, potentially, because they are in a superior position to solve social problems of coordination or cooperation.[36] A foreign judge, to the extent that he or she is in a position to bring these qualities to bear on constitutional adjudication, has legitimate authority, or at least the same degree of legitimate authority, as does any other judge. For example, the impartiality of foreign judges makes them just as capable as citizen judges of fairly resolving legal disputes.

The legal expertise of foreign judges means that they are in a position to state authoritatively what the law is. It is here, however, that the kinds of knowledge imputed to foreign judges might affect their legitimacy, depending on what the law is understood to be. Where law is understood to be based on legal sources, foreign judges with access to those sources can determine what the law is. In this book, this is illustrated by the preference of foreign judges to look to familiar and reasonably clear sources, such as the constitutional text and the shared common law, when adjudicating constitutional issues.[37] Moving away from positivist conceptions of law, a foreign judge might also be able to speak to the moral content of law, particularly where that content is understood to be universal. One example might be where foreign judges apply international human rights norms, which, although a relatively uncommon approach to constitutional adjudication in the Pacific region, might support legitimacy in other contexts.[38]

A problem for legitimacy arises when judges are required to speak to what are (to them) foreign sources of law or a different morality, based, for example, on the customs, habits and common views of a community.[39] The most pressing example considered in this book is custom, which is a source of law in all Pacific legal systems. Conscious of the limitations of their knowledge, foreign judges understandably tend not to deal too closely with custom in the course of constitutional adjudication, preferring instead to draw on more familiar sources of law or to defer to the decisions of local authorities.[40] The risk that foreign judges will overlook or marginalise custom can have serious ramifications. The community's response to the *Teonea* case in Tuvalu, in which the Court's decision was seen to undermine the customary authority of the *Falekaupule*, demonstrates

[35] ibid.

[36] SJ Shapiro, 'Authority' in JL Coleman and SJ Shapiro (eds), *The Oxford Handbook of Jurisprudence and Philosophy of Law* (Oxford, Oxford University Press, 2002) 382, 405–06.

[37] Ch 5, section IV.

[38] Ch 5, section III.A.

[39] J Raz, *The Authority of Law: Essays on Law and Morality*, 2nd edn (Oxford, Oxford University Press, 2009) 46, fn 7.

[40] Ch 5, section IV; Ch 7, section IV.

the kinds of social tensions that can arise when foreign judges rule on customary matters in a way that does not accord with community understandings.[41]

Problems for legitimacy also arise when judges are required to address gaps in the law, or to choose between different possible meanings or applications of a constitutional provision. Such cases test the legitimate authority of all courts because they take courts beyond the core judicial function of resolving disputes according to law and into the realm of law making. There is a range of views about how judges should decide difficult cases of this kind.[42] MacCormick proposes that judges should choose between different possible rulings by considering the effect on the coherence and consistency of the legal system and on society.[43] Dworkin suggests that judges should decide on grounds of principle, seeking an interpretation that fits the law with the political morality of the community.[44] Noting the institutional constraints on judicial law making, Raz suggests that judges should choose between partial reform and conservatism, rather than carry out wide-ranging reforms.[45] All of these views require the judges deciding such cases to be in a position to determine the effect of their decisions on society, the community's political morality or the relationships between political institutions. When they come from within the national community, judges can draw on the understandings embedded in a common history, tradition and practice, and on their own knowledge and experience of institutional relationships and community expectations.[46] Judges from outside the national community, however, are in a more tenuous position to assess not only the law but also its operation in practice. It is difficult to claim that foreign judges are in position equal to or better than that of local judges to determine the right reasons for action that apply to subjects, making the legitimacy of their authority questionable in these circumstances.

B. Democratic Legitimacy

The democratic account provides that an authority is legitimate to the extent that its procedures for decision making or its decisions themselves treat all citizens fairly and with equal respect.[47] Constitutional judicial review challenges

[41] *Teonea v Kaupule* [2005] TVHC 5; *Teonea v Pule o Kaupule of Nanumaga* [2009] TVCA 2, discussed in Ch 7, section IV.

[42] W Lucy, 'Adjudication' in Coleman and Shapiro (eds) (n 36) 207, 208–21.

[43] N MacCormick, *Legal Reasoning and Legal Theory* (Oxford, Clarendon Press, rev edn 1993, 1978) 100, cited by Lucy (n 42) 217.

[44] R Dworkin, *Law's Empire* (London, Fontana, 1986) 255–56, cited by Lucy (n 42) 218.

[45] Raz (n 39) 200–01, cited by Lucy (n 42) 220.

[46] R Dworkin, 'Discussion: International Criminal Justice' in R Badinter and S Breyer (eds), *Judges in Contemporary Democracy: An International Conversation* (New York, New York University Press, 2004) 189, 215.

[47] T Christiano, 'Authority' in Zalta (ed) (n 33) pt 7.

the legitimacy not just of foreign judges but of all judiciaries, because it involves judges who lack the trappings of democratic accountability overruling the determinations of the democratically elected legislature and executive.[48] The pressures on legitimacy are heightened when it is acknowledged that judges not only apply the law, but sometimes also extend or make the law in the course of constitutional adjudication. In the Pacific, as elsewhere, these challenges to legitimacy are most apparent when judges are called upon to adjudicate issues on which there is real social and political contestation.

One response to the democratic objection to judicial review is to emphasise the democratic credentials of judges. This claim, outlined in greater detail in chapter 4, is that the citizenship of judges provides a form of democratic responsiveness, because judges who are citizens are bound by the laws they have a hand in shaping and are invested in their community and their constitution. As citizens, they share in the community's responsibility for the law as it stands and as it might become.[49] While the judge's citizenship does not make judicial *procedures* more democratic, it does signify a representative connection to the people, found in a shared national identity and common membership of the national community.

Foreign judges lack this connection to the people. In the absence of the ties of identity and membership implicit in citizenship, the clearest points of connection between a foreign judge and the people are found in the judge's oath of office and allegiance, and the fact that his or her appointment is, at least formally, in the hands of a body responsible to the people.[50] The use of foreign judges stretches, and sometimes breaks, the range of representative connections between the people on one hand and judges on the other, connections that support the judiciary's engagement in law making and reform. All judges, when engaging in law making, do not score highly on democratic measures of legitimacy, but foreign judges are at an even greater disadvantage.

C. Tethering the Legitimacy of the Foreign Judge

On both accounts, the legitimacy of foreign judges is tested when the conception of judging moves away from a technical understanding of judging as the impartial resolution of disputes through the application of pre-existing law. It is when

[48] J Waldron, *Law and Disagreement* (Oxford, Clarendon Press, 1999) 239–43.

[49] P Kahn, 'Independence and Responsibility in the Judicial Role' in IP Stotzky (ed), *Transition to Democracy in Latin America: The Role of the Judiciary* (Boulder, CO, Westview Press, 1993) 73; RA MacDonald, 'Exercising Judgement' in *Which Judge for Which Society? Proceedings of the 2008 Judges' Conference* (Québec City, 2008) 51, 60, challenging the assumption that judges 'necessarily have a personal agenda that is untethered to the society and community within which they live'.

[50] Ch 7, section III.

the role requires judges to go beyond a technical knowledge of the law, or to take account of the political and social effects of a decision or community values and expectations, that the pressures on legitimacy emerge.[51]

It is in light of these concerns about legitimacy that the predominant conception of the foreign judge as an impartial expert professional assumes significance. Tying the approach to constitutional adjudication to pre-existing laws derived from clear and familiar sources, such as the constitutional text and shared common law, means that foreign judges are understood to have the relevant knowledge and expertise to determine constitutional questions. The emphasis placed on the impartiality of foreign judges and the sense that foreign judges are representatives of a profession rather than the people or the state, further bolster the conception of the foreign judge as impartial expert, with skills that are transferrable across national borders. This conception also supports the transition rationale for the use of foreign judges, by presenting foreign judges as having the necessary expertise and impartiality to temporarily stand in the place of local judges and provide essential judicial services to Pacific communities.

This idea of the foreign judge as a professional, impartial expert resonates with the characterisation of other kinds of international involvement in the governance of independent states. In his study of the expanding powers of international organisations such as the United Nations and the World Bank, Sinclair shows how the deployment of international personnel (including judges) to positions within the governments of independent states came to be seen not as political interference but rather as 'technical assistance'.[52] One way in which international involvement of this kind was justified was through a conception of the 'international civil servant', with the 'ideal combination of personal virtue, specialist knowledge and fidelity to law'.[53] Highlighting the moral purpose, expertise and legality of international personnel helped to legitimate the expanding mandates of international organisations and refute charges of imperialism and interference. The emphasis on the expertise, professionalism and impartiality of foreign judges operates in a similar way to justify the use of foreign judges in the Pacific, a practice that in many other states would be regarded as problematic if not illegitimate.

This conception of the foreign judge is, of course, a construct that requires glosses and omissions to maintain. In this, foreign judges share with all judges an *appearance* of legitimacy, based on notions of expertise, impartiality and

[51] This finding reflects Shapiro's thesis that the burdens on legitimacy increase as judges move beyond the core function of dispute resolution: MM Shapiro, *Courts: A Comparative and Political Analysis* (Chicago, IL, University of Chicago Press, 1981) ch 1.

[52] GF Sinclair, *To Reform the World: International Organizations and the Making of Modern States* (Oxford, Oxford University Press, 2017) 72–73.

[53] ibid 19.

purported neutrality, all of which support public confidence in the judiciary.[54] However, applying this conception to *foreign* judges carries its own distinctive risks. One is the risk that casting foreign judges as neutral, professional experts can imply that citizen judges do not have these qualities. Another is that this conception informs an approach to constitutional adjudication that confines it too closely to constitutional text and fails to give a sufficient role to constitutional and customary values, creating a law that is out of step with the understandings and values of Pacific polities.

IV. GOOD PRACTICE INITIATIVES

The discussions in this book have identified a range of benefits and challenges that arise from the use of foreign judges in the Pacific. In this section, I suggest some good practice initiatives that would support the legitimacy and effectiveness of foreign judging. The initiatives I outline here are deliberately non-prescriptive. It is a matter for each Pacific state, in consultation with stakeholders, including the states and organisations that provide foreign judges, to develop its own laws and practices to address the issues that arise as a result of the use of foreign judges. It is important to also note that this book has assessed the use of foreign judges by considering the implications for *constitutional* adjudication, and that different issues might arise if the focus were to shift to commercial litigation or criminal law for example. The five good practice initiatives set out here are therefore generally framed and intended to respond to the most pressing issues arising from the use of foreign judges in the Pacific.

A. Localisation

Efforts towards localisation – that is, the appointment of citizen judges – serve to support the legitimacy of foreign judges and the sustainability and effectiveness of Pacific judiciaries. The transition and capacity-building rationales make sense only where there is a local judiciary and legal profession. Local judges, whether sitting on single-judge trials or as members of the bench of the court of appeal, provide direct knowledge and experience of local law, custom and community values, helping courts to adjudicate constitutional cases and develop the law in ways that meet community expectations. Local judges are resident, full-time and appointed for longer and more secure terms, providing stability to the judiciary. They are citizens as well as judicial officers, and thus have the distinctive commitments to the law and the community that membership

[54] Lucy (n 42) 265–66.

entails. Finally, the presence of local judges increases the extent to which Pacific judiciaries reflect the communities they serve, supporting public confidence.

Across Pacific states, there do not appear to be any express policies that seek to marry legal frameworks and procedures for judicial appointment with the objective of localisation. In Papua New Guinea, the Constitutional Planning Committee and the Law Reform Commission considered the value of localisation and laws and practices to facilitate it.[55] These efforts, however, were initiated in the 1970s and were somewhat overtaken by the hurried localisation in the aftermath of the Rooney affair. In other states that have achieved a degree of localisation, such as Samoa, Solomon Islands and Vanuatu, this seems due mainly to the efforts of Chief Justices and the authorities responsible for judicial appointments, rather than to a specific policy.

A localisation policy would commit the state to the appointment of local judges and perhaps even nominate a timeline for meeting that goal. The policy could identify necessary steps towards localisation, such as supporting legal education and professional experience; developing progression paths for citizens to judicial office; and addressing the barriers to the taking up of judicial appointments by qualified citizens (such as remuneration or a low mandatory retirement age). It might provide guidance to ensure that appointing authorities first consider local candidates whenever a judicial position is vacant.[56] A localisation policy could also assist courts themselves in the management of judicial workload. For example, a court might consider ways to enable more local judges to sit alongside foreign judges on courts of appeal, whether by increasing the size of the bench (as in Vanuatu) or by including a local judge on the bench where possible (as in Samoa). By setting out the actions required to support localisation, a policy would also guide donor states and organisations, and promote forms of external assistance that are most likely to help the state in its transition from a judiciary predominantly composed of foreign judges to one that is predominantly local.

In some Pacific states, particularly the smallest states of Nauru and Tuvalu, the appointment of local judges is some time away. Even here, however, a localisation policy would be valuable. In Tuvalu, for example, the constitutional provision setting out the requirements for eligibility for appointment to judicial office appears to preclude a person who has served as a Magistrate in Tuvalu, thus cutting off a significant pathway for citizens to judicial appointment.[57] A localisation policy might encompass efforts to identify and amend such laws, making the appointment of a citizen judge possible in the future.

[55] Narokobi (n 10); Constitutional Planning Committee Papua New Guinea, *Final Report of the Constitutional Planning Committee* (1974) ch 8.

[56] An example is *High Court Judges (Salaries and Allowances) Act 2017* (Kiribati), s 4, which states that 'provided that having been qualified [for appointment] and without prejudice, special consideration may be afforded where possible to an I-Kiribati'.

[57] *Constitution of Tuvalu 1986*, s 124; ch 3, section II.C.

B. Regionalisation

The recruitment of foreign judges from other Pacific island states is a growing trend.[58] The appointment of Pacific Islander judges may be seen as a half-way step towards localisation, especially in the smallest Pacific states where the appointment of citizen judges is not yet possible. Judges from within the Pacific region bring knowledge and experience of comparable jurisdictions, and an awareness of the social and cultural issues that arise in conditions of legal pluralism. The use of regional judges on national courts also builds upon shared Pacific identities, making Pacific judiciaries more reflective of the communities they serve. In addition, the appointment of foreign judges from within the region is more likely to evolve into a genuine judicial 'exchange' between judiciaries, in contrast to the unidirectional movement of foreign judges from outside the region.

Intra-regional exchanges have to date been limited by the low number of local judges. Pacific courts are understandably reluctant to release their judges to sit overseas where that diminishes their own capacity. Exchanges are, however, likely to increase as national judiciaries become more localised, and as Pacific judges reach the statutory retirement age and make themselves available for service overseas.[59]

The creation of a regional court of appeal is sometimes mooted as a way to address some of the concerns arising from the practice of foreign judging. Advocates argue that a single Pacific Court of Appeal could operate in place of the Judicial Committee of the Privy Council and national courts of appeal, and provide a cost-effective appeals mechanism. It is also claimed that a regional court comprising judges from within the region would promote the development of a Pacific jurisprudence based on an understanding of Pacific society, customs and culture.[60] Depending on its structure, a regional court might also protect judicial independence by taking decisions about the appointment, renewal and removal of judges out of the direct control of national executives.[61] The idea has a long history, encompassing several pre-independence models and post-independence proposals.[62] It has not, however, received widespread

[58] Ch 7, section V.B.

[59] For example, Justice Lesatele Vaai was appointed a Judge in Nauru following his retirement from the Supreme Court of Samoa in 2017; Justice Daniel Fatiaki was appointed a Judge and later Chief Justice of Nauru following his retirement from the Supreme Court of Vanuatu in 2019.

[60] P MacFarlane, 'Some Challenges Facing Legal Strengthening Projects in Small Pacific Island States' (2006) 4(1) *Journal of Commonwealth Law and Legal Education* 103, 111; M Pulea, 'A Regional Court of Appeal for the Pacific' (1980) 9(2) *Pacific Perspective* 1, 1, 7–8.

[61] Interview F20. See also W Veenendaal, *Politics and Democracy in Microstates* (Abingdon, Routledge, 2015) 120 in relation to the Eastern Caribbean Supreme Court.

[62] Pulea (n 60) 3–6; J Logan, 'A Regional Final Court of Appeal for the South Pacific?', Paper presented at the 21st Pacific Judicial Conference 2014: Equal Access to Justice (9 March 2014) 2–6. The Pacific Islands Forum explored the possibility in 2011: L Kershaw, 'Presentation to Pacific Constitutions and the Rule of Law Conference' (Auckland, 7 December 2011).

support from Pacific states. One concern is that a regional court will not have the capacity to deal with distinctively national issues and customs. Pacific states are reluctant to relinquish jurisdiction and sovereignty, while donor states and organisations are concerned about the costs and viability of a regional court.[63] These concerns are significant, although, as Powles notes, some of them also apply to the use of foreign judges on domestic courts.[64]

Because the establishment of a regional court appears to have little traction in the Pacific at present, encouraging the recruitment of foreign judges from within the Pacific to sit on existing national courts seems the most feasible way of realising the advantages of regionalisation.

C. Stability

The practice of foreign judging in the Pacific introduces an element of instability to Pacific judiciaries, as positions are filled by a succession of foreign judges serving for short terms, sometimes on a part-time, non-residential basis. 'Fly-in, fly-out' judging can exacerbate concerns about foreign judges' knowledge gap in relation to local law and conditions, as visiting foreign judges have limited opportunity to gain firsthand knowledge of the Pacific state and its community. The stability of the bench is also important for capacity building – if that is what is sought from foreign judges – as it provides judges with an opportunity to establish the relationships and trust required to build capacity in a sustainable way.

One way to address these concerns is to encourage greater continuity and stability in the cohort of foreign judges serving in the judiciaries of each state. A good start would be to provide greater security of tenure and longer terms of appointment. Another useful strategy would be to foster formal connections between particular Pacific and donor courts, thereby building a cohort of foreign judges with knowledge of and connections to a particular country. Finally, a smaller, settled pool of foreign judges appointed to serve on courts of appeal would also encourage greater stability. For example, in Tonga until 2013, only three judges at a time held commissions for the Court of Appeal and would visit Tonga for every sitting of the Court. A small pool of foreign appeal judges also reduces the risk of 'judge shopping', or any perception of preference in the assignment of appeal cases.

[63] Pulea (n 60) 8; I Mataitoga, 'South Pacific Court of Appeal: Some Critical Issues' (1981) 11(1) *Pacific Perspective* 70.

[64] G Powles, 'Law, Courts and Legal Services in Pacific Societies' in G Powles and M Pulea (eds), *Pacific Courts and Legal Systems* (Suva and Clayton, University of the South Pacific and Monash University, 1988) 6, 26.

D. Judicial Independence

Chapter 6 identified the risks to judicial independence arising from the appointment of foreign judges for short renewable terms and the susceptibility of foreign judges to extra-constitutional removal from office. While these features of foreign judging do not, in and of themselves, compromise judicial independence, they can, in combination with other factors, put judicial independence at risk. Such factors include circumstances where most, if not all, judges serve for short renewable terms; where the individuals appointed to Pacific courts depend on that position for career progression or financial security; and where executives or other appointing authorities have demonstrated that they will act to remove judges who have made decisions that are perceived to be against their interests.

In chapter 6, I argued that the appointment of foreign judges on short terms is justifiable where the judge is, in effect, an acting judge to meet a temporary need, or to support localisation so that there will be positions available on the bench for qualified citizens.[65] A localisation policy could provide appointing authorities within states, as well as external donor agencies, with clearer direction about the circumstances that justify the appointment of a foreign judge on a short term. If, for example, the localisation policy identifies that the appointment of local judges will take a significant number of years, there is less justification for appointing a foreign judge for a short term.

If legal measures are required, comparative experience provides some possible options to limit or reduce the involvement of the political branches in decisions about the renewal of a judge's appointment, thereby mitigating the risks to judicial independence. One option is to limit or prohibit the renewal of judicial contracts. Short-term contracts would still be available, but once the term expired, the judge could not be reappointed.[66] In Seychelles, a small island state that also uses foreign judges, a constitutional provision specifies that foreign judges are to be appointed for one term not exceeding seven years, with reappointment only in 'exceptional circumstances'.[67] An alternative approach

[65] Ch 6, section III.

[66] The South African Constitutional Court has held that the authorities responsible for appointing judges do not have the discretion to renew a judge's appointment after the expiry of the term: *Justice Alliance of South Africa v President* 2011 (5) SA 388. A similar decision was made by the High Court of Botswana but overturned on appeal: *National Amalgamated Local Central Government and Parastatal Workers Union v President* (Botswana High Court, 16 February 2017) [66]; *President v National Amalgamated Local Central Government and Parastatal Workers Union* (Botswana Court of Appeal, June 2017).

[67] *Constitution of the Republic of the Seychelles 1993*, s 131(3), (4). The reappointments of several foreign judges have been challenged before the courts with mixed success. The Court of Appeal held that it has the power to determine whether 'exceptional circumstances' exist (*Bar Association of Seychelles v President* [2004] SCCA 1, 42–43), but it will give the phrase 'exceptional circumstances' a wide interpretation to encompass all circumstances relevant to a particular reappointment (*Michel v Dhanjee* [2012] SLR 1, 19).

is to create a presumption that a judge's appointment will be renewed. This approach was taken by the Court of Appeal of Timor Leste, which held that a foreign judge has a legal expectation that his or her contract will be renewed as long as there is a need for the judge in the legal system.[68] Other proposals include contractual provisions for automatic renewal or renewal at the option of the judge,[69] and a legal requirement that appointing authorities must give reasons for non-renewal.[70]

These considerations should also inform the approach of external organisations that recruit and fund foreign judges, guiding the selection of candidates and the terms on which they are engaged. Providing a foreign judge on a fixed-term contract to fill what is in essence a permanent judicial position supports neither the independence nor the stability of the judiciary. If the status and protections afforded to judges in their home state are relevant to the independence of foreign judges, it might be preferable to direct aid funding to secondment programmes between courts, such as the long-standing programme between the Supreme Court of Vanuatu and the District Court of New Zealand, rather than the ad hoc recruitment of individuals to specific judicial positions. Providing development aid funds through judicial institutions, rather than directly to judges, also dilutes the link between the funder and individual judges, which might be perceived as a channel for improper influence.

E. Exchange of Knowledge

Foreign judging can sometimes be characterised as a one-way process, in which foreign judges provide skills and expertise to Pacific courts. However, foreign judges face knowledge gaps of their own, most notably in relation to national laws, including custom, and the wider context in which the law operates. The analysis in chapter 5 showed how this knowledge gap can affect the way in which foreign judges approach constitutional adjudication. One risk is that the use of judges unfamiliar with custom and the legal context of Pacific jurisdictions can hamper efforts to develop an indigenous jurisprudence.

A final good practice initiative is therefore to assist foreign judges to gain knowledge of the legal system, including custom, in the states in which they sit. One way in which this can be done on courts of appeal is to ensure that local

[68] *Decision regarding the appeal of Judge Ivo Rosa against the non-renewal of his Contract by the Superior Council for the Judiciary* (Timor Leste Court of Appeal, 31 December 2008).

[69] CB Ingram, 'The Length of Terms of Judges in the Pacific and Its Impact on Judicial Independence' in *Land Law and Judicial Governance in the South Pacific: Comparative Studies* (Wellington, New Zealand Association for Comparative Law, 2011) 375, 377; D Schofield, 'Maintaining Judicial Independence in a Small Jurisdiction' in J Hatchard and P Slinn (eds), *Parliamentary Supremacy and Judicial Independence: A Commonwealth Approach* (London, Cavendish Publishing, 1999) 73, 76. Two judges noted in interviews that they had negotiated such terms: Interviews F1, F6.

[70] Schofield (n 69) 76.

and foreign judges sit together on panels, where there are sufficient numbers of local judges available, as a way to share local judges' knowledge of law, custom and context with foreign judges.[71] There is also a range of possible procedures to assist courts to understand custom, from adjusting the rules of evidence to encouraging submissions from amicus curiae or the involvement of assessors.[72]

Another way is to provide specific training for foreign judges, or to include foreign judges in court-wide judicial education programmes.[73] Foreign lawyers who wish to practise in Papua New Guinea are required to pass an exam covering customary law, land law and constitutional law.[74] There is no similar requirement for foreign judges in Papua New Guinea or anywhere else in the Pacific. However, in Papua New Guinea, foreign judges participate in judicial training and conferences alongside local judges, including a series on the development of the underlying law. Writing in the Samoan context, Mulitalo recommends joint training on law and custom for judges of the Supreme Court and the Land and Titles Court, as well as the development of a reference guide or bench book on customary law and practice.[75] Initiatives such as these are important for ensuring that foreign judges have the expertise necessary to adjudicate according to Pacific law, and for building collegiality between foreign and local judges.

V. GLOBAL SIGNIFICANCE

While it has historical roots and takes a particular form in the Pacific, the use of foreign judges is part of a wider story of contemporary globalisation. The use of foreign judges is most prevalent in small states, where, as in the Pacific, foreign judges are used because of the limited numbers of qualified citizens able to accept judicial appointment. It is not, however, confined to such circumstances, but is rather a growing and evolving global trend. States transitioning from conflict or authoritarian rule have turned to foreign judges to administer domestic judiciaries while the state rebuilds its institutions.[76] International peace-brokers have advocated, and at times required, that foreign judges sit on

[71] Interviews F1, F2, F7, F12, F20.

[72] New Zealand Law Commission, 'Converging Currents: Custom and Human Rights in the Pacific', *Study Paper SP17* (2006) 194–202.

[73] ibid 204–05.

[74] *Lawyers Act 1986* (PNG), s 25; *Lawyers (Examination) Regulation 1992* (PNG); APEC Legal Services Initiative, *Inventory: Papua New Guinea* (2010) available at www.legalservices.apec.org/inventory/papua_new_guinea.html.

[75] TLS Mulitalo Seumanutafa, *Law Reform in Plural Societies* (Cham, Springer, 2018) 133–34, 136.

[76] eg in Timor Leste: H Strohmeyer, 'Policing the Peace: Post-Conflict Judicial System Reconstruction in East Timor' (2001) 24 *University of New South Wales Law Journal* 171; in Kosovo: ME Hartmann, 'International Judges and Prosecutors in Kosovo: A New Model for Post-Conflict Peacekeeping', *Special Report 112* (United States Institute of Peace, 2003).

domestic constitutional courts in countries with deeply entrenched societal conflict.[77] Foreign judges have been proposed, although not always accepted, to sit on transitional justice tribunals.[78] In countries seeking to address entrenched corruption, foreign judges and legal personnel are regarded as a way to provide integrity to a judiciary and legal system tainted by corruption.[79] Finally, the globalisation of commerce and investment has led several states to establish specialist commercial courts staffed by foreign judges.[80] These developments suggest that, far from declining as decolonisation proceeds, the practice of foreign judging is evolving and becoming more diverse.

Despite the expansion of the practice, the use of foreign judges receives limited attention in the literature on judicial institutions and globalisation and in comparative constitutional law and policy. To conclude this book, I identify how greater study of the practice of foreign judging across different contexts contributes to pressing debates in these areas of scholarship.

A. Globalisation

The use of foreign judges is part of the phenomenon of judicial globalisation, traced by Slaughter and developed by others,[81] in which judges interact across national boundaries in various ways. Slaughter identified a range of interactions, including the citation of foreign judgments, engagements with foreign courts in determining transnational legal disputes, and face-to-face meetings of judges through judicial conferences and exchange programmes. While she does not mention the practice of foreign judging, it is clearly an example of judicial globalisation, connecting judges and legal systems across national borders.

The emphasis, identified in this book, on foreign judges as representatives of a profession rather than a state, resonates with Slaughter's study of judges in

[77] eg in Bosnia Herzegovina and Kosovo: C Grewe and M Riegner, 'Internationalized Constitutionalism in Ethnically Divided Societies: Bosnia-Herzegovina and Kosovo Compared' (2011) 15 *Max Planck Yearbook of United Nations Law* 1; in Cyprus: H Faustmann and A Varnava (eds), *Reunifying Cyprus: The Annan Plan and Beyond* (London, IB Tauris, 2009) 33, 76–77,102.

[78] eg in Colombia: K Ambos and S Aboueldahab, 'Foreign Jurists in the Colombian Special Jurisdiction for Peace: A New Concept of Amicus Curiae?' on *EJIL Talk: Blog of the European Journal of International Law* (19 December 2017); in Sri Lanka: B Fonseka and L Ganeshathasan, *Hybrid vs Domestic: Myths, Realities and Options for Transitional Justice in Sri Lanka* (Colombo, Centre for Policy Alternatives, 2016) 4–8.

[79] eg in Honduras: 'Agreement between the Government of the Republic of Honduras and the General Secretariat of the Organization of American States for the Establishment of the Mission to Support the Fight against Corruption and Impunity in Honduras' (signed 19 January 2016), art 2.1.1.

[80] In Singapore, Qatar and Dubai: A Godwin, I Ramsay and M Webster, 'International Commercial Courts: The Singapore Experience' (2017) 18 *Melbourne Journal of International Law* 219.

[81] A-M Slaughter, 'A Global Community of Courts' (2003) 44(1) *Harvard International Law Journal* 191; S Muller, S Richards and L Henderson (eds), *Highest Courts and Globalisation* (The Hague, Hague Academic Press, 2010).

conditions of globalisation. She claims that judicial globalisation changes how judges think about their role by fostering a sense of judging as a global profession, in which 'judges see each other not only as servants and representatives of a particular polity, but also as fellow professionals in an endeavour that transcends national borders'.[82] For Slaughter, transnational interactions between individual judges can create a 'global community of courts', fostering dialogue and exchange that enriches the jurisprudence of each nation.

The practice of foreign judging in the Pacific, however, introduces at least two significant points of tension overlooked in Slaughter's vision of a community of judicial professionals. First, aside from the examples of intra-Pacific and south–south judicial exchange, foreign judges tend to travel from large developed states to smaller, developing states and rarely if ever in reverse. Although the *movement* of foreign judges tends to be unidirectional, *influence* is not necessarily also one way, as the presence of a foreign judge on a Pacific court creates a site of interaction and mutual influence. It does, however, speak to constraints on the mobility of citizens of the Global South and inequalities in the status of national judiciaries that limit their full participation in 'global' judicial networks, and which make metaphors of 'dialogue' and 'exchange' inapt.[83] In the Pacific, the increasing diversity of the countries from which foreign judges are recruited reflects, in part, efforts to change this.[84]

Second, this book highlights some of the risks that arise from the idea of judging as, first and foremost, a profession. The connections between judges and states, for which citizenship serves as the proxy, continue to be important. The qualities of membership and identity implied in citizenship are significant to the way in which judges understand the responsibilities of judicial office and approach adjudication, and to the way in which the public perceives the judges on its national courts. Taken to an extreme, the vision of a global judicial profession de-identifies and de-nationalises judges, such that one judge can easily stand for another, losing the sense that *who* a judge is matters, because it serves to connect judicial office with the law, the state and the people.

B. Internationalisation

The use of foreign judges is also part of the story of the internationalisation of constitutional systems. Internationalisation refers to the impact of international and supranational norms, institutions and processes on domestic constitutional arrangements, through vertical interactions between international law and

[82] Slaughter (n 81) 193.

[83] MA Jayatilake, 'The Global Judicial Network: Towards New Hope for Development, Democracy and Equality in the Global Era' (2009) 21 *Sri Lanka Law Journal* 137.

[84] Ch 2, section V.

state law, horizontal interactions between states, and transnational networks of constitutional actors. The usual understanding is that the structure and composition of constitutional institutions is exclusively a matter for the state concerned. However, the use of foreign judges on national courts shows how domestic constitutions and institutions may be subject to a range of external influences and sources of regulation.

Constitutional and legislative provisions in each of the nine Pacific states set out the legal framework for their judiciaries. However, giving effect to these provisions through the use of foreign judges exposes the judiciary to many kinds of external influence. The use of foreign judges also opens up constitutional jurisprudence to a range of national and international influences, as foreign judges cite foreign law and bring constitutional understandings shaped in their home jurisdictions to bear on the interpretation of Pacific constitutions. Choices about which foreign judges to appoint, and on what terms and conditions, are influenced by personal relationships between judges, formal and informal relations between courts, international relations between states, and global market forces. Legal frameworks are supplemented (and sometimes bypassed) by contractual relationships between governments, courts, donor organisations and foreign judges themselves. Lines of accountability flow in various different directions – to professional peers, foreign judges' home states, Pacific states and Pacific communities. Allegiances are multiplied, 'scrambled' even, as citizens move across national borders to take up constitutional office in foreign states.[85]

The use of foreign judges provides a complex, somewhat messy example of internationalisation, which exposes Pacific judges and judiciaries to gaps in regulation, instability, and multiple and potentially competing sources of influence. It shows that the channels of international influence on national constitutions are varied and indirect, and not without their costs.

C. Comparative Insights

Foreign judges sit on domestic courts in a range of diverse jurisdictions around the globe. The course of decolonisation suggests that the use of foreign judges on state courts might be contracting, as the number of local candidates for judicial appointment increases and states pursue policies of localisation. However, as this study of the Pacific has shown, decolonisation is a slow process and foreign judges are likely to feature on the courts of some states for an extended time. Meanwhile, the use of foreign judges in other contexts, such as post-conflict transitional justice, specialised anti-corruption mechanisms and international commercial courts, seems likely to continue and even expand. The framework

[85] S Benhabib, *The Rights of Others: Aliens, Residents, and Citizens* (Cambridge, Cambridge University Press, 2004) 174.

provided in this book, developed by identifying the points at which nationality or citizenship is relevant to the task and the role of the judge, can, with care for relevant differences, be applied to analyse the use of foreign judges in contexts beyond the Pacific.

Despite the continuing use of foreign judges on national courts, it is still an exceptional phenomenon. It remains the case that the global norm is that the judges on courts of constitutional jurisdiction will be citizens of the state they serve. This fact is often taken for granted, to the point that the citizenship of judges is treated either as the default assumption or as irrelevant in global studies of judicial independence and in theories of constitutional adjudication. The study of the use of foreign judges in this book not only sheds light on a distinctive practice in the Pacific region. It also opens the way for an examination of widespread, but often unarticulated, presumptions about the significance of nationality to the functions and qualities of constitutional judges. In identifying the implications of the use of foreign judges to constitutional adjudication, judicial independence, and the connections between judges and judiciaries and the state and its people, this book shows how a judge's nationality is important to understanding the role of judges, even in constitutional systems that use only citizen judges. It may be that the requirement of nationality, whether imposed by law or practice, in the majority of the world's constitutional systems deserves more critical study and justification, particularly in contemporary conditions of globalisation.

Fiji, Kiribati, Nauru, Papua New Guinea, Samoa, Solomon Islands, Tonga, Tuvalu and Vanuatu have been largely overlooked in comparative constitutional studies. This book demonstrates that the constitutional experiences of Pacific states are important to understand, not just in their own right, but also for the contribution they can make to global understandings of constitutional practice and to the development of constitutional theory. The use of foreign judges on courts of constitutional jurisdiction is just one aspect of the rich and distinctive constitutional histories and practices of the Pacific region, which deserve greater recognition and reward further study.

Bibliography

ABC News (Sydney), 'Aust, NZ Judges Quit Fiji's Appeal Court' (4 September 2007)

——, 'Fiji Expels Envoys over Interference Claims' (4 November 2009)

——, 'Chief Magistrate Says Foreigners No Solution to Solomons Shortage' (21 October 2013)

Adams, M, 'Doing What Doesn't Come Naturally: On the Distinctiveness of Comparative Law' in M Van Hoecke (ed), *Methodologies of Legal Research* (Oxford, Hart Publishing, 2011) 229

Adlam, G, 'New Zealand's Judiciary and Gender' (New Zealand Law Society, 11 November 2015)

——, 'Snapshot of the Profession' (2018) 915 *LawTalk* 43

Aleck, J, 'Beyond Recognition: Contemporary Jurisprudence in the Pacific Islands and Common Law Tradition' (1991) 7 *Queensland University of Technology Law Journal* 137

Alexy, R, 'Balancing, Constitutional Review, and Representation' (2005) 3(4) *International Journal of Constitutional Law* 572

Alford, RP, 'In Search of a Theory for Constitutional Comparativism' (2005) 52(3) *UCLA Law Review* 639

Allott, A, 'The Independence of the Judiciary in Commonwealth Countries: Problems and Provisions' (1994) 20(4) *Commonwealth Law Bulletin* 1428

Ambos, K and Aboueldahab, S, 'Foreign Jurists in the Colombian Special Jurisdiction for Peace: A New Concept of Amicus Curiae?' on *EJIL Talk: Blog of the European Journal of International Law* (19 December 2017)

Amet, A, 'Severing the Umbilical Cord from the Common Law' in J Rannells and J Aleck (eds), *Custom at the Crossroads* (Faculty of Law, University of Papua New Guinea, 1995) 62

Anderson, B, *Imagined Communities: Reflections on the Origin and Spread of Nationalism* (London, Verso, rev edn, 2006)

Anderson, M, Luma, J and Voigt-Graf, C, 'Recent Developments Regarding Non-Citizen Technical Advisers in Papua New Guinea', *Issues Paper 24* (National Research Institute Papua New Guinea, March 2017)

Angelo, AH, '"Steady as She Goes": The Constitution and Court of Appeal of Samoa' (2012) 18 *New Zealand Association for Comparative Law Yearbook* 145

Anghie, A, *Imperialism, Sovereignty and the Making of International Law* (Cambridge, Cambridge University Press, 2005)

APEC Legal Services Initiative, *Inventory: Papua New Guinea* (2010)

Apinelu, E, 'Societal Culture and Constitutions: The Case of Tuvalu' in *Implications of Culture for Constitution Building* (International IDEA and Constitution Transformation Network, 2018)

Appleby, G et al, *Temporary Judicial Officers in Australia: A Report Commissioned by the Judicial Conference of Australia* (2017)

Arcioni, E, 'Identity at the Edge of the Constitutional Community' in F Jenkins, M Nolan and K Rubenstein (eds), *Allegiance and Identity in a Globalised World* (Cambridge, Cambridge University Press, 2014) 31

Arnold, M, 'PNG Judiciary Honors Late Justice Foulds' *Post Courier* (Port Moresby) (8 October 2018)

Atkinson, B, 'Regional Co-Operation in the Courts: A Tuvalu View' in G Powles and M Pulea (eds), *Pacific Courts and Legal Systems* (Suva and Clayton, University of the South Pacific and Monash University, 1988) 241

Baird, N, 'Judges as Cultural Outsiders: Exploring the Expatriate Model of Judging in the Pacific' (2013) 19 *Canterbury Law Review* 80

Banivanua-Mar, T, 'Frontier Space and the Reification of the Rule of Law: Colonial Negotiations in the Western Pacific, 1870–74' (2009) 30 *Australian Feminist Law Journal* 23

——, *Decolonisation and the Pacific: Indigenous Globalisation and the Ends of Empire* (Cambridge, Cambridge University Press, 2016)
Baragwanath, D, 'Judging: A Butterfly View' (2010) 16 *Canterbury Law Review* 243
Barak, A, 'The Role of the Supreme Court in a Democracy' in MT Andenæs, Lord Slynn of Hadley and D Fairgrieve (eds), *Judicial Review in International Perspective* (The Hague, Kluwer Law International, 2000) 121
Barmes, L and Malleson, K, 'Lifting the Judicial Identity Blackout' (2018) 38(2) *OJLS* 357
Bayne, P, 'The Constitution and the Franchise in Western Samoa' (1985) 1 *Queensland Institute of Technology Law Journal* 201
Bayne, PJ, 'Judicial Method and the Interpretation of Papua New Guinea's Constitution' (1980) 11 *Federal Law Review* 121
Bellamy, R, *Political Constitutionalism: A Republican Defence of the Constitutionality of Democracy* (Cambridge, Cambridge University Press, 2007)
Benhabib, S, *The Rights of Others: Aliens, Residents, and Citizens* (Cambridge, Cambridge University Press, 2004)
Berkovic, N, 'Judge Criticised over Fiji Posting' *The Australian* (Canberra) (10 March 2008) 4
Bilimoria, NN, 'Choices for the South Pacific Region's Bar Associations and Law Societies?' in P Butler and C Morris (eds), *Small States in a Legal World* (Cham, Springer International Publishing, 2017) 245
Black, V and Pitel, SGA, 'Out of Bounds: Can a Court Sit Outside Its Home Jurisdiction?' (2013) 41 *Advocates' Quarterly* 503
Bobbitt, P, *Constitutional Fate: A Theory of the Constitution* (Oxford, Oxford University Press, 1982)
Bogdandy, A von and Venzke, I, *In Whose Name? A Public Law Theory of International Adjudication* (Oxford, Oxford University Press, 2014)
Boyd, S, 'Australian Judges at Work Internationally: Treason, Assassinations, Coups, Legitimacy of Government, Human Rights, Poverty and Development' (2003) 77 *Australian Law Journal* 303
Brennan, G, 'Speech on Swearing in as a Chief Justice' (1995) 183 *CLR* ix
Briguglio, L, 'Small Island Developing States and Their Economic Vulnerabilities' (1995) 23 *World Development* 1615
Brown, D, 'Judicial Independence: An Examination' (1986) 58(4) *The Australian Quarterly* 348
Brown, K and Corrin Care, J, 'More on Democratic Fundamentals in Solomon Islands: Minister for Provincial Government v Guadalcanal Provincial Assembly' (2001) 32 *Victoria University of Wellington Law Review* 653
Brown, M, '"An Unqualified Human Good"? On Rule of Law, Globalization, and Imperialism' (2018) 43(4) *Law and Social Inquiry* 1391
Bruch, EM, 'Hybrid Courts: Examining Hybridity through a Post-Colonial Lens' (2010) 28(1) *Boston University International Law Journal* 1
Bukurura, SH, 'A Judiciary in Transition: Reflections on the Selection of Judges in Namibia' in PH Russell and K Malleson (eds), *Appointing Judges in an Age of Judicial Power: Critical Perspectives from around the World* (Toronto, University of Toronto Press, 2006) 313
Cahill-O'Callaghan, RJ, 'Reframing the Judicial Diversity Debate: Personal Values and Tacit Diversity' (2015) 35(1) *Legal Studies* 1
Cappelletti, M, *The Judicial Process in Comparative Perspective* (Oxford, Clarendon Press, 1989)
Casey, M, 'New Zealand Judges in Overseas Courts' in I Barker and G Wear (eds), *Law Stories: Essays on the New Zealand Legal Profession 1969–2003* (Wellington, LexisNexis NZ, 2003) 89
Chen, EM, 'The Judiciary, Diversity, and Justice for All' (2003) 91(4) *California Law Review* 1109
Chief Justice Lunabek, 'Speech on the Official Opening of the Courts of Vanuatu' (Port Vila, 27 January 2012)
Chitty, J, *A Treatise on the Law of the Prerogatives of the Crown* (London, J Butterworth, 1820)
Christiano, T, 'Authority' in EN Zalta (ed), *The Stanford Encyclopedia of Philosophy* (Stanford, CA, Stanford University, 2013)

Cohen, D and Lipscomb, L-A, 'Justice at the Crossroads in Timor-Leste', *Report No 22* (Institute for Policy Analysis of Conflict, 7 September 2015)

Cohen, M, 'Judicial Colonialism Today: The French Overseas Courts' (2020) 8(2) *Journal of Law and Courts* 247

Colvin, E, 'Criminal Procedure in the South Pacific' (2004) 8(1) *Journal of South Pacific Law*, available at www.usp.ac.fj/index.php?id=13266

Commonwealth Magistrates' and Judges' Association, 'Judicial Independence and Human Rights Issues: Nauru' (2014) 35 *CMJA News* 3

Commonwealth Secretariat, 'Evaluation of the Commonwealth Fund for Technical Cooperation' (London, Commonwealth Secretariat, 2008)

——, 'Report of the Commonwealth Secretary-General 2011–2013' (London, Commonwealth Secretariat, 2013)

Constitutional Planning Committee Papua New Guinea, *Final Report of the Constitutional Planning Committee* (1974)

Cook Islands News (Rarotonga), 'Tuvalu Judge Unable to Transit via Fiji' (24 January 2014) 4

Corrin Care, J, 'Cultures in Conflict: The Role of the Common Law in the South Pacific' (2002) 6 *Journal of South Pacific Law*

——, 'Finding the Right Balance in Plural Systems: Training Lawyers in the South Pacific' (2006) 4(2) *Journal of Commonwealth Law and Legal Education* 171

——, 'Negotiating the Constitutional Conundrum: Balancing Cultural Identity with Principles of Gender Equality in Post-Colonial South Pacific Societies' (2006) 5 *Indigenous Law Journal* 51

——, 'Discarding Relics of the Past: Patriation of Laws in the South Pacific' (2009) 39(4) *Victoria University of Wellington Law Review* 635

Corrin Care, J and Paterson, D, *Introduction to South Pacific Law*, 2nd edn (London, Routledge-Cavendish, 2008)

Corrin, J, 'Breaking the Mould: Constitutional Review in Solomon Islands' (2007) 13 *Revue Juridique Polynésienne* 143

——, 'Judge or Be Judged: Accepting Judicial Appointment in an Unlawful Regime' (2009) 16(2–3) *International Journal of the Legal Profession* 191

——, 'Moving beyond the Hierarchical Approach to Legal Pluralism in the South Pacific' (2009) 59 *Journal of Legal Pluralism and Unofficial Law* 29

——, 'A Question of Identity: Complexities of State Law Pluralism in the South Pacific' (2010) 61 *Journal of Legal Pluralism and Unofficial Law* 145

——, 'Getting Down to Business: Developing the Underlying Law in Papua New Guinea' (2014) 46(2) *The Journal of Legal Pluralism and Unofficial Law* 155

Cotterrell, R, *Law, Culture and Society: Legal Ideas in the Mirror of Social Theory* (Aldershot, Ashgate, 2006)

Cox, M, Duituturaga, E and Scheye, E, 'Solomon Islands Case Study: Evaluation of Australian Law and Justice Assistance' (Australian Government Office of Development Effectiveness, Ausaid, 2012)

Dale, G, 'Appealing to Whom? Australia's "Appellate Jurisdiction" Over Nauru' (2007) 56(3) *ICLQ* 641

Dam, KW, *The Law-Growth Nexus: The Rule of Law and Economic Development* (Washington, DC, Brookings Institution Press, 2006)

Dann, P, Riegner, M and Bönnemann, M, 'The Southern Turn in Comparative Constitutional Law: An Introduction' in *The Global South and Comparative Constitutional Law* (Oxford, Oxford University Press, 2020) 1

Dannenbaum, T, 'Nationality and the International Judge: The Nationalist Presumption Governing the International Judiciary and Why It Must be Reversed' (2012) 45(1) *Cornell International Law Journal* 77

Davidson, JW, *Samoa Mo Samoa: The Emergence of the Independent State of Western Samoa* (Melbourne, Oxford University Press, 1967)

De, R, '"A Peripatetic World Court" Cosmopolitan Courts, Nationalist Judges and the Indian Appeal to the Privy Council' (2014) 32 *Law and History Review* 821
De Smith, SA, *The New Commonwealth and Its Constitutions* (London, Stevens & Sons, 1964)
Dickinson, LA, 'The Promise of Hybrid Courts' (2003) 97 *American Journal of International Law* 295
Dixon, R and Jackson, V, 'Hybrid Constitutional Courts: Foreign Judges on National Constitutional Courts' [2019] *Columbia Journal of Transnational Law* 283
Domah, SB, 'Judicial Assistance to Small Jurisdictions in the Commonwealth: The Case for a Special Chapter and Forum' (2011) 37(4) *Commonwealth Law Bulletin* 605
Donne, G, 'Introduction' in G Powles and M Pulea (eds), *Pacific Courts and Legal Systems* (Suva and Clayton, University of the South Pacific and Monash University, 1988) 3
Dorney, S, *The Embarrassed Colonialist* (Melbourne, Penguin Group Australia, 2016)
Draunidalo, T, 'The Rule of Law and Judicial Independence amidst the Coups and Attempted Coups in Fiji since 1987' in J Fraenkel, S Firth and BV Lal (eds), *The 2006 Military Takeover in Fiji: A Coup to end all Coups* (Canberra, ANU Press, 2009) 311
Du Bois, F, 'Judicial Selection in Post-Apartheid South Africa' in PH Russell and K Malleson (eds), *Appointing Judges in an Age of Judicial Power: Critical Perspectives from Around the World* (Toronto, University of Toronto Press, 2006) 280
Duff, P, 'The Evolution of Trial by Judge and Assessors in Fiji' (1997) 21 *Journal of Pacific Studies* 189
Dworkin, R, *Law's Empire* (London, Fontana, 1986)
——, 'Discussion: International Criminal Justice' in R Badinter and S Breyer (eds), *Judges in Contemporary Democracy: An International Conversation* (New York, New York University Press, 2004) 189
Dyzenhaus, D, 'Are Legislatures Good at Morality? Or Better at It than the Courts?' (2009) 7(1) *International Journal of Constitutional Law* 46
Dziedzic, A, 'Foreign Judges and Hong Kong's New National Security Law' (2020) 25(2) *Commonwealth Judicial Journal* 27
——, '"To Join the Bench and Be Decision-Makers": Women Judges in Pacific Island Judiciaries' in M Crouch (ed), *Women and the Judiciary in the Asia-Pacific* (Cambridge, Cambridge University Press, 2021) 29
——, 'Foreign Judges of the Pacific as Agents of Global Constitutionalism' (2021) 10(2) *Global Constitutionalism* (forthcoming)
Eames, G, 'The Rule of Law in Nauru: An Evolving Concept?', Paper presented at Law Society of South Australia Criminal Law Conference, McLaren Vale (24 October 2014)
Ellett, R, *Politics of Judicial Independence in Lesotho* (Johannesburg, Freedom House Southern Africa, 2012)
——, *Pathways to Judicial Power in Transitional States: Perspectives from African Courts* (Abingdon, Routledge, 2013)
Ellis, G, 'Life on the Bench in PNG' [2010] *Bar News: The Journal of the New South Wales Bar Association* 96
Epstein, L, Knight, J and Shvetsova, O, 'The Role of Constitutional Courts in the Establishment and Maintenance of Democratic Systems of Government' (2001) 35(1) *Law and Society Review* 117
Etherton, T, 'Liberty, the Archetype and Diversity: A Philosophy of Judging' [2010] *Public Law* 727
Farran, S, *Human Rights in the South Pacific: Challenges and Changes* (London, Routledge-Cavendish, 2009)
Faustmann, H and Varnava, A (eds), *Reunifying Cyprus: The Annan Plan and Beyond* (London, IB Tauris, 2009)
Feingold, ER, *Colonial Justice and Decolonization in the High Court of Tanzania, 1920–1971* (Cham, Palgrave Macmillan, 2018)
Feldman, D, 'The Independence of International Judges in National Courts: Lessons from Bosnia Herzegovina' in CF Forsyth and S Shetreet (eds), *The Culture of Judicial Independence: Conceptual Foundations and Practical Challenges* (Boston, MA, Martinus Nijhoff Publishers, 2011) 215

Ferejohn, J, 'Independent Judges, Dependent Judiciary: Explaining Judicial Independence' (1999) 72 *Southern California Law Review* 353

Ferreyra, A, Mabsout, R and United Nations Office of the High Representative for the Least Developed Countries, Landlocked Developing Countries and Small Island Developing States, *Best Practices in the Implementation of the Brussels Programme of Action for the Least Developed Countries for the Decade 2001–2010* (New York, United Nations, 2008)

FijiLive (Suva), 'Fiji Judge Urges Lawyers to Speak Out' (25 January 2008)

Fiji Women's Rights Movement, *Herstory: Celebrating 25 Years of Balancing the Scales 1986–2011* (Suva, 2011)

Fok, J, 'The Use of Non-Local Judges in Overseas Jurisdictions' (2017) 23(1) *Journal of the Commonwealth Magistrates' and Judges' Association* 28

Fonseka, B and Ganeshathasan, L, *Hybrid vs Domestic: Myths, Realities and Options for Transitional Justice in Sri Lanka* (Colombo, Centre for Policy Alternatives, 2016)

Fonua, P, 'Controversial Bill to Amend Constitution' *Matangi Tonga* (Nuku'alofa) (22 September 2020)

——, 'Parliament Amends Tongan Constitution to Include Unwritten "Customs"' *Matangi Tonga* (Nuku'alofa) (17 October 2020)

Forsyth, M, 'Beyond Case Law: Kastom and Courts in Vanuatu' (2004) 35 *Victoria University of Wellington Law Review* 427

——, *A Bird That Flies with Two Wings: The Kastom and State Justice Systems in Vanuatu* (Canberra, ANU Press, 2009)

——, 'Understanding Judicial Independence in Vanuatu', *Discussion Paper 2015/9, State, Society and Governance in Melanesia* (Canberra, Australian National University, 2015)

——, 'The Vanuatu Judiciary: A Critical Check on Executive Power' in HP Lee and M Pittard (eds), *Asia-Pacific Judiciaries: Independence, Impartiality and Integrity* (Cambridge, Cambridge University Press, 2017) 354

Fraenkel, J, Madraiwiwi, J and Okole, H, *The RAMSI Decade: A Review of the Regional Assistance Mission to Solomon Islands, 2003–2013* (Solomon Islands Government and Pacific Islands Forum, 2014)

Frame, A, 'The Tahitian Pomare Code of 1819: First Steps to Written Law in the Pacific', Paper presented at the Pacific Judicial Conference, Auckland (9–12 March 2014)

Frankenberg, G, 'Critical Comparisons: Re-Thinking Comparative Law' (1985) 26 *Harvard International Law Journal* 411

French, R, 'Judicial Exchange: Debalkanising the Courts' (2006) 15 *Journal of Judicial Administration* 142

——, 'Judges in Fiji Face "Interim" Problem' *The Australian* (Canberra) (2 May 2008)

Gans, C, 'Citizenship and Nationhood' in A Shachar et al (eds), *The Oxford Handbook of Citizenship* (Oxford, Oxford University Press, 2017) 107

Garoupa, N and Ginsburg, T, *Judicial Reputation: A Comparative Theory* (Chicago, IL, University of Chicago Press, 2015)

George, N, 'Contending Masculinities and the Limits of Tolerance: Sexual Minorities in Fiji' (2008) 20(1) *The Contemporary Pacific* 163

Ghai, Y, 'Themes and Arguments' in Y Ghai and SNM Young (eds), *Hong Kong's Court of Final Appeal* (Cambridge, Cambridge University Press, 2013) 1

Glenn, HP, 'Transnational Common Laws' (2005) 29(3) *Fordham International Law Journal* 457

Godwin, A, Ramsay, I and Webster, M, 'International Commercial Courts: The Singapore Experience' (2017) 18 *Melbourne Journal of International Law* 219

Goldsmith, J and Levinson, D, 'Law for States: International Law, Constitutional Law, Public Law' (2009) 122(7) *Harvard Law Review* 1792

Goldsworthy, J, 'Constitutional Interpretation' in M Rosenfeld and A Sajó (eds), *The Oxford Handbook of Comparative Constitutional Law* (Oxford, Oxford University Press, 2012) 689

Government of Nauru, 'Expression of Interest Sought for Appointment as Judge to the Supreme Court of Nauru' (October 2013)

——, 'Nauru Government Sets the Record Straight', *Media Release* (24 February 2014)
——, 'Nauru Announces Court of Appeal' *Media Release* (24 July 2018)
——, 'PNG's Nicholas Kirriwom Sworn in as Judge to Nauru Appeals Court', *Media Release* (12 November 2018)
Government of Tuvalu, 'Te Kakeega III: National Strategy for Sustainable Development 2016 to 2020' (March 2016)
Grewe, C and Riegner, M, 'Internationalized Constitutionalism in Ethnically Divided Societies: Bosnia-Herzegovina and Kosovo Compared' (2011) 15 *Max Planck Yearbook of United Nations Law* 1
Grimm, D, *Constitutionalism* (Oxford, Oxford University Press, 2016)
Groppi, T and Ponthoreau, M-C (eds), *The Use of Foreign Precedents by Constitutional Judges* (Oxford, Hart Publishing, 2013)
Hamburger, P, 'Judicial Office' (2011) 6 *Journal of Law, Philosophy and Culture* 53
Hartmann, ME, 'International Judges and Prosecutors in Kosovo: A New Model for Post-Conflict Peacekeeping', *Special Report 112* (United States Institute of Peace, 2003)
Hassall, G and Saunders, C, *Asia-Pacific Constitutional Systems* (Cambridge, Cambridge University Press, 2002)
Hau'ofa, E, 'Our Sea of Islands' in E Hau'ofa, E Waddell and V Naidu (eds), *A New Oceania: Rediscovering our Sea of Islands* (Suva, University of the South Pacific in association with Beake House, 1993)
Healy, AM, 'Colonial Law and Metropolitan Defence: The Curious Case of Australia in New Guinea' in H Hiery and JM MacKenzie (eds), *European Impact and Pacific Influence: British and German Colonial Policy in the Pacific Islands and the Indigenous Response* (London, Tauris Academic Studies, 1997) 214
Heuschling, L, 'Why Should Judges Be Independent? Reflections on Coke, Montesquieu and the French Tradition of Judicial Dependence' in KS Ziegler, D Baranger and AW Bradley (eds), *Constitutionalism and the Role of Parliaments* (Oxford, Hart Publishing, 2006)
Hewitson, M, 'First Female Pacific Island Judge Ready to Be Tough but Caring' *New Zealand Herald* (Auckland), 13 September 2002
Hezel, FX, 'Pacific Island Nations: How Viable Are Their Economies?' *Pacific Islands Policy No 7* (Honolulu, East-West Center, 2012)
Hobbs, H, 'Hybrid Tribunals and the Composition of the Court: In Search of Sociological Legitimacy' (2016) 16(2) *Chicago Journal of International Law* 482
Honig, B, *Democracy and the Foreigner* (Princeton, NJ, Princeton University Press, 2001)
Horwitz, P, 'Three Faces of Deference' (2008) 83 *Notre Dame Law Review* 1061
——, 'The Constitutional Marriage of Personality and Impersonality: Office, Honor, and the Oath' (2018) 33 *Constitutional Commentary* 101
Hoster, P, 'Understanding the Value of Judicial Diversity through the Native American Lens' (2011) 36 *American Indian Law Review* 457
Howard, RE, 'Legitimacy and Class Rule in Commonwealth Africa: Constitutionalism and the Rule of Law' (1985) 7(2) *Third World Quarterly* 323
Ibhawoh, B, *Imperial Justice: Africans in Empire's Court* (Oxford, Oxford University Press, 2014)
Ingram, CB, 'The Length of Terms of Judges in the Pacific and Its Impact on Judicial Independence' in *Land Law and Judicial Governance in the South Pacific: Comparative Studies* (New Zealand Association for Comparative Law, 2011) 375
International Bar Association, *Under Pressure: A Report on the Rule of Law in The Gambia* (August 2006)
——, *Dire Straits: A Report on the Rule of Law in Fiji* (2009)
Iyer, V, 'The Judiciary in Fiji: A Broken Reed?' in HP Lee and M Pittard (eds), *Asia-Pacific Judiciaries: Independence, Impartiality and Integrity* (Cambridge, Cambridge University Press, 2017) 109
Jackson, VC, 'Paradigms of Public Law: Transnational Constitutional Values and Democratic Challenges' (2010) 8 *International Journal of Constitutional Law* 517

——, *Constitutional Engagement in a Transnational Era* (Oxford, Oxford University Press, 2010)
Jacobsohn, GJ, 'Constitutional Values and Principles' in M Rosenfeld and A Sajó (eds), *The Oxford Handbook of Comparative Constitutional Law* (Oxford, Oxford University Press, 2012) 777
Jakab, A, Dyevre, A and Itzcovich, G, *Comparative Constitutional Reasoning* (Cambridge, Cambridge University Press, 2017)
Jamieson, L, 'Theorising Identity, Nationality and Citizenship: Implications for European Citizenship Identity' (2002) 34(6) *Sociologia* 507
Jayatilake, MA, 'The Global Judicial Network: Towards New Hope for Development, Democracy and Equality in the Global Era' (2009) 21 *Sri Lanka Law Journal* 137
Jeffries, C, *The Colonial Empire and Its Civil Service* (Cambridge, The University Press, 1938)
Judge's Chambers Supreme Court of Nauru, 'Geoffrey Eames Resigns as Chief Justice of Nauru' (Media Release, No 5, 13 March 2014)
Kahn, P, 'Independence and Responsibility in the Judicial Role' in IP Stotzky (ed), *Transition to Democracy in Latin America: The Role of the Judiciary* (Boulder, CO, Westview Press, 1993) 73
Kama, B, *Reconceptualising the Role of the Judiciary in Papua New Guinea's 'Home-Grown' Constitution*, PhD Thesis (Canberra, Australian National University, 2019)
Kaplan, M, 'Promised Lands: From Colonial Lawgiving to Postcolonial Takeovers in Fiji' in SE Merry and DL Brenneis (eds), *Law and Empire in the Pacific: Fiji and Hawaiì* (Santa Fe, NM, School of American Research Press, 2004) 153
Kautoke, RL, 'The Jury System in Tonga' (2009) 13(1) *Journal of South Pacific Law* 8
Kavanagh, A, 'Defending Deference in Public Law and Constitutional Theory' (2010) 126 *Law Quarterly Review* 222
——, 'The Lure and the Limits of Dialogue' (2016) 66(1) *University of Toronto Law Journal* 83
Keith, K, 'Reflections on Some Pacific Constitutions' (2012) 18 *New Zealand Association for Comparative Law Yearbook* 133
Kempton, H, 'A Busy and Varied Career in Law' *The Mercury* (Hobart) (8 June 2015)
Keniapisia, JA, 'Judges from Other Commonwealth Jurisdictions Serving in the High Court and Court of Appeal of Solomon Islands', Paper presented at the 20th Commonwealth Law Conference, Melbourne (22 March 2017)
Kershaw, L, 'Presentation to Pacific Constitutions and the Rule of Law Conference' (Auckland, 7 December 2011)
King, K, 'Order from the Court: Judiciaries as a Bulwark Against Legislative Corruption in Vanuatu' *The Global Anticorruption Blog* (2015)
Koval, R, 'Geoffrey Eames, Former Nauru Chief Justice' *The Saturday Paper* (21 March 2015)
Kurukulasuriya, U, 'Can We Expect Justice and Independence from Servants of Military Dictators?' *Colombo Telegraph* (Colombo) (30 October 2011)
Kusapa, J, 'Expatriate Judges, Not an Answer: Chief Justice' *Island Sun* (Honiara) (21 January 2015)
——, 'High Court Receives Video Conferencing Equipment' *Island Sun News* (Honiara) (2 October 2020)
Kymlicka, W, 'Citizenship in an Era of Globalization' in I Shapiro and C Hacker-Cordón (eds), *Democracy's Edges* (Cambridge, Cambridge University Press) 112
Lal, BV, *A Time Bomb Lies Buried: Fiji's Road to Independence, 1960–1970* (Canberra, ANU Press, 2008)
——, *Historical Dictionary of Fiji* (Lanham, MD, Rowman & Littlefield, 2016)
Langwenya, M, *Swaziland Justice Sector and the Rule of Law: A Review by AfriMAP and the Open Society Initiative for Southern Africa*, (Johannesburg, Open Society Initiative, 2013)
Larkins, CM, 'Judicial Independence and Democratization: A Theoretical and Conceptual Analysis' (1996) 44(4) *American Journal of Comparative Law* 605
Lātūkefu, S, *The Tongan Constitution: A Brief History to Celebrate Its Centenary* (Nuku'alofa, Tonga Traditions Committee, 1975)
——, 'Constitution-Making in the Pacific Islands in the Nineteenth Century' in PG Sack (ed), *Pacific Constitutions: Proceedings of the Canberra Law Workshop VI* (Canberra, Australian National University, 1982) 21

Law Reform Commission of Papua New Guinea, 'Declaration and Development of Underlying Law', *Working Paper No 4* (1976)

Lee, HP and Pittard, M (eds), *Asia-Pacific Judiciaries: Independence, Impartiality and Integrity* (Cambridge, Cambridge University Press, 2017)

Lee, I, 'Practice and Predicament: The Nationality of the International Arbitrator (With Survey Results)' (2008) 31 *Fordham International Law Journal* 603

Leubsdorf, J, 'Theories of Judging and Judge Disqualification' (1987) 62 *New York University Law Review* 237

Leung, G, 'The Erosion of Judicial Independence' in J Fraenkel, S Firth and BV Lal (eds), *The 2006 Military Takeover in Fiji: A Coup to End All Coups?* (Canberra, ANU Press, 2009) 301

——, 'The Impact of the Coup on Fiji's Judiciary' in J Fraenkel, S Firth and BV Lal (eds), *The 2006 Military Takeover in Fiji: A Coup to End All Coups?* (Canberra, ANU Press, 2009) 291

——, 'Some Challenges to the Rule of Law in Fiji' (Paper presented at the 36th Australian Legal Convention, Perth, 18 September 2009)

Levine, S, 'Constitutional Change in Tuvalu' (1992) 27(3) *Australian Journal of Political Science* 492

Lilomaiava-Doktor, S, 'Beyond "Migration": Samoan Population Movement (Malaga) and the Geography of Social Space (Vā)' (2009) 21(1) *Contemporary Pacific* 1

Lin, F, 'The Expatriate Judges and Rule of Law in Hong Kong: Its Past, Present and Future' in S Shetreet and W McCormack (eds), *The Culture of Judicial Independence in a Globalised World* (Leiden, Brill Nijhoff, 2016) 279

Logan, J, 'A Regional Final Court of Appeal for the South Pacific?', Paper presented at the 21st Pacific Judicial Conference 2014: Equal Access to Justice (9 March 2014)

——, 'A Year in the Life of an Australian Member of the PNG Judiciary', *SSGM Discussion Paper 2015/16, State, Society and Governance in Melanesia Program* (Canberra, Australian National University, 2015)

——, 'Law and Justice in Papua New Guinea', Paper presented at the Australian Institute of International Affairs, Brisbane (23 June 2015)

Loop PNG, 'Senior PNG Judge Sworn in as Nauru Judge' (18 November 2018)

Lord Cooke of Thorndon, 'The Dream of an International Common Law' in C Saunders (ed), *Courts of Final Jurisdiction: The Mason Court in Australia* (Annandale, Federation Press, 1996) 138

——, 'Final Appeal Courts: Some Comparisons', *Occasional Paper No 7* (New Zealand Centre for Public Law, 2001)

Lord Reid, 'The Judge as Lawmaker' (1972) 12(1) *Journal of the Society of Public Teachers of Law* 22

Lucy, W, 'Adjudication' in JL Coleman and SJ Shapiro (eds), *The Oxford Handbook of Jurisprudence and Philosophy of Law* (Oxford, Oxford University Press, 2002) 207

MacCormick, N, *Legal Reasoning and Legal Theory* (Oxford, Clarendon Press, rev edn 1993, 1978)

MacDonald, RA, 'Exercising Judgement' in *Which Judge for Which Society? Proceedings of the 2008 Judges' Conference* (Québec City, 2008) 51

MacDonald, RA and Kong, H, 'Judicial Independence as a Constitutional Virtue' in M Rosenfeld and A Sajó (eds), *The Oxford Handbook of Comparative Constitutional Law* (Oxford, Oxford University Press, 2012)

MacFarlane, P, 'Some Challenges Facing Legal Strengthening Projects in Small Pacific Island States' (2006) 4(1) *Journal of Commonwealth Law and Legal Education* 103

Mackenzie, R et al, *Selecting International Judges: Principle, Process, and Politics* (Oxford, Oxford University Press, 2010)

Marko, J, 'Foreign Judges: A European Perspective' in Y Ghai and SNM Young (eds), *Hong Kong's Court of Final Appeal* (Cambridge, Cambridge University Press, 2013) 637

Markovic, M, 'International Criminal Trials and the Disqualification of Judges on the Basis of Nationality' (2014) 13 *Washington University Global Studies Law Review* 1

Mason, A, 'Reflections of an Itinerant Judge in the Asia-Pacific Region' (2000) 28 *International Journal of Legal Information* 311

——, 'Sharing Expertise with the Developing World' (2001) 26 *Alternative Law Journal* 7
Mataitoga, I, 'South Pacific Court of Appeal: Some Critical Issues' (1981) 11(1) *Pacific Perspective* 70
Matangi Tonga (Nuku'alofa), 'Tonga's Appeal Court Proceeds via Teleconference' (24 March 2020)
McCrone, D and Kiely, R, 'Nationalism and Citizenship' (2000) 34(1) *Sociology* 19
McHugh, MH, 'The Judicial Method' (1999) 73 *Australian Law Journal* 37
McIntyre, J, *The Judicial Function: Fundamental Principles of Contemporary Judging* (Singapore, Springer, 2019)
Meleisea, M, *The Making of Modern Samoa: Traditional Authority and Colonial Administration in the History of Western Samoa* (Suva, University of the South Pacific, 1995)
Mellor, T and Jabes, J, *Governance in the Pacific: Focus for Action, 2005–2009* (Manila, Asian Development Bank, 2004)
Menski, W, *Comparative Law in a Global Context: The Legal Systems of Asia and Africa*, 2nd edn (Cambridge, Cambridge University Press, 2006)
Merritt, C, 'Jocelynne Scutt Cleared of Misconduct' *The Australian* (Canberra) (8 August 2008)
——, 'Sacked Fiji Judges Warn Expats on Treason' *The Australian* (Canberra) (13 April 2009)
——, 'When Backlogs Lead to Payback' *The Australian* (Canberra) (1 May 2009)
Merritt, C and Berkovic, N, 'Fiji's Democracy Lobby Tries to Scuttle Scutt Appointment' *The Australian* (Canberra) (14 March 2008)
Merry, SE, *Colonizing Hawai'i: The Cultural Power of Law* (Princeton, NJ, Princeton University Press, 2000)
Meti, L, *Samoa: The Making of the Constitution* (Apia, National University of Samoa, 2002)
Miles, WFS, *Bridging Mental Boundaries in a Postcolonial Microcosm: Identity and Development in Vanuatu* (Honolulu, University of Hawaii Press, 1998)
Miller, D, *On Nationality* (Oxford, Oxford University Press, 1997)
Millett, P, *As in Memory Long* (London, Wildy, Simmonds & Hill Publishing, 2015)
Ministry of Justice, *The District Courts of New Zealand* (2008)
Mitchell, P, 'The Privy Council and the Difficulty of Distance' (2016) 36(1) *OJLS* 26
Mulitalo Seumanutafa, TLS, *Law Reform in Plural Societies* (Cham, Springer, 2018)
Muller, S, Richards, S and Henderson, L (eds), *Highest Courts and Globalisation* (The Hague, Hague Academic Press, 2010)
Muria, J, 'The Role of the Courts and Legal Profession in Constitutional and Political Disputes in the Pacific Islands Nations' (2002) 6 *Journal of South Pacific Law*, available at www.informit.org/doi/abs/10.3316/agispt.20031163
Murray, S, 'Dual Federal and State Judicial Appointments: An Australian Impossibility?' (2014) 25 *Public Law Review* 284
Mutua, M, 'Justice under Siege: The Rule of Law and Judicial Subservience in Kenya' (2001) 23(1) *Human Rights Quarterly* 96
Naidu, R, 'Coup and Crisis: Comments on the Fiji Experience', Paper presented at the 20th Annual Conference of the Australian Institute of Judicial Administration, Brisbane (13 July 2002)
Nanau, GL, 'Solomon Islands' in SI Levine (ed), *Pacific Ways: Government and Politics in the Pacific Islands*, 2nd edn (Wellington, Victoria University Press, 2016) 291
Narokobi, B, 'The System of Selecting Judges of the National and Supreme Courts: A Proposal', *Occasional Paper No 7* (Law Reform Commission of Papua New Guinea, 1978)
——, 'How Independent Are the Courts in Papua New Guinea? The Somare/Rooney Affair' (1980) 9(2) *Pacific Perspective* 12
——, 'In Search of a Melanesian Jurisprudence' in P Sack and E Minchin (eds), *Legal Pluralism: Proceedings of the Canberra Law Workshop VII* (Canberra, Australian National University, 1986) 215
——, *Lo Bilong Yumi Yet: Law and Custom in Melanesia* (Papua New Guinea, Melanesian Institute for Pastoral and Socio-Economic Service University of the South Pacific, 1989)
Narokobi, V, *The Implementation of Papua New Guinea's National Goals and Directive Principles and Basic Social Obligations*, PhD thesis (Victoria University of Wellington, 2016)
Nauru Constitutional Review Committee, *Naoero Ituga: Report* (2007)

Neuberger, D, 'The Judicial Committee of the Privy Council in the 21st Century' (2014) 3(1) *Cambridge Journal of International and Comparative Law* 30

New Zealand Law Commission, 'Converging Currents: Custom and Human Rights in the Pacific', *Study Paper SP17* (2006)

Nimbtik, G, 'The Struggles of Adoption and Adaptation in the Governance Space of Vanuatu: The Incorporation of Jifly Authority and Kastom Governance into the Legal-Rational System' in JI Lahai and H Ware (eds), *Governance and Societal Adaptation in Fragile States* (Cham, Palgrave Macmillan, 2020) 237

Nonggorr, J, 'The Maintenance of Judicial Independence and Integrity in Papua New Guinea: Some Recent Developments' (1992) 18(3) *Commonwealth Law Bulletin* 1181

——, 'Development of an "Indigenous Jurisprudence" in Papua New Guinea: The Past Record and Future Prospects' in J Rannells and J Aleck (eds), *Custom at the Crossroads* (Faculty of Law, University of Papua New Guinea, 1995) 68

Ntumy, MA (ed), *South Pacific Islands Legal Systems* (Honolulu, University of Hawaii Press, 1993)

NZ Herald (Auckland), 'NZ Lawyers Should Not Work for Fiji Regime, Law Society Says' (21 April 2009)

Office of the Attorney-General, *Country Report of the Office of the Attorney General Tuvalu* (Report to the 34th Pacific Islands Law Officers' Network Meeting, October 2015)

Osii, A, 'Agreement Signed for PNG Judge to Sit in Nauru's Appeals Court' *The National* (Port Moresby) (26 July 2018)

Pacific Judicial Development Programme, *Toolkit for Review of Guidance on Judicial Conduct* (Federal Court of Australia and New Zealand Ministry of Foreign Affairs and Trade, 2014)

Pacific Scoop (Wellington), 'Fiji's Chief Justice Condemns Australian, NZ "Interference" and "Hostility"' (3 November 2009)

Palley, C, 'Rethinking the Judicial Role: The Judiciary and Good Government' (1969) 1 *Zambia Law Journal* 1

Palmer, A, 'The Ethnic Conflict in Solomon Islands' in U Dolgopol and JG Gardam (eds), *The Challenge of Conflict: International Law Responds* (Leiden, Martinus Nijhoff Publishers, 2006) 49

Pannick, D, *Judges* (Oxford, Oxford University Press, 1987)

Parrish, AL, 'Storm in a Teacup: The US Supreme Court's Use of Foreign Law' [2007] *University of Illinois Law Review* 637

Perju, V, 'Constitutional Transplants, Borrowing and Migrations' in M Rosenfeld and A Sajó (eds), *Oxford Handbook of Comparative Constitutional Law* (Oxford, Oxford University Press, 2012) 1304

Peter, F, 'Political Legitimacy' in EN Zalta (ed), *Stanford Encyclopedia of Philosophy* (Stanford, CA, Stanford University, 2010)

Pettit, P, 'Varieties of Public Representation' in I Shapiro et al (ed), *Political Representation* (Cambridge, Cambridge University Press, 2009) 61

Phillips, A, *The Politics of Presence* (Oxford, Clarendon Press, 1995)

Pimental, D, 'Reframing the Independence v Accountability Debate: Defining Judicial Structure in Light of Judges' Courage and Integrity' (2009) 57 *Cleveland State Law Review* 1

Pitkin, HF, *The Concept of Representation* (Berkeley, CA, University of California Press, 1967)

Poole, T, 'Back to the Future? Unearthing the Theory of Common Law Constitutionalism' (2003) 23(3) *OJLS* 435

Powles, G, 'Traditional Institutions in Pacific Constitutional Systems: Better Late or Never?' in PG Sack (ed), *Pacific Constitutions: Proceedings of the Canberra Law Workshop VI* (Canberra, Australian National University, 1982) 345

——, 'Law, Courts and Legal Services in Pacific Societies' in G Powles and M Pulea (eds), *Pacific Courts and Legal Systems* (Suva and Clayton, University of the South Pacific and Monash University, 1988) 6

——, 'The Common Law as a Source of Law in the South Pacific: Experiences in Western Polynesia' (1988) 10 *University of Hawaii Law Review* 105

Pratihba, J, 'Judiciary Independent: Chief Justice' *Fiji Sun* (Suva) (28 August 2018)
Premdas, RR, 'The Dynamics of Ethnic Minority Domination in Fiji' in EP Kaufmann (ed), *Rethinking Ethnicity: Majority Groups and Dominant Minorities* (London, Routledge, 2004) 195
Pulea, M, 'A Regional Court of Appeal for the Pacific' (1980) 9(2) *Pacific Perspective* 1
——, 'Pacific Courts and Personnel' in G Powles and M Pulea (eds), *Pacific Courts and Legal Systems* (Suva and Clayton, University of the South Pacific and Monash University, 1988) 37
Rackley, E, *Women, Judging and the Judiciary: From Difference to Diversity* (Abingdon, Routledge, 2013)
Radio New Zealand (Wellington), 'NZ Judge Praised for Work Samoa' (27 June 2014)
——, 'Nauru Magistrate Departs after Contract Non Renewed' (12 December 2016)
——, 'Nauru Bringing in Australian Judge for "Riot" Trial' (1 August 2017)
——, 'Nauru Justice Minister Attacks Nauru 19 Lawyers' (15 August 2018)
Raz, J, 'The Problem of Authority: Revisiting the Service Conception of Authority' (2006) 90 *Minnesota Law Review* 1003
——, *The Authority of Law: Essays on Law and Morality*, 2nd edn (Oxford, Oxford University Press, 2009)
Reeves, P, Vakatora, TR and Lal, BV, 'The Fiji Islands: Towards a United Future Report of the Fiji Constitution Review Commission 1996' (Parliamentary Paper No 34 of 1996, Parliament of Fiji, 1996)
Rehfeld, A, 'Towards a General Theory of Representation' (2006) 68(1) *Journal of Politics* 1
Republic of Vanuatu Chief Justice's Chambers, 'Guidance Note for Remote Hearings – Vanuatu Court of Appeal' (28 April 2020)
Resnik, J, 'Law as Affiliation: Foreign Law, Democratic Federalism, and the Sovereigntism of the Nation-State' (2008) 6 *International Journal of Constitutional Law* 33
Robertson, B, 'Judicial Independence in the Pacific' in *Land Law and Judicial Governance in the South Pacific: Comparative Studies* (Wellington, New Zealand Association for Comparative Law, 2011) 267
Robinson, T and Bulkan, A, 'Constitutional Comparisons by a Supranational Court in Flux: The Privy Council and Caribbean Bills of Rights' (2017) 80 *MLR* 379
Roughan, N, 'The Legitimacy of Whom?' in K Walton, W Sadurski and M Sevel (eds), *Legitimacy: The State and Beyond* (Oxford, Oxford University Press, 2019) 82
Russell, PH, 'Toward a General Theory of Judicial Independence' in DM O'Brien and PH Russell (eds), *Judicial Independence in the Age of Democracy: Critical Perspectives from around the World* (Charlottesville, VA, University Press of Virginia, 2001)
——, 'Judicial Recruitment, Training and Careers' in P Cane and HM Kritzer (eds), *The Oxford Handbook of Empirical Legal Research* (Oxford, Oxford University Press, 2010)
Russell, PH and Malleson, K (eds), *Appointing Judges in an Age of Judicial Power: Critical Perspectives from around the World* (Toronto, University of Toronto Press, 2006)
Rutgers, MR, 'The Oath of Office as Public Value Guardian' (2010) 40(4) *American Review of Public Administration* 428
Salevao, I, *Rule of Law, Legitimate Governance and Development in the Pacific* (Canberra, ANU Press, 2005)
Samararatne, D, 'Reframing Feminist Imperatives in Adjudication through a Reading of Sri Lankan Jurisprudence' in M Crouch (ed), *Women and the Judiciary in the Asia-Pacific* (Cambridge, Cambridge University Press, 2021) 66
Samoa Law Reform Commission, 'Samoa Mo Samoa: Fetuunai Muniao', *Research Report*, vol 1 (2020)
Sapolu, FM, 'Adjudicators in Western Samoa' in G Powles and M Pulea (eds), *Pacific Courts and Legal Systems* (Suva and Clayton, University of the South Pacific and Faculty of Law, Monash University, 1988) 60
Sapolu, PF et al, 'Law and Custom' in M Meleisea, P Schoeffel Meleisea and E Meleisea (eds), *Samoa's Journey 1962–2012: Aspects of History* (Wellington, Victoria University Press, 2012) 18
Saunders, C, 'Towards a Global Constitutional Gene Pool' (2009) 4(3) *National Taiwan University Law Review* 1

——, 'Judicial Engagement with Comparative Law' in T Ginsburg and R Dixon (eds), *Comparative Constitutional Law* (Northampton, Edward Elgar, 2011) 571

——, 'Common Law Public Law: Some Comparative Reflections' in J Bell et al (eds), *Public Law Adjudication in Common Law Systems: Process and Substance* (Oxford, Hart Publishing, 2015) 353

Saunders, R, *The Concept of the Foreign: An Interdisciplinary Dialogue* (Lanham, MD, Lexington Books, 2003)

Schauer, F, 'Formalism' (1987) 97 *Yale Law Journal* 509

Scheppele, KL, 'Constitutional Ethnography: An Introduction' (2004) 38 *Law and Society Review* 389

Schofield, D, 'Maintaining Judicial Independence in a Small Jurisdiction' in J Hatchard and P Slinn (eds), *Parliamentary Supremacy and Judicial Independence: A Commonwealth Approach* (London, Cavendish Publishing Limited, 1999) 73

Schwartz, A, 'International Judges on Constitutional Courts: Cautionary Evidence from Post-Conflict Bosnia' (2019) 44 *Law and Social Inquiry* 1

Scott, M, 'Fiji's Judicial Department: A Review' in MA Ntumy (ed), *South Pacific Islands Legal Systems* (Honolulu, University of Hawaii Press, 1993)

Shany, Y, 'Dédoublement Fonctionnel and the Mixed Loyalties of National and International Judges' in F Fontanelli, G Martinico and P Carrozza (eds), *Shaping Rule of Law through Dialogue: International and Supranational Experiences* (Groningen, Europa, 2010) 27

Shapiro, MM, *Courts, A Comparative and Political Analysis* (Chicago, IL, University of Chicago Press, 1981)

Shapiro, SJ, 'Authority' in JL Coleman and SJ Shapiro (eds), *The Oxford Handbook of Jurisprudence and Philosophy of Law* (Oxford, Oxford University Press, 2002) 382

Shetreet, S, 'Judicial Accountability: A Comparative Analysis of the Models and the Recent Trends' (1986) 11(2) *International Legal Practitioner* 38

——, 'The Challenge of Judicial Independence in the Twenty-First Century' (2000) 8(2) *Asia Pacific Law Review* 153

Shihata, IFI, *The World Bank in a Changing World* (Dordrecht, M Nijhoff Publishers, 1991)

Sinclair, GF, *To Reform the World: International Organizations and the Making of Modern States* (Oxford, Oxford University Press, 2017)

Sirimanna, B, 'Fiji Courts Want 6 of Our Judges' *Sunday Times* (Colombo) (16 August 2009)

Slaughter, A-M, 'A Global Community of Courts' (2003) 44(1) *Harvard International Law Journal* 191

Smellie, R, *Few Regrets: Reflections on a Life in the Law* (Auckland District Law Society, 2008)

Smilov, D, 'The Judiciary: The Least Dangerous Branch?' in M Rosenfeld and A Sajó (eds), *The Oxford Handbook of Comparative Constitutional Law* (Oxford, Oxford University Press, 2012) 859

Smith, SE, 'The Way We Do Things Back Home: Do Expatriate Judges Preferentially Cite the Jurisprudence of Their Home Countries?' (2013) 13(2) *Oxford University Commonwealth Law Journal* 331

Statistics for Development Division, Pacific Community, *2018 Pocket Statistical Summary* (2018)

Stone, A, 'Judicial Reasoning' in C Saunders and A Stone (eds), *Oxford Handbook of the Australian Constitution* (Oxford, Oxford University Press, 2018) 472

Strohmeyer, H, 'Policing the Peace: Post-Conflict Judicial System Reconstruction in East Timor' (2001) 24 *University of New South Wales Law Journal* 171

Supreme Court of Tasmania, *Report of the Chief Justice of the Supreme Court of Tasmania: Annual Report 2005–2006* (2006)

Swanson, M, 'Trial of the "Nauru 19"' [2018] *Bar News: Journal of the NSW Bar Association* 83

Tamanaha, BZ, *Understanding Law in Micronesia: An Interpretive Approach to Transplanted Law* (Leiden, EJ Brill, 1993)

——, 'Understanding Legal Pluralism: Past to Present, Local to Global' (2008) 30(3) *Sydney Law Review* 375

——, 'Battle between Law and Society in Micronesia' in D Galligan and M Versteeg (eds), *Social and Political Foundations of Constitutions* (Cambridge, Cambridge University Press, 2013) 584

Terris, D, Romano, C and Swigart, L, *The International Judge: An Introduction to the Men and Women Who Decide the World's Cases* (Waltham, MA, Brandeis University Press, 2007)

Territory of Nauru, 'Record of Proceedings of the Constitutional Convention' (3–29 January 1968, 19 April–17 May 1968)

The Economist Intelligence Unit (London), 'The Political Scene: More Supreme Court Judges Resign' (1 October 2010)

The National (Port Moresby), 'Pay Disparity a Thorny Issue' (6 December 2011)

——, 'PNG, SI Sign Agreement on Judiciary Cooperation' (24 August 2017)

Tierney, S, *Constitutional Law and National Pluralism* (Oxford, Oxford University Press, 2004)

Troper, M, 'Sovereignty' in M Rosenfeld and A Sajó (eds), *Oxford Handbook of Comparative Constitutional Law* (Oxford, Oxford University Press, 2012) 1304

Tui Atua Tupua Tamasese Efi, *Su'esu'e Manogi In Search of Fragrance: Tui Atua Tupua Tamasese Ta'isi and the Samoan Indigenous Reference* (Apia, Centre for Samoan Studies, National University of Samoa, 2008)

Tupufia, LT, 'Court Tackles Drugs and Alcohol Abuse' *Samoa Observer* (Apia) (28 February 2016)

Turenne, S, *Fair Reflection of Society in Judicial Systems: A Comparative Study* (Cham, Springer, 2015)

Tushnet, M, 'The Possibilities of Comparative Constitutional Law' (1999) 108 *Yale Law Journal* 1225

——, 'Judicial Accountability in Comparative Perspective' in N Bamforth and P Leyland (eds), *Accountability in the Contemporary Constitution* (Oxford, Oxford University Press, 2013) 57

Twining, W, 'Diffusion of Law: A Global Perspective' (2004) 49 *Journal of Legal Pluralism and Unofficial Law* 1

——, *General Jurisprudence: Understanding Law from a Global Perspective* (Cambridge, Cambridge University Press, 2009)

United Nations Development Programme, Bangkok SURF, 'Global Experiences Using Expatriate Judges' (Substantive Research Piece – East Timor, UNDP, August 2002)

United Nations Office of the High Representative for the Least Developed Countries, Landlocked Developing Countries and Small Island Developing States, *About the Small Island Developing States* (2015)

Urbis, *National Profile of Solicitors* (Report prepared for the Conference of Law Societies of Australia, June 2019)

Va'ai, A, 'The Idea of Law: A Pacific Perspective' (1997) 21 *Journal of Pacific Studies* 225

Van Dyke, JM, 'The Pacific Judicial Conference: Strengthening the Independent Judiciary and the Rule of Law in the Pacific' (2011) 22(1–2) *Western Legal History* 127

Vanberg, G, 'Constitutional Courts in Comparative Perspective: A Theoretical Assessment' (2015) 18 *Annual Review of Political Science* 167

Veenendaal, W, *Politics and Democracy in Microstates* (Abingdon, Routledge, 2015)

Voigt, S, Ebeling, M and Blume, L, 'Improving Credibility by Delegating Judicial Competence: The Case of the Judicial Committee of the Privy Council' (2007) 82(2) *Journal of Development Economics* 348

VonDoepp, P, 'Context-Sensitive Inquiry in Comparative Judicial Research: Lessons from the Namibian Judiciary' (2008) 41(11) *Comparative Political Studies* 1515

Vyas, Y, 'The Independence of the Judiciary: A Third World Perspective' (1992) 11 *Third World Legal Studies* 127

Waldron, J, *Law and Disagreement* (Oxford, Clarendon Press, 1999)

Weisbrot, D, 'Judges and Politicians' (1979) 4 *Legal Service Bulletin* 240

Williams, G, 'McPherson JA in the Solomon Islands' in A Rahemtula (ed), *Justice According to Law: A Festschrift for the Honourable Mr Justice BH McPherson CBE* (Brisbane, Supreme Court of Queensland Library, 2006) 632

Winter, G, 'Judicial Guidelines: The Five Way Test' (2006) 1(2) *International Judicial Monitor*, available at www.judicialmonitor.org/archive_0506/globaljudicialdialogue.html

Zorn, J, 'Custom Then and Now: The Changing Melanesian Family' in A Jowitt and T Newton Cain (eds), *Passage of Change: Law, Society and Governance in the Pacific* (Canberra, Pandanus Books, 2003) 95

Zorn, JG and J Corrin Care, 'Barava Tru: Judicial Approaches to the Pleading and Proof of Custom in the South Pacific' (2002) 51 *International and Comparative Law Quarterly* 611

Zyl Smit, J van, *The Appointment, Tenure and Removal of Judges under Commonwealth Principles: A Compendium and Analysis of Best Practice* (London, Commonwealth Secretariat, 2015)

Index